Uncle John's
BATHROOM
READER®
PLUNGES INTO
HOLLYWOOD

Uncle John's BATHROOM READER® PLUNGES INTO HOLLYWOOD

The Bathroom Readers'
Hysterical Society

San Diego, California

Uncle John's Bathroom Reader
Plunges into Hollywood

www.bathroomreader.com

The Bathroom Readers' Hysterical Society
Portable Press
5880 Oberlin Drive, San Diego, CA 92121
e-mail: unclejohn@advmkt.com

ISBN 10: 1–59223–497–6
ISBN 13: 978–1–59223–497–4

Library of Congress Catalog-in-Publication Data is available.

Printed in the United States of America
First printing: December 2005

06 07 08 09   10 9 8 7 6 5 4 3 2

PROJECT TEAM

Amy Briggs, Project Editor
Stephanie Spadaccini, Editor
Allen Orso, Publisher
JoAnn Padgett, Director, Editorial and Production
Jennifer Browning, Production Manager
Michael Brunsfeld, Cover Design
Robin Kilrain, Copy Editor
Tamar Schwartz, Proofreader

The Bathroom Readers' Hysterical Society sincerely
thanks the following people whose advice and
assistance made this book possible.

Brian Boone
Cynthia Francisco
Mary Lou GoForth
Kristine Hemp
Gordon Javna
Rebecca Kaiser
Dan Mansfield
Julia Papps
Sydney Stanley
Jennifer Thornton
Connie Vazquez

HYSTERICAL SCHOLARS

The Bathroom Readers' Hysterical Society sincerely thanks the following talented people who contributed selections to this work.

Amy Briggs
Jen Crawford
Kathleen Duey
Padriac Duffy
Kathy Grogman
Vickey Kalambakal
Kerry Kern
Megan Kern
Robin Kilrain
Lea Markson
Debbie Pawlak
William Dylan Powell
John Scalzi
Terri Schlichenmeyer
Stephanie Spadaccini
Sue Steiner
Diana MoesVandeHoef

CONTENTS

HOLLYWOOD GOES TO WAR

HOLLYWOOD HISTORY

HOLLYWOOD LEGENDS

HOWL AT THE MOON

I SPY

IT'S ALIVE!

PREFACE

Welcome to our latest addition to the Bathroom Reader family—*Uncle John's Bathroom Reader Plunges into Hollywood*. One afternoon at the Bathroom Reader, someone was making popcorn. As the hot, buttery aroma wafted through the air, it got JoAnn, one of our editors, thinking about the movies. And the more popcorn she smelled, the more she thought about her favorite films. And then it hit her. The next topic we needed to plunge into was Hollywood—the movies, the myths, the moguls, and the magic behind it all.

So everyone got together, ate popcorn, and began thinking "Hollywood." We called in our writers, pulled some of our favorite articles from previous *Bathroom Readers*, and put together this comprehensive collection of Hollywood history and Tinseltown trivia. We learned a lot along the way, like who created the first Snow White cartoon (page 106) and what movie was first shown on an airplane (page 146).

Want some more coming attractions?

- **The Stars:** Read all about Bogie, Grant, and Monroe by the numbers; tales of stars' discoveries and stories of their tragic demise

- **The Movies:** Go behind the scenes of the epics *The Longest Day* and *Cleopatra*, bone up on the *Thin Man* series, and spot our favorite bloopers and on-screen goofs

- **The Landmarks:** Read the stories behind the Hollywood sign, Frederick's of Hollywood, the Hollywood Walk of Fame, and Grauman's Chinese Theatre

- **The Biz:** Learn how to break into show business, the meanings behind the credits; and how to translate those *Variety* headlines

- **The Legends:** Get the answers to the questions: Is the Hollywood sign haunted? Is there really a curse on Dracula? And who killed the Black Dahlia?

As always, it's a collaborative effort here at the Bathroom Reader. And everyone deserves a big thank you.

- To Allen, JoAnn, Gordon, and Brian, our resident Hollywood experts and content czars, for their expertise, suggestions, input, and ideas
- To Sydney and Christian, for having an exceptional Hollywood library and the generosity to open it up to us
- To Stephanie, for expert editing and superb polishing
- To Jennifer Browning, Jennifer Thornton, and Rebecca Kaiser, for all the editorial excellence and production perfection you bring to the table. We couldn't have made it without you.
- To Michael, for putting our name in lights (on the cover)

But like an Academy Awards acceptance speech, I've gone on too long. So before the orchestra cuts me off, let's get started. Sit back, get comfortable, and come with us as we visit the Dream Factory, the Magic Store, or just plain Hollywood.

As always, go with the flow.

Cousin Amy
Editor

MARILYN MONROE:
BY THE NUMBERS

Despite a short and tragic life, Marilyn Monroe remains
popular; the beautiful actress's star has continued to
rise since her untimely, mysterious death in 1962.

1

Number of Best Actress Golden Globes won by Monroe. She had
been nominated twice, for *Bus Stop* (1956) and *Some Like It Hot*
(1959). She won for the latter. In 1954 and 1962 she was awarded
two other Golden Globes as Female World Film Favorite but was
never nominated for an Oscar.

2

Years that Norma Jeane Mortensen spent at the Los Angeles
Orphans Home, from ages 9 to 11. Most of her childhood was
spent in various foster homes because her biological mother,
Gladys, a former film cutter with RKO studios, was in a mental
institution.

3

Number of times per week Joe DiMaggio had fresh roses delivered
to Monroe's crypt for 20 years after her death.

4

Number of years Monroe was married to *Death of a Salesman* playwright Arthur Miller. He later said that he was sorry about the
divorce, but that it had been necessary: "If I hadn't, I would be
dead."

5

Number of times a week that Monroe met with a psychiatrist while
living in New York and attending the Actors Studio in the mid-
1950s. She continued with analysis thereafter, seeing doctors in
both New York and Los Angeles until her death.

The boots eaten by Charlie Chaplin in *The Gold Rush* (1925) were made of licorice.

8
Number of months it took Monroe to file for divorce from Joe DiMaggio in 1954. Biographers cite his possessiveness, temper, and insistence that she give up show business as the main causes of their split. Until the end, the legendary ballplayer remained devoted to her and hoped to win her back.

16
Age at her first marriage to Jimmy Dougherty, a merchant marine who, from all reports, was a nice guy. A family friend had suggested the marriage, and since Marilyn had nowhere else to turn, she married him. She might still be married to Dougherty if she hadn't been discovered a few years later while working in a factory and been offered a job as a model.

20
Number of Nembutal capsules that Monroe was taking per day during the filming of *The Misfits* (1961), the last film she completed. She would prick them with a pin to make them work more quickly.

26
Age at which Monroe started work on *Gentlemen Prefer Blondes* (1953), the film that established her as a major comedic star.

30
The number of films in which Monroe appeared. *Dangerous Years* (1947) was her first; *Something's Got to Give* (1962) was the last. She died before it could be completed.

36
Age at which Monroe died from an overdose of sedatives in 1962.

37-24-35
Monroe's measurements for most of her career, according to *Celebrity Sleuth* magazine.

40
As reported by actor Jack Lemmon, the number of takes required for some of Monroe's scenes during the filming of *Some Like It Hot*.

"Over? Did you say 'over?' Nothing is over until we decide it is."

45
Age of President John F. Kennedy when Monroe sang "Happy Birthday, Mr. President" to him in 1962. (The First Lady did not attend that celebration.)

69
Age of Joe Schenck, the chairman of the board of Twentieth Century Fox, when he became Monroe's first powerful benefactor in the movie business. Uncle Joe, as she called him, got her a contract with Columbia Pictures in 1948.

500
In dollars, the amount that Hugh Hefner paid for the rights to the famous nude photo of Monroe taken in 1949. Hefner used the photo as his centerfold to help launch the first issue of *Playboy*. Monroe had been paid $50 for the photo session.

1956
The year Norma Jeane officially changed her name to Marilyn.

6778
Hollywood Boulevard address of Monroe's star on the Walk of Fame.

1,267,000
The Guinness World Record–setting price fetched by the sparkly gown Monroe wore as she serenaded JFK in 1962. Christie's auctioned it off in 1999, along with other items that belonged to Monroe, when the gown set the record for most valuable dress.

1,600,000
In dollars, the value of Monroe's estate when she died. She bequeathed 75 percent of it to Lee Strasberg of the Actors Studio, and 25 percent to Dr. Marianne Kris, her New York psychoanalyst. A trust fund provided her biological mother with $5,000 a year.

8,000,000
In dollars, the amount earned by Monroe's estate in 2004. (She was 6th on the *Forbes* list of top-earning dead celebrities. Elvis was first, with $40 million.)

—Bluto Blutarksy (John Belushi), *Animal House* (1978)

THE WILHELM SCREAM

Have you ever heard a sound effect in a film—a screeching eagle, a car crash, or a laughing crowd—that you swear you've heard before in other movies? You're probably right. Here's the story behind Hollywood's most famous "recycled" sound effect.

SOUNDS FAMILIAR

Like most American kids growing up in the 1950s, Ben Burtt went to the movies . . . *a lot.* Movie budgets were much smaller back then, and film studios reused whatever they could—props, sets, stock footage, sound effects, everything. If you watched and listened to the movies carefully, you might have noticed things you'd seen and heard in other movies. Burtt noticed. He was good at picking out sounds—especially screams, and especially one scream in particular. "Every time someone died in a Warner Bros. movie, they'd scream this famous scream," he says.

By the 1970s, a grown-up Burtt was working in the movie business himself, as a sound designer—the guy who creates the sound effects. Years had passed, but he'd never forgotten that classic Warner Bros. scream. So when he got the chance, he decided to track down the original recording. It took a lot of digging, but he eventually found it on an old studio reel marked "Man Being Eaten by an Alligator." It turns out it had been recorded for the 1951 Warner Bros. western *Distant Drums* and used at least twice in that movie: once in a battle with some Indians, and then—of course—when a man is bitten and dragged underwater by an alligator.

A STAR IS BORN

No one could remember what actor had originally been hired to record the scream, so Burtt jokingly named it after a character in the 1953 movie *Charge at Feather River.* The character, named Wilhelm, screams the scream after he is struck in the leg by an arrow. The "Wilhelm Scream" was used two more times in that film: once when a soldier is struck by a spear, and again when an Indian is stabbed and then rolls down a hill.

The Wilhelm Scream is now more than 50 years old, but if you heard it you'd probably recognize it, because Burtt, who's worked on almost every George Lucas film, uses it often—including in his Academy Award–winning sound design for *Star Wars*. "That scream gets in every picture I do, as a personal signature," he says.

So when you hear a Wilhelm Scream in a film, can you assume that Burtt did the sound effects? No. When other sound designers heard what he was doing, they started inserting the scream into their movies, too. Apparently, Burtt isn't the only person good at noticing reused sound effects, because movie buffs have caught on to what he is doing and discovered at least 66 films that use the Wilhelm Scream. A few examples:

AHHHHHHHHHHEEEEEIIIIII!!!

Star Wars (1977) Just before Luke Skywalker and Princess Leia swing across the Death Star's chasm, a stormtrooper falls in.

The Empire Strikes Back (1980) 1) In the battle on the ice planet Hoth, a rebel soldier screams when his big satellite-dish laser gun is struck by laser fire and explodes. 2) As Han Solo is being frozen, Chewbacca knocks a stormtrooper off the platform.

Return of the Jedi (1983) 1) In the desert scene, Luke slashes an enemy with his light saber. The victim screams as he falls into the Sarlac pit. 2) Later in the film, Han Solo knocks a man over a ledge. The man is Ben Burtt himself, making a cameo appearance—and that's him impersonating the Wilhelm Scream . . . with his own voice.

Batman Returns (1992) Batman punches a clown and knocks him out of the way. The clown screams.

Toy Story (1995) Buzz Lightyear screams when he gets knocked out of the bedroom window.

Titanic (1997) In the scene where the engine room is flooding, a crew member screams when he's hit with a jet of water.

Spaceballs (1987) Barf uses a section of tubes to reflect laser bolts back at three guards. The last one screams.

The Lord of the Rings: The Two Towers (2002) A soldier falls off the wall during the Battle of Helm's Deep . . . and lets out a Wilhelm.

THE WORLD'S FASTEST STUDIO TOUR

From cinema's earliest days, just a few studios have monopolized movie production. Who are they, and how have they managed to stay on top (or not, as the case may be)?

STUDIO: UNIVERSAL STUDIOS
Origin: The home of classic horror films dates back to 1909, when Carl Laemmle created the Independent Moving Picture Company (IMP). He did this to get around the Motion Picture Patents Company, the Thomas Edison–fronted organization that had a monopoly on film at the time. IMP became the Universal Film Manufacturing Company in 1912, and subsequently Universal Pictures, which in its early existence would be branded a low-rent producer of B movies.

Studio Mogul: Carl Laemmle Jr. was promoted by his father to production chief on his twenty-first birthday. In the late 1920s, Laemmle Jr. tried to upgrade the studio's reputation through a series of high-toned productions, including *All Quiet on the Western Front*, and by introducing the wildly successful series of monster films that kicked off with *Dracula* and *Frankenstein* in 1931. The "high-toned" plan backfired when the 1936 production of *Show Boat* (based on the Kern and Hammerstein musical) flopped at the box office, forcing the Laemmles to relinquish control of Universal to the Standard Chartered Bank. Carl Jr. went independent with little success, and the studio went back to the cheap stuff; it would bounce back and forth between cheap and good until the 1970s.

Best Picture Wins: Eight, including coproductions with other studios: *All Quiet on the Western Front* (1930), *The Sting* (1973), *The Deer Hunter* (1978), *Out of Africa* (1985), *Schindler's List* (1993), *Shakespeare in Love* (1998), *Gladiator* (2000), *A Beautiful Mind* (2001). Notice the 43-year gap between *All Quiet* and *The Sting*.

Yes, sir! "If there's anything I can't stand, it's yes-men. When I say no, I want . . ."

Other Notable Films:

- *Frankenstein* (1931) The highest-grossing film of the year.
- *My Man Godfrey* (1936) The first film to ever receive four acting nominations (William Powell, Carole Lombard, Mischa Auer, and Alice Brady) at the Academy Awards—and in the year that the supporting categories were first introduced. None of the film's nominees won.
- *To Kill a Mockingbird* (1962) Gregory Peck called this his best and favorite film.
- *Jaws* (1975) The top-grossing movie of the year and Stephen Spielberg's ticket to the big time.
- *E.T. The Extra-Terrestrial* (1982) The top-grossing movie of the year.
- *Apollo 13* (1995) Its rerelease in 2005 into IMAX theaters marked the first use of a remastering process that converts conventional films into IMAX format.

Today: Universal is majority-owned by General Electric as part of its NBC Universal media arm. Prior to this, Universal was owned by the French company Vivendi, who got it when it acquired Seagram. Seagram bought it from Japanese manufacturer Matsushita, who bought it from MCA, which owned it for a couple of decades.

STUDIO: PARAMOUNT PICTURES
Origin: Paramount dates back to 1912, when Adolph Zukor founded the Famous Players Film Company. One year later, Zukor invested in Paramount Pictures, a film distribution company founded by W. W. Hodkinson. Then, in 1916, another film production company, Jesse L. Lasky Company, merged with Famous Players. All three finally consolidated under the name Paramount Pictures.

Studio Mogul: Adolph Zukor made a name for Paramount Pictures in two ways: first by getting (or creating) big stars like Mary Pickford and Rudolph Valentino for his movies, and second by strong-arming theater owners into agreeing to show Paramount movies for an entire year in order to get the films. Zukor's bright idea would get Paramount investigated by the government for anti-trade practices. His aggressive policies in general put Paramount into financial trouble in the 1930s and got him "bumped upstairs" as chairman emeritus in 1935, a position he held for forty-one years until his death at age 103.

Best Picture Wins: Eleven, including coproductions: *Wings* (1927–28), which was the first movie to win an Oscar, *Going My Way* (1944), *The Lost Weekend* (1945), *The Greatest Show on Earth* (1952), *The Godfather* (1972), *The Godfather Part II* (1974), *Ordinary People* (1980), *Terms of Endearment* (1983), *Forrest Gump* (1994), *Braveheart* (1995), *Titanic* (1997).

Other Notable Films:

- *Roman Holiday* (1953) Audrey Hepburn's first American movie, for which she won the Best Actress Oscar.
- *White Christmas* (1954) The first film produced in VistaVision, Paramount's wide-screen process.
- *The Ten Commandments* (1956) Cecil B. DeMille's last film and the highest-grossing film of the year.
- *Psycho* (1960) Director Alfred Hitchcock used the crew from his TV series, *Alfred Hitchcock Presents*, to save time and money; the film cost $800,000 to make and has earned more than $40 million.
- *Chinatown* (1974) Robert Towne's script won the Oscar, Golden Globe, and Writers Guild Award for his original screenplay.
- *Witness* (1984) No Amish people appeared in this movie, but they did enjoy watching while it was filmed.

Today: Paramount is owned by media conglomerate Viacom.

STUDIO: WARNER BROS.
Origin: The three eldest Warner brothers (Harry, Albert, and Sam) began by exhibiting films in 1903. By the end of World War I, in 1918, they had opened their Sunset Boulevard studio with younger brother Jack. The company formally incorporated as Warner Brothers Pictures, Inc. in 1923.

Studio Mogul: Darryl F. Zanuck, before he helped found 20th Century Fox, was the go-to guy for Warner Bros. As production chief, he helped the studio make the transition to sound. In the early 1930s it became established as the place where gritty crime

---

Director John Ford's last words: "May I please have a cigar?"

films and other melodramas got made. Zanuck resigned in 1933 when he realized that he'd never have as much power as any of the Warners. His successor, Hal Wallis, found the situation to be the same: Wallis quit the studio after an incident at the 1943 Academy Awards, when Jack Warner headed him off at the pass to accept the Best Picture Oscar for *Casablanca*.

Best Picture Wins: Seven, including coproductions: *The Life of Emile Zola* (1937), *Casablanca* (1943), *My Fair Lady* (1964), *Chariots of Fire* (1981), *Driving Miss Daisy* (1989), *Unforgiven* (1992), *Million Dollar Baby* (2004).

Notable Films:

- *Porky's Duck Hunt* (1937) Daffy Duck's first screen appearance, and the first time that Mel Blanc voiced Porky Pig. Initially, Warner Bros. handled only the distribution of Looney Tunes and Merrie Melodies until they bought the animation studio that produced them in 1944.
- *The Maltese Falcon* (1941) This was fledgling director John Huston's first collaboration with Humphrey Bogart. It was also Sydney Greenstreet's movie debut at 61 years old and 285 pounds.
- *A Streetcar Named Desire* (1951) With *Network*, the only film to win three acting Oscars (Vivien Leigh, Kim Hunter, Karl Malden—not Brando!)
- *Who's Afraid of Virginia Woolf?* (1966) The first movie to receive the "Suggested for Mature Audiences" tag from the MPAA, the Motion Picture Association of America.
- *The Exorcist* (1973) The top-grossing movie of the year.
- *Harry Potter and the Sorcerer's Stone* (2001) The top-grossing movie of the year.

Today: Warner Bros. has been part of Time Warner since 1988, when Warner Communications (the company that owned the studio) merged with Time, Inc. (owner of *TIME* magazine and other book and media properties).

STUDIO: UNITED ARTISTS
Origins: This is the most unusual film studio in that it was the brainchild of actual filmmakers, not just producers. United Artists

---

was founded in 1919 by Charlie Chaplin, Douglas Fairbanks, Mary Pickford, D. W. Griffith, and cowboy star William S. Hart. The studio acted more like a distributor for independently produced films for much of its existence, giving its filmmakers a wider creative latitude than they had at other Hollywood studios.

Studio Mogul: Excepting the famous founders, none.

Best Picture Wins: Eleven, including coproductions: *Rebecca* (1940), *Marty* (1955), *Around the World in Eighty Days* (1956), *The Apartment* (1960), *West Side Story* (1961), *In the Heat of the Night* (1967), *Midnight Cowboy* (1969), *One Flew Over the Cuckoo's Nest* (1975), *Rocky* (1976), *Annie Hall* (1977), *Rain Man* (1988).

Other Notable Films:

- *Modern Times* (1936) The last film appearance of Charlie Chaplin's Little Tramp.
- *Doctor No* (1962) The first James Bond film.
- *A Hard Day's Night* (1964) The Beatles' first feature film.
- *A Fistful of Dollars* (1964) Sergio Leone's first spaghetti Western, its tagline, referring to the Clint Eastwood character, and probably directly translated from the Italian, was "In his own way he is perhaps, the most dangerous man who ever lived!"
- *Bowling for Columbine* (2002) Michael Moore's Best Documentary Oscar winner, and the highest grossing documentary in history, until Moore beat his own record with *Fahrenheit 9/11* in 2004.

Today: After a good run in the 1970s, United Artists famously crashed and burned at the end of the decade thanks to the expensive megaflop, 1980's *Heaven's Gate*, directed by Michael Cimino. The studio, which had been owned by Transamerica since 1967, was sold to MGM, where it remained a production arm until the sale of MGM to Sony in 2005.

STUDIO: COLUMBIA PICTURES
Origin: Columbia was founded in 1920 as the production-distribution company CBC Film Sales by brothers Harry and Jack Cohn and Joe Brandt; the CBC stood for Cohn-Brandt-Cohn,

but was more commonly known in the trade press as "Corned Beef and Cabbage," a reflection of its low-budget ventures. CBC changed its name to Columbia in 1924 as part of an attempt to develop a more upscale reputation. Nevertheless, the studio's reputation for churning out B movies changed only gradually. (The improvement was thanks largely to Frank Capra.)

Studio Mogul: Harry Cohn was probably the most feared and hated man in Hollywood. He was the toughest of the studio heads, notorious for his ruthlessness and vulgarity. He spied on his employees through informers and hidden microphones, and frequently clashed with his stars, directors, and writers. His fights with his brother, Jack, who ran the company headquarters in New York, culminated in an attempt by Jack to oust him in 1932. Harry came out ahead in the skirmish and thereby solidified his position as the real boss of the studio. What he lacked in gentility, he made up for in an uncanny sense of what made for a good movie. That, the luck of finding director Frank Capra, and the sense to leave him alone to direct his movies his way, made Columbia into a major studio by the 1930s. (Cohn gave Frank Capra the opportunity to direct his first hit, 1928's *That Certain Thing*, because the director was first on an alphabetical list of available directors.)

As disliked as he was, there was a big turnout for Harry Cohn's 1958 funeral, prompting comedian Red Skelton to crack, "Give the people what they want, and they'll come out."

Best Picture Wins: Twelve, including coproductions: *It Happened One Night* (1934; directed by Capra), *You Can't Take It With You* (1938; Capra again), *All the King's Men* (1949), *From Here to Eternity* (1953), *On the Waterfront* (1954), *The Bridge on the River Kwai* (1957), *Lawrence of Arabia* (1962), *A Man for All Seasons* (1966), *Oliver!* (1968), *Kramer Vs. Kramer* (1979), *Gandhi* (1982), *The Last Emperor* (1987).

Other Notable Films:

- *Woman Haters* (1934) The first short the Three Stooges did for Columbia, to be followed by 200 or so more, until the 1965 feature film *The Outlaws Is Coming*.
- *Mr. Smith Goes to Washington* (1939) The Frank Capra film was bitterly denounced by Washington power brokers, but in 1942, when the German occupiers in France announced that they were

—Travis Coates (Tommy Kirk), *Old Yeller* (1957)

going to ban the showing of American films, *Mr. Smith* was deliberately the last one shown, and loudly cheered by the audience.

- *Guess Who's Coming to Dinner* (1967) The studio's top-grossing feature in theatrical release to date; it was Spencer Tracy's last film (he died 10 days after the filming wrapped).
- *Easy Rider* (1969) The counterculture indie that inspired the big studios to hand over the controls to younger directors.
- *Ghost Busters* (1984) The top-grossing movie of the year.
- *Spider-Man* (2002) The top-grossing movie of the year.

Today: Columbia was purchased from Coca-Cola in 1989 by Sony Corporation, and is part of Sony Pictures Entertainment.

STUDIO: METRO-GOLDWYN-MAYER
Origin: MGM, the most glamorous of the classic studios and the home of some of Hollywood's most lavish musicals, was formed in 1924 as a merger between Metro Pictures Corporation (founded in 1916), Goldwyn Picture Corporation (1917), and Louis B. Mayer Pictures (1918).

Studio Mogul: Louis B. Mayer got his start in the movie business in 1907, when he opened a theater in Haverhill, Massachusetts. Mayer's taste for big, gaudy film events helped make MGM the studio to beat in the 1930s; the studio was so successful that Mayer became the first American executive to get a million-dollar salary. But he clashed with his underlings, including legendary producer Irving Thalberg (who preferred literary works to Mayer's crowd-pleasers), and later, with production chief Dore Schary (who wanted the studio to make more "message" pictures). In 1948 Mayer told MGM owner Loews, Inc. that they would have to choose between Schary or him; to his shock, they chose Schary and promoted him to Mayer's old job.

Best Picture Wins: Nine, including coproductions: *The Broadway Melody* (1929), *Grand Hotel* (1932), *Mutiny on the Bounty* (1935), *The Great Ziegfeld* (1936), *Gone With the Wind* (1939), *Mrs. Miniver* (1939), *An American in Paris* (1951), *Gigi* (1958), *Ben-Hur* (1959).

Other Notable Films:
- *The Wizard of Oz* (1939) It's been televised annually at Thanksgiving, Christmas, and/or Easter since its second showing

in December 1959, and has probably been seen by more people worldwide than any other movie.

- *The Women* (1939) The more than 130 roles in this sophisticated comedy were all written for and played by women.

- *Singin' in the Rain* (1952) It didn't win one Academy Award, but the American Film Institute voted it the #10 movie of all time, the highest rated musical on the list.

- *Doctor Zhivago* (1965) Nominated for 10 Academy Awards, it helped save MGM from bankruptcy as the second top-grossing movie of the year (just behind *The Sound of Music*).

- *Network* (1976) With *A Streetcar Named Desire*, the only film to win three acting Oscars (Faye Dunaway, Peter Finch, Beatrice Straight).

- *Moonstruck* (1987) In which Cher, an Armenian/Cherokee actress, turns in an Oscar-winning performance as an Italian American from Brooklyn.

Today: MGM's glory days have long since been over. Under the ownership of Kirk Kerkorian of Las Vegas, the once-proud studio sold virtually all its valuable props and memorabilia (from Ben-Hur's chariot to Dorothy's ruby slippers) to an auctioneer at the bargain basement price of $1.5 million. The 1970 auction brought in $12 million. In 1981 the company acquired United Artists and became MGM/UA Entertainment. Turner Broadcasting System bought the company in 1986, sold off most of its subsidiaries, but kept and preserved the huge library of unforgettable films that made the studio great. A few deals and creditors later, what was left of the studio was bought by Sony Entertainment in 2005.

STUDIO: TWENTIETH CENTURY FOX

Origin: This now anachronistically named studio was the result of a 1935 merger between two competing studios: Twentieth Century Pictures, formed in 1932, and the older Fox Film Corporation, founded in 1915. (The studio has no plans to update its name—despite the fact that it also owns the "21st Century Fox" trademark, just in case.)

Studio Mogul: Darryl F. Zanuck helped create Twentieth Century Pictures and after the 1935 merger took an active role in editing and producing films. In the late 1950s, in the throes of a midlife crisis, Zanuck left the studio—and his wife—to become an independent producer in Europe. After the success of *The Longest Day* (1962), which Fox had hired him to produce, Zanuck was begged to return to the studio. When cost overruns on *Cleopatra* (1963) threatened to shut down production, Zanuck bailed out the studio with his own money. A power struggle with the board of directors in the late 1960s led to Zanuck being forced out of the studio in 1971.

Best Picture Wins: Eight, including coproductions: *How Green Was My Valley* (1941), *Gentleman's Agreement* (1947), *All About Eve* (1950), *The Sound of Music* (1965), *Patton* (1970), *The French Connection* (1971), *Braveheart* (1995), *Titanic* (1997).

Other Notable Films:

- *Miracle on 34th Street* (1947) Darryl Zanuck insisted that the movie be released in June because more people went to the movies in the summer.
- *The Robe* (1953) The first movie released in the wide-angle CinemaScope format.
- *Cleopatra* (1963) When adjusted for inflation, the most expensive movie ever made.
- *Star Wars* (1977) Now subtitled *Episode IV—A New Hope*, the second-highest-grossing movie in the United States; *Titanic* is first.
- *Home Alone* (1990) The highest-grossing comedy film.

Today: Twentieth Century Fox is owned by News Corporation, headed by billionaire Rupert Murdoch.

* * *

QUIET ON THE SET!

When sound first made its way into Hollywood, it wasn't an easy transition. Too much extra noise could ruin a shot, even noise from airplanes flying overhead. To solve the problem, MGM floated a red "silence" balloon and flew red flags to warn aircraft to stay away while they were shooting. Eventually agreements were made with the Department of Commerce, the California Aircraft Operators Association, and the studios to help overhead aviators avoid messing up a movie take.

Ella Fitzgerald tested for the role of the piano player (Sam) in *Casablanca.*

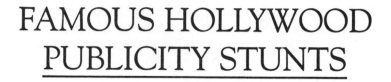

FAMOUS HOLLYWOOD PUBLICITY STUNTS

Publicity is the mother's milk of Hollywood, and over the years it has been refined to an art by a handful of practitioners. Here are three publicity stunts that built Hollywood legends.

I VANT TO BE ALONE

Background: When Greta Garbo came to Hollywood from Sweden in the 1920s, she didn't realize how conservative America was. In her first newspaper interview, she mentioned casually that she was living with director Mauritz Stiller. Today that's no big deal, but in the 1920s, it was a shocking revelation.
Publicity Stunt: When MGM head Louis B. Mayer heard about the interview, he was furious. He banned Garbo from ever speaking to the press again. That suited Garbo fine—she was shy anyway. But how to explain it to the press? Someone in the MGM publicity department came up with the famous quote: "I vant to be alone."

THE SEARCH FOR SCARLETT

Background: Producer David O. Selznick wanted the perfect actress to play Scarlett O'Hara in the film adaptation of *Gone With the Wind*, so he launched a nationwide talent search that lasted (coincidentally) for the two years it took to prepare for filming. Joan Crawford, Bette Davis, and Tallulah Bankhead all wanted the part. So did Katharine Hepburn, who told Selznick, "The part was practically written for me." "I can't imagine Rhett Butler chasing you for ten years," Selznick replied.

"George Cuckor, the intended director, was sent scurrying southward to scout locations, but also, supposedly, to check out high school plays for ingenues," explains a film historian. "To keep the game of who-will-play-her alive, every female willing to try out was tested." Newspapers and radio stations kept the country updated on the progress of the search. According to legend, just when the search seemed hopeless, Selznick's brother escorted a young British actress named Vivian Leigh onto the set. They signed her on the spot.

Director Quentin Tarantino played an Elvis impersonator on TV's *The Golden Girls*.

Publicity Stunt: Selznick had Leigh in mind for the part from the very beginning. But there were two problems: Leigh was a foreigner, which might not go over well with Southern audiences, and she was in the middle of a scandalous affair with actor Laurence Olivier (both were married to other people at the time). M. Hirsch Goldberg writes in *The Book of Lies:*

A scenario was devised in which Vivian Leigh would be discovered at the last minute after an extensive search for the right Scarlett had not been successful. In this way the foreign-born aspect would be diffused, especially since Scarlett, the character, and Vivien, the actress, shared the same Irish-French background. And with Olivier and Leigh agreeing not to move for a divorce at the time, the scandal would be abated in the flurry of good news that the Scarlett part had finally been settled.

WONG KEYE, PIANO TUNER

Background: When Barbra Streisand announced that she wouldn't give any interviews to promote *On a Clear Day You Can See Forever*, publicity man Steve Yeager was stuck—if the star wouldn't cooperate, he'd have to find another publicity angle.

Publicity Stunt: Yeager called AP gossip columnist Jim Bacon and "suggested we do a story on one Wong Keye, a mythical tone-deaf Chinese piano tuner who was tuning all the pianos on the Streisand movie." Bacon agreed. According to Bacon, in his book *Made in Hollywood:* "The story was written with appropriate tongue-in-cheek. It told how Wong Keye had started out in life as a fortune-cookie stuffer in a Chinatown bakery, then sold exotic fish for awhile until he found his niche tuning pianos. Since then he had been in great demand because he was such a superb piano tuner."

What Happened: It worked—the story ran all over the country, and was picked up by the London *Daily Mirror*, which even ran a photo (an actor hired to dress up in Chinese costume). Bacon even got calls from piano owners asking how they could get in touch with Keye. "But the funniest repercussion of all," Bacon writes, "came when Streisand—who had refused to give interviews in the first place—complained to the producer because the piano tuner in the movie was getting more publicity than the star."

If she had kept her birth name, you'd know Jane Seymour as Joyce Frankenberg.

THE ONE-MAN USO

When you think USO, you think Bob Hope.
For most people, they're as closely linked as bacon
and eggs. That's because, for nearly 50 years, U.S.
troops could count on Bob for their entertainment, a
taste of home, and a little welcome relief from the war.

AY, SOLDIER . . . SHOW YOU A GOOD TIME?
In early 1940, when World War II began to heat up, the U.S.
government instituted a peacetime draft. Military training
camps sprung up throughout the United States. Suddenly, soldiers
from all over the country found themselves on bases in small towns
far away from home. Because many of these towns didn't have the
resources to keep the boys entertained, representatives from several
organizations—the YWCA, the YMCA, the National Catholic
Community Service, the National Jewish Welfare Board, the
Salvation Army, and the Travelers Aid Association—joined
together in New York City. They formed the United Service
Organizations for National Defense, later simply called the USO.

After Pearl Harbor was bombed and the United States entered
the war officially, Hollywood stars leapt into action. Many joined
the armed services, while others worked on the home front with
the USO and with Camp Shows, an organization that worked with
the Screen Actors Guild to allow actors and actresses to perform
for the troops for free. More than 7,000 performers, including some
of Hollywood's best-loved and biggest stars, donated their time and
talent to put smiles on servicemen's faces. One star in particular
would become synonymous with the USO's mission to entertain
troops and boost their morale. That man was Bob Hope.

WHAT ABOUT BOB?
The star of the popular *On the Road* movie series (with costar Bing
Crosby), Bob Hope was already a comedic star in his own right. He
also had a popular weekly radio show (sponsored by Pepsodent)
that brought him into people's homes. In 1941 Hope broadcast his
radio show and performed live for servicemen at March Field in
California. His ratings went through the roof. Pepsodent, excited

---

Actress Charlize Theron and her mother have matching fish tattoos.

by the results, encouraged him to do more shows from military bases—and thus began a tradition that would last for 50 years (through four wars), and entertain millions of American soldiers.

On his first official wartime USO tour, Hope visited what he called the Great White Way (Alaska and the Aleutian Islands). He brought along his sidekick, Jerry Colonna, and the beautiful singer Frances Langford; they sang, danced, and told jokes for American troops in the North Pacific. Hope and his troupe would travel all over the world for the soldiers, inching as close to the front as they could get. In 1943 they took their first combat-zone trip to North Africa. Later, in Palermo, Italy, Hope saw real combat when the Germans staged an air raid next to his hotel.

With the exception of two instances when he was ill, Bob Hope broadcast all his radio shows from service bases around the world during the war years of 1941–1945. The soldiers loved seeing him and his troupe. "Seeing his show made me feel like I was back home in the USA," recalled one soldier stationed in Naples, Italy. "I completely forgot about the war." But even as combat ended, Hope's services were still needed. In 1948 Air Force Secretary Stuart Symington asked Hope to entertain the troops involved in the Berlin airlift. The show would air at Christmastime—and mark the beginning of another Hope tradition, the annual Christmas show.

TROUPES FOR THE TROOPS
Hope continued to entertain U.S. armed forces via the USO during the 1950s. His formula remained the same: tell some jokes, sing some songs, play some music, and then bring out the stars from back home—like Marilyn Monroe, Gina Lollobrigida, Steve McQueen, and Jayne Mansfield. During the Korean War and after (opinion surveys showed that the USO was needed not just during wartime, but also during times of peace), Hope entertained in hospitals, on bases, and on ships. In 1954 the USO and Bob Hope presented the first televised USO show (one of his Christmas shows) from Thule Air Force Base in Greenland. When the Vietnam conflict arose in the early 1960s, the USO quickly set up four USO clubs there. By the war's end, there were 24 clubs in Vietnam and Thailand. Bob Hope brought his annual Christmas show to Vietnam in 1964 and continued to perform there for the next seven years.

Much like World War II military troops, Hope and his troupes faced their fair share of danger. In the early stages of the Korean War, his group first flew to Tokyo and then on to the Sea of Japan—and straight into the war zone. During another flight, Hope's plane accidentally landed in Communist-occupied Wonson before the U.S. Marines had even captured the beach. When Hope and his team toured Vietnam, they came under fire too. On Christmas Eve 1964, a Vietcong truck loaded with dynamite exploded near the hotel where Hope and his entourage were staying. Once he even performed under enemy sniper fire. Three times his planes were attacked by Vietnamese forces, and he almost became a casualty of a bombing raid.

Hope even tried to reach the soldiers behind enemy lines. In 1971 he tried to obtain a visa to enter North Vietnam so that he might entertain POWs and possibly negotiate for their release. Hope traveled to Vientiane, Laos, to meet with the North Vietnamese representative, Nguyen Van Thanh. He even offered to put on a charity show in the United States to raise $10 million for a Vietnamese children's charity. Thanh posed for pictures with Hope, but the visa was ultimately denied. Undeterred, Hope tried again in 1975. Again, he was refused entrance to Hanoi.

THE SHOW MUST GO ON
Following the Vietnam War, Bob Hope continued to do performances for the USO whenever he was needed. In 1983 he took his Christmas show to Lebanon. In 1987 he and his entertainment troupe visited the Persian Gulf. In 1990 he performed in Frankfurt, Germany, and in Cambridge, England. His road tour went to the Berlin Wall and Moscow, then to Kuwait to entertain Americans deployed to that country. In 1990 Hope took a tour to Saudi Arabia on the eve of Operation Desert Storm; it would be his last.

MEMORIES
When he died on July 29, 2003, at age 100, Bob Hope had been honored by several government agencies and other organizations for service to his country through his USO performances. He received the George Foster Peabody Award for excellence in broadcasting in 1943 for the "high level of entertainment of his camp tours." He received the Silver Buffalo Award from the Boy

---

Sophia Loren was called *Stechetto* (Italian for "stick") as a girl because she was so skinny.

Scouts of America in 1959 and again in 1967. He was awarded the Presidential Medal of Freedom in 1969. On May 30, 1985, the Bob Hope USO Center and World Headquarters was opened in Washington, DC. In 1985 he received Kennedy Center Honors. In 1997, the United States Naval Service *Bob Hope* was christened by the navy and *The Spirit of Bob Hope* cargo plane was christened by the air force. And on Hope's 100th birthday, President George W. Bush established the Bob Hope American Patriot Award.

* * *

STATISTICS ON BOB HOPE'S SERVICE TO THE USO

- Went to Vietnam nine times.
- Did 24 consecutive Christmas tours, starting in 1948.
- Entertained for the USO every year from 1942 to 1990.
- Headlined approximately 60 tours.
- First Bob Hope Christmas Tour was in 1943; visited military bases each December for the next 34 years.
- Started carrying his trademark golf club during his 1969 USO tour.
- Became an honorary veteran, by a 1997 act of Congress signed by President Bill Clinton.

* * *

YOU "AUDIE" BE IN PICTURES

Audie Murphy, the most decorated U.S. soldier in World War II, appeared on the cover of *Life* magazine on July 16, 1945. Actor James Cagney saw him on the cover and invited him out to Hollywood to try acting. After a few small parts, Murphy found success, starring as himself in *To Hell and Back* (1955). His career included 43 other films.

THE CURSE OF
DRACULA

*In every film about Dracula, there's a curse. But did the
curse extend beyond the screen . . . and actually affect the
people involved with bringing the character to life? Don't
dismiss the idea. Read these stories . . . and then decide.*

HORACE LIVERIGHT

The stage producer who brought *Dracula*—and later
Frankenstein—to America made a fortune doing it. But he
was a terrible businessman and spent money as fast as it came in.
He made more than $2 million on Dracula alone, but was so slow
to pay author Bram Stoker's widow, Florence, the royalties she was
due that he lost control of the stage rights in a dispute over a
delinquent payment . . . of a mere $678.01. He died drunk, broke,
and alone in New York in September 1933.

HELEN CHANDLER
She was only 20 when she signed on to play the female lead Mina
Murray in the 1931 film version of *Dracula*, but she was already
close to the end of her film career. It was tragically shortened by a
bad marriage and addictions to alcohol and sleeping pills. By the
mid-1930s she was no longer able to find work in Hollywood, and
in 1940 she was committed to a sanitarium. Ten years later she was
severely burned after smoking and drinking in bed, in what may
have been a suicide attempt. She died in 1965.

DWIGHT FRYE
In the 1931 film, Frye played Renfield, the character who goes
insane after meeting Dracula and spends the rest of the movie as
Dracula's slave. He performed so well in that part that he was
offered a similar role in the movie version of *Frankenstein*, as Dr.
Frankenstein's hunchback assistant, Ygor.

Unfortunately for him, he took it—and was promptly typecast as
the monster's/mad scientist's assistant for the rest of his career. He
didn't get a chance to play any other type of role until 1944, when

—Lorelei (Marilyn Monroe), *Gentleman Prefer Blondes* (1953)

he was cast as the Secretary of War in the film *Wilson*. Not long after he won the part, Frye had a heart attack on a Los Angeles bus and died before he was able to appear in the film.

CARL LAEMMLE, JR.

As president of Universal Pictures, he did more than anyone else to establish Universal as the horror movie studio of the 1930s. He left the studio after it was sold in 1936 and tried to establish himself as an independent producer. He never succeeded. A notorious hypochondriac, Laemmle eventually did come down with a debilitating disease—multiple sclerosis—in the early 1960s. He died in 1979—40 years to the day after the death of his father.

BELA LUGOSI

Worn out by years of playing *Dracula* in New York and on the road, Lugosi was already sick of the vampire character by the time he began work on the film version; the indignity of being paid less than his supporting cast only made things worse. Reporter Lillian Shirley recounted one incident that took place in Lugosi's dressing room between scenes:

> I was with him when a telegram arrived. It was from Henry Duffy, the Pacific Coast theatre impresario, who wanted Mr. Lugosi to play Dracula for sixteen weeks. "No! Not at any price," he yelled. "When I am through with this picture I hope never to hear of Dracula again. I cannot stand it. . . . I do not intend that it shall possess me. No one knows what I suffer for this role."

But like a real vampire, Lugosi was trapped in his role. *Dracula* was a box-office smash when it premiered in 1931 and Universal, eager to repeat its success, offered Lugosi the part of the monster in *Frankenstein*. It was the first in a series of planned monster movie roles for Lugosi that Universal hoped would turn Lugosi into "the new Lon Chaney," man of a thousand monsters.

Foolishly, Lugosi turned down the role of the Frankenstein monster because there was no dialogue—Frankenstein spoke only in grunts—and the makeup would have obscured his features, which he feared would prevent fans from knowing that he was the one under all that makeup.

The role went instead to an unknown actor named William Henry Pratt . . . who changed his name to Boris Karloff and within a year eclipsed Lugosi to become Hollywood's most famous horror star of the 1930s.

"Thereafter," David Skal writes in V *Is for Vampire*, "Lugosi was never able to negotiate a lucrative Hollywood contract. *Dracula* was the height of his Hollywood career, and also the beginning of its end." His last good role was as the monster keeper Ygor in the 1939 film *Son of Frankenstein*, considered to be the finest performance of his entire career.

Lugosi played Count Dracula for a second and final time in the 1948 Universal film *Abbot and Costello Meet Frankenstein*, his last major-studio film. After that he was reduced to appearing in a string of low-budget films, including the Ed Wood film *Bride of the Monster* (1956). Wood also had cast Lugosi in his film *Plan 9 From Outer Space* (1958), but Lugosi died on August 16, 1956 (and was buried in full Dracula costume, cape, and makeup), so Wood recycled some old footage of Lugosi and hired a stand-in, who covered his face with his cape so that viewers would think he was Lugosi. When he died, Lugosi left an estate valued at $2,900.

FLORENCE STOKER

Mrs. Stoker was nearly broke when she sold Universal the movie rights to *Dracula*, a sale that, combined with the royalties from the novel and the London and American plays, enabled her to live in modest comfort for the rest of her life. But she never did get rich off of the property that would bring wealth to so many others. When she died in 1937, she left an estate valued at £6,913.

Then again, Mrs. Stoker may have been luckier than she knew: After her death it was discovered that when Bram Stoker was issued a copyright for *Dracula* in 1897, he or his agents neglected to turn over two copies of the work to the American copyright office as was required by law; and the Stoker estate failed to do so again in the 1920s when the copyright was renewed in the U.K. Since Stoker failed to comply with the requirements of the law, *Dracula* was technically in the public domain, which meant that anyone in the United States could have published the novel or adapted it into plays, movies, or any other form without Mrs. Stoker's permission and without having to pay her a cent in royalties.

For more on Dracula, turn to page 341.

Sigourney Weaver was named Susan. She took her stage name from *The Great Gatsby*.

MUCHO MONEYMAKERS

How do the biggest box office champs stack up against each other? We did a little math (and some adjusting for inflation) to find out just how much moola the biggest earners pulled in.

ALL-TIME BOX OFFICE CHAMP
It shouldn't be too surprising that the biggest box office earner of all time is *Gone With the Wind*, released in 1939. Its lifetime box office take: $1,293,085,600.

LUKE MAKES LOOT
The Force is still with *Star Wars* (1977), which pulled in $1,139,965,400. It's the second-highest earner, next to *Gone With the Wind*. *The Empire Strikes Back* is also the highest-earning sequel of all time with earnings of $628,356,100.

THE SOUND OF MONEY
The Sound of Music brought studios some of their favorite things: profits. The musical made $911,458,400, the third-highest all-time earner on our list.

GROSSEST MOVIE WITH THE HIGHEST GROSS
The Exorcist pulled audiences in (and drove some away) with its head-spinning and pea soup–soaking action. It made $707,639,500.

ANIMATED EARNERS
Feature-length cartoons make big bucks. And the top earner was the very first one: *Snow White and the Seven Dwarfs* tops out at $697,600,000. The next biggest cartoon? The popular *101 Dalmations*, which came in just behind *Snow White* with $639,470,000 in earnings.

BIG YUKS EQUALS BIG BUCKS
The Sting has made the most money by making people laugh. This criminal caper earned $570,514,300.

HOW SUPERHEROES STACK UP
Beating out *Superman* and *Batman*, your friendly neighborhood *Spider-Man* takes top honors. The wall-crawling web-slinger brought in $444,702,400.

WINNING WESTERN
Butch Cassidy and the Sundance Kid is the biggest moneymaker in the West. The movie made $451,570,300.

BIGGEST MOVIE ABOUT CROSS-DRESSING
More people paid to see Dustin Hoffman dress like a woman in *Tootsie* than paid to see Robin Williams do the same in *Mrs. Doubtfire*. *Tootsie* earned $364,185,200 compared to *Doubtfire*'s $337,180,100.

* * *

QUOTES OF EVIL
Some favorite lines from our favorite villains.

"You beasts! But I'm not beaten yet. You've won the battle, but I'm about to win the wardrobe."
—Cruella De Vil (Glenn Close),
101 Dalmations (1996)

"Choose your next witticism carefully Mr. Bond, it may be your last."
—Auric Goldfinger (Gert Frobe),
Goldfinger (1964)

"I am your number one fan."
—Annie Wilkes (Kathy Bates),
Misery (1990)

* * *

"It's the movies that have really been running things in America ever since they were invented. They show you what to do, how to do it, when to do it, how to feel about it, and how to look how you feel about it."
—Andy Warhol

YOUR GUIDE TO
THE THIN MAN

He was a retired detective and she was a wealthy heiress; they traveled through life with Asta, their wirehaired terrier, happily anticipating their next adventure . . . and their next cocktail.

The first thing you should know (if you don't already) is that the Thin Man of the title refers to the murder victim in the first movie. But since everyone seemed to think it referred to detective Nick Charles, the producers—in typical Hollywood fashion—decided to use it in all the sequels.

MEET THE AUTHOR
Dashiell Hammett wrote *The Thin Man*, the successful novel on which the movie series was based. He modeled Nick and Nora after himself and his significant other, playwright Lillian Hellman, to whom the 1934 novel *The Thin Man*—which would prove to be his fifth and final book—is dedicated. Even though Hammett didn't write the screenplays for the movie series, much of the dialogue— that delightfully flippant repartee—is taken straight from the book.

MEET THE CAST AND CREW
Other actors have played Nick and Nora over the years, on radio and TV (including Peter Lawford and Phyllis Kirk in the TV series in the 1950s), but William Powell and Myrna Loy defined the cocktail-swigging couple for generations to come.

When director W. S. "Woody" Van Dyke was hired to direct *The Thin Man*, he had just finished directing Powell and Loy in *Manhattan Melodrama*. He knew great chemistry when he saw it, and he wanted them for *The Thin Man*. But MGM boss Louis B. Mayer had some objections. In his opinion, Powell was too old for the part and Loy, who'd long been typecast as an exotic vamp, wasn't the right type to play the witty Nora. Van Dyke insisted and Mayer eventually relented. Van Dyke shot the movie in just

Tom Hanks collects typewriters from the 1940s.

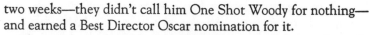

two weeks—they didn't call him One Shot Woody for nothing—
and earned a Best Director Oscar nomination for it.

The movie was hugely successful and cemented the stardom of
Powell and Loy. Despite their chemistry, the two were never lovers,
nor were they married, as a lot of moviegoers thought. But they
were lifelong friends and virtually inseparable from the two characters they played. Powell claimed that Nick was as close to his personality as a screen character could ever get. Fans identified Loy
with Nora for most of her life; in her 1987 autobiography she
wrote, "Recently, the boy who delivers my afternoon paper
returned my payment with a note: 'Never a charge for Nora
Charles.' Now, that's immortality!"

THE INSIDE GUIDE

Like any good series, *The Thin Man* movies are sprinkled with
familiar little details. Here's what to look for:

Alcohol. And lots of it. Thanks to the repeal of Prohibition a few
years before the series began, Nick and Nora are free to enjoy their
cocktail hour, with Nick usually doing the mixing. His secret to a
well-concocted drink: "The important thing is the rhythm! Always
have rhythm in your shaking. Now a Manhattan you shake to fox-
trot time, a Bronx to two-step time, a dry martini you always shake
to waltz time."

Asta. The female Schnauzer in Hammett's novel became a male
wirehaired terrier in the movie. Asta helps out with the sleuthing;
sometimes he'll even find an important clue. But he's no dummy—
he'll scoot into the nearest hiding place when danger threatens.

A dog named Skippy played Asta in the first four films; he was
also featured in the classics *Bringing Up Baby* and *The Awful Truth*.
Skippy wasn't the friendliest of dogs; his trainer Frank Weatherwax
(brother of Lassie's trainer, Rudd Weatherwax), kept him away
from his costars, so he never really got to know either Powell or
Loy—except to bite them on several occasions.

Criminal acquaintances. Because of Nick's past as a private detective, he has a lot of old cronies from the seamy side of life. With
nicknames like Creeps, Meatballs, and Spider, they're primarily
petty criminals—whom Nora is usually delighted to meet. One of
her catchphrases to Nick is, "You know the nicest people!"

The working title of *Pretty Woman* (1990) was "$3,000."

Nora being ditched. Nora always wants to be involved in the sleuthing, but Nick fears for her safety and tries to sideline her—often by sending her on a wild-goose chase. It usually doesn't work; the resourceful Nora always ends up thwarting his plans and joining in the fun, anyway.

The payoff. At the end of each film, the whole group of suspects is called together, and Nick, after a few well-directed questions, solves the case.

THE MOVIES TO WATCH

There are six films in the series. Most critics agree that the first few are the best.

The Thin Man (1934)

Set in New York City at Christmastime, the original Thin Man tale centers on an absentminded inventor and his neurotic family. They pull the Charleses into a cluster of crimes including embezzlement, bigamy, and several murders.

After the Thin Man (1936)

Set in San Francisco, a New Year's Eve celebration takes a deadly turn involving money, matrimony, and murder. Nick is wrangled into investigating when Nora's cousin Selma is accused of killing her husband. A young Jimmy Stewart plays one of the suspects.

Another Thin Man (1939)

Nick, Nora, and Asta investigate a murder on Long Island. When they arrive back in Manhattan, son Nicky Jr. celebrates his first birthday at a party thrown for him by some of the "nicest people."

Shadow of the Thin Man (1941)

A day at the races turns into a murder investigation when a jockey is found shot to death. Nick Jr., now a scene stealer at about three years old, forces Nick Sr. to drink milk with him at the dinner table—much to Nick's dismay, Nora's amusement, and their maid's amazement.

The Thin Man Goes Home (1945)

Nick and Nora visit Nick's hometown, where Nick gets to solve a

Hitchcock's *The Birds* (1963) was a relative flop when released in theaters . . .

crime and impress his parents, who disapprove of his chosen profession as a detective. This was the only film that Myrna Loy made during World War II; she devoted all her other energies during the war years to the Red Cross.

Song of the Thin Man (1947)
Nick and Nora mingle with musicians they meet while on a gambling boat. Love and money—or lack thereof—lead to murder and madness in the world of jive-talking hipsters. Nick Jr., who's now old enough (around seven) for piano lessons, baseball, and going to the movies, is played by Dean Stockwell (*Blue Velvet*, and TV's *Quantum Leap*).

IT'S AN HONOR JUST TO BE NOMINATED
The series didn't win any Academy Awards, but it did receive five nominations. *The Thin Man* was nominated for Best Picture; Best Actor in a Leading Role; Best Director; and Best Writing, Adaptation. *After the Thin Man* was nominated in the category of Best Writing, Screenplay.

* * *

LOOK, UP IN THE SKY!
Searchlights were first used at a Hollywood movie premier in 1922. *Robin Hood*, starring Douglas Fairbanks, opened at Grauman's Egyptian Theatre that night. But in 1942 Hollywood premieres could no longer use them. During World War II, West Coast citizens had to dim their lights at night to prevent enemy attacks and minimize opportunities for surveillance. After the war, the lights were put back on.

* * *

HALLOWEEN IN HOLLYWOOD
The City of West Hollywood holds the largest Halloween street celebration every October. The Halloween Costume Carnaval is held on Halloween night on a one-mile stretch of Santa Monica Boulevard that is packed with more than 350,000 revelers every year.

but on TV (NBC, 1968), it got the highest ratings of any movie at that time.

BOX OFFICE BLOOPERS

We all love bloopers. Here are a bunch of movie
mistakes to look for in popular films.

MOVIE: *Terminator 2: Judgment Day* (1991)
SCENE: As Arnold Schwarzenegger's cyborg character heads
toward a bar, he passes a parked car.
BLOOPER: Arnie's cranial read-out says the car he's scanning is a
Plymouth sedan. It's actually a Ford.

MOVIE: *Forrest Gump* (1994)
SCENE: In a sequence set around 1970, someone is shown reading
a copy of *USA Today*.
BLOOPER: The newspaper wasn't established until 1982.

MOVIE: *Wayne's World* (1992)
SCENE: Wayne and Garth are filming their cable access show.
BLOOPER: The exterior shot of the house shows it's night. Look
out the window of the interior shot: it's daytime.

MOVIE: *The Invisible Man* (1933)
SCENE: Claude Rains, in the title role, strips completely naked
and uses his invisibility to elude police.
BLOOPER: The police track his footprints in the snow. But check
out the footprints—they're made by feet wearing shoes.

MOVIE: *The Story of Robin Hood* (1952)
SCENE: In one scene, Maid Marian (played by Joan Rice) wears a
dress with a zipper in the back.
BLOOPER: Did they have zippers in the 12th century?

MOVIE: *Wild Wild West* (1999)
SCENE: After thwarting the plans of the evil Loveless (Kenneth
Branagh), Jim West (Will Smith) and Artemus Gordon (Kevin
Kline) ride off into the sunset heading back to Washington, D.C.
BLOOPER: A romantic notion, but impossible: Washington is in
the east and the sun sets in the west.

MOVIE: *Field of Dreams* (1989)
SCENE: Shoeless Joe Jackson is shown batting right-handed.
BLOOPER: The real Shoeless Joe was left-handed.

MOVIE: *The Wizard of Oz* (1939)
SCENE: Before the Wicked Witch of the West sends her flying monkeys to capture Dorothy and friends in the Haunted Forest, she tells the head monkey that she has "sent a little insect on ahead to take the fight out of them." What does she mean by that? She's referring to a song-and-dance sequence featuring "The Jitterbug," a bug that causes its victims to dance wildly until they are exhausted.
BLOOPER: The sequence was cut from the film before its release.

MOVIE: *Face-Off* (1997)
SCENE: The hero (John Travolta) learns that a bomb is about to go off somewhere. But where? He's got six days to pry the information from the villain. We then see the bomb—it shows 216 hours.
BLOOPER: Do the math: 216 hours equals *nine* days. Did someone forget to tell us we've gone to 36-hour days?

MOVIE: *Entrapment* (1999)
SCENE: Catherine Zeta-Jones's character says she needs 10 seconds to download computer files that will steal billions of dollars from an international bank. She states further that after 11:00 p.m. her computer will steal 1/10th of a second every minute, totaling ten seconds by midnight.
BLOOPER: More Hollywood math: One-tenth of a second per minute for 60 minutes equals only six seconds . . . four shy of the required ten.

* * *

I LOVE A PARADE

Some actors crave Oscars, but George C. Scott didn't. In 1962 he called the award meaningless and turned down his nomination for Best Supporting Actor in *The Hustler* (it was largely moot since he didn't win). But nine years later Scott stayed true even after he won the Best Actor Oscar for *Patton*. This time, not only did he refuse the award, he called the ceremony a "meat parade."

TAXI DRIVER, STARRING NEIL DIAMOND

Some roles are so closely associated with a specific actor that it's hard to imagine he or she wasn't the first choice. But it happens all the time. Can you imagine, for example . . .

KEVIN KLINE AS BATMAN (*Batman*—1989) Many fans were puzzled when Michael Keaton was cast as Batman, but it could have been stranger: Kline was the first choice. Lacking confidence in his action-star abilities, Kline passed on the role and made *A Fish Called Wanda* instead, for which he won an Academy Award. Other actors offered the role of Batman: Alec Baldwin, Charlie Sheen, Pierce Brosnan, Mel Gibson, Bill Murray, and Tom Hanks.

WILL SMITH AS NEO (*The Matrix*—1999) After *Independence Day* and *Men in Black*, Smith was Hollywood's biggest action star. He was offered the lead role in a new action-adventure series called *The Matrix*, but turned it down. Why? Smith didn't want to be involved in an obscure, dense, low-budget science-fiction mess. Instead, he chose to make *Wild Wild West*, which bombed.

GWYNETH PALTROW AS ROLLERGIRL (*Boogie Nights*—1997) Director Paul Thomas Anderson liked Paltrow's performance in his first film, *Hard Eight*, so much that he considered her for the part of Rollergirl in *Boogie Nights*, a movie about the 1970s adult film industry. Paltrow was still relatively unknown and was picking her roles with care. She turned *Boogie Nights* down because of the sex scenes and nudity. Heather Graham got the part.

BILL MURRAY AS FORREST GUMP (*Forrest Gump*—1994) Murray was strongly considered for the role, but lost it to Tom Hanks, whose work in *Philadelphia* proved he was capable of drama. Murray, on the other hand, was still considered a comic actor.

Christopher Walken spent the summer of 1960 as an assistant lion tamer.

NEIL DIAMOND AS TRAVIS BICKLE (*Taxi Driver*—1976)
When Brian De Palma planned to direct the film, he almost cast Diamond, at that time a very successful singer. Producers thought *Taxi Driver* would be an ideal debut for Diamond. His dismal screen test proved otherwise. De Palma dropped out and was replaced by Martin Scorcese, who chose Robert De Niro to star.

ERIC STOLTZ AS MARTY MCFLY (*Back to the Future*—1985)
Michael J. Fox was the first choice to play Marty McFly, but he said he was too busy filming the TV series *Family Ties*, so the producers cast Eric Stoltz (*Mask*, *Some Kind of Wonderful*). When Fox had a change of heart, they fired Stoltz even though they'd already filmed several scenes.

MEG RYAN AS VIVIAN (*Pretty Woman*—1990)
Ryan was the queen of romantic comedy in the late 1980s, and the first choice for *Pretty Woman*. But producers didn't think audiences would find her believable in the role of a prostitute, so they went with a relatively unknown actress instead. The role made Julia Roberts a superstar. (1980s teen movie star Molly Ringwald was also considered.)

WARREN BEATTY AS BILL (*Kill Bill, Vols I & II*—2003/2004)
Quentin Tarantino wrote the Bill character with Warren Beatty in mind, but when discussing the character with Beatty, Tarantino repeatedly insisted he play the part "more like David Carradine." Beatty finally suggested that Tarantino just cast David Carradine. After nearly going with Kevin Costner, Tarantino took Beatty's advice and hired Carradine.

ROD STEWART AS THE PINBALL WIZARD (*Tommy*—1975)
Stewart declined the chance to appear in the film version of The Who's rock opera. Why? His friend Elton John convinced him he'd look ridiculous in the garish costumes and psychedelic musical numbers. Plus, said John, the movie was sure to bomb and would ruin Stewart's career. So who ended up playing the Pinball Wizard? Elton John. He'd wanted the role all along and purposely talked Stewart, the producers' first choice, out of taking it.

You'll find more on page 285.

Thousands of berets were sold after Faye Dunaway wore them in *Bonnie and Clyde*.

CROCETTI AND LEVITCH?

It may be lonely at the top for some people, but these successful duos and trios would beg to differ. These teams worked together, but success may have been more elusive if they had used their real names.

DYNAMIC DUOS
Fred Astaire and Ginger Rogers
Real Names: Frederic Austerlitz Jr. and Virginia Katherine McMath

Stan Laurel and Oliver Hardy
Real Names: Arthur Stanley Jefferson and Oliver Norvell Hardy

George Burns and Gracie Allen
Real Names: Nathan Birnbaum and Grace Ethel Cecile Rosalie Allen

Dean Martin and Jerry Lewis
Real Names: Dino Paul Crocetti and Jerome Levitch

Bud Abbott and Lou Costello
Real Names: William Alexander Abbott and Louis Francis Cristillo

TERRIFIC TRIOS
The Marx Brothers: Groucho, Chico, and Harpo Marx
Real Names: Julius, Leonard, and Adolph (later changed to Arthur) Marx

The Three Stooges: Larry Fine, Moe Howard, and Curly Howard
Real Names: Louis Feinberg, Moses Horwitz, and Jerome Horwitz

"The Road" Trio: Bing Crosby, Bob Hope, and Dorothy Lamour
Real Names: Harry Lillis Crosby, Leslie Townes Hope, and Mary Leta Dorothy Slaton

"You imbecile! You bloated idiot! You stupid fathead!"

WOMEN WHO CALLED THE SHOTS

"There is nothing connected with the staging of a motion picture that a woman cannot do as easily as a man, and there is no reason why she cannot completely master every technicality of the art." —Alice Guy

Despite Alice Guy's declaration, the history of film direction has largely been *his*-story. Of the thousands of features made between 1930 and 1979, fewer than 25 were directed by women. But against long odds, these pioneers managed to leave a legacy for women in film.

THIS LADY'S FIRST: Alice Guy (1873–1968)
Who was she? In 1896 Alice Guy was a secretary with a Parisian camera company that made moving picture cameras. Guy convinced her boss that she could make films to demonstrate the new contraption. Her works were so good that she began making films full time as the head of a newly formed film production department. Then, in 1907, she married Herbert Blaché, and the couple headed to the United States. They settled in Fort Lee, New Jersey, where Alice set up Solax studios to make more films.

What did she accomplish? The title of the world's first film director—normally given to Frenchman Georges Méliès—may actually belong to a Frenchwoman. According to some sources, the first narrative film was Alice Guy's *The Cabbage Fairy*, produced in 1896—a few months before Méliès's *A Trip to the Moon*. Without a doubt however, Guy was the world's first female film director and the first woman to head her own studio. From 1896 to 1920, she directed between 30 and 40 films—some with early experiments in color and synchronized sound (recorded on wax cylinders)—and she supervised more than 300 others. Her legacy had been largely overlooked for many years, until the French government awarded her the badge of the Legion of Honor in 1953.

Her movies: Among Guy's films are: *The Spring Fairy* (1906), one of the first to be shot in color, and *The Pit and the Pendulum* (1913), perhaps the first Edgar Allan Poe story on film. She also

---

—Joel Cairo (Peter Lorre), *The Maltese Falcon* (1941)

worked on some of the first romantic comedies, such as
Matrimony's Speed Limit (1913), about a wedding-hungry woman
who tricks her groom into marriage. She also pioneered another
Hollywood favorite—the car chase. *The Lure* (1914) contained an
exciting scene where a car chases a train.

STAR SHOOTER: Dorothy Arzner (1897–1979)

Who was she? A Hollywood native by birth, Dorothy Arzner grew
up in Los Angeles and planned to become a doctor. Medical school
didn't agree with her, and she dropped out. Arzner turned to ste-
nography to earn a living and found a job at a production company
that would eventually become Paramount Pictures. After a quick
promotion to script girl, she was promoted again to cutting and
editing film (a rare move in those days as that department was usually staffed by men). Arzner's talent captured attention, especially
her work on a famous bullfighting scene in the Rudolph Valentino
picture *Blood and Sand*. From there she began working with director James Cruze on *The Covered Wagon;* Cruze labored behind the
scenes to get Arzner a directorship of her own. In 1927 she got her
chance with *Fashions for Women*, and she went on to direct films
for the next 16 years.

What did she accomplish? Arzner began her work in the silent
era, when there were other female directors. But after the advent
of sound, she was the only woman left standing behind the camera.
Arzner was the first woman to enter the newly formed Director's
Guild of America, and she remained the only woman in the Guild
during her entire career.

Hollywood can thank Arzner for the boom mike. When she
directed Paramount's first talkie, *The Wild Party* (1929), Arzner
wanted to give her leading lady, Clara Bow, more freedom of movement. So Arzner attached a microphone to a fishing pole and followed the actress around with it—the first boom was invented.

Her movies: Arzner's work showcased actresses and made stars
out of some up-and-comers. *Christopher Strong* (1933) was
Katherine Hepburn's first starring role and brought her compar-
isons to Greta Garbo. *Craig's Wife* (1936) was a tour de force for
Rosalind Russell, who played a cold, materialistic housewife: *TIME*
magazine called her direction "distinguished for giving pace without apparent effort to a picture that might, with less expert treatment, have seemed pedestrian."

THE MOTHER OF US ALL: Ida Lupino (c. 1916–1995)

Who was she? Born in London into a famous theatrical family, Ida Lupino became a performer herself. She came to Hollywood in 1934, groomed by Paramount Pictures—they dyed her hair platinum—to be the British Jean Harlow. Not interested in copying another actress, Lupino pushed her way into nonglamorous, gritty roles. She first made her mark as a prostitute out for revenge in 1939's *The Light That Failed*. After a successful decade playing "tough girl" roles—most notably opposite Humphrey Bogart in *High Sierra* (1941)—she decided to try life on the other side of the camera.

In 1949 Lupino left acting and became a partner in a production company, The Filmmakers. When the director of one of its films (*Not Wanted*, which Lupino had co-written) had a heart attack, Lupino took over and was so successful that she continued directing. She directed feature films and expanded into television episodes in a multitude of series—everything from *Bewitched* to *Alfred Hitchcock Presents*.

What did she accomplish? When it came to the content of her movies, Lupino was known for controversial themes and working-class drama. She also earned the nickname, the Female Hitch, for her tough-minded ability to create thrilling suspense and action onscreen.

Behind the camera, Lupino was anything but tough. To succeed in a man's world where women weren't supposed to give orders, Lupino developed a unique directing method: "I'd say, 'Darlings, Mother has a problem. I'd love to do this. Can you do it? It sounds kooky, I know. But can you do this for Mother?'" Her approach worked so well for the director that she had the back of her chair printed with the title: "The Mother of Us All."

Her movies: Among Lupino's most notable films are: *Outrage* (1950), which tackled the controversial subject of rape and *The Hitch-Hiker* (1953), the only true film noir ever directed by a woman, and her biggest financial success.

A STAND-UP GAL: Elaine May (1932–)

Who is she? Elaine May faced the footlights at an early age, working with her father, who was a Yiddish theater actor. In 1957 she and Mike Nichols became an improvisational comedy team that found fame on radio and television, and on Broadway in the

The Fly (1986), starring Jeff Goldblum and Geena Davis.

comedy showcase, An Evening with Mike Nichols and Elaine May. When the comedy team split up in 1961, May turned to playwriting, screenwriting, and performing in films.

Then in 1971 she directed (and acted in) her first feature, A New Leaf. That screwball comedy about a ditzy heiress and a con man (played by Walter Matthau) garnered a Golden Globe nomination for Best Comedy. May went on to direct three more films.

What did she accomplish? So far May's career illustrates some of the pitfalls that plague even the most talented movie makers. Her original three-hour version of A New Leaf was recut (some say butchered) by Paramount executives, and May disavowed the released movie—Golden Globes and all. And though May directed two more critically acclaimed comedies and brought in Oscar nominations, her fourth film Ishtar (1987) was a legendary flop, losing more than $40 million. The film's stars, Dustin Hoffman and Warren Beatty, rebounded from the disaster, but May hasn't directed since.

Her movies: May also directed The Heartbreak Kid (1972) and Mikey and Nickey (1978). Both were acclaimed comedies, and The Heartbreak Kid brought Oscar nominations for supporting actor, Eddie Albert, and May's own daughter, Jeannie Berlin. It did take awhile but there was life after Ishtar for May. In 1996 she teamed up again with Mike Nichols; May wrote and he directed The Bird Cage, an adaptation of the French comedy La Cage aux Folles. It starred Robin Williams and Nathan Lane and was a smash.

THE NEW BREED: (1980 and beyond)

Though higher numbers of women have entered the Director's Guild of America since the 1980s, their numbers remain small— they make up only less than five percent of the total membership. But women continue to make strides forward as they make good movies.

Martha Coolidge: Valley Girl (1983), Real Genius (1985), Rambling Rose (1991)
The first female president of the Director's Guild (2002–2003).

Penny Marshall: Big (1988), Awakenings (1990), A League of Their Own (1992)
The first woman to direct a movie that grossed over $100 million.

Nora Ephron: *Sleepless in Seattle* (1993), *You've Got Mail* (1998)
Ephron's first two outings as director grossed an average of $121
million per film.

Jane Campion: *The Piano* (1993), *The Portrait of a Lady* (1996), *In
the Cut* (2003)
The second woman to be nominated for the Oscar for Best
Director. Italian filmmaker Lina Wertmüller was the first, for
Pasqualino Settebellezze (Seven Beauties) in 1975

Sofia Coppola: *The Virgin Suicides* (1999), *Lost in Translation*
(2003), *Marie Antoinette* (2006)
The third woman, and first American woman, to be nominated for
the Best Director Oscar, for *Lost in Translation*

* * *

"In Hollywood now when people die they don't say 'Did he leave a
will?' but 'Did he leave a diary?'"

—Liza Minnelli

"Hollywood has always been a cage . . . a cage to catch our
dreams."

—John Huston

"Hollywood is a place where people from Iowa mistake each other
for stars."

—Fred Allen, comedian

* * *

HIS REAL NAME
You may know him now as Albert Brooks (*Broadcast News*,
Finding Nemo) but when he came into this world on July 22, 1947,
he had a different name: Albert Einstein.

—Trent (Vince Vaughn), *Swingers* (1996)

HOLLYWOOD SCANDAL: 1921, PART 1

*A woman is found dead . . . a well-known celebrity is charged
with murder . . . the whole world follows the trial. O. J. Simpson?
Nope—Fatty Arbuckle. In its day, the Arbuckle trial was as
big as the Simpson trial. Here's the story.*

KNOCK AT THE DOOR

On the morning of Saturday, September 10, 1921, two men from the San Francisco sheriff's office paid a visit to Roscoe "Fatty" Arbuckle, then Hollywood's most famous comedian, at his home in Los Angeles. One of the men read from an official court summons:

"You are hereby summoned to return immediately to San Francisco for questioning. . . . You are charged with murder in the first degree."

Arbuckle, thinking the men were pulling a practical joke, let out a laugh. "And who do you suppose I killed?"

"Virginia Rappé."

Arbuckle instantly knew that this was no joke. He'd just returned from a trip to San Francisco, where he'd thrown a party over the Labor Day weekend to celebrate his new $3 million movie contract—then the largest in Hollywood history—with Paramount Pictures. A 26-year-old bit actress named Virginia Rappé had fallen ill at the party, presumably from drinking too much bootleg booze. Arbuckle had seen to it that the woman received medical attention before he returned to L.A., but now Rappé was dead—and Arbuckle had somehow been implicated in her death. Whatever doubts he may still have had about the summons vanished the following morning as he read the three-inch headlines in the *Los Angeles Examiner*:

ARBUCKLE HELD FOR MURDER!

The autopsy report showed that Rappé died from acute peritonitis, an inflammation of the abdominal lining brought on by a ruptured bladder. Why was Arbuckle a suspect in the death? Because Maude "Bambina" Delmont, another woman at the party, had filed

Three vegetarian stars: Reese Witherspoon, Alicia Silverstone, and Natalie Portman.

a statement with San Francisco police claiming that she had seen Arbuckle drag Rappé into his bedroom against her will and assault her. As she later explained to newspaper reporters:

"I could hear Virginia kicking and screaming violently and I had to kick and batter the door before Mr. Arbuckle would let me in. I looked at the bed. There was Virginia, helpless and ravaged. When Virginia kept screaming in agony at what Mr. Arbuckle had done, he turned to me and said, 'Shut her up or I'll throw her out a window.' He then went back to his drunken party and danced while poor Virginia lay dying."

The 265 pound comedian had supposedly burst Rappè's bladder with his weight during the assault. And because the injury had gone undiagnosed and untreated, it developed into a massive abdominal infection, killing Rappè.

PRESSING CHARGES

After Delmont's statement was filed, San Francisco District Attorney Matthew Brady ordered Arbuckle's arrest and issued a public statement to the press:

"The evidence in my possession shows conclusively that either a rape or an attempt to rape was perpetrated on Miss Rappè by Roscoe Arbuckle. The evidence discloses beyond question that her bladder was ruptured by the weight of the body of Arbuckle either in a rape assault or an attempt to commit rape."

FALSE WITNESS

Brady's case was based almost entirely on Delmont's police statement. And the case certainly appeared substantial—at least until Brady looked into Maude Delmont's background after she gave her statement. Then he discovered a police record containing more than 50 counts of bigamy, fraud, racketeering, extortion, and other crimes (including one outstanding bigamy warrant, which Brady would later use to his advantage).

WHAT REALLY HAPPENED

Brady later learned from other guests at the party that a very drunk Maude Delmont had actually been locked in a bathroom with Lowell Sherman, another party guest, during the entire time that she claimed to have witnessed Arbuckle with Rappé. She could not have seen any of the things she claimed to have seen—and if

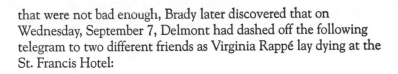

that were not bad enough, Brady later discovered that on Wednesday, September 7, Delmont had dashed off the following telegram to two different friends as Virginia Rappé lay dying at the St. Francis Hotel:

> WE HAVE ROSCOE ARBUCKLE IN A HOLE
> HERE CHANCE TO MAKE MONEY OUT OF HIM

BLIND AMBITION
District Attorney Brady had no case—there wasn't a shred of physical evidence to indicate that Arbuckle had committed any crime against Rappé; his only "witness" was a woman with a long criminal record; and the telegrams demonstrated clearly that Delmont's police statement was part of an attempt to blackmail Arbuckle.

Despite all this, Brady decided to bring the case to trial. Why? One theory: Brady, whom acquaintances described as a "self-serving, arrogant, ruthless man with blind ambition and a quick temper," was gearing up to run for governor of California. He probably figured that winning a murder conviction against Hollywood's biggest comedian would score points with the public.

JUDGE NOT
Still, the case would not have gone to trial if the police judge, Sylvain Lazarus, had dismissed the case due to lack of evidence. But Judge Lazarus refused to throw it out, citing the "larger issues" surrounding the case:

> I do not find any evidence that Mr. Arbuckle either committed or attempted to commit rape. The court has been presented with the merest outline. . . . The district attorney has presented barely enough facts to justify my holding the defendant on the charge which is here filed against him.

> But we are not trying Roscoe Arbuckle alone; we are not trying the screen celebrity who has given joy and pleasure to the entire world; we are actually, gentlemen, trying ourselves.

> We are trying our present-day morals, our present-day social conditions, our present-day looseness of thought and lack of social balance. . . .

> I have decided to make a holding on the ground of manslaughter.

Winston Churchill, Mussolini, and Pope John Paul II all wrote movie scripts.

The judge suspected Arbuckle was innocent, the district attorney *knew* Arbuckle was innocent, and yet the case still went to trial.

EXTRA!

Much like the Menendez brothers trials and the O.J. Simpson trials of the 1990s, the media—which in the 1920s consisted mostly of newspapers—had a field day with the Arbuckle trial. Unlike the Simpson trial, however, the lack of evidence in the Arbuckle trial led most newspapers to conclude that Arbuckle was innocent. Most papers, that is, except for those owned by media baron William Randolph Hearst. His papers loudly attacked Arbuckle's character, insinuated his guilt, and ran as many as six special editions per day to keep readers up-to-date on the latest developments in the case.

The Hearst papers published the most lurid accounts of the crime and the trial, and even stooped to publicizing totally unsubstantiated rumors about the case—the most famous of which was that Arbuckle, supposedly too impotent from booze to rape Rappé himself, had used a Coke bottle (some accounts said it was a champagne bottle) instead, causing her bladder to rupture. "Nowhere in any testimony in the court transcripts, police reports, or personal interviews did this story appear," Andy Edmonds writes in *Frame Up! The Untold Story of Roscoe "Fatty" Arbuckle.* "Everyone connected with the case vehemently denied it, yet it is the most popular story, and one of the most ugly lies, still connected with the ordeal. The fabrication haunted Roscoe throughout the remainder of his life."

The story is continued on page 157.

* * *

"I was born at the age of twelve on a Metro-Goldwyn-Mayer lot."
—Judy Garland

Samuel L. Jackson was called Machine Gun as a boy because of his childhood stutter.

DISASTER AND DE NILE, PART 1

They don't make epics like Cleopatra *any more—for good reason.*

THE MOVIE: CLEOPATRA (1963)

THE STORY
The Egyptian queen Cleopatra seduces Julius Caesar. After he is stabbed to death in the Roman senate, she seduces his second-in-command, Roman general Mark Antony, who is then defeated in battle by Caesar's successor, Octavian. Antony and Cleopatra commit suicide—but not before one last big love scene!

THE CONCEPT
In the late 1950s, 20th Century Fox was looking for a hit. The studio was in financial trouble, so execs searched the Fox script library for a proven property that could be remade quickly and at minimal expense. Studio president Spyros Skouras chose the 1917 *Cleopatra*, starring Theda Bara, which had made a lot of money for the studio back then. It seemed a sure thing to make some quick cash for Fox. Now all they needed was a producer willing to handle the project.

THE PRODUCER
Luckily for Fox, in October 1958 veteran producer Walter Wanger (rhymes with "ranger") approached Fox with a project he'd been wanting to do for years: the story of Cleopatra. Skouras practically kissed him and then gave him a little less than $2 million and the run of the back lot. He expected a finished movie within 64 days. But Wanger had a bigger vision: he used his own money to hire a set designer and then presented the studio with a more grandiose plan. Impressed by his presentation, Fox execs increased *Cleopatra's* budget to $5 million. They went ahead and started building a replica of ancient Alexandria, Egypt, on Fox's back lot. Now all they needed was a star.

THE STAR, TAKE ONE! ELIZABETH TAYLOR
Wanger didn't want to pick among the bevy of relative unknowns under contract to the studio. He wanted an A-lister to play the

---

Though a major star, John Wayne had only one line in *The Greatest Story Ever Told.*

Egyptian queen; he wanted Elizabeth Taylor. When he offered her the role, Taylor joked that she'd do it for $1 million—an unheard-of amount at the time. She was surprised when Wanger agreed. Fox and Taylor signed a contract, one that would bring Taylor a lot of money (and begin the process of Fox studio's hemorrhaging it). In addition to her salary, she also stipulated that:

- the movie would be shot in Todd-AO, a 70mm film process pioneered by her late husband, Mike Todd, and which she now owned;
- the movie would be shot outside the United States;
- her $1 million salary was for sixteen weeks of work, after which she would go on salary at $50,000 a week;
- she would also receive ten percent of the film's gross;
- the studio would provide $3,000 per week living expenses, plus food and lodging, and first-class airline tickets for herself, three adults (husband Eddie Fisher and two nannies), and three children.

THE DIRECTOR, TAKE ONE! MAMOULIAN

Rouben Mamoulian was hired to direct and began filming at London's Pinewood Studios on September 28, 1960. The studio had been chosen as a cost-saving measure; at the time Britain was offering a tax subsidy to filmmakers who would employ British actors and crews.

CLEOPATRA, TAKE ONE! LONDON

On the first day of shooting, the hairdressers on the set walked out to protest the presence of Taylor's personal hairdresser, Sydney Guilaroff. A deal had to be struck whereby Guilaroff would only do Taylor's hair at her hotel, and the union would take over for the rest of the day's shooting.

Then it started to rain, causing damage to the sets; the papier-mâché statues and facades started peeling and had to be repainted every day. Worse than that, Taylor immediately caught a bad cold, with fever. Mamoulian had to shoot around his Cleopatra until all the scenes that didn't require her—and there weren't many—were done. By October 24, 1960, the production was losing $100,000 a day, so it shut down for a month to give Liz a chance to recover. Mamoulian used the time to work on the script, which, by the way, Taylor despised.

All of Grace Kelly's films were prohibited in Monaco, by order of Prince Rainier.

When she complained about the script, the studio hired veteran screenwriter Nunnally Johnson (*How to Marry a Millionaire*, *The Man in the Gray Flannel Suit*) to fix it. But Johnson ended up collecting his fee of $140,000 for nothing because Mamoulian liked his unfinished script just the way it was. Things came to a head: when the director threatened to resign, the studio looked at what they had so far—sixteen weeks, $7 million spent, 10 minutes of useable footage—and fired Mamoulian.

THE DIRECTOR, TAKE TWO! MANKIEWICZ

Taylor's contract had also included a previously unheard-of clause giving her director approval. There were only two men she wanted to replace Mamoulian: One was George Stevens, who'd directed her in *Giant*, but he was busy working on *The Greatest Story Ever Told*. The other was Joseph L. Mankiewicz, who'd directed Taylor in *Suddenly, Last Summer* and had won back-to-back Best Writing and Best Director Oscars for *A Letter to Three Wives* (1949) and *All About Eve* (1950).

Spyros Skouras made a series of phone calls begging Mankiewicz to take on the job. He finally accepted, to the tune of $1.5 million. His remarks on seeing Mamoulian's sets for the first time were that they were a "garish nightmare." Finding that there was still no finished script, Mankiewicz started writing one himself. Which kept him busy while Taylor recovered from yet another illness—this time a pneumonia so severe that she was in and out of comas and needed a tracheotomy.

THE STARS, TAKE TWO! CAESAR & ANTONY

It was during this period that the production reached the $12 million mark. Because of Liz's delicate health, Mankiewicz decided to move the shoot to warmer, sunnier Italy. Actors Peter Finch and Stephen Boyd (who'd been hired to play Julius Caesar and Mark Antony, respectively) had prior commitments and dropped out of the picture. Rex Harrison was hired to replace Finch. But who would play Mark Antony? Mankiewicz decided that he had to have Richard Burton, who was starring in *Camelot* on Broadway at the time. No problem. The studio bought out Burton's contract for $250,000 and signed him to *Cleopatra* for $300,000.

The action is continued on page 363.

Mickey Mouse was banned in Romania in 1935 on the grounds that . . .

"I SPY"
AT THE MOVIES

*You probably remember the kids' game "I spy with my
little eye . . ." Moviemakers have been playing it for years.
Want to play? Here are some in-jokes and gags you can
look for the next time you see these films.*

SPIDER-MAN (2002)
I Spy . . . Lucy Lawless, star of *Xena: Warrior Princess*
Where to Find Her: She appears as the red-haired punker who
makes the astute observation: "A man with eight arms? Sounds like
a good time to me!" (*Spider-Man* director Sam Raimi worked as a
producer on *Xena*.)

AMERICAN PIE (1999)
I Spy . . . Blink 182
Where to Find Them: During the Internet scene, the popular
band can be seen watching the Webcast. Their song "Mutt" is
playing in the background.

HOW THE GRINCH STOLE CHRISTMAS (2000)
I Spy . . . Director Ron Howard's favorite hat
Where to Find It: On the Grinch's head—when he is "directing"
his dog Max to become a reindeer. Legend has it that Jim Carrey
stole the hat and ad-libbed an imitation of Howard. Howard
thought the bit was funny and left it in the movie, hat and all.

ERIN BROCKOVICH (2000)
I Spy . . . The real Erin Brockovich
Where to Find Her: When the fake Erin (Julia Roberts) is in a
restaurant with her kids, their waitress is the real Erin. Her name
tag reads "Julia."

THE MATRIX (1999)
I Spy . . . Andy and Larry Wachowski, the film's directors
Where to Find Them: They're the two window washers outside
the office where Neo is being chastised for arriving late to work.

. . . he was frightening to children.

SPIES LIKE US (1985)
I Spy . . . Blues legend B.B. King
Where to Find Him: He's one of the CIA agents at the drive-in theater/missile silo. In the credits, he's listed as "Ace Tomato Agent."

FERRIS BUELLER'S DAY OFF (1986)
I Spy . . . References to several of director John Hughes's movies
Where to Find Them: On the license plates of various cars. VCTN (*National Lampoon's Vacation*), TBC (*The Breakfast Club*), MMOM (*Mr. Mom*), and 4FBDO (*Ferris Bueller's Day Off*).

MONSTERS, INC. (2001)
I Spy . . . Pixar's phone number
Where to Find It: At the end of the simulation that begins the film, a monster reaches for a knob on the control panel. Just below it and to the left is a series of 10 numbers. Dial them and you'll reach Pixar, the studio that made the movie.

THE SHAWSHANK REDEMPTION (1994)
I Spy . . . A photograph of Morgan Freeman's son
Where to Find It: The parole papers that repeatedly receive a rejected stamp show a picture of Red (Morgan Freeman) when he was a young man. Morgan's son Alfonzo was used for the shot.

GEORGE LUCAS MOVIES
I Spy . . . THX-1138
Where to Find It: *THX-1138* was the name of Lucas's first feature film, and he has paid homage to it throughout his career. A license plate in *American Graffiti* reads "1T1H3X8." Luke Skywalker rescued Princess Leia from Cell Block 1138 in *Star Wars*. In *Raiders of the Lost Ark*, a loudspeaker in the submarine dock states, "Ein, Ein, Drei, Acht" ("One, one, three, eight" in German). A battle droid in *The Phantom Menace* has the designation—you guessed it—1138. (Note: We don't know if there are any references to it in *Howard the Duck*—we couldn't make it through a complete viewing.)

THOROUGHLY MODERN MAE

To say that Mae West had a way with words would be a serious understatement. A master comedienne, screenwriter, and a woman with men on her mind, here are some bits of wisdom from her.

"I'm no angel, but I've spread my wings a bit."

"There was a time when I didn't know where my next husband was comin' from."

"A man in love is like a clipped coupon—it's time to cash in."

"I always say, keep a diary and someday it'll keep you."

"When women go wrong, men go right after them."

"Don't let a man put anything over on you—outside of an umbrella."

"A man in the house is worth two in the street."

"Give a man a free hand and he'll try to put it all over you."

"Every man I meet wants to protect me. I can't figure out what from."

"Too much of a good thing can be wonderful."

"Anytime you got nothin' to do—and a lot of time to do it—come on up."

"I see you're a man with ideals. I guess I better be going while you've still got them."

"When I'm good, I'm very good. But when I'm bad, I'm better."

"I generally avoid temptation unless I can't resist it."

"When choosing between two evils, I always like to pick the one I never tried before."

"It's not the men in my life, but the life in my men."

"There are no good girls gone wrong, just bad girls found out."

"Too many girls follow the line of least resistance—but a good line is hard to resist."

"Is that a gun in your pocket, or are you just glad to see me?"

—Otto (Kevin Kline), *A Fish Called Wanda* (1988)

A TRAGIC END FOR A COMIC STAR

This 70-year-old mystery began on December 16, 1935, when movie actress Thelma Todd was found dead in her garage. Reddened from carbon monoxide poisoning, her body was slumped over in the front seat of her car. At first it looked like a suicide, but that made her broken bones and bruises tough to explain. Was she murdered? Was it an accident?

Thelma Todd was one of Hollywood's most successful comediennes in the 1930s. Nicknamed Hot Toddy and the Ice Cream Blonde, this pretty actress had a talent for comedy and worked for Hal Roach Studios. There she was cast in several Stan Laurel and Oliver Hardy films, including 1929's *Unaccustomed as We Are* (their first talkie) and *Another Fine Mess* (1930). Two of her best films (among the more than 100 movies she appeared in) were the Marx Brothers' *Monkey Business* (1931) and *Horse Feathers* (1932).

Two days before her body was found in her garage, Thelma had been at a party held at the Café Trocadero on Sunset Boulevard. Todd loved a good time and was known for her hard-partying ways. This night would be no different. She drank quite heavily and stayed at the party until 2:45 a.m. Her chauffeur drove her home, but she refused his help in walking to her apartment and sent him home. He was the last known person to see her alive. Her success made the suicide theories difficult to believe, and a look into her personal life made a strong case for foul play.

IN OVER HER HEAD
Despite an on-screen life full of laughs, Todd's offscreen life was full of drama, intrigue, and crime. Todd was attracted to powerful men, and both Pat DiCicco and Lucky Luciano intrigued her. The two men were involved with organized crime. In 1930s Los Angeles, control of gambling, drugs, prostitution, and restaurant unions was heatedly fought for by various factions and attracted gangsters like Luciano from as far away as New York City.

The average number of letters used in a film title is 17.

Todd married DiCicco in 1932. DiCicco was unfortunate enough to introduce Todd to Lucky Luciano. Interested in the pretty blond actress, Luciano found reasons to send DiCicco on errands to New York. With her husband often away, Thelma was pressured into becoming Lucky's date and, eventually, his lover.

Roland West, one of Todd's former lovers, had been involved with about a dozen films, mainly silent. But his career had come to an end in 1931 after he directed and produced *Corsair*, an unsuccessful bid to launch Thelma Todd as a dramatic star. Casting around for other ways to make money, West proposed a new business venture to Todd—a restaurant.

In August 1934 Thelma Todd's Sidewalk Café opened. A Spanish-style, three-story building housed the restaurant on the main floor, a private bar and a couple of apartments on the second floor, and storage on the smaller third floor. As planned, West ran the place; his wife, actress Jewel Carmen, was a silent partner and financial backer; and Thelma Todd's fame drew the crowds. What seemed to be a positive step in Todd's life, however, may have been the beginning of the end for the actress-entrepreneur.

HOT TODDY IN HOT WATER

Todd divorced her husband in 1934, but her relationship with Luciano was not so easily dissolved. Luciano soon wormed his way into the café's business. His growing influence with the unions allowed his organization to manipulate deliveries of food and drink, driving up prices and making the restaurant more costly to operate. West and the café's treasurer were allegedly pressured into complying—something they kept from Todd. Luciano also insisted on opening an illegal gambling parlor on the building's secluded third floor, which Todd vehemently opposed. Instead, she wanted to open a steak house there; that way, she and West could keep control of the third floor by making it physically unavailable to Luciano. But Luciano still tried to "persuade" West and Todd by sending his associates to the restaurant to repeat his demands.

Fed up with the pressure and demands from Luciano, Todd decided to fight back. She had made an appointment with the district attorney's office for December 17 at 11:30 a.m. (coincidently—or not—one day after she died). Although Luciano thought he

A 1955 film made in India was titled *Ha Ha Hee Hee Hoo Hoo*.

could control her, Todd was presumably ready to spill all she knew about the mobster in order to protect herself and her business. She also planned an independent audit of the café's records for the beginning of the new year. Busy as it was, the restaurant still wasn't making money, and West and the café's treasurer weren't giving her the answers she demanded about the finances.

Luciano's plans for the new year were quite different. A few days before Thanksgiving, fellow diners at the Brown Derby restaurant overheard this exchange between the mobster and the actress:

"You do what you have to do. But I will open the gambling casino by the first of the year."

"You'll open a gambling casino in my restaurant over my dead body!" Todd shouted.

"That can be arranged," Luciano calmly responded.

Perhaps it was.

REASONABLE DOUBTS?

After Todd's body was discovered, the *Los Angeles Times* front-page headline screamed, "Body of Thelma Todd Found in Death Riddle." Just days later, on December 19, 1935, a grand-jury panel convened on the fifth floor of the Los Angeles Hall of Justice to answer that riddle. With national media camped outside, the jury called more than 40 witnesses to explain the circumstances leading up to Todd's death.

After the jury reviewed the evidence, they ruled her death accidental (rather than suicide) and decided that she had probably died sometime Sunday evening (rather than more than 12 hours earlier).

Accidental death presumed that an intoxicated Todd (her blood alcohol content was confirmed at 0.13 percent) had taken refuge in her car after having been locked out of her apartment above the café—either by forgetting her keys or by having been intentionally locked out by West (who lived in the adjoining apartment). West was said to have been fed up with her late-night carousing and the amount of time she was spending away from the restaurant. Perhaps Todd had simply turned on the engine for heat and fallen asleep. If that was the case, though, what would explain the blood and bruises found on her body? And would she suffer cracked ribs from merely slumping over a steering wheel?

The first ruling by the medical examiner, suicide by carbon monoxide, discounts the gala opening planned for the steak house in little more than two weeks, to say nothing of Todd's flourishing film career. Alice Todd, Thelma's mother, initially offered an explanation favored by many: "My daughter was murdered." One theory? A beating knocked Todd unconscious; the killer placed her in her car, turned on the ignition, and shut the door. Carbon monoxide poisoned her as she lay on the front seat.

THE THEORIES

Among the leading suspects were the three main men in Todd's life: Luciano, West, and DiCicco. Their motives were all clear. Luciano wanted his illegal casino and orchestrated her murder to get it; suspiciously, Luciano had flown out of town on the morning of December 17 and reportedly never returned to Los Angeles. He also allegedly knew about Todd's pending appointment with the DA and was not pleased by the news. Roland West came under suspicion as a jealous ex-lover or greedy business partner; perhaps a fight with Todd turned deadly. Todd's ex-husband, Pat DiCicco, drew police attention because he unsuccessfully tried to convince Todd to involve him in the steak house venture. But no hard evidence could link any of these men to her death, and no one was ever arrested. Alice Todd's only solace would be taking her daughter's cremated remains back to their hometown with her. After Alice's death, the two were buried together in the Todd family plot in Lawrence, Massachusetts. The full story behind Thelma Todd's death still remains untold. Perhaps the riddle will never be solved.

* * *

FOUR MOST COPIED HOLLYWOOD NOSES

1. Heather Locklear
2. Nicole Kidman
3. Marisa Tomei
4. Catherine Zeta-Jones

Debra Winger's first role: Debbie in *Slumber Party '57* (1975).

WRITTEN IN STONE

Hollywood stars' tombstones are chiseled with
final thoughts, permanent publicity, and last laughs.

Jack Lemmon: In

Gene Autry: America's Favorite Cowboy, American Hero, Philanthropist, Patriot and Veteran, Movie Star, Singer, Composer, Baseball Fan and Owner, 33rd Degree Mason, Media Entrepreneur, Loving Husband, Gentleman, A Believer In Our Western Heritage.

Billy Wilder: I'm A Writer But Then Nobody's Perfect

Mary Pickford: America's Sweetheart

Ernie Kovacs: Nothing in Moderation

Ed Wynn: Dear God, Thanks.

Frank Sinatra: The Best Is Yet To Come

Billy Barty: In loving memory of Billy Barty, who always thought big.

Sammy Davis Jr.: The Entertainer: He Did It All.

Francis X. Bushman (a star of silent films and the original *Ben-Hur*): King of the Movies

Bonzo (the chimp from *Bedtime for Bonzo*): He made us laugh.

Fred Astaire: I will always love you my darling. Thank You.

Gracie Allen and George Burns: Together Again

Sammy Cahn: Sleep With a Smile

Rodney Dangerfield: There Goes the Neighborhood

Mel Blanc: That's All Folks!

Kate Hudson was originally cast as William's sister in *Almost Famous* (2000).

THE WORST FILMMAKER OF ALL TIME

*There are good movies, and there are bad movies. And then
there are movies that are so bad, they're good. Nobody mastered
the art of the so-good-it's-bad movie quite like 1950s director Ed
Wood, whose creations feature many great examples of all the
"don'ts" of film direction. Follow us on our short journey
through the works of the Worst Filmmaker of All Time.*

From the time he was 7 years old, Edward D. Wood Jr. wanted
to make movies. After seeing *Dracula* (1931), Ed started cutting school to spend as much time as he could at the theater.
He got his first camera as a teenager, and one day hoped to be a
writer, director, and actor—just like his idol, Orson Welles.

FIRST FILM

After enlisting and serving in the marines during World War II,
Wood moved to Hollywood to pursue his filmmaking dream. There
were a few false starts, including one failed production company and
an uncompleted Western. But Ed Wood's big break came in 1952.
He heard that George Weiss, a producer of low-budget exploitation
films, was planning on making a movie out of the Christine
Jorgensen sex-change story. Weiss wasn't able to obtain the official
story rights, but hired Ed anyway to make a movie tentatively called
I Changed My Sex! It was later retitled *Glen or Glenda*.

Wood was overjoyed to work on a subject so close to his heart. His
mother, for reasons unknown, had frequently dressed Ed as a girl
when he was a child, a behavior that Wood continued independently
for most of his life. (He had a lifelong fondness for angora sweaters,
mostly due to a comforting memory of being wrapped in one as a
child.). Wood wrote, directed, and starred in the movie. He was also
thrilled to work with Bela Lugosi, the star of *Dracula*. Lugosi had
fallen on hard times and needed work, so he gladly played a mad doctor in the movie (although some say his character is supposed to
represent God).

She took over the Penny Lane role when Sarah Polley dropped out of the film.

Wood starred as Glen, a transvestite (with a similar attachment to pink angora) struggling with the decision to reveal his secret to his fiancée, played by Wood's real-life girlfriend, Dolores Fuller. During the filming of the movie, Wood prevented Fuller from ever seeing him in drag. It wasn't until the premiere that she got the full effect. Although the fiancée in the film accepts Glen's transvestitism, Fuller was mortified. She didn't break off her relationship with Wood then but admitted that she never married him because of his cross-dressing. They broke up in 1955.

Wood's resulting film was a sincere yet incoherent plea for acceptance of transvestitism. But the movie bombed. Maybe America in the 1950s just wasn't ready to accept cross-dressing. Or maybe it was Wood's nonsensical insertion of stock footage of buffalo, or Bela Lugosi's odd rambling lines (like, "Beware of the big green dragon that sits on your doorstep. He eats little boys, puppy dog tails, and big, fat snails") that caused the film's downfall. Or maybe it was the 20-minute-long, silent dream sequence featuring the devil and an overturned couch!

MORE MOVIES
After *Glen or Glenda*, Wood made several more films:

Jail Bait (1954) A criminal lures a teen into a life of crime, and then blackmails his plastic surgeon father to alter his face to evade arrest. The title and the tagline ("DANGER! These Girls are Hot!") have nothing to do with the plot.

Bride of the Monster (1955) In this film, Lugosi stars as the evil Dr. Vornoff, who hopes to use atomic energy to create an army of supermen—a standard plot for a supervillian. What's not so standard is that Varnoff dies in the arms of a giant rubber octopus!

The Bride and the Beast (1958) Laura, a new bride, has a problem. She's more interested in her husband's gorilla than her husband, Dan. Hypnosis reveals that she was Queen of the Gorillas in a former life.

Night of the Ghouls (1959) This sequel to *Bride of the Monster* has a phony psychic summoned to Dr. Varnoff's house for a séance. The movie wasn't released until 1981 (when, finally, Wood paid the film lab's processing fee).

Plan 9 From Outer Space (1959) After eight tries to take over Earth, evil aliens have designed a terrifying ninth plan: to conquer with an army of zombies. Features lousy acting, stilted dialogue, flying saucers made of hubcaps on string, wobbly cardboard tombstones, and a terrifying zombie army of . . . three. (This is Lugosi's last movie; he died before filming wrapped.)

DECLINE AND FALL

After *Plan 9*, which like all his other films made no money and was mostly ignored at the time, Wood continued to make low-budget schlock. In the early 1960s he started publishing pulp novels. No one's sure how many Ed Wood wrote, since he often used a pseudonym, but he published at least 75 novels with titles like *Death of a Transvestite* and *Hell Chicks*. His films became more and more exploitative, and fell into the realm of adult entertainment. But he kept working until he died in 1978 from a heart attack. His death passed without any public notice; no trade papers ran his obituary, and his ashes were scattered at sea.

UNDISCOVERED GENIUS?

Ed Wood died just a few years before his name would become a household word among fans of B movies. When Michael and Harry Medved wrote a book called *The Golden Turkey Awards* in 1981, they asked their readers to write in to vote for the Worst Film of All Time. *Plan 9 From Outer Space* won in a landslide and continues today to be considered the worst movie ever made.

ART IMITATES LIFE . . . OR IS IT THE OTHER WAY AROUND?

In the ultimate irony, director Tim Burton turned the story of Ed Wood's life into an Oscar-winning movie starring Johnny Depp as Wood. Filmed in black and white, *Ed Wood* (1994) was a loving tribute to the oddball director. Burton spent take after take meticulously recreating the gaffs and bloopers in Ed Wood's films, mistakes that Wood left in his movies because he didn't like to spend more than two takes on any one scene. The budget for *Ed Wood* was more than the budget for every film Ed Wood ever created—combined. Burton's title sequence alone cost more than all of *Plan 9 From Outer Space*. Like Wood's movies, Burton's film didn't perform well at the box office, but it has since become a cult hit (much like *Plan 9*) with fans at home.

Turn to page 131 for more on Ed Wood.

Clint Eastwood's salary for the 1964 spaghetti Western **A *Fistful of Dollars*: $15,000.**

A TOWN CALLED TOMBSTONE

Tombstone, Arizona, located 70 miles from Tucson, was a silver mining boomtown in the 1870s and 1880s. Folks—including Wyatt Earp, his brothers, and gambler Doc Holliday—came from all over to strike it rich. The silver boom quickly faded, but the Tombstone legend lives on—thanks to the shoot-out at the O.K. Corral . . . and the many movies that followed.

A LITTLE HISTORY

In 1881 the Earp brothers and their rivals, the Clanton gang, had been feuding for months over control of Tombstone before things came to a head. Town marshal Virgil Earp and his brothers had faced many deadly threats from the Clantons, a group they felt was nothing but cattle rustlers and thieves. The Clantons thought no better of the Earps, calling them pimps for the local business interests.

The situation exploded on October 26, 1881, when Virgil Earp, his brothers, and Earp's friend Doc Holliday went to the O.K. Corral to disarm the Clanton gang, who were in violation of a local firearms law. There they found the Clanton brothers (Ike and Billy), the McLaury brothers (Tom and Frank), and Billy Claiborne, all armed and dangerous. When the Earp gang arrived, they told everyone to drop their weapons; a short standoff ensued, and then someone opened fire. Shots flew for 30 seconds. When it was all over, two Earps were wounded, and Billy Clanton and the McLaury brothers lay dead.

The notorious shoot-out remains one of history's most hotly contested events. The Earp faction said they were on the side of law and order; the Clantons said the Earps were murderers. The Earp brothers and Holliday stood trial but were acquitted—mostly because of unverifiable accounts of who fired first; most witnesses were too biased to be trusted. The shoot-out became legendary, thanks to Wyatt Earp and his wife, Josie, writing best-sellers that told their side of the story: the white-hatted Earps were saving Tombstone from the black-hatted Clanton gang. This version, and the friendship between Wyatt and Doc Holliday, captured the public's imagination.

Hollywood took notice of the fascination with Tombstone and has cranked out many movies about it over the years. Some movies stuck closely to the history—while others—like *Cheyenne Autumn* (1964) and *The Outlaw* (1943)—got creative and placed Wyatt and Doc in places they'd never been, with people they'd never known. Studios found that sticking the word *Tombstone* in a movie title brought in an audience. More than 20 movies have *Tombstone* in the title, but most have nothing to do with actual events at the O.K. Corral or the Earps themselves. So if you're looking for Earps, you'll want to avoid: *Tombstone Canyon* (1932), *Tombstone Terror* (1935), *Sheriff of Tombstone* (1941), *Bad Men of Tombstone* (1949), *Toughest Gun in Tombstone* (1958), and *Five Guns to Tombstone* (1970).

AN EARP IS AN EARP IS AN EARP

Wyatt Earp has been portrayed by many actors, including A-listers Henry Fonda, Burt Lancaster, Kevin Costner, Kurt Russell, Hugh O'Brien, James Stewart, and Buster Crabbe. Some of the best-known Doc Hollidays were Kirk Douglas, Val Kilmer, Dennis Quaid, Victor Mature, and Walter Huston.

Other interesting casting choices include DeForest Kelley (Dr. "Bones" McCoy, from the original Star Trek series) as Morgan Earp in *Gunfight at the O.K. Corral* (1957), and Marie Osmond as Josie, Wyatt's wife in the made-for-television *I Married Wyatt Earp* (1983). The award for Most Ironic Casting goes to the producers of 1993's *Tombstone*. Actor Wyatt Earp (fifth cousin to and descendant of the very famous lawman) played Billy Claiborne—one of men killed at the O.K. Corral.

ON LOCATION—NOT

Since Tombstone, Arizona, is a real place and many historic 19th-century buildings still stand, you might assume that most of the movies about Wyatt and his brothers were shot there. But that'd be wrong, tenderfoot.

Kevin Costner's *Wyatt Earp* (1994) for example, was shot in New Mexico. John Ford's classic *My Darling Clementine* (1946) was filmed in Monument Valley, Utah. *Hour of the Gun* (1967) was done entirely in Mexico. Many Westerns were shot in Arizona—

—Gunnery Sgt. Hartman (R. Lee Ermay), *Full Metal Jacket* (1987)

including those about Wyatt Earp—at Old Tucson Studios (conveniently located in Tucson). Built in 1939, this elaborate set represented Tombstone in *Gunfight at the O.K. Corral* and *Tombstone*. About the only movie that used the real town itself was *Wyatt Earp, Return to Tombstone*, a 1994 movie that spliced in scenes from the 1950s TV show *The Life and Legend of Wyatt Earp* as flashbacks.

WANNA WATCH A MOVIE?

Now that we've whetted your appetite, here's a list of our favorite movies about Wyatt and the gang in Tombstone:

Frontier Marshal (1939), starring Randolph Scott and Cesar Romero

Tombstone, the Town Too Tough to Die (1942), starring Richard Dix and Kent Taylor

My Darling Clementine (1946), starring Henry Fonda and Victor Mature

Gun Belt (1953), starring George Montgomery and Tab Hunter

Gunfight at the O.K. Corral (1957), starring Burt Lancaster and Kirk Douglas

The Outlaws Is Coming (1965), starring the Three Stooges

Hour of the Gun (1967), starring James Garner and Jason Robards

Doc (1971), starring Stacy Keach, Faye Dunaway, and Harris Yulin

Tombstone (1993), starring Kurt Russell and Val Kilmer

Wyatt Earp (1994), starring Kevin Costner and Dennis Quaid

* * *

HOME, SICK

On October 15, 1918, leading film studios decided to stop releasing movies. Why? Because of the flu. An influenza epidemic caused many theaters nationwide to close, to try to halt the spread of the sickness. The studios stopped releasing films until the theaters opened again.

Stars who once worked as extras: Marilyn Monroe, Clark Gable, Sophia Loren.

THEIR BIG BREAKS, PART 1

*Big Hollywood stars occupy their places in the firmament
so comfortably that we tend to forget that they were once
relatively unknown—until that one big break came along.*

THE STAR: BRAD PITT
THE FILM: *THELMA & LOUISE* **(1991)**
Who isn't familiar with the handsome face of the ex–Mr. Aniston?
Achilles himself of *Troy*. Mr. Smith, in *Mr. & Mrs. Smith*. A-list
member of *Ocean's Eleven*. But not everyone remembers that Mr.
Pitt first registered on our radar in the film *Thelma & Louise*
(1991). He had a small but memorable role as J.D., the sexy, sweet-
talking hitchhiker picked up by the title characters. What isn't
generally known is that George Clooney, who hadn't yet found his
own big break, auditioned five times for the part of J.D. How's that
for a difficult decision for director Ridley Scott to make!

THE STAR: MERYL STREEP
THE FILM: *THE DEER HUNTER* **(1978)**
Widely acclaimed as one of the premier actresses of her generation,
Meryl Streep got her big break playing the stateside love interest of
two of the three buddies whose lives are irreparably changed when
they ship out to the Vietnam War. Streep, an enormously talented
and multifaceted actress, improvised most of her lines in this Best
Picture Oscar–winning film. The following year, Streep went on to
play Woody Allen's lesbian ex-wife in *Manhattan*.

THE STAR: HARRISON FORD
THE FILM: *STAR WARS* **(1977)**
How many stars have two breakout roles? Harrison Ford came
pretty close. *American Graffiti* was the launching pad for several
movie careers (you may have heard of its director, George Lucas—
he went on to make a few films called *Star Wars*). For his role as
Bob Falfa, Ford was asked to cut his hair. He refused, saying the
part was too small for such a sacrifice. He told the director he

---

Chewbacca in *Star Wars* (1977) was modeled partly after George Lucas's dog, Indiana.

would be willing to wear a hat instead, which is just what he did.

In spite of his charismatic presence in *Graffiti*, no impressive movie offers came Ford's way in the years immediately following. To pay the rent and support his wife and two kids, Ford worked as a carpenter. In 1975 he was building some cabinets for George Lucas when the director was auditioning actresses for parts in his new film, to be named *Star Wars*. Lucas asked Ford to help out by reading dialogue opposite aspiring actors. At the time, Lucas had been considering a number of actors for the role of Han Solo, including Kurt Russell, Nick Nolte, Christopher Walken, and Al Pacino. But when Ford read the Han Solo lines—even though he wasn't auditioning for the part—Lucas realized that he was perfect for the role. The rest, as they say, is history.

THE STAR: PAUL NEWMAN
THE FILM: *THE LONG HOT SUMMER* (1958)

The Long Hot Summer led to two life-altering events in Paul Newman's life. It was his performance in this screen adaptation of William Faulkner writings—two stories and a novel (*The Hamlet*)—that brought Newman and his blue eyes to the public's attention. Playing Ben Quick, a down-at-the-heels drifter who moves into a sleepy southern town and becomes involved with the town's richest man (Orson Welles) and his family, Newman gave a nuanced and sensitive performance. After that, it wasn't long before he became one of the most respected and sought-after actors in the business. And it was during the filming that Newman met his future wife, Joanne Woodward—they were married the year the film was released. They have enjoyed a rare Hollywood marriage that has survived to this day; that's 47 years and counting.

THE STAR: ANGELA LANSBURY
THE FILM: *GASLIGHT* (1944)

Nowadays known primarily to generations of TV watchers as Jessica Fletcher of *Murder, She Wrote*, Angela Lansbury has had a long and distinguished cinema career. She made her screen debut in 1944 in *Gaslight*, playing the part of Nancy Oliver, the maid of characters played by Ingrid Bergman and Charles Boyer. She was just 17.

A psychological thriller, *Gaslight* depicts a young wife (Bergman) being driven insane by her husband. For the film, Lansbury wore high platform shoes so she could tower menacingly over Bergman.

In *Sitting Bull* (1954), the Native Americans and U.S. Cavalry were played by Mexicans.

A key scene has the maid defiantly lighting a cigarette—but, by law, the film could not show a minor smoking. Filming of the scene had to wait until Lansbury turned 18, which was celebrated on the set. For her role in this film, Lansbury was nominated for an Oscar. Not bad for her very first outing.

THE STAR: JACK NICHOLSON
THE FILM: *EASY RIDER* (1969)
Jack Nicholson won his part in this film only after Rip Torn and Bruce Dern dropped out. He played George Hanson, the ACLU lawyer who meets the movie's two leads (Peter Fonda and Dennis Hopper) when they are thrown in jail. The filmmakers had wanted a genuine Texan for the part, and Nicholson, born in New Jersey, did not fit the bill. Nonetheless, many critics felt that he stole the movie.

Nicholson has said that he studied clips of President Lyndon Baines Johnson, with his Texas drawl and downhome manner, as preparation for the role. It has also been said that the pot shown being smoked in the film by Nicholson and his costars wasn't oregano; it was the real McCoy.

For more big breaks, turn to page 385.

* * *

TOP 10 GREATEST AMERICAN
MOVIES OF ALL TIME
From the American Film Institute's "100 Years, 100 Movies" list

1. *Citizen Kane* (1941)
2. *Casablanca* (1942)
3. *The Godfather* (1972)
4. *Gone With the Wind* (1939)
5. *Lawrence of Arabia* (1962)
6. *The Wizard of Oz* (1939)
7. *The Graduate* (1967)
8. *On the Waterfront* (1954)
9. *Schindler's List* (1993)
10. *Singin' in the Rain* (1952)

The name that actress Sandra Dee was born with: Alexandra Cymboliak Zuck.

BATHROOMS ON THE BIG SCREEN, PART 1

In honor of our favorite room in the house, we've put together this collection of powder room quotations from the movies.

"One bathroom for nine people? And I never did see a toilet."
—Mr. Steve Yeager (James Avery), *The Brady Bunch Movie* (1995)

"Did you scrub the bathroom floor today? DID YOU?"
—Joan Crawford (Faye Dunaway), *Mommie Dearest* (1981)

"I'm not apologizing to Buzz. I'd rather kiss a toilet seat!"
—Kevin McCallister (Macaulay Culkin), *Home Alone 2: Lost in New York* (1992)

"Hey, listen, I want somebody good—and I mean very good—to plant that gun. I don't want my brother coming out of that toilet with just his **** in his hands, alright?"
—Sonny Corleone (James Caan), *The Godfather* (1972)

"Your cat can flush?"
—Roz Focker (Barbra Streisand) *Meet the Fockers* (2004)

"It has come to my attention that the maintenance staff is switching our toilet paper from Charmin . . . to generic. All those opposed to chafing, please say 'Aye.'"
—Elle Woods (Reese Witherspoon), *Legally Blonde* (2001)

SHAGGY: "What do you care? You drink out of the toilet."
SCOOBY-DOO: "So do you." *Scooby-Doo* (2002)

"Do you see a wedding ring on my finger? Does this place look like I'm . . . married? The toilet seat's up, man!"
—The Dude (Jeff Bridges), *The Big Lebowski* (1998)

Good decision! Why Herbert Lom changed his name to something a bit shorter:

THE OPENING CREDITS

Opening credits may seem like just a simple list—the title, the director, and the actors, right? Actually, it's more complicated than that. These credits are the source of a lot of Hollywood headaches and negotiations. Deciding the order of names and logos, who gets credit for what and when, can be just as contentious and complicated as the making of a movie itself. Relax. Uncle John will help you decipher this secret language and get some insight into the Hollywood biz.

MOVIEMAKERS

The first names on-screen are usually the production companies, the businesses that make and distribute the film itself. The order of appearance gives clues as to what each one did on the film. The first name and logo to appear is usually the studio that distributes the film. Next will be the name of the company that ran the physical production. That is followed by the group of investors who fronted the money to make the picture (this credit is usually preceded by the phrase, "In association with . . ."). After each company splashes its name across the screen (and maybe a "Film by" credit appears—if the director has worked it into his contract), we then come to the stars.

A GOOD CAST

In the early years of film, studios did not even allow actors to appear in the credits, feeling it would devalue the importance of the movie itself and give actors too much power and prestige. Actors were simply employees and often worked in other departments. For example, Florence Lawrence was both an actress and a seamstress for the Vitagraph Film Company in 1908. She was lucky enough to be stolen away from Vitagraph by director D. W. Griffith, who was at the time running Biograph Studios. He made her a recognizable face, but no one knew her name; she was simply called the Biograph Girl.

It wasn't until 1910 that this actress's name would become famous. A young Carl Laemmle—who would later found Universal Pictures—lured Lawrence away from Biograph to his studio—with the promise of a screen credit. He began to promote her name with a bold publicity campaign: he started a rumor that the Biograph

Girl had been run over by a streetcar. Following the frenzy of publicity, Laemmle then announced that she had been "found" alive and well . . . and filming a new movie for his studio. His announcement publicized her real name, and Lawrence's film credit in 1910's *The Broken Oath* was the first one for an actor.

For the next six decades, how an actor's name appeared was decided by the studios. After the studio system's collapse in the 1970s actors began using their contracts to articulate exactly how they wanted their names to appear at the beginning of a film. And it's been crazy ever since.

ME FIRST!

Now actors spend much energy jockeying for an "above title" credit, one that comes before the name of the movie. Battles also break out over whether their names appear on a "separate card" (all alone on the screen) or if they must settle for a "shared card." Font size is another important detail because it determines how big one actor's name is compared to the title and to the names of other actors. How long the name stays on the screen and its color are all negotiated too.

Unfortunately, seemingly impossible situations can arise, such as when two stars each insist that his or her name has to be the biggest. One solution is the "favored nations" agreement, which decrees that all names receive equal treatment. Another compromise might be to feature an actor's name alone but in a smaller font. One imaginative solution was reached for the credits of 1974's *The Towering Inferno*, which had to satisfy megastars Steve McQueen and Paul Newman: while Newman's name appeared above his costar's, McQueen's was indented more to the left. (Since English is read left to right, McQueen's name would be seen first.) Negotiations like these are held privately well in advance of production, so many juicy details are never made public.

But if actors become so unhappy that they don't want their names to appear at all, they can resort to a pseudonym: traditionally, it's a variation on the name George Spelvin. There are a few stories about this pseudonym's origin—some say it was a naughty joke based on "Georgina Spelvin," the star of the X-rated film *The Devil in Miss Jones* (1973). Others say the tradition has its roots in late 19th-century theater; George or Georgina Spelvin's name would appear in a program if the cast member's name was not known when it was printed.

Shirley Temple failed a screen test for the *Our Gang* movie comedies.

PRODUCER PARADE

After the actors comes the title of the movie, followed by the supporting cast . . . and then come the producers. While executive producers are usually the individuals who secured the investors, a "Produced by" credit often goes to those who did the legwork, shopped the script around, and put the entire package together. But there is often a long list of producers and associate producers that haven't really done as much work on the film, if anything at all. They might be simply friends, personal trainers, or even assistants of the stars. So when a movie has an all-star cast, things can get out of hand fairly quickly: 1995's Sylvester Stallone action flick *Assassins* had 17 producers listed, as did 2001's *The Caveman's Valentine*, starring Samuel L. Jackson. The movie *Quiz Show* originally was slated to have 14 producers, but two were so embarrassed with how little work they did that they withdrew their names. In an attempt to limit the plethora of producers, the Producers Guild of America (PGA) decided to create guidelines to ensure that producers actually produce, but their rules are still largely voluntary.

WRITERS

After the producers come the writers' names. Unlike the PGA, the Writers Guild of America is very strict with credits. Although dozens of writers may work on a film, only three will get credit for the screenplay. When their names appear on screen, they must be separated by the word "and" in the credits. If a screenwriting team (such as the Coen Brothers) writes the script, then the team counts as one writer.

The listings become even more complicated if one of the screenwriters also came up with the story on which the script is based: Those lucky few get a "Story by" credit in addition to their screenplay credit. Their names will also appear first—unless another writer made substantial changes to the story. If that's the case, then the latter writer's name appears on-screen first. While this may seem way too technical, remember that these strict rules keep everything in order.

DIRECTORS

Saving the best for last (in some people's opinions), the director finally shows up. With even stricter rules than the Writers Guild, the Directors Guild of America only allows one director to be listed. (There are a few exceptions—such as the *Matrix* trilogy's Wachowski brothers—but teams must prove they are bona fide.) This not only gives more prestige to the director, but protects the careers of those who might have been fired (or quit) during production: Richard Stanley went uncredited for his work on 1996's box office disaster *The Island of Dr. Moreau*. Stanley, an up and coming director, was fired early into production and replaced by John Frankenheimer, who got the director's "credit" for the flop.

And when no director wants to take credit for a film, the Directors Guild has pseudonyms for them to hide behind. But directors cannot disown a movie just because they think the film is poor. They must make a very strong case that their artistic vision has been corrupted—either by the studio's editing or some other wrongdoing. While lobbying to remove their names, directors can't badmouth the film publicly. The whole process protects everyone: the director's reputation will be saved from a bad movie, while the studio's movie will be safe from bad publicity.

A DIRECTOR BY ANY OTHER NAME

Until being outed in 1999, the DGA used the fictional name Alan Smithee for movies that nobody wanted. Smithee had about 50 movies on his resume (not bad for someone who doesn't exist), the first being 1969's *Death of a Gunfighter*. His identity—or lack thereof—remained an industry secret until two movies spilled the beans. The first movie, *An Alan Smithee Film: Burn, Hollywood, Burn!* (1997), was not a big success, but it spelled out explicitly what Smithee's name was and why it existed. Joe Esterhas wrote the mockumentary about a movie director (played by Eric Idle) whose name really is Alan Smithee. In the movie, Idle's character wants to remove his name from a film, but the problem is that it will only be replaced by the fictional Alan Smithee's name.

In another odd twist, Arthur Hiller, the real director of *Burn, Hollywood, Burn*, was so unhappy with the studio's edit of the film, he took his name off the project, and replaced it with . . . Alan Smithee. So the before the title credit turned out to be correct after all.

But it was *American History X* (1998) that fully exposed Smithee's "existence." In 1998 New Line Cinema allowed starring actor Edward Norton to do the final edit on the film, a decision that infuriated the director, Tony Kaye. Kaye took out an ad in

While visiting his native London, Charlie Chaplin received 73,000 letters in two days.

Variety to protest and lobbied the DGA to replace his name with Alan Smithee. Because his *Variety* ad bad-mouthed the film publicly, Kaye's name stayed attached. But the whole battle attracted so much attention, that Alan Smithee's identity had been revealed to outsiders. Once audiences knew that Smithee would only be attached to troubled productions, the DGA realized that the name had become a liability. Alan Smithee's name was retired, and several new false identities were created. So who are these new "bad" directors? The DGA's not telling.

* * *

WHAT WAS THE NAME OF THAT MOVIE?

Look at each clue in order and try to figure out the name of the film in question. How many clues will it take you?

1. It was nominated in both the Best Picture and Best Foreign Language Film categories in 1969.
2. It won in the latter category.
3. It has the shortest title of any film to ever win an Oscar.
4. Its title is a letter of the alphabet.

Answer: The movie was Z, a political thriller based on a real-life incident.

* * *

WANNA GO TO A MOVIE?

In 1946 100 million Americans, out of a total population of 141 million, attended the movies every week. In 1947 it dropped to 90 million. In 1950 it was 60 million; in 1957 it was 40 million. It leveled out at about 15 million in the 1970s. Today weekly attendance is 25 million—out of a population of 295 million people.

A newspaper critic on Faye Dunaway's first movie: "[Her] rib cage looks marvelous."

GREGORY PECK:
BY THE NUMBERS

*Tall, dark, and handsome, Gregory Peck was much more
than the latest heartthrob: he specialized in roles that were steadfast,
noble, and dignified. It was these traits that made him a star.*

1
Number of Peck's Oscar wins for Best Actor. He was nominated
four times before for *The Keys of the Kingdom* (1944), *The Yearling*
(1946), *Gentleman's Agreement* (1947), and *Twelve O'Clock High*
(1949). He finally won for *To Kill a Mockingbird* (1963).

2
Number of *Cape Fear* movies Peck appeared in. The first, his own
production in 1962, lost close to $1 million and finished his career
as a producer. The second was a cameo role in Martin Scorsese's
1991 remake.

2
Number of things Ernest Hemingway liked in the film version of
his story *The Snows of Kilimanjaro* (1952) in which Peck starred:
"The only two good things in it were Ava Gardner and the hyena."

3
Number of Peck's favorite leading ladies: Ingrid Bergman, Ava
Gardner, and Audrey Hepburn.

4
Along with an F, the military classification that gave Gregory Peck
the opportunity to break into Hollywood during World War II
(most big stars were in the Armed Forces, but Peck couldn't
enlist). His deferment can be traced back to a dance lesson: His
teacher, the legendary Martha Graham, told him to put his legs
straight out on the floor and touch his head to his knees. Then she
put her knee against his back and pushed—hard—rupturing a disk.
The snapping sound was so loud that the other students heard it.

5
Grade in elementary school in which Peck first appeared onstage. In a school play about the legend of Pandora's box, he wore a green velvet vest and played the unfortunate one who opened the box.

6
Age at which, after his parents were divorced, Peck traveled by train—alone—from his father's house in La Jolla, California, to his newly married mother's house in St. Louis, Missouri.

12
In feet, the height of the waves in the sea off the coast of Ireland when Peck, playing Captain Ahab, floated off into the fog, clinging to a huge rubber model of the white whale Moby Dick. The camera boat eventually rescued him.

17
Age at which Peck shot up from 5 foot 4 inches to 6 foot 2 inches tall.

19
Age of Veronique Passani when she first met Peck while interviewing him for a magazine article in 1952.

19
Number of hours after his divorce from first wife, Greta, was final before Peck married Veronique in 1955.

21
Age at which Eldred Gregory Peck dropped the Eldred and insisted from that day forward on being known simply as Gregory Peck.

26
In dollars, Peck's tuition for a full semester at University of California, Berkeley, where he majored in literature.

40
Number of actors (including Spencer Tracy, Franchot Tone, and Gene Kelly) that Darryl Zanuck tested for the lead in *The Keys of the Kingdom*, before choosing Peck. It was only Peck's second

—The Caller (voice of Tony Beckley), *When a Stranger Calls* (1979)

movie but, besides lots of critical praise, it earned him a $25,000 bonus from the studio and his first Academy Award nomination.

44
Age at which Peck starred in *The Guns of Navarone* (1961), with David Niven, 50; Anthony Quinn, 45; and Anthony Quayle, 47. One critic described the film as "an elderly gang goes to war."

1,000
Minimum number of books about Abraham Lincoln that Peck owned by 1982, the year that he played Lincoln in *The Blue and the Gray*, his first dramatic TV role.

3,000
Average number of fan letters Peck received every week after his starring role in Alfred Hitchcock's *Spellbound* (1945).

4,575,000
In dollars, the (then record-setting) cost of making *Duel in the Sun* (1946), which starred Peck opposite Jennifer Jones, the mistress of big-spending producer David O. Selznick.

* * *

AND THE ENDING IS . . .
Love (1927) starring Greta Garbo and John Gilbert was a silent version of *Anna Karenina*. But Hollywood producers were concerned that audiences wouldn't like the original tragic ending. So two endings were filmed—and released. Theater owners were the ones to choose from *Love's* two endings—one was happy, the other sad.

* * *

SPLAT
In the silent film *A Noise from the Deep* (1913) Mabel Normand creamed Fatty Arbuckle in the face with a pie, the first pie-in-the-face gag on film.

Courteney Cox and David Arquette met and fell in love on the set of *Scream* (1996).

THE HOLLYWOOD BLACKLIST, PART 1

How the Red Scare of the late 1940s and early 1950s led to the blacklisting of hundreds of Hollywood actors, writers, and directors.

I n the days following World War II, America began to look with suspicion on one of its former wartime allies, the Soviet Union, and to fear that the U.S. government was riddled with Communist infiltrators and spies. The Red Scare, as it became known, was fueled by certain radical and/or self-seeking politicians, but the idea caught on like wildfire, and pretty soon Americans thought there was a Communist under every bed. A saying of the times was, "Better dead than Red."

THE SPIES AMONG US

In Washington, the House Un-American Activities Committee (HUAC), which had been established in 1938 to investigate German-American involvement in Nazi and Ku Klux Klan activity, became a standing (i.e., permanent) committee. Its new aim was to investigate subversion and propaganda in general, and Communist infiltrators and sympathizers working within the government in particular.

In 1947 the committee turned its attention to Hollywood, to investigate what it considered "Communist propaganda" in the movies and the possibility of infiltration into Hollywood's labor unions.

RADICAL CHIC

It's important to know that in the 1930s, at the height of the Depression and as the Nazis were rising to power in Europe, a large group of Americans (mostly intellectuals) had joined, or flirted with the idea joining, the Communist Party. It's safe to say that every artist or intellectual in America at the very least knew someone who belonged to the party. So that when the Commie-seeking spotlight landed on Hollywood, it found more than it was looking for.

Jack Nicholson's first job in Hollywood: office boy in MGM's cartoon department.

ROUND ONE

The congressional investigation began in October 1947. The committee, headed by right-wing congressman J. Parnell Thomas, interviewed two groups. The so-called friendly witnesses, who were willing to testify about Communist activity, were allowed to read prepared statements and were treated with respect. They included actors Gary Cooper, Robert Taylor, Robert Montgomery, and Ronald Reagan. These witnesses also included studio heads Jack Warner, Louis B. Mayer, and Walt Disney, whose employees had recently unionized and held a strike, which, Disney told the committee, had been instigated by Communists. Disney named a few former employees and recommended outlawing labor unions for their un-American tendencies.

THE HOLLYWOOD ELEVEN

The second group were screenwriters, actors, and directors who were either alleged or admitted members of the American Communist Party. Nineteen of these "unfriendly" witnesses were subpoenaed; 11 were called to testify. German playwright and songwriter Bertolt ("Mack the Knife") Brecht was the only one of the 11 to answer any questions on the stand. He claimed he was not a Communist; but after testifying, he immediately left Hollywood to return to East Germany.

AND THEN THERE WERE TEN

The remaining 10, mostly screenwriters, refused to testify, citing the First Amendment, which forbids Congress to infringe on the right of free speech. For refusing to divulge their political affiliations past or present, they were cited for contempt of Congress on November 24 and convicted in 1948; the Hollywood Ten were sent to prison for terms ranging from six months to one year, and fined $1,000.

The men who made up the Hollywood Ten were the following:

- Alvah Bessie (Oscar-nominated screenwriter of 1945's *Objective, Burma!*)
- Herbert Biberman (screenwriter of *The Master Race* and husband of actress Gale Sondergaard, who won the first Best Supporting Actress Oscar and was also blacklisted)

Jude Law told Jay Leno that his name came from the Beatles song "Hey Jude."

- Lester Cole (screenwriter with Alvah Bessie on *Objective, Burma!* and cofounder of the Screen Writers Guild—now the Writers Guild of America)
- Edward Dmytryk (director of *The Caine Mutiny*; Oscar nominated for 1947's *Crossfire*)
- Ring Lardner Jr. (screenwriter, Oscar winner for the 1942 screenplay of *Woman of the Year*)
- John Howard Lawson (screenwriter, Oscar nominated for 1938's *Blockade*, and cofounder of the Screen Writers Guild and its first president)
- Albert Maltz (screenwriter, Oscar nominated for 1945's *Pride of the Marines*)
- Samuel Ornitz (screenwriter of 1937's *It Could Happen to You!* and cofounder of the Screen Writers Guild)
- Adrian Scott (producer of the Oscar-nominated *Crossfire* in 1947)
- Dalton Trumbo (screenwriter, Oscar nominated for 1940's *Kitty Foyle*)

ADDING INSULT TO INJURY

The rest of Hollywood scurried to catch the wave. The Motion Picture Association of America issued a press release known as the Waldorf Statement; it declared that the members of the Hollywood Ten would not be permitted to work in Hollywood again until they were either acquitted or purged of their contempt charges and swore that they weren't Communists. The Screen Actors Guild decided to require its officers to pledge that they weren't Communists. A few years later, in 1952, the guild additionally declared that members who hadn't been cleared of suspicion of Communist leanings by Congress could have their names stripped from previous film credits.

For more on the story, turn to page 178.

Director John Ford: "Don't ever forget what I'm going to tell you: Actors are crap."

ON LOCATION IN SOUTHERN CAL

Even if you've never been to Southern California,
you've visited plenty of its landmarks on film.

Union Station, Los Angeles
This station first opened for business in 1939, in the heyday of
train travel. Its architecture is a beautiful blend of art deco and
Spanish revival, which makes the station perfect for period pieces,
like *Pearl Harbor*, *Bugsy*, and *Dead Men Don't Wear Plaid*. Its classy
noir look also made it the perfect setting for: Captain Picard's
holodeck detective fantasy in *Star Trek: First Contact*; the police
station in *Blade Runner*; and Demi Moore's boudoir and lair in
Charlie's Angels: Full Throttle.

The Hotel del Coronado, San Diego
Designated a National Historic Landmark in 1977, "The Del"
served as the Miami Beach hotel in *Some Like It Hot* and was also
featured in 1980's *The Stunt Man*. Built in 1888 in whimsical
Queen Anne revival style, it's said that the Del was the inspiration
for the design of Oz's Emerald City: L. Frank Baum, who wrote *The
Wonderful Wizard of Oz*, was a frequent guest. The hotel also
inspired the romantic novel (and the movie based on it)
Somewhere in Time. The 1980 adaptation starred Christopher
Reeve and Jane Seymour, but the movie was not filmed at the
inspirational Del in Southern California at all, but at the Grand
Hotel on Mackinac Island in Michigan.

Los Angeles County Arboretum & Botanic Garden, Arcadia
The lush green forests on the grounds have served as exotic back-
drops for scores of films, including *The Road to Singapore*, *The Man
in the Iron Mask* (1939), and more than a few of Johnny
Weissmuller's Tarzan and Jungle Jim movies. More recent flicks
filmed there include *Marathon Man*, *Wayne's World*, *Anaconda*, and
Terminator 2: Judgment Day. Television viewers have been to the
arboretum courtesy of classic TV shows like *Lassie*, *Mission*

At $79 million, *Cold Mountain* (2003) was the costliest film Miramax financed on its own.

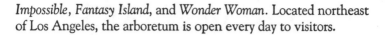

Impossible, *Fantasy Island*, and *Wonder Woman*. Located northeast of Los Angeles, the arboretum is open every day to visitors.

The Bradbury Building, Los Angeles
The exterior of the Bradbury at Third and Broadway in downtown L.A. is anything but photogenic. But its visually stunning interior, featuring a glass roof that illuminates an indoor courtyard lined with ornate staircases and open elevators, makes it a natural for either period pieces or futuristic films. Built in 1893, the Bradbury is the oldest commercial building in downtown Los Angeles. The first movie filmed there was the 1950 noir classic *D.O.A.*, starring Edmund O'Brien. Then there was *Chinatown*, among others, and most famously, *Blade Runner*.

The Santa Anita Racetrack, Arcadia
Opened for business in 1934, the Santa Anita Racetrack is an art deco treasure that was not only a source of entertainment for real-life gentlemen gamblers Clark Gable, Cary Grant, and Fred Astaire, but the perfect authentic backdrop for recent releases like *Seabiscuit* and old favorites like the Marx Brothers's *A Day at the Races*. It was also featured in the 1937 and 1954 versions of *A Star Is Born*. The track is open year-round; its racing season runs from late December through April.

The RMS *Queen Mary*, Long Beach
The *Queen Mary* is a ship with a story that could rival anything Hollywood might dream up. After a life of romance and adventure on the high seas—as an ocean liner and as a transport ship during and after World War II (the boat made thirteen voyages in 1946 carrying war brides and their children to the U.S. and Canada)—the *Queen Mary* docked on the shores of Long Beach, California. Since then it's served as the backdrop for movies like *The Poseidon Adventure*, *Death Cruise*, *Chaplin*, and *Pearl Harbor*. *Mary* is also a hotel with restaurants, shops, and a museum.

* * *

TRANSLATION, PLEASE?
In MGM's logo, "*Ars Gratia Artis*" appears in the banner surrounding Leo the Lion's head. It means "Art for Art's Sake."

THE LONG AND SHORT OF IT

*If a picture is worth a thousand words, how many words is
a moving picture worth, especially in a title? Uncle John took a
look at some of the longest and shortest titles around
to see how they matched up.*

DRAWN OUT
Long titles don't guarantee success. By the time some of
these lengthy winners were posted on the marquee, the
movies had completed their run, but a few have become true classics. The longest we could find were:

11 Words: *The Incredibly Strange Creatures Who Stopped Living and
Became Mixed-Up Zombies!!?* (1964) Also known as: *The Incredibly
Strange Creature: Or Why I Stopped Living and Became a Mixed-up
Zombie*

12 Words: *The Englishman Who Went Up a Hill but Came Down a
Mountain* (1995)

13 Words: *Dr. Strangelove or: How I Learned to Stop Worrying and
Love the Bomb* (1964)

14 Words: *Don't Be a Menace to South Central While Drinking Your
Juice in the Hood* (1996)

14 Words: *Who Is Harry Kellerman and Why Is He Saying Those
Terrible Things About Me?* (1971)

15 Words: *Oh Dad, Poor Dad, Mama's Hung You in the Closet and
I'm Feeling So Sad* (1967)

17 Words: *The Saga of the Viking Women and Their Voyage to the
Waters of the Great Sea Serpent* (1957)

20 Words: *Those Magnificent Men in Their Flying Machines, or How
I Flew from London to Paris in 25 hours 11 minutes* (1965)

Mel Gibson on *Hamlet:* "It's a great story. It's got some great things in it. I mean . . ."

And the longest is the 41-word *Night of the Day of the Dawn of the Son of the Bride of the Return of the Revenge of the Terror of the Attack of the Evil, Mutant, Alien, Flesh Eating, Hellbound, Zombified Living Dead Part 2: In Shocking 2-D* (1991).

KEPT BRIEF

Ranking the shortest titles comes down to number of letters and digits in the title:

Three: *She* (1935), *Hud* (1963), *UHF* (1989), *X-15* (1961)

Two: *It* (1927), *If . . .* (1969), *10* (1979), *I.Q.* (1994), *Go* (1999), *FX* (2001)

One and a Half: *8 1/2* (1963)

One: M (1931, 1951), $ (1971), W (1974), Z (1969), π (1998)

OSCARS AND RAZZIES

The shortest title of an Oscar-winning Best Picture was *Gigi* (1958). Just one letter away is the shortest title to win the Razzie for Worst Picture: *Gigli* in 2003.

The longest of the best and worst? The longest Oscar-winner is *The Lord of the Rings: The Return of the King* (2003). Before then, it was a tie between *One Flew Over the Cuckoo's Nest* (1975) and *Around the World in Eighty Days* (1956). The longest title to capture a Razzie for Worst Picture? It's *An Alan Smithee Film: Burn, Hollywood, Burn!* (1998).

* * *

ON PLAYING THE COWARDLY LION

"That was my one big Hollywood hit, but, in a way, it hurt my picture career. After that, I was typecast as a lion, and there just weren't many parts for lions."

—Bert Lahr

HATS OFF TO HARRYHAUSEN

The man behind some of the most memorable movie monsters, Ray Harryhausen was a pioneer in the world of special effects. Here's a brief look at the life and work of the animation legend who brought us the ape in Mighty Joe Young, *the cyclops in* The 7th Voyage of Sinbad, *and the army of sword-wielding skeletons in* Jason and the Argonauts. *And it all began with a great big ape.*

When 13-year-old Ray Harryhausen first saw *King Kong* in 1933, he knew exactly what he wanted to do with his life: be an animator. He got a pair of free tickets to the Hollywood debut of *King Kong* at the Chinese Theatre from his aunt, who worked for the mother of famous film producer Sid Grauman. After seeing the huge ape on the screen, Ray began a crash course in stop-motion animation (instead of drawings, actual models are filmed one frame at a time). He said, "That picture changed my life. It was so novel, and I didn't know how it was done."

When *King Kong* was rereleased in 1938, Harryhausen obsessively returned to watch it night after night, even trying to convince the theater manager to give him the film stills that hung in the lobby. Though the theater manager insisted that they were not his to give, he did put Harryhausen in contact with their owner, Forrest J. Ackerman (who would later become famous as both the editor of the popular 1950s movie magazine *Famous Monsters of Filmland*, as well as for coining the term *sci-fi*). Ackerman let Ray make copies of the stills, and their friendship quickly blossomed. Soon Ackerman was bringing Harryhausen along to meetings of the Los Angeles Science Fiction Society, where he would start up a lifelong friendship with a then young Ray Bradbury.

After a stint in the army during World War II, during which his unit produced army training films, Harryhausen began to assist on George Pal's popular Puppetoons series. There Ray found himself working alongside his idol, Willis O'Brien, the man responsible for

Early job for French actor Gerard Depardieu: door-to-door soap salesman.

the monsters in *King Kong*. When O'Brien began work on his 1949 classic *Mighty Joe Young*, Harryhausen was part of his staff and ended up doing about 80 percent of the actual animation. Ray was now ready to go out on his own—and the world of special effects would forever change because of it.

THE RHEDOSAURUS
Independent producer Jack Dietz was looking for an animator to work on a new monster epic and, fearing that O'Brien would be too expensive, decided to go with his protégé, Harryhausen. *The Beast from 20,000 Fathoms* was based on a story by Harryhausen's friend, Ray Bradbury; it was about a frozen dinosaur that thaws out and terrorizes the human race. In honor of himself, Harryhausen dubbed his dinosaur model the Rhedosaurus, beginning the name with his initials.

Ray made his name on this movie, thanks to his innovative model making and filming methods that resulted in breathtaking animation. And it cost relatively little money: instead of building expensive miniature sets, his stop-motion creatures were shot in front of previously filmed live-action backgrounds. While it was still a time-consuming process (it can take several hours to film one second of stop-motion), monsters could now appear to interact realistically with live actors. The head of Warner Bros., Jack Warner, was so amazed by the film that he snatched it up for his studio, and the picture went on to be their biggest hit of 1953. It would quickly be remade by a Japanese production company into the immensely popular *Gojira*, which American audiences would come to know as Godzilla.

A LEGEND IS BORN
Harryhausen's career skyrocketed as he made a string of sci-fi classics with producer Charles Schneer for more than 20 years, such as *It Came from Beneath the Sea* (1955), *Earth vs. the Flying Saucers* (1956), *20 Million Miles to Earth* (1957), and 1958's *The 7th Voyage of Sinbad*, his first foray into color. As part of marketing his films, the term *Dynamation* was coined to describe his unique combination of live action and stop-motion.

By the 1960s no one in Hollywood rivaled Harryhausen. Yet with one particular film, 1969's *The Valley of Gwangi*, he showed that he had not forgotten what got him there: it was a movie

Willis O'Brien had dreamed of making and, as an homage to his mentor, Harryhausen had his monster scratch his ear when it first appears—just as O'Brien had done with his creation years earlier in *King Kong*. Harryhausen's last major film was the popular *Clash of the Titans* in 1981, starring Laurence Olivier, Claire Bloom, Dame Maggie Smith, Ursula Andress, and Burgess Meredith. But the actors weren't the main attraction; Harryhausen's creations—the slithering, scaly Medusa, the flying horse Pegasus, and the sea monster the Kraken—took center stage.

HIS LEGACY

Despite his retirement, legions of fans continue to celebrate Harryhausen's work, even in today's world of computer-generated special effects. And every so often he is coaxed out of retirement: he did a cameo in 1985's *Spies Like Us*, directed by his friend John Landis, and appeared at the 1992 Academy Awards, where he was given an honorary Oscar for technical achievement. Filmmakers like Steven Spielberg, George Lucas, Tim Burton, and Peter Jackson all cite Harryhausen as a source of influence and inspiration.

Harryhausen remains a strong advocate for stop-motion animation—a bold stance in the face of today's computer-generated effects. According to Harryhausen, the older technique "adds this dream quality to a film . . . You know it is not real, but it looks real. It's like a nightmare or something in a dream." Computer effects, he feels, can almost be too real to be memorable: "You bring it down to the level of the mundane."

FUN FACTS

- Harryhausen grew up near the La Brea Tar Pits in California and developed a fascination with dinosaurs. His earliest test films are of dinosaurs and cave bears chasing each other.
- Harryhausen was the best man at Ray Bradbury's wedding.
- In addition to movies, Harryhausen also created TV ads for Lucky Strike cigarettes.
- When creating a plant-eating dinosaur, Harryhausen ate nothing but celery to get into character.
- In 2003 Harryhausen was awarded a star on the Hollywood Walk of Fame.

AT THE OSCARS

*You've got a front-row seat. Vote for your
favorite answer from the choices given.*

1. In 1972 Marlon Brando rejected the Oscar for his performance
in *The Godfather* by sending Sacheen Littlefeather to read his reasons (mostly having to do with America's treatment of Native
Americans). Ms. Littlefeather turned out to be
   a. Brando's mistress
   b. Brando's daughter
   c. an actress named Maria Cruz
   d. Sacheen Littlefeather

2. In 1973, during the famous streaker incident, a man named
Robert Opal raced naked across the stage as what actor was introducing the next presenter?
   a. David Niven
   b. Charlton Heston
   c. Rock Hudson
   d. Jim Nabors

3. In 1984, when Sally Field gushed, "And I can't deny the fact
that you like me . . . right now . . . you like me," it was because
she'd just won the second of two Best Actress Oscars. For what two
films?
   a. *Sybil* and *Norma Rae*
   b. *Norma Rae* and *Places in the Heart*
   c. *Places in the Heart* and *Soapdish*
   d. *Soapdish* and *Smokey and the Bandit*

4. In 1997, when John Cameron shouted, "I'm king of the world!"
in his acceptance speech when he won the Best Director Oscar for
Titanic, he was quoting
   a. one of the real survivors of the *Titanic* disaster
   b. a line from the film
   c. a poem by Rudyard Kipling
   d. himself, in front of the mirror every morning

—Ty Webb (Chevy Chase), *Caddyshack* (1980)

5. When Adrien Brody won the Oscar as Best Actor for his role in 2002's *The Pianist* he
   a. gave Halle Berry a long, passionate kiss
   b. said, "C'mon guys, I only get one shot at this," when the orchestra tried to drown him out
   c. became the youngest to win a Best Actor Oscar
   d. all of the above

6. For 21 years actors Richard Burton and Peter O'Toole shared a distinction—they were each nominated for seven acting Oscars, but neither had won. Until
   a. Burton won in 1977 for *Equus*
   b. O'Toole won in 1982 for *My Favorite Year*
   c. Burton was presented with a Lifetime Achievement Award in 1991 (Burton died in 1984 after starring in his last feature film, *Nineteen Eighty-Four*, in 1984)
   d. O'Toole was presented with a Lifetime Achievement Award in 2002

7. Woody Allen has been nominated countless times as Best Director and for Best Writing (Screenplay Written Directly for the Screen), and once as Best Actor. But has he ever appeared at an Oscar ceremony?
   a. No
   b. Only once: in 1977 when he was nominated for Best Actor, Director, and Screenplay for *Annie Hall*
   c. Only once: in 2002, as part of a tribute to New York after the 9/11 attacks
   d. Twice, for b and c above

8. Which actress holds the record for the most acting nominations in the categories of both Best Actress and Supporting Actress?
   a. Meryl Streep
   b. Katharine Hepburn
   c. Bette Davis
   d. Mary Pickford

Turn to page 485 for the answers.

The working title for *Some Like It Hot* (1959) was *Not Tonight, Josephine.*

BEFORE HIS TIME: JAMES DEAN

*Although he only starred in three feature films, James Dean
made a permanent impression on the Hollywood
screen before his death at age 24.*

James Byron Dean was born in Indiana in 1931 after his parents Winton and Millie had been married for just six months. When Jimmy was five, his mother signed him up for violin and dance lessons. His father, a dental technician at a VA hospital, was offered a promotion and a transfer to Los Angeles. But Jimmy's first trip to L.A. was short-lived. After his mother died in 1940 of cervical cancer, his father sent him back to Indiana to live with an aunt and uncle on a farm. He spent the rest of his childhood there, living the life of a Hoosier farm boy. A fall from the loft of a barn knocked out his two front teeth and forced him to wear a bridge for the rest of his life, but that didn't spoil his pretty-boy looks. Neither did the glasses that he habitually wore offscreen.

From all reports he was a good kid and a good student, quiet but friendly, and reasonably popular. There was no sign yet of that brooding, rebellious side he became famous for. He played basketball and appeared in a couple of school plays. At night he would listen to the radio and dream about becoming a movie star.

After high school, he moved back to L.A. to live with his father, but his decision to attend UCLA (with the inevitable switch from prelaw—his father's preference—to a major in acting) caused a rift between them that fueled Jimmy's rebelliousness. UCLA turned out to be a disappointment, so he dropped out and started looking for work. He did a Pepsi commercial, played John the Baptist in an Easter special on a local TV station, and won a few bit parts in films, but he made most of his money parking cars on the CBS lot.

In 1952 he left Hollywood for New York City. He became one of the youngest students ever accepted into the famous Actors Studio,

---

Mexican-born Salma Hayek is of Lebanese descent (her father is Lebanese Mexican).

where he confronted another difficult father figure, Studio founder Lee Strasberg. Jimmy dropped out of the studio for a while after Strasberg criticized one of his performances. He eventually returned because he knew that acting was his life—it was what animated him. Out of that milieu, Dean was uptight and could be obnoxious.

A CAREER IN ONE PLAY, THREE MOVIES

Things converged in early 1954: on opening night of *The Immoralist*, his first starring Broadway role, Dean gave an extraordinary performance. He also gave producer Billy Rose his two-week notice of resignation because Elia Kazan had offered him the lead in a movie, *East of Eden*. Dean packed his belongings into two brown paper bags and hopped a plane back to L.A.

East of Eden was John Steinbeck's modernization of the biblical story of Cain and Abel. Both Kazan and Steinbeck thought Dean was perfect for the role of Cal, the rebellious son who couldn't win the love of his stern father, a role Dean understood only too well. In fact, Kazan deliberately chose an actor for the role of Cal's father that he knew Dean could not get along with. Raymond Massey played the stern Adam Trask for the edge it would add to the story.

On March 7, 1955, *Life* magazine ran a series of photos of Dean, entitled "Moody New Star." When *East of Eden* premiered two days later, everyone but Jimmy showed up. "I know I was good," he said later, "and having people tell me would only embarrass me." His absence contributed to a growing mystique surrounding him.

He had already been campaigning for—and had landed—a part in the upcoming production of *Giant*. But when a schedule complication with Elizabeth Taylor caused a delay, Warner Bros. let Dean star in *Rebel Without a Cause*, a drama about 24 hours in the lives of a group of delinquent teenagers. Because *East of Eden* had opened to good reviews, Warner decided to upgrade *Rebel* from a B to an A picture, which meant that it could be shot in color. Dean decided that instead of the black motorcycle jacket, he'd wear a red nylon jacket, which, with the white T-shirt, blue jeans, and black boots, became the *Rebel* trademark. Filming began on March 28 and wrapped on May 26.

Dean had just three days off before he had to be on the set of what would be his last movie, *Giant*. George Stevens directed and

Largest number of extras used in a film: more than 300,000, in *Gandhi* (1982).

for the first time Dean was not allowed to experiment with his character. Worse, by the end of the first week of shooting, Stevens had reprimanded him in front of the cast and crew. Despite their differences, the two managed to make it through the filming. Dean turned in a strong performance and was set to star in *Somebody Up There Likes Me*, a film about boxer Rocky Graziano.

THE END IS NEAR

Back in Indiana, they had called him "one-speed Dean," because the only speed he drove was fast. No wonder, then, that he used his Hollywood money to buy racing cars and enter competitions. The studio was aware of his reputation and prohibited him from racing during the filming of *Giant*. But days after the film wrapped, on September 30, 1955, Dean hopped into his silver Porsche 550 Spyder with his friend and mechanic Rolf Wutherich and zoomed out of L.A., bound for a race in Salinas.

After being pulled over briefly for a speeding ticket, the Spyder headed westbound on Highway 466, just outside the town of Cholame. As they approached the dusty intersection of Highway 41, they saw a car coming from the opposite direction looking like it might be about to turn left. Probably thinking that the other car saw the Spyder and would stop, Dean kept driving straight on. But the other car turned in front of them, and the cars collided. The other driver walked away unhurt, but Rolf Wutherich was badly injured and Dean died instantly. He was 24.

POSTMORTEM

At the time of his death, James Dean was considered a promising actor with good potential. Only one of his three movies had been released, so he had been receiving a trickle of fan mail. But when the news stories and his obituary made their way across the world, his legend grew. Almost every article about him compared him to Marlon Brando.

Rebel Without a Cause was released on October 27, 1955, less than a month after the accident. His portrayal of a rebellious but vulnerable teenager captured the imagination of a growing audience of adoring fans. The fan letters started pouring in to Warner Bros., a few hundred a month at first, then thousands. In January the studio received 7,000 fan letters for the dead actor. In February the Academy nominated him for a Best Actor Oscar. The fact that he

Kissing is still banned in films made in Iran.

lost to Ernest Borgnine, who won for *Marty*, didn't lessen the enthusiasm of Dean's fans—in fact, it galvanized them. Hundreds of thousands of "Deaner" fan clubs sprang up. The death cult was, as *Giant* coproducer Henry Ginsberg observed, "bigger than Valentino."

THE LEGEND
Fifty years later, the Deaners still flock to Jimmy's grave in Fairmount, Indiana. He has been memorialized in books, festivals, biopics, and songs like the Beach Boys's "A Young Man Is Gone." In 1977 wealthy Tokyo businessman Seita Ohnishi erected the James Dean Memorial at the site of the accident, a $15,000 stylized concrete and steel sculpture that bears the dates and hours of Dean's birth and death, and a quote from his favorite book, Antoine de Saint-Exupery's *The Little Prince:* "What is essential is invisible to the eye."

* * *

"I'm a serious-minded and intense little devil, terribly gauche, and so tense I don't see how people can stay in the same room with me."
—James Dean

* * *

DO WHAT I SAY, NOT WHAT I DO
Shortly before his crash, Dean made a public service announcement with fellow actor Gig Young. Wearing his cowboy hat and taking a break from filming *Giant*, Dean told kids to "Take it easy driving; the life you might save could be mine."

* * *

SEVEN ACTORS IN *THE MAGNIFICENT SEVEN*
1. Robert Vaughn
2. Steve McQueen
3. Brad Dexter
4. James Coburn
5. Horst Bucholz
6. Yul Brynner
7. Charles Bronson

"An army without leaders is like a foot without a big toe."

THE BIGGEST CULT MOVIE OF ALL TIME

Imagine the boy next door trading in his Levi's for fishnet stockings, his all-American sister sporting a sexy French maid's outfit. It's a scene that's played out at movie theaters around the world every Saturday at midnight—all because starving actor/ playwright Richard O'Brien needed to pay the rent.

DON'T DREAM IT, BE IT

In the early 1970s, Richard O'Brien had just been fired as a chorus boy in a musical on London's version of Broadway, the West End. With no money, a wife and child to support, and lots of time on his hands, O'Brien penned a bizarre musical about cross-dressing, sex-starved aliens. He called it *The Rocky Horror Show*. And somehow, this weird show actually got produced. It opened at London's Royal Court Theatre in 1973 and was an amazing success; it was even named the best musical of the year.

Shortly after its debut, producer Lou Adler bought the play and moved it across the Atlantic to Los Angeles' Roxy Theater, where it met with critical and audience acclaim. It also caught the eye of filmmakers at 20th Century Fox, who were sure that they could transform it into a hit movie. The film version starred newcomers Tim Curry, Susan Sarandon, Barry Bostwick, and the singer Meat Loaf. It took eight weeks to shoot and cost $1 million to make. But before the movie was released, the play opened in New York . . . and flopped.

COLD FEET

Because the play had bombed, 20th Century Fox spent very little on publicity for the film, and it played in very few theaters. The movie initially had about as much success as the Broadway show— critics hated it and audiences stayed away in droves. It appeared that *The Rocky Horror Picture Show* was dead in the water.

But because of the play's early success at the Roxy, the movie

—John Winger (Bill Murray), *Stripes* (1981)

did well in Los Angeles, so Adler and a few others were convinced that the film just hadn't found its audience. In 1976 a Twentieth Century Fox employee named Tim Deegan persuaded New York's Waverly Theater, in the heart of bohemian Greenwich Village, to begin midnight showings. The tactic was tried in other select cities across the country as well. The hope was that it would catch on with cult audiences, just as offbeat films like *El Topo* and George Romero's horror classic *Night of the Living Dead* had done.

JUST A JUMP TO THE LEFT

Within months a phenomenon began to take hold. Audiences decided to tear down the invisible wall that separated them from the on-screen action. They weren't content just watching the movie from their seats—they began to dress as their favorite characters and perform along with the film, creating a show within a show. Seeing the movie became an interactive adventure; the *Rocky* experience was now part movie, part sing-along, part fashion show, and all party. Being in the audience at *The Rocky Horror Picture Show* now involved shouting lines at the screen, covering up with newspapers during scenes with rain, squirting water pistols to simulate rain in the theater, throwing rice during the wedding sequences, and dancing in the aisles doing the "Time Warp," the film's contagious anthem.

The *Rocky* phenomenon spread across the United States, giving birth to a midnight movie industry that spanned from major metropolitan areas right through to the straightlaced suburbs of America's heartland.

Almost 30 years after its initial debut in the attic of London's Royal Court Theatre, *Rocky* still plays every weekend at midnight in theaters across the United States and around the world. And in November 2000 *The Rocky Honor Show* returned to Broadway . . . this time to critical praise and commercial success. It was nominated for several Tony Awards, including Best Revival.

LAUNCHING PAD

Can you picture actor Russell Crowe in high heels and a black bustier? In the 1980s, the Academy Award–winning star of *Gladiator* toured Australia and New Zealand singing and dancing through more than 400 performances of *The Rocky Horror Show*, including several times as the cross-dressing Dr. Frank N. Furter.

MORE "I SPY" AT THE MOVIES

*Here are more in-jokes and gags you can look for
the next time you watch these films (from Reel Gags, by
Bill Givens and Television In-Jokes, by Bill van Heerden).*

SCREAM (1996)
I Spy . . . Wes Craven, the film's director
Where to Find Him: He's the school janitor, wearing a Freddy Krueger sweater from his *Nightmare on Elm Street* movie.

E.T. THE EXTRA-TERRESTRIAL (1982)
I Spy . . . Harrison Ford
Where to Find Him: He's the biology teacher who explains that "the frogs won't feel a thing." Screenwriter Melissa Mathison wrote this bit part for her husband. You won't see his face, because his back is to the camera.

BEETLEJUICE (1988)
I Spy . . . Elwood (Dan Aykroyd) and Jake (John Belushi) Blues from the *Blues Brothers*
Where to Find Them: The scene in which Barbara (Geena Davis) and Adam (Alec Baldwin) go to their caseworker's office. Elwood and Jake are peeking through the blinds.

THE ROCKY HORROR PICTURE SHOW (1975)
I Spy . . . Easter eggs
Where to Find Them: Various places during the movie. For example, one is under Frank's throne, one is in a light fixture in the main room, and you can see one when the group goes into an elevator to the lab. What are they doing there? The film crew had an Easter egg hunt on the set, but didn't find all the eggs . . . so they show up in the film.

TRUE ROMANCE (1993), PULP FICTION (1994), FOUR ROOMS (1995), FROM DUSK TILL DAWN (1996)

I Spy . . . Big Kahuna burgers and Red Apple cigarettes
Where to Find Them: They're writer/director Quentin Tarantino's special signature on his work. They first showed up in *True Romance*. "In *Pulp Fiction*," says Bill Givens in his book, *Reel Gags*, "Samuel L. Jackson recommends Big Kahuna burgers and both Bruce Willis and Uma Thurman smoke Red Apple cigarettes. In *From Dusk Till Dawn*, George Clooney carries a Big Kahuna burger bag, and you can spot a pack of Red Apples in his car. In *Four Rooms*, Red Apple smokes are near the switchboard."

THE ADDAMS FAMILY (1991)

I Spy . . . Barry Sonnenfeld, the film's director
Where to Find Him: The scene in which Gomez (Raul Julia) is playing with his train set. When he looks into the window of a train car, a tiny commuter looks back up at him. That's Sonnenfeld.

THE LOST WORLD: JURASSIC PARK (1997)

I Spy . . . Ads for some improbable new movies: *King Lear*, starring Arnold Schwarzenegger; *Jach and the Behnstacks*, starring Robin Williams; and *Tsunami Surprise*, with Tom Hanks's head attached to a surfer's body
Where to Find Them: In the window of a video store.

CLOSE ENCOUNTERS OF THE THIRD KIND (1977)

I Spy . . . The Grateful Dead's Jerry Garcia
Where to Find Him: Among the masses in the Indian crowd scene.

HALLOWEEN (1978)

I Spy . . . William Shatner
Where to Find Him: On the psycho's face. The film's budget was so small, they couldn't afford a custom-made mask. So they bought a William Shatner mask, painted it white, and teased out the hair.

In Mexico, *The Sound of Music* (1965) was titled *The Rebel Novice Nun.*

HOORAY FOR HOWLYWOOD

Hollywood directors love working with dogs: what other kind of movie star would be happy with an occasional pat on the head and a doggy treat? Here's a look at the biggest names in doggy stardom.

FIRST DOG STAR

The first canine on film, billed as Blair the Dog, appeared in 1905 in the British short *Rescued by Rover*. In it, the heroic family dog saves a kidnapped baby from gypsy thieves. Rover was an uncommon dog name at the time, but it gained widespread popularity after this screen debut. Since then, dogs of all sizes, shapes, and colors have earned a big place in cinematic history.

FIRST DOG SUPERSTAR

Strongheart was a pedigreed German shepherd (and a year or so older than his cinematic rival Rin Tin Tin). He was born in Germany during World War I, and trained as a police dog for the military. So, when American director Laurence Trimble found him (at three years old and 125 pounds), it took months of retraining and socialization before Strongheart was ready to star in his first film, *The Silent Call*, in 1921. The movie made Strongheart a star, adored by fans of movies and dogs everywhere.

He made four more films, including *White Fang* in 1925 and *The Return of Boston Blackie* in 1927, but an accident ended his career. He slipped and was burned by a studio light during filming; the burn turned into a tumor and the big guy died in 1929. But Strongheart survives—his handsome face still graces the labels of the dog food named for him all those years ago.

RIN TIN TIN TO THE RESCUE

Strongheart was popular, but Rin Tin Tin, the German shepherd who starred in 26 pictures for Warner Bros., went all the way: he became the studio's top-grossing "actor" and saved the studio from ruin in the 1920s. The original Rin Tin Tin was just a puppy when U.S. Air Corporal Lee Duncan found him at the end of World War I

In China, the British film *The Full Monty* (1996) was retitled *Six Naked Pigs*.

in a bombed-out building in France. Duncan brought the dog to the United States, named him Rin Tin Tin (after the tiny finger puppets that French children gave American soldiers for luck), and started training him.

Duncan and Rin Tin Tin were trying to break into the movies when they stumbled onto a set where a director was trying to get a wolf to perform. Duncan told the director that his dog could do it in one take, which he did—and Rin Tin Tin got his first film role, as the Wolf-Dog in 1923's *Where the North Begins*. By 1926 he was the top box office draw in the country. At the height of his career, Rinty was pulling in 12,000 fan letters a week; was making $6,000 a month; and had his own chauffeur, chef, and 18 stand-ins. He died in 1934 after a long life and successful career—and, according to Hollywood legend, took his last breath in the arms of his neighbor Jean Harlow. Duncan returned Rinty's remains to his birthplace in France and had him interred in the Cimetière des Chiens ("Cemetery of Dogs") near Paris.

Rin Tin Tin's legacy lived on through his offspring. Rin Tin Tin II (known as Junior) made three serials and traveled the country with Duncan promoting Rin Tin Tin films. When Duncan formed the first military K-9 Corps, Rin Tin Tin III helped him train some 5,000 dogs. Rin Tin Tin IV starred in *The Adventures of Rin Tin Tin* TV series that ran from 1954 to 1959. The bloodline continues to this day, with most Rin Tin Tin offspring now being used in the ARFkids (A Rinty for Kids) program, which provides service dogs to disabled children nationwide.

LASSIE COMES ALONG

Lassie's personal story isn't as dramatic as Strongheart's or Rin Tin Tin's—but it is typical Hollywood. The ever-faithful Lassie character in the original short story "Lassie Come Home" (published in 1938 in the *Saturday Evening Post*) was a female tricolor collie, i.e., similar to our concept of Lassie, but with black markings. When it came to casting the part for the 1943 movie, the winning candidate—the Lassie we know and love—turned out to be the familiar two-color rough collie, and a male. (And yes, there's a variety called the smooth collie; it looks like Lassie with a 1-inch crew cut.)

About 300 dogs auditioned for the starring role in the movie *Lassie Come Home*. The part went to Pal, an unpedigreed one-year-old male owned by Hollywood dog trainer Rudd Weatherwax. In fact, all the movie Lassies were played either by Pal or one of his descendants. And all were male. Male collies have thicker coats; when they shed in summer, these dogs still looked as big and heroic as Lassie should.

Pal performed perfectly in the role of the beloved collie who, after being sold to a rich nobleman so that her English family could pay their rent, finds her way back home over several hundred miles. The movie not only made Lassie famous but also launched the careers of Roddy McDowall and 11-year-old Elizabeth Taylor.

Pal provided the bark for the Lassie radio show that ran in the late 1940s, but the whining, growling, and panting were done by human actors. The TV series *Lassie* ran from 1954 to 1974.

POUND PUPPIES

The American Humane Association estimates that nearly 80 percent of the dogs used in films come from animal adoptions, like the pooches who appeared in such movies as the following:

Benji: The first Benji, aka Higgins, was rescued from the Burbank Animal Shelter in 1960 by veteran animal trainer Frank Inn (who also trained Tramp, the family dog on *My Three Sons*, and Arnold, the family pig on *Green Acres*). In fact, Inn's love for his animals was so strong that their ashes, which he kept in urns at his home, were buried with him. After the success of *Benji*, it was estimated that nearly 1 million similar-looking dogs were adopted from shelters.

Harry Potter: A 150-pound Neapolitan mastiff named Bully is one of four dogs that play Hagrid's intimidating but cowardly boarhound, Fang, in the *Harry Potter* movies. One of the movies' trainers originally found Bully in a junkyard; he adopted the dog after filming ended.

Air Bud: A golden retriever named Buddy was rescued from the pound and transformed into the heroic, basketball-shooting dog in the Disney film *Air Bud*. Buddy died of cancer shortly after the filming was over, and six dogs were needed to replace the talented pooch for the sequel, *Air Bud: Golden Receiver*.

How the Grinch Stole Christmas: Max, the Grinch's trusted companion, was played by six different dogs, all mixed-breed rescues from animal shelters. The American Humane Association monitored the filming to make sure the animals adjusted properly to their costuming and were not frightened by costar Jim Carrey's scary green makeup.

Dr. Dolittle and Dr. Dolittle 2: Sammy, a mixed breed, was rescued from the East Valley Shelter in Los Angeles and went on to star as Lucky, the doc's scruffy right-hand pooch.

FURRY FACTS

- Spike, the dog who played Old Yeller, was trained by Bob Weatherwax, son of Lassie's trainer, Rudd Weatherwax.
- Shirley Temple demanded that her Pekingnese pup, Ching-Ching II, be included in her film *Just Around the Corner*—and be paid as an extra.
- George Lucas named the character Indiana Jones after his Alaskan malamute.
- Pete the Pup, a pit bull mix that appeared in the *Our Gang* shorts, had a fresh circle drawn around his right eye before every shoot.
- Bullet, Roy Roger's trusty German shepherd, is stuffed and on display at the Roy Rogers–Dale Evans Museum in Branson, Missouri, next to Trigger, Roy's also-stuffed horse.
- Toto wasn't the only pooch in Oz. A Saint Bernard named Buck shows up in Munchkinland pulling a wagon.
- In *As Good as It Gets*, the role of Greg Kinnear's Brussels griffon, Verdell, was played by six dogs: Jill, Billy, Debbie, Timer, Sprout, and Parfait.
- The *Lassie* theme song is simply named "Whistle."
- Three dogs have been awarded a star on the Hollywood Walk of Fame: Strongheart, Rin Tin Tin, and Lassie.

* * *

ANCIENT WONDERS

Talos, the giant bronze statue in *Jason and the Argonauts*, was inspired by the Colossus of Rhodes, one of the Seven Wonders of the Ancient World.

Ian Fleming modeled his James Bond character partially with Cary Grant in mind.

MURDEROUS MACHINES

Humans love their modern conveniences. But this isn't always true in the movies, especially when the machines come to life and turn on their creators. Watch a few of these flicks and you might not look at your car (or your refrigerator) the same way again.

THE CAR (1977)
The 1977 cult classic *The Car* is a must-see for commuters everywhere. It tells the tale of a small-town sheriff as he tries to catch the driver of a mysterious black car that keeps killing people. He has a tough time of it, naturally, since there is no driver of the mean-looking converted Lincoln Mark III.

THE HEARSE (1980)
Trish Van Devere stars as a woman who relocates to a small town after a bad divorce and nervous breakdown. She moves into the house of her dead aunt, a woman rumored to have been a witch. The local townsfolk are cold and distant to the new arrival, who soon finds herself terrorized by a menacing black hearse with a disfigured driver. Joseph Cotten appears in one of his last film roles as a crusty old lawyer.

CHRISTINE (1983)
Unlike the Lincoln in *The Car*, the 1958 Plymouth Fury *Christine* has a driver. High school nerd Arnie Cunningham (Keith Gordon) becomes obsessed with restoring—and protecting—his new hot rod. Soon Arnie's obsession with his car turns him from wimp to predator, as the car starts killing everyone who isn't on Arnie's side, including the bullies who pick on him at school. Over 25 Plymouth Furys and Belvederes were used (and crashed) in the filming of *Christine*, angering some collectors, because there were so few of the cars to begin with.

MAXIMUM OVERDRIVE (1986)
This is the coup de grace of killer machines. The earth passes through the tail of a mysterious comet that causes every machine,

---

Later, when offered the role of Bond, Grant turned it down.

from electric knives to diesel trucks to soda machines, to come to life and go into a murderous rage against humans. The movie soon focuses on the Dixie Boy truck stop, where an assortment of salt-of-the-Earth people congregate to keep from becoming murdered by the hands—er—gears of their tormentors. Between the AC/DC soundtrack and the killer ice cream truck, this is a staple for everyone who wants to see mankind punished by machines.

ATTACK OF THE KILLER REFRIGERATOR (1990)

No, Uncle John isn't kidding. The tagline of this underground short film says it all: "Oh no! I just HATE cold cuts!" It's a tale of a very uncool icebox exacting revenge on the teenagers who vandalized it. Starring actors as unknown as that thing wrapped in aluminum foil way in the back, this hard-to-find flick can be purchased only online.

THE MANGLER (1995)

There've been a lot a of deaths at Blue Ribbon Laundry, where employees keep falling into a giant washing machine. Local authorities suspect foul play on the part of the owner (played by Robert Englund, who also played Freddy Kreuger in the *Nightmare on Elm Street* movies). But evil forces have possessed the giant washing and folding machine, nicknamed the Mangler. Now it demands blood sacrifices and will stop at nothing to get them. There's even a chase scene where the Mangler pursues those who are trying to exorcise it.

MURDERCYCLE (1999)

Take some meteors, add the CIA and a motorcycle with deadly intentions and you've got this flick. It all starts when a meteor somehow "becomes one" with a motorcycle and its rider—turning the combination into an unstoppable killing machine that can shoot lasers, run people over, and do gratuitous stunts. It is unclear what the Murdercycle is really after (world domination perhaps?), but a team of experts, including an ex-Marine and a psychic doctor, are brought in to stop it—before it pops wheelies of death again.

Dylan McDermott's stepmother is Eve Ensler, author of *The Vagina Monologues*.

BOX OFFICE BLOOPERS

Everyone loves bleepers, er, bloppers, er, we mean bloopers.
Here are a few great ones from the silver screen.

MOVIE: *Lethal Weapon 2* (1989)
SCENE: Martin Riggs (Mel Gibson) is placed in a straitjacket and thrown into a river.
BLOOPER: Struggling to escape from the straitjacket, Riggs purposely dislocates his left shoulder. Back on dry land, he slams his *right* shoulder against a car to put it back in place.

MOVIE: *Fear.com* (2002)
SCENE: The entire movie is about a woman who is a hemophiliac.
BLOOPER: This is one of our favorites—the whole movie is a blooper. How so? It's physically impossible for women to be hemophiliacs. They are carriers of the disease, but only males can contract it.

MOVIE: *Terminator 2* (1991)
SCENE: The Terminator (Arnold Schwarzenegger), Sarah Connor (Linda Hamilton), and John Connor (Edward Furlong) escape from a mental hospital in a car, driving in reverse.
BLOOPER: The stunt driver is driving from the trunk of the car, and you can see his head pop up just inside the rear window.

MOVIE: *Panic Room* (2002)
SCENE: When the group of robbers first enters the house, Meg (Jodie Foster) runs into her daughter's room and dumps a bottle of water on the girl to wake her up.
BLOOPER: They quickly make their way to the panic room, but once they're inside, the girl is completely dry.
BONUS BLOOPER: The survival pack inside the panic room is well stocked with almost everything they need—except food. (It does have another "essential," though: sugar-free breath mints.)

Rachel Weisz, "I have absolutely no empathy for camels. . . . They don't like people."

MOVIE: *Gladiator* (2000)
SCENE: After the battle with the Germans, Maximus (Russell Crowe) feeds his horse an apple.
BLOOPER: You can see a crewman standing in the background (wearing blue jeans).

MOVIE: *One Hour Photo* (2002)
SCENE: Nina (Connie Nielsen) drops off three rolls of film.
BLOOPER: Although the film she drops off is clearly labeled "Fuji Superior," when Sy (Robin Williams) runs the film through the machine all the negatives say "Kodak."

MOVIE: *The Last of the Mohicans* (1992)
SCENE: The British troops leave Fort Henry.
BLOOPER: As the Huron warriors begin to attack the British, the camera moves behind the procession, and in the middle of the commotion a man in a blue hat can be seen raising a megaphone.

MOVIE: *Star Wars* (1977)
SCENE: Stormtroopers break into the control room.
BLOOPER: One unfortunate trooper rushes in and slams his head against the door frame.

MOVIE: *The Lord of the Rings: The Two Towers* (2002)
SCENE: Just before the final battle at Helm's Deep, the villagers run into caves for safety.
BLOOPER: As the camera pans the rocky interior, one of the villagers leans against a stalactite . . . which wobbles back and forth.

MOVIE: *The Scorpion King* (2002)
SCENE: Opening narration.
BLOOPER: The film is said to have taken place long before the time of the pyramids, yet all the swords seem to be made of steel, which would not be invented for thousands of years to come.

MOVIE: *Signs* (2002)
SCENE: Merrill (Joaquin Phoenix) is in an Army recruiting office.
BLOOPER: The "Army" poster in the background shows a soldier in a Marine Corps uniform.

HARD-BOILED
LINGO LESSONS

*Watching vintage detective movies of the 1930s and 1940s can
get confusing—not because of the mysteries, but because
of the slang. Here's the low-down from A to Z.*

Ameche, Horn: Telephone

Bean Shooter, Rod, Roscoe: Gun

The Big House: Prison

Bracelets: Handcuffs

Butt: Cigarette

Cabbage, Dough, Kale, Mazuma, Scratch, Sugar: Money

Canary: (1) Female singer (2) A snitch

Cheese it (as in "Cheese it, the cops!"): Hide

Chick, Dame, Dish, Doll, Frail, Jane, Tomato (pronounced tuh-MAY-tuh): Woman

Clam up: Stop talking

Dick, Gumshoe: Private detective

Finger, Put the finger on: Identify

Flatfoot: Police officer

Flimflam: Swindle

Glad rags: Fancy clothes

In stir: In prison

Kisser, Yap: Mouth

Large: $1,000

Meat wagon: Ambulance

Mitts, Paws: Hands

Monicker: Name

On the level, Square: Fair or honest

Palooka: Man (especially a dumb one)

Paste: Punch

Pills, Slugs: Bullets

Pinch: Arrest

Pump metal, squirt metal: Shoot a gun

Puss: Face

Racket: Business

Send up the river: Send to prison

Sing: Confess

Take a powder: Leave

Tight: Tipsy, Drunk

Weak sister: Someone who's a pushover

Wooden kimono: Coffin

Zotzed: Killed

—Belle Rosen (Shelley Winters), *The Poseidon Adventure* (1972)

SUPER SCI-FI

What would make your list of the top ten science fiction films?
These critically acclaimed science fiction films get our vote.

METROPOLIS (1927)

Even though this is a silent picture, it remains one of the most visually influential films ever. Many sci-fi films (including several on this list) have drawn images, characters, and situations directly from this movie. Director Fritz Lang imagines a futuristic world where the clean and happy ruling class lives in gleaming cities, while the masses live in the depths, slaving away at big machines. Maria (Brigitte Helm) becomes the revolutionary leader of the masses but is kidnapped and turned into a robot, a false Maria, to manipulate the people. Roger Ebert credits the movie's lasting power to its "creating a time, place and characters so striking that they become part of our arsenal of images for imagining the world."

A Lasting Legacy: A famous (and oddly attractive) female robot from this film was the model for *Star War's* C-3PO, who was designed as a male version (although not as sexy).

THE BRIDE OF FRANKENSTEIN (1935)

A science fiction film with two mad scientists: Dr. Frankenstein (Colin Clive) and Dr. Pretorius (Ernest Thesiger) bring the monster his mate through judicious use of electricity and dead body parts. Critics agree this sequel is better than the 1931 *Frankenstein*, and it is generally regarded as the best "classic" horror film ever made. Although not really scary, it is surprisingly witty. Elsa Lanchester gives a memorable performance as the hissing, reluctant bride with the really big hair.

Hair-Raising: An ancient bust of Egyptian queen Nefertiti inspired the Bride's distinctive hair-do. The stand-up-straight effect was accomplished by attaching braids to a wire cage and brushing Lanchester's own hair over it.

Mervl Streep's role in *Out of Africa* (1985) was first offered to Audrey Hepburn.

THE DAY THE EARTH STOOD STILL (1951)

The 1940s were a fallow period for science fiction films, but the 1950s were a golden age—and this is one of the films that kick-started the genre. In this film a gentle alien visitor comes to Washington, DC, where Earthlings immediately shoot and wound him. The film holds up more for its message of the need for peace and brotherhood than for its special effects, although when Gort the robot shoots lasers from his eyes, it still looks pretty cool.

Moonlighting Robot: Lock Martin, the 7-foot-tall actor who played Gort, had another career as the doorman at Grauman's Chinese Theatre.

INVASION OF THE BODY SNATCHERS (1956)

The pod people from outer space come to a California town and begin replacing the inhabitants with zoned-out, look-alike aliens. The hero (Kevin McCarthy) realizes the threat and tries to warn society—but no one believes him. This suspenseful thriller has been seen over the years as either a metaphor for the dangers of communism or the dangers of McCarthyism (it depends on the historian you ask). But the director insists that it's just a movie about aliens. The idea of identity-stealing extraterrestrials has proved powerful enough to spawn several remakes—the most notable starring Donald Sutherland in 1978.

Bit Part: When watching the original movie, see if Charlie the meter reader looks familiar. Director and actor Sam Peckinpah plays him.

2001: A SPACE ODYSSEY (1968)

This movie dropped the hysteria and made science fiction serious. People had a hard time deciphering the flick (at the movie's premiere, Rock Hudson was famously heard to exclaim, "Will someone tell me what the hell this is about?"), but the realistic view of space travel released just one year before the Moon landings captivated audiences (plus hippies loved the psychedelic special effects of the last third of the movie). And then there was HAL, the homicidal computer, whose flat, calm delivery helped make him one of the most memorable movie villains ever. An American and

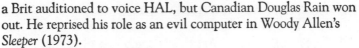

a Brit auditioned to voice HAL, but Canadian Douglas Rain won out. He reprised his role as an evil computer in Woody Allen's *Sleeper* (1973).

Say What? The film *2001* makes very spare use of dialogue. Nobody even speaks a line until 40 minutes into the picture.

STAR WARS (1977)

A long time ago (about 30 years), filmed at a location far, far away (Great Britain and Tunisia), George Lucas cobbled together a little film that would change movies forever. Borrowing story-telling elements from the 1930s Flash Gordon adventure serials and marrying them with groundbreaking special effects, Lucas created a fun, fast-paced, and adventure-filled movie that audiences couldn't get enough of. The film solidified the concept of the summer blockbuster, introduced the era of the special effects–driven film, and made Lucas (who kept the merchandising and sequel rights) very, very rich.

Always a Bridesmaid: *Star Wars* is one of the few science fiction films to be nominated for Best Picture (it lost to *Annie Hall*).

ALIEN (1979)

Alien was a different kind of sci-fi adventure: a monster movie set in outer space. The story: A lurking, ravenous alien creature eliminates, one by one, the members of a trapped crew on a derelict spaceship; it's up to Ellen Ripley (Sigourney Weaver), one of the first onscreen sci-fi heroines, to kill it—using both her brains and brawn to survive. In 1979, a female action hero was unusual, and Ripley's status shocked audiences—although not quite as much as what emerged from John Hurt's stomach (we won't ruin it—you'll need to see the movie).

Tag Line: "In Space, No One Can Hear You Scream."

BLADE RUNNER (1982)

Blade Runner was a commercial disappointment when it came out, but since then its reputation has more than redeemed its box office performance. The reasons: its eye-popping visual design, which updated the *Metropolis* look by way of film noir, and its dispassionate look at what makes us human. Harrison Ford stars as Deckard, a Los Angeles cop in 2019 who has to hunt down and destroy four replicants (artificial humans with four-year life spans) who are attempting to prolong their own lives.

Another Note: You can watch two versions of *Blade Runner*—the theatrical release and the Director's Cut (which removed some narration, ditched a studio-imposed happy ending, and is now generally regarded by fans as the "official" version).

E.T. THE EXTRA-TERRESTRIAL (1982)

This story of a suburban boy and his alien friend is still undeniably moving and effective, courtesy of Steven Spielberg's smart direction (most of the film is shot at kid height), Melissa Mathison's sweet but smart script, and the performance of Henry Thomas as Elliott, which is one of the great child performances in film. **Becoming an Icon:** The flying bicycle with Elliott and E.T. has become the logo for the production company, Amblin Entertainment (named for Spielberg's first commercial movie, 1968's *Amblin*).

THE MATRIX (1999)

When *The Matrix* first hit screens, audiences had never seen action like that before. Advances in cinematography and computer-generated effects allowed characters to effortlessly maneuver under and around bullets and to skitter up and down walls like spiders. Cameras rotate seamlessly around the actors, giving a panoramic view of the action. In the movie, computer hacker Neo (Keanu Reeves) discovers that his everyday world is actually just a facade created by evil, intelligent machines that draw power for themselves from subdued humans. A band of rebels contact Neo and enlist his aid in the fight against the machines. Audiences kept coming back, helping the movie gross more than $170 million. **Production Note:** To recover from the intensive martial arts scenes in the movie, Reeves had to soak in bathtubs full of ice.

Now that you know the sci-fi films to pop in your VCR, are you interested in what to avoid? For the worst in sci-fi, turn to page 353.

Al Pacino's grandparents were natives of Corleone, Sicily.

THE FIRST
SNOW WHITE

While Walt Disney Studios created the first feature-length version of the fairy tale, it didn't create the first animated Snow White. That distinction belongs to the Fleischer brothers, once the Disney studio's biggest rival.

In 1921 the Fleischer brothers, Dave and Max, founded an animation company in New York City. The brothers were pioneers in the business, developing and inventing many animation processes that became industry standards. One innovation, called rotoscoping, is still used today: live action was filmed, and then the footage was traced onto animation cells to produce extremely lifelike cartoon movements. The Fleischers were also early experimenters with recorded sound in cartoons, as well as the inventors of the bouncing ball for their sing-a-long cartoons.

In its prime in the 1920s and early 1930s, the brothers' studio was Walt Disney's biggest competition; its stable of characters—Betty Boop, Koko the Clown, Popeye the Sailor, and Superman—were huge box office draws. Popeye was so popular that theaters gave him billing equal to or even above the main feature. And Betty Boop, the first female cartoon character, had a sexual charm that no other toon could match. Her short skirt and bobbed hair gave her a very modern yet cute sensibility.

STARRING BETTY BOOP
Five years before Disney's creation, the Fleischers and animator Roland C. Crandall created the first Snow White cartoon. Their black-and-white version, released in 1933, lasts for just seven minutes, but that was long enough to tell a slightly altered version of the familiar fairy tale.

The cartoon is simply called *Snow-White* and stars sexy Betty Boop in the leading role. In this version, a magic mirror tells Betty that she's the fairest in the land, which infuriates the queen, who orders her guards—Bimbo (a dog) and Koko the Clown—to behead Betty. After this point, the cartoon deviates from the familiar story. The two henchmen fail to kill Betty and fall down a hole into the "Mystery Cave." Betty escapes but tumbles into an ice-cold river and freezes into a solid block of ice. The seven dwarfs discover her frozen body and take it to the Mystery Cave to bury her. There they find Koko and Bimbo. The queen eventually shows up, transforms into a monster, and chases everyone around the cave. She is defeated, and Betty is brought back to life.

Unlike the Disney version, this Snow White's plot seems secondary. The animators used it as more of a backdrop for a bunch of clever sight gags and bits, much like other animated shorts of the day. But the highlight of the cartoon is the somber, spooky rendition of "Saint James Infirmary," sung by Koko when Snow White is believed dead and her funeral procession descends into the cave. Cab Calloway, who voiced the clown, also provided the smooth dance steps for Koko. The Fleischers rotoscoped a Calloway dance routine to animate Koko's movements.

RECOGNITION

The cartoon short was largely forgotten after Disney released his *Snow White and the Seven Dwarfs* in 1937. But in 1994 the U.S. government recognized the work of the Fleischers as "culturally significant" and placed their *Snow-White* in the National Film Registry. Why? Because it features "some of the most imaginative animation and background drawings from the Fleischer Studio's artists."

FLEISCHER FACTS

- Cab Calloway was not the only star to appear in Fleischer cartoons; Louis Armstrong and Ethel Merman put in appearances, as well.

- When Betty Boop made her debut in the short "Dizzy Dishes," she was supposed to be a dog. When the Fleischers decided to make her a human, her long ears were reworked into hoop earrings.

For more on Snow White on the big screen, turn to page 203.

Director-actor Woody Allen won't use a shower if the drain is in the middle.

DESTINATION: ON LOCATION

Hey, movie fans, how about planning your next vacation around the spot where your favorite film was shot?

The Mouth of Truth, Rome, Italy
Roman Holiday (1953)
Gregory Peck brings Audrey Hepburn to a church to show her La Bocca della Verità (the Mouth of Truth), a large face engraved in stone with a slot for its mouth. As he slips his hand inside the mouth, he tells her, "The legend is that if you're given to lying, you put your hand in there and it will be bitten off." With that, he pulls his arm back—and his hand's gone! Hepburn screams, and Peck shows her how he's hidden it inside his sleeve. The mouth is located in Rome's 6th-century church of Santa Maria in Cosmedin.

Bodega Bay, California
The Birds (1963)
Hitchcock fans flock (you should excuse the expression) to this northern California town to look for sites like the café where the frightened, bird-beset citizens take cover and the schoolhouse where the teacher (played by Suzanne Pleshette) and her students are attacked by a gang (or, as it is called, a "murder") of crows. The café has been remodeled, but the schoolhouse exterior, now a private residence, looks largely the same. If you find the latter—and we're not going to tell you where it is—please do not disturb the occupants.

Aghios Ioannis (St. John's Beach), Mykonos, Greece
Shirley Valentine (1989)
Visit the location where Pauline Collins, as Shirley, decides to trade in the drab life of a Liverpool housewife to become an island waitress. The beach still has all the necessary elements, including George's Bar, which served as the taverna owned by Costas (Tom Conti). You may decide to stay, too.

For her *Dark Angel* role on TV, Jessica Alba studied martial arts and did weight training.

Devils Tower, Wyoming
Close Encounters of the Third Kind (1977)
Remember the giant rock formation that Richard Dreyfuss was channeling by building a mountain of mashed potatoes? You can visit the real thing—the mountain, not the mashed potatoes—where the world's first official alien encounter takes place. Over 3,000 climbers try to scale the tower every year, but only about half of them reach the summit. Don't bother looking for the landing strip: the entire facility was re-created in an airplane hangar in Alabama.

Chattooga River, Georgia/South Carolina
Deliverance (1972)
In one of life's inexplicable ironies, the river-rafting business in the area perked up after the release of the Burt Reynolds–Jon Voight movie about four tourists who are viciously attacked while canoeing on a scenic river. So try to put that nasty story line out of your mind, and just enjoy the breathtaking views and superior rafting that Sumter National Forest and the Chattooga River have to offer.

Marfa, Texas
Giant (1956)
The movie classic about Texas oil barons left its giant footprints all over town, and the El Paisano Hotel has been maintained as a monument to the film. A grand tour includes the room James Dean slept in and a *Giant* memorabilia room (where the movie plays in a constant loop).

Port Antonio, Jamaica
Cocktail (1988)
Want to meet the people who shake their cocktail shakers where Tom Cruise used to shake his? The Dragon Bay Beach Resort in Port Antonio is the beachside paradise for you. This out-of-the-way resort and its "Cruise Bar" are a great way to get away from the rat race. And when you're not hanging out at the bar, you can swim, scuba dive, and play tennis.

"I'm not going around kicking ass," she said at the time. "But it's nice to know I can."

Woodstock, Illinois
Groundhog Day (1993)
Bill Murray's character is forced to relive the same day over and over again, but not in Punxsutawney, Pennsylvania, that mecca of groundhog watchers. Instead, the movie was filmed in a faithfully re-created version of the town, some 500 miles to the west. Remembrances of scenes are scattered around Woodstock, including a plaque on one of the buildings designating it as Ned's Corner—the spot where actor Stephen Tobolowsky's character appeared every day to try to sell Murray a life insurance policy.

Squam Lake, Holderness, New Hampshire
On Golden Pond (1981)
Sorry to burst your pretty balloon, but there is no Golden Pond. The peaceful spot where Katharine Hepburn and Henry Fonda played a couple spending their last summer together is called Squam Lake, just two hours from Concord, Massachusetts. You'll know you are getting close when you start to see signs for the Golden Pond Country Store, the Inn on Golden Pond, the Manor on Golden Pond, and . . . you get the picture.

Matera, Italy
The Passion of the Christ (2004)
The crucifixion scenes were filmed in this gem of a city located in the instep of Italy's boot. Mel Gibson chose the site purely for its looks: gray, bleak hillsides spotted with *sassi*, houses and caves dug out of the porous rock. Abandoned in the 1950s when the government relocated residents to modern housing, the *sassi* are slowly being repopulated as trendy digs by artistic types.

Dunnottar Castle, Aberdeenshire, Scotland
Hamlet (1990)
Mel Gibson again, this time doing his Shakespeare thing in a castle just 15 miles from the city of Aberdeen. Built in 1392 and shot to pieces by Oliver Cromwell's cannons during his invasion of Scotland in 1650, the gorgeous ruin is perched high on a cliff surrounded on three sides by the sea. Open year-round.

Rapid City, South Dakota
Dances With Wolves (1990)
If you're planning a North by Northwest pilgrimage to Mount Rushmore, you might as well stop in nearby (15 miles) "Fort Hays," where Kevin Costner's character makes his decision to set off for the wilderness. The movie fort has been preserved as a tourist attraction called the Fort Hays Chuckwagon *Dances With Wolves* Film Set, where you can catch a cowboy show, shop for souvenirs, and even grab some cowboy grub served on tin plates.

Eberbach Monastery, Kiedrich, Germany
The Name of the Rose (1986)
Umberto Eco's book of the same name was set in an Italian monastery in the 14th century, but the movie's interior scenes of murder by candlelight were shot in this 12th-century monastery in Germany. The monks are gone, but the buildings remain: explore the cloisters and try a variety of monastic wines.

Savannah, Georgia
Midnight in the Garden of Good and Evil (1997)
Fodors.com has put together a two-hour walking tour of the city that covers all the main sites in the true story as told in the novel by John Berendt. The tour includes the Mercer House, home of wealthy antiques dealer Jim Williams (Kevin Spacey) and scene of the murder of Danny Hansford (called Billy Carl Hanson in the movie, and played by Jude Law). Visitors are encouraged to take another hour to meander around the Bonaventure Cemetery, Danny Hansford's final resting place.

National Radio Astronomy Observatory, Socorro, New Mexico
Contact (1997)
The giant satellite dishes from the Jodie Foster film based on the Carl Sagan book scan the skies for intelligent life while collecting and analyzing the data. The facility's Very Large Array (VLA) telescopes, as shown in the movie, were actually collecting data from outer space during filming! Guided tours are available.

With several Toronto cops, police buff Dan Aykroyd owns a Toronto bar called Crooks.

FREDERICK'S OF HOLLYWOOD UNHOOKED

Before Frederick Mellinger came along, women could get underwear in any color they wanted—as long as it was white. The colorful visionary founded Frederick's of Hollywood and forever changed the way women "support themselves."

Frederick Mellinger always liked women's underwear. At 14 years old, the tailor's son from lower Manhattan lied about his age to work in an intimate apparel business during the Depression. Serving overseas in the army during World War II, Frederick's unabated interest in undergarments was even further stimulated by Betty Grable pinups and the exotic, black, lacy undergarments of European women. He and his fellow soldiers wished that their girlfriends back home could wear the same revealing, nonwhite lingerie. After the war ended, Frederick returned to the States, opened his first lingerie shop in New York, and began selling unmentionables. Frederick's of Fifth Avenue specialized in black lingerie and was a huge success.

GO WEST, YOUNG MAN
One year later, Mellinger decided that the real market in ladies' underwear was Tinseltown. He packed his bags, headed out to Los Angeles, and changed the store's name to Frederick's of Hollywood. His idea was to give every woman the chance to dress like a movie star, even if she didn't have the body of one; all she needed was a little support in just the right places. One of his first pieces, and a true advance in brassiere technology, was the first push-up bra. Invented in 1948, Frederick's called it the Rising Star ("You cup your breasts IN, arrange them UP, and SNAP!").

Believing in better cleavage through engineering, Frederick's of Hollywood began to turn support into a science and even had a team from the Army Corps of Engineers working on designs. Technological advances in underwear included the Three-Way

Flatterer corset, the Fanny Former girdle, the padded Cadillac Bra (it promised customers that they could "Come in Looking Like a Chevy, Leave Looking Like a Cadillac"), and the Marabou-Trim Babydoll, a nightie designed in the 1950s and a consistent Valentine's Day best-seller. Celebrity clientele that flocked to the store included stars like Joan Crawford, Marilyn Monroe, Jayne Mansfield, and Lana Turner.

Another big breakthrough came when Mellinger imported the bikini (in a leopard-skin print) from France to California. The bathing suits sold quickly. When a Frederick's of Hollywood bikini customer was arrested on Venice Beach for indecent exposure, someone snapped her picture. The photograph of the bikini-clad woman being led away in handcuffs appeared in the newspapers and turned out to be great publicity. Business boomed.

ON EXHIBIT

Today Frederick's of Hollywood is still open at its original location on Hollywood Boulevard. It is also home to the Celebrity Lingerie Hall of Fame, billed as "a tribute to the stars who glamorized lingerie." The free exhibit displays Marilyn Monroe's corset from *Let's Make Love*, Natalie Wood's petite lavender bra from *Bob & Carol & Ted & Alice*, and Kathleen Turner's beige teddy from *Undercover Blues*. Also on display are negligees, petticoats, slips, and sundry other undies from Ingrid Bergman, Lana Turner, Judy Garland, Kim Basinger, and Zsa Zsa Gabor. Fans of *Austin Powers* can see the pink Marabou-Trim Babydolls worn by the Fembots. Madonna donated a black bustier with gold tassels. (Madonna has actually donated two bustiers; the first one was stolen during the Los Angeles riots in 1992.)

Like Madonna's tassels, the exhibit rotates its collection. At various times, visitors may also see Susan Sarandon's garter belt from *Bull Durham*, bras worn by Cher, Tom Hanks's boxers from *Forrest Gump*, and the bra worn by Tony Curtis in his cross-dressing performance in the classic comedy *Some Like It Hot*.

* * *

COSTUME COPY

Every year since the release of *The Seven Year Itch*, at least one fashion designer has reproduced Marilyn Monroe's halter dress.

—George McFly (Crispin Glover), *Back to the Future* (1985)

BAD HISTORY! BAD!

Eleven reasons why you shouldn't get your history from Hollywood.

A night at the movies is a fine way to amuse yourself and support America's $6 billion a year film industry, but it's a bad way to learn anything useful about history. Even when you throw out the obviously historically inaccurate comedies or special effects–laden fantasies, the supposedly more "accurate" genre of historical drama is still chock-full of bad history or history "reedited" to make the story less confusing, more exciting, or to accommodate the availability of some top box office actor. Even Oscar-winning films are replete with inaccuracies that would make your history teacher sick. As proof, here are 11 historical dramas that have played fast and loose with the past.

PEARL HARBOR (2001): Before the attack on Pearl Harbor in the film, Japanese Zeros are shown flying low over wholesome American kids playing baseball; they would have to have gotten up pretty early to play ball, since the attack occurred just before 8 a.m. Commander-in-Chief of the Pacific Fleet, Admiral Husband Kimmel, is likewise shown golfing, as if to emphasize his utter unpreparedness for the attack. In fact he was nowhere near the greens when the attack occurred. (Kimmel, the Navy's fall guy, was relieved of command after the attack; he's since been exonerated.)

Movie heroes Ben Affleck and Josh Hartnett are shown taking flight and doing battle with attacking Japanese Zeros; in the real world, it was Army pilots Kenneth Taylor and George Welch who managed to get into the air. Later, Affleck and Hartnett fly in Doolittle's raid over Tokyo; no actual pilots flew in both battles. Affleck is also shown serving in Britain's Eagle Squadron. While the squadron did include Americans, they were all civilians.

Final small inaccuracy: In one scene a sailor displays a dollar bill with the word "HAWAII" on it; those bills, introduced in Hawaii so they could be declared illegal if the Japanese invaded, came out in July 1942—long after the Pearl Harbor attack.

THIRTEEN DAYS (2000): The film in which Kevin Costner averts nuclear war during the Bay of Pigs, with a little help from

John Fitzgerald Kennedy (JFK). Most historians and participants of the event suggest that Costner's character, JFK adviser Kenny O'Donnell, was not nearly as pivotal a character in the crisis as he's shown to be. Indeed, several critical scenes in the film show O'Donnell doing things he never did in real life—taking Bobby Kennedy to meet the Soviet ambassador, giving pep talks to pilots before they overfly Cuba, and having a moment with JFK himself before a Kennedy television address.

The film also had an embarrassing flap over its newspaper ads, which featured F-15 Eagle fighter jets and a Spruance class destroyer. But neither of these saw military service until the 1970s. The error was on the part of the ad agency, not the film producers. Stupid ad agencies.

GLADIATOR (2000): This Oscar-winning toga flick is a historical mess right down to the Latin somebody chipped into the Coliseum. First off, there is no historical general to match Russell Crowe's Maximus. There was of course a real Marcus Aurelius, whose son was named Commodus. However, Commodus didn't smother Marcus Aurelius to death when he learned he wouldn't be chosen as emperor, if for no other reason than he already was emperor (or more accurately co-emperor) when his father died in A.D. 180. Moreover, while Commodus did in fact enjoy prancing about as a gladiator, much to the scandal of the higher classes, he was not killed by a revenge-crazed former general during gladiatorial battle. His real death in 192 is even weirder: he was strangled by a champion wrestler hired as an assassin by his advisers.

Oh, and the Roman Empire didn't become a republic again after Commodus's death, as intimated in the movie. Commodus was succeeded as emperor by one Publius Helvius Pertinax, who lasted all of three months before his assassination. Tough gig.

THE PATRIOT (2000): Neither Mel Gibson's character Benjamin Martin nor the chief baddie William Tavington are actual historical characters, but both are based loosely on real people: Francis "Swamp Fox" Marion and British Lieutenant Colonel Banastre Tarleton, respectively. The operative phrase here is "loosely," since Francis Marion owned slaves and loved a good fight (a far cry from Gibson's Martin, who was reluctant to go to war and paid free black citizens to work on his plantation).

True Grit (1969) was the only film for which John Wayne ever won an Oscar.

Tarleton, while earning the nickname "Bloody Ban," didn't set fire to churches while the parishioners were still in them. He also didn't die in the film's climactic Battle of Cowpens; he lived until 1833.

The Battle of Cowpens, it should be noted, hadn't nearly the amount of heavy firepower as is portrayed in the film. There were only two light cannons, brought by the British. Other than that, it was muskets and swords—still bloody enough. Incidentally, British commander Lord Cornwallis, portrayed in the movie as a somewhat stuffy older man, was actually only 42 at the time of the battle, in which he did not take part. The British forces were led by Tarleton, who led badly—he lost 600 out of 1,500 men, while the colonists lost a mere 72. Oops.

U-571 (2000): You know that part in the movie, when the crack team of U.S. soldiers launches a surprise attack on a German submarine and steals the sub's Enigma code generator? Never happened. The U.S. had no part in capturing the naval Enigma machine; that honor belongs to the British, who clambered aboard the German sub U-110 on May 9, 1941, to recover a working Enigma machine, its cipher keys, key books, and other cryptological records.

The Germans subsequently made their naval Enigma machines more complicated, requiring the Brits to perform the same maneuver again on October 30, 1942, when British sailors boarded the U-559. Two soldiers drowned in the attempt to bring up the sub's Enigma machine, but the signal key books were retrieved, which allowed the Allies to crack the naval Enigma code. Americans did board the German sub U-505 in 1944, retrieving sensitive papers, maps, and whatnot (earning the leader of the boarding crew, Lt. Albert David, the Congressional Medal of Honor), but it just wasn't the same.

There was a German submarine with the designation U-571 that patrolled the waters off the U.S. Eastern shore, sinking several merchant ships between 1942 and 1943. It sunk in the North Atlantic on January 28, 1944, after getting into a fight with an Allied aircraft and losing. All hands were lost.

ELIZABETH (1998): Lots of people in this film are in the wrong place at the wrong time, or simply shouldn't be there at all.

Bishop Stephen Gardiner, shown leading the Catholic Church opposition to Queen Elizabeth, died three years before she was crowned. Sir William Cecil was not an old man when Elizabeth came to the throne, as he is in the film, but a spry 38; he remained one of the queen's closest advisers until his death in 1598. Sneaky Francis Walsingham, portrayed as two or more decades older than the queen, was in fact only one year older. Robert Dudley, Elizabeth's fallen lover in the film, never really fell, but rather remained one of the queen's closest friends until his death in 1588. Other time-slip issues include Elizabeth's excommunication by the pope, which happened far later, in 1570.

AMISTAD (1997): While the majority of the characters in this retelling of the famous slave ship rebellion are based on real-life people, Theodore Joadson, played by Morgan Freeman, is not. The *Amistad* is shown making port in the winter; in the real world, it made port in August 1839. (Interestingly, in 1839, slavery was still legal in Connecticut, where the *Amistad* made port; a general emancipation in the state was not enacted until 1848. The film, rather conveniently, doesn't bring up the fact of a northern state still allowing slavery.) The film also shows the leader of the Africans, Cinque, peppering his lawyers (who included former president John Quincy Adams) with legal questions and helping create the defense. But there's no real evidence that he did this.

BRAVEHEART (1995): Oh, lots to complain about here, but for the sake of keeping things brief, let's focus on the film's portrayal of the relationship between William Wallace (Mel Gibson) and Princess Isabella (Sophie Marceau). In the movie, she's seen negotiating with Wallace for English king Edward I before she eventually jumps his bones and ultimately (one assumes) places his child on the English throne as Edward III.

Wallace was captured by the English and very messily dispatched (the movie got that right) in 1305. Isabella was born in 1292, making her 13 at the time of Wallace's death. She didn't wed Edward II until 1308—by which time, incidentally, he was already king. (Isabella would, however, play a primary role in deposing her husband in 1327.)

The movie fiddles with the death of Edward I, who died in 1307, not immediately after Wallace's death, and certainly not due to apoplexy from the idea of a Scotsman one day gaining his throne. Also, it should be noted that Edward I wasn't in the habit of throwing his son's gay lovers out of windows.

HOFFA (1992): Jimmy Hoffa's bosom buddy in this flick, Bobby Ciaro (played by director Danny DeVito), goes through every bump and turn of the union boss's tumultuous career with him. That's loyalty, or would be if Bobby Ciaro actually existed, which he did not—he's an alleged composite of several different real-life people. This film also shows Hoffa (and Ciaro) getting snuffed in Hoffa's car and then being tossed into the back of a moving truck, never to be seen again. Since no one actually knows what happened to Hoffa (except possibly those few who did it to him, and Hoffa himself, all too briefly), this is also total fiction.

JFK (1991): So many historical inaccuracies that it's hard to know where to begin. For example, the film features David Ferrie (Joe Pesci) confessing knowledge of the Kennedy assassination; in real life Ferrie consistently denied knowing anything. In presenting Dealey Plaza evidence, the film contends 51 people heard shots from the "Grassy Knoll," while the U.S. House Select Committee notes only 20. The film presents witness Lee Bowers telling the Warren Commission about seeing a "flash of light" and "smoke"; Bowers actually told this to author Mark Lane well after his Warren Commission testimony. The film has the Dallas mayor changing the motorcade route; the route was planned for days and was even published in newspapers. And so on and so on. People will be fighting about this one for years to come.

FAT MAN AND LITTLE BOY (1989): This re-creation of the birth of the nuclear bomb features a scene in which scientist Michael Merriman, working with others prior to the bomb's creation, stops an inadvertent nuclear reaction from detonating. As a result he receives massive radiation exposure and expires. This would be sad if "Michael Merriman" were a real person, but he's not; he's yet another "composite" character designed to push the plot along. An event like this did happen, bringing about the death of a real Manhattan Project scientist—Canadian physicist Louis Slotkin, but it happened in 1946, nine months after the nuclear bombs from which this movie gets its name were dropped on Japan.

Shrek (2001) is also the Yiddish word for **"monster."**

STARGAZING ON THE SIDEWALK

People dream of seeing their names up in lights, in splashy headlines . . . and on the sidewalk? Even Hollywood royalty like Jack Nicholson (he wept at his induction ceremony) dreams of landing a star on Hollywood's great Walk of Fame.

A s television boomed in the 1950s, Hollywood began to worry about losing its luster. Even the Hollywood Chamber of Commerce grew concerned. But Harry Sugarman (a local businessman and chamber member) figured out a way to restore a little shine to Hollywood. Inspired by the celebrity hand- and footprints outside Grauman's Chinese Theatre, Sugarman proposed to put the names of the stars *in* stars on the sidewalk as a tourist attraction. He called his idea the Hollywood Walk of Fame. Property owners along Hollywood and Vine (the selected route) liked the idea and raised $1.25 million to cover the construction costs. The Walk of Fame was born.

THE WORLD'S MOST FAMOUS SIDEWALK
The original Walk of Fame contained more than 2,500 empty spots. More than half of them were filled with names within 18 months of its opening in 1960 (mostly by directors, comedians, and stars of the silent era). Another 150 blanks were added in 1994, when the Walk expanded to 18 blocks: down both sides of Hollywood Boulevard from Gower to La Brea, and both sides of Vine Street, from Yucca to Sunset. While the limited space outside Grauman's is carefully allotted only to Hollywood royalty, the Walk has a lot more room and can include more names. Officially designated a historical landmark in 1978, the Walk of Fame had nearly 2,300 occupied stars by 2005.

The Walk originally honored achievements in motion pictures, but the guidelines quickly expanded to include other performing arts such as television, music, radio, and live theater. Set in a 3-foot square of terrazzo and brass, each pink, five-pointed star bears a name and an emblem that shows the person's specialty: a motion

The villain in *Scream* (1996) was based on a Florida serial killer, the Gainesville Ripper.

picture camera (the movies), a television set (TV), a phonograph record (music), a microphone (radio), and the twin comedy/tragedy masks (live stage performance).

GETTING A STAR

So how can you get your own pink star on the Walk of Fame? All you need is five years experience in entertainment and someone to nominate you. (And you don't have to be a real person to receive a star: Mickey Mouse, Bugs Bunny, Donald Duck, the Simpsons, Big Bird, and Godzilla all have them.) After a lengthy approval process (including the Walk of Fame Committee, the Hollywood Chamber of Commerce's board of directors, the Los Angeles Board of Public Works, and the Los Angeles City Council), the honoree must schedule and attend the dedication ceremony. There is also the little matter of a $15,000 fee to help out with installation and upkeep.

Celebrities can request a specific location for a star—if it is available; Ed McMahon requested (and got) a spot next to W. C. Fields. For other honorees, the committee will use the star's bio to determine the location; Drew Barrymore has a spot near her famous family members, Lionel, Ethel, John D., and John. But once a star is dedicated, there is no guarantee that it will always remain in the same spot. Some have had to be moved to accommodate street or subway construction, and others have been shifted to oblige the wishes of the honorees. Merv Griffin was fortunate enough to have his star relocated to lie in front of his studio.

Blank stars can still be found on the streets, and impatient wannabes have been known to skip the formalities and to stencil their names onto an available star—usually at night, with gold spray paint. This fame is usually very fleeting, however, as the imposter names are power-washed off as soon as discovered.

SEEING STARS

The First Star to have a Star: Actress Joanne Woodward, dedicated February 9, 1960. (Her husband, Paul Newman, had to wait until 1994 for his star, one of 134 stars installed en masse when the Walk was extended to La Brea).

The Star with the Most Stars: Gene Autry is the only person with five separate stars; he's got one in each category. Bob Hope and Mickey Rooney are second with four.

Early jobs for Russell Crowe: street performer, bingo caller, fruit picker, bartender.

Moon and Stars: A special plaque was placed on the corner of Hollywood and Vine to honor the *Apollo 11* astronauts: Neil Armstrong, Buzz Aldrin, and Michael Collins. They were given a special star in the television category—for their telecast from the moon.

Stars Without Stars: As of 2005, Al Pacino, Clint Eastwood, Mel Gibson, Francis Ford Coppola, Robert Redford, Jane Fonda, and Julia Roberts are not on the Walk of Fame.

* * *

OTHER WALKS OF FAME

Hollywood is not the only place with sidewalks dedicated to the stars. Check out these other cities and their walks of fame.

The Canadian Walk of Fame

Location: King Street West (between John St., & Simcoe St.). Toronto, Ontario

How to Get a Star: Nominees must be Canadian or have spent their formative years in Canada. Anyone can nominate an artist, and a selection committee reviews.

The Walk: Honorees are inducted in an annual ceremony where their bronze sidewalk stars are unveiled.

A Few Honorees: Mary Pickford (America's sweetheart was Canadian), Louis B. Mayer (he emigrated from Minsk to New Brunswick when he was 3), William Shatner, Arthur Hiller, Leslie Nielson, Mike Myers, and Dan Akroyd

St. Louis Walk of Fame

Location: Delmar Boulevard, St. Louis, Missouri

How to Get a Star: Anyone can be nominated just as long as they were born in St. Louis or spent a significant amount of time there. They must also have made an impact on national culture with their achievements in entertainment, architecture, literature, journalism, politics, civil rights, education, science, or sports.

The Walk: Each honoree gets a large brass star with his or her name and a brass plaque describing his or her contributions.

A Few Honorees: Josephine Baker, Kevin Kline, Phyllis Diller, Shelley Winters, Harold Ramis, and Vincent Price

---

Number 1 on the AFI's "100 Greatest American Movies" list: *Citizen Kane* (1941).

CARY GRANT:
BY THE NUMBERS

*Once a circus performer named Archie Leach, Cary
Grant went on to become one of the most debonair, charming,
sophisticated, and comedic leading men of all time.*

0
Number of acting Oscars won by Cary Grant. Nominated twice:
for *Penny Serenade* (1941) and *None But The Lonely Heart* (1944).
Grant received an honorary Oscar in 1970 for his life's work.

1
Cary Grant's rank in *Premiere* magazine's Greatest Movie Stars list.

2
His rank in the American Film Institute's Greatest (Male) Screen
Legends list. (Humphrey Bogart was #1.)

5
Number of Cary Grant's wives, the first four of whom divorced
him: actress Virginia Cherrill (1934–1935); heiress Barbara Hutton
(1942–1945); actress Betsy Drake (1949–1962); actress Dyan
Cannon (1965–1968), with whom he had a daughter, Jennifer. He
married non-actress Barbara Harris in April 1981; they were married until his death in November 1986.

6
The number of Grant's films on the American Film Institute's list
of America's Top Romances: *An Affair to Remember, The
Philadelphia Story, To Catch a Thief, Bringing Up Baby, The Awful
Truth,* and *Notorious.* Of all leading men, Grant had the most films
on the list.

007
Role that Cary Grant was offered, but refused, before the producers
settled on Sean Connery.

At the end of *Lost in Translation* (2003), Bill Murray whispers something . . .

13
Age at which Grant ran away from home to join a traveling acrobatic troupe.

17
Number of months after their marriage that Dyan Cannon sued for divorce on the grounds of "cruel and inhuman treatment."

27
Age at which Cary Grant sang in 12 operettas (during the summer of 1931) in St. Louis.

28
Age at which he arrived in Hollywood in January 1932 and picked his stage name, Cary Grant.

37
In cents, the value of the "Legends of Hollywood" commemorative postage stamp with Grant's picture on it (issued October 2002).

72
Number of films Cary Grant made in his 34-year career in movies. That's a little over two pictures per year.

73.5
Cary Grant's height in inches (that's about 6 feet 1 1/2 inches or 1.87 meters).

100
Number of times, according to Grant, that he took LSD. He began taking the mind-expanding drug as part of an experimental psychotherapy program, under the encouragement of third wife, Betsy Drake. After their divorce, he continued taking the drug and said that he benefited greatly from it overall.

150
In dollars, Grant's salary for one of his earliest movies, *Singapore Sue* (1932).

1904
The year of Cary Grant's birth. He was born on January 18.

1942
Year that Archie Leach officially changed his name to Cary Grant (and became a U.S. citizen).

100,000
In dollars, his salary for *Arsenic and Old Lace* (1944). After Uncle Sam took his share, Grant donated the remainder to the U.S. War Relief Fund.

150,000
In dollars, Grant's salary for *The Philadelphia Story* (1940), which he donated, after taxes, to the British war effort.

4,000,000
In dollars, Grant's salary for *That Touch of Mink* (1962), which—as far as anyone knows—he donated to himself.

10,000,000
In dollars, the amount for which Grant sued Chevy Chase after the comic called Grant a "homo" on Tom Snyder's talk show *Tomorrow* in 1980. As his defense, Chase used the First Amendment right of free speech and the "protective cloak of satire." The suit was settled out of court, for a reported $1 million.

* * *

LEADING LEGENDS
The top five male and female legends, according to the American Film Institute:

MEN	WOMEN
1. Humphrey Bogart	1. Katharine Hepburn
2. Cary Grant	2. Bette Davis
3. James Stewart	3. Audrey Hepburn
4. Marlon Brando	4. Ingrid Bergman
5. Fred Astaire	5. Greta Garbo

"Love means never having to say you're ugly."

A NOVEL TAKE ON HOLLYWOOD

Warning! These novels contain passages unsuitable for the dreamy, the naive, or the faint of heart. Only Hollywood is powerful enough—or weird enough—to have a genre of fiction all its own—filled with down and dirty looks at the movie biz and its most conniving characters.

THE FIRST HOLLYWOOD NOVEL

The Title: *Merton of the Movies* (1922)

The Plot: Stargazing Merton leaves the Midwest to become a hero on-screen. He arrives in a cynical Hollywood that he never read about in fan magazines. Merton ultimately does achieve stardom—as a comedian—because his melodramatic acting is so bad it's funny. But his sleazy comedy director never lets Merton know that he should take acting lessons.

Insider connections: Author Harry Leon Wilson moved to Carmel, California, in 1910. He worked in the movie biz, and out of his experiences came the first, much-read Hollywood novel. Wilson introduced two character types that would constantly reappear in other movieland satires—the naive outsider and the sleazy opportunist.

Go figure—they made it into a movie: *Merton of the Movies* became a successful comedy on Broadway (it is sometimes revived even today) before it made it on-screen. Red Skelton played Merton in the popular 1947 movie adaptation of the book.

THE DARKEST HOLLYWOOD NOVEL

The Title: *They Shoot Horses* (1935)

The Plot: Robert comes to Hollywood during the Depression to become a director. He and his penniless partner Gloria join a marathon dance contest where Robert hopes to meet a producer among the Hollywood glitterati in the audience. Couples are allowed only a 10-minute break every two hours and dance for hundreds of hours—until they drop in painful exhaustion or even death. The last couple standing wins, but Robert and Gloria find their own terrible way out of Hollywood desperation.

—Dr. Anton Phibes (Vincent Price), *The Abominable Dr. Phibes* (1971)

Insider Connections: Author Horace McCoy was a successful Dallas newspaperman and pulp fiction writer who played leading-man roles in local theater. After being offered a screen test, he came to Hollywood in 1931. Instead of becoming a successful actor, McCoy struggled in Depression-era Hollywood and eventually became a screenwriter. He had plenty of chances to observe the cruelty and despair that fueled his famous novel.

Go figure—they made it into a movie: McCoy's pain-filled work was critically acclaimed in Europe but often unappreciated at home. It wasn't until 1969 that director Sidney Pollack took a risk and put the novel on film; he won an Oscar for his efforts. Gig Young also got a statue for his role as the epitome of sleaze—the MC of the dance marathon. The popular movie starred Jane Fonda, who was Oscar nominated for her gritty portrayal of Gloria.

THE ULTIMATE HOLLYWOOD NOVEL

The Title: *The Day of the Locust* (1939)

The Plot: Tod Hackett has a job as a movie scene designer. In his off-hours he comes in contact with a bizarre string of Hollywood's lost souls: a promiscuous actress wannabe, her vaudeville has-been father, and a dwarf. These hopefuls and hangers-on are frustrated in their desire to be part of the glamorous fantasies they see on-screen. And their frustration explodes into violence at a Hollywood premiere.

Insider Connections: In 1933 novelist Nathanael West came to Hollywood. He worked on more than 30 screenplays including the hit *Five Came Back* about some unprepared city folk whose plane crashes in a jungle filled with headhunters. *Locust* presents such a sinister view of moviemaking and its influences that critics have called it the ultimate Hollywood novel.

Go figure—they made it into a movie: *The Day of the Locust* was released as a film in 1975. A friend of the late Nathanael West, the renowned Waldo Salt (*Midnight Cowboy; Serpico*) wrote the script. Karen Black starred as a sexy but talentless actress—and showed enough talent to be nominated for a Golden Globe. Burgess Meredith, who played her father, was nominated for a Golden Globe and an Oscar.

THE DOG-EAT-DOGGIEST HOLLYWOOD NOVEL
The Title: *What Makes Sammy Run?* (1941)
The Plot: Sammy Glick starts out as a newspaper office boy.
Surrounded by writers, he plagiarizes their work to make his way
into the film business. Of course, he fits right in. The book reveals
a Hollywood where executives trample artists to line their own
pockets, and Sammy rises to mogul status—until he meets his
comeuppance in the form of a banker's beautiful daughter.
Insider Connections: Author and screenwriter Budd Schulberg,
the son of a Paramount producer, grew up with an insider's knowledge of Hollywood. His father begged Budd not to publish *What
Makes Sammy Run?* predicting it would terminate Budd's screenwriting career. Fortunately Dad was wrong, and his son went on to
win an Oscar for penning the 1954 classic *On the Waterfront*.
(Schulberg may be best known for Marlon Brando's famous line, "I
coulda been a contender.")
Go figure—they *didn't* make it into a movie: Many Hollywood
villains have made it big in theaters. Why not Sammy? In 1941
studio executives loathed being compared to the backstabbing
Glick, and they refused to put his saga on film. A decade later,
Schulberg (a disillusioned ex-communist) testified before the
House of Un-American Activities Committee about his communist colleagues. That action, unpopular with many in Hollywood,
may have hindered filming of his acclaimed novel. Whatever the
reason, Sammy has just "run" on the small screen, in 1949 and
1959 TV dramatizations.

EQUAL OPPORTUNITY HOLLYWOOD NOVELS
The Titles: *Play It As It Lays* (1970); *Hollywood Wives* (1984)
The Plots: Lest you suppose that Hollywood's bad guys are all guys,
these two best-sellers have a feminine touch. In *Play It As It Lays*,
the temptations of Hollywood are too much for the troubled Maria,
an actress turned model. She drifts through days that are full of
casual sex, alcohol, and drugs, but which are ultimately empty of
pleasure and meaning.

As for *Hollywood Wives*, these gorgeous trophy wives don't clean
or cook. They "do lunch" in Beverly Hills and shop on Rodeo
Drive. They don't have much time to play with their kids, either.
They're much too busy playing with pool boys.

All the President's Men **was the first film Jimmy Carter watched as president.**

Insider Connections: Joan (*Play It As It Lays*) Didion came to Southern California with her husband John Gregory Dunne, who was researching a book about Twentieth Century Fox. The couple stayed on to write screenplays.

Jackie (*Hollywood Wives*) Collins was born in London. But she took in the glitz of Hollywood in her teens, after her parents sent her to live with her sister, actress Joan Collins. She has written a series of best-selling Hollywood (s)exposes.

Go figure—they made them into movies and mini-series: In 1972 Didion collaborated with her hubby on the script for *Play It As It Lays*. Tuesday Weld played Maria and earned critical praise and a Golden Globe nomination for her performance. In 1985 *Hollywood Wives* was made into a four-hour-plus miniseries on ABC, starring Candice Bergen and Anthony Hopkins.

THE "STILL THE SAME OLD HOLLYWOOD" NOVEL
The Title: *The Player* (1988)
The Plot: Griffin is senior vice president of production at a major Hollywood studio and determined to be head honcho. Meanwhile, he has it all, a glam job, money, and the power to either cash in on the work of toiling scriptwriters or give them a quick brush off. But one anonymous and angry screenwriter writes that he is out for blood, Griffin's blood.

Insider Connections: Author Michael Tolkin grew up in the entertainment industry. Dad wrote comedy for TV, and Mom was an executive lawyer for Paramount. Young Michael himself was a sitcom writer when he published his first novel, *The Player*. The book was immediately acclaimed for its deadly aim at the studio system—which still had not lost its power to provoke disgust in readers.

Go figure—they made it into a movie: Michael Tolkin was Oscar nominated for his screenplay adaptation of his novel. Directed by Robert Altman (also nominated) *The Player* (1992) became a critical and box office success. Starring Tim Robbins, the movie is filled with lots of cameo performances by movie stars (Julia Roberts, Burt Reynolds, Susan Sarandon, and Bruce Willis to name a few). Some of them worked for free just to appear in this classic trashing of Hollywood higher-ups.

Jeremiah Johnson (1972) was based on the life of real-life trapper John Johnston.

SIX DEGREES OF KEVIN BACON

In which we explore who—among all the actors in the
world—deserves the title "Center of the Hollywood Universe."

Six Degrees of Kevin Bacon was someone's playful turn on the
phrase "six degrees of separation," based on the idea that
everyone in the world can be linked to anyone else in the
world in just six steps—that your Aunt Betty's dentist's son's
teacher lives next door to the guy who was the president of your
high school senior class way back when. And so on.

FOUR DEGREES
For the uninitiated, the object of Six Degrees of Kevin Bacon is to
link any actor or actress, through the movies they've appeared in,
to Kevin Bacon in less than six steps. For example, O. J. Simpson
was in *Naked Gun* with Priscilla Presley, who was in *The
Adventures of Ford Fairlane* with Gilbert Gottfried, who was in
Beverly Hills Cop II with Paul Reiser, who was in the movie *Diner*
with Kevin Bacon. That's four steps.
   And it works with most actors you can name.

THE LAW OF AVERAGES
A computer scientist, Brett Tjaden at the University of Virginia,
was curious about what the average "Bacon number" would be for
the nearly 500,000 or so actors and actresses listed in IMDb, the
Internet Movie Database, so he applied a theorem to the database
and found that the average number came out to an amazing 2.917
steps. In other words, anyone who has ever acted professionally can
be linked to Bacon in an average of under three steps.

THE CENTER OF THE UNIVERSE
It's the nature of science (and scientists) to try to take things one
or more steps further. Tjaden then wondered who, if anyone, was
more "linkable" than Bacon; who—he asked himself—was closer
to the center of the Hollywood Universe? When he did the math,

Robert Redford didn't see *The Sting* (1973) until June 2004.

he found that there were 1,048 other actors who were even better centers than Kevin Bacon, that is, who could be linked to the largest number of actors in fewer steps. Bacon is still in the 99th percentile, but he was beaten out by Shelley Winters, for instance, who can be linked to every other actor in the world in an average of 2.75 steps.

THE TOP 20
By now you might be wondering who among all the actors in the world is the center of the Hollywood Universe. Here's the list of the top 21, followed by the average number of steps it takes to link them with all the other actors in the known universe.

1. Rod Steiger (2.678695)
2. Christopher Lee (2.684104)
3. Dennis Hopper (2.698471)
4. Donald Sutherland (2.701850)
5. Harvey Keitel (2.705573)
6. Donald Pleasence (2.707490)
7. Max von Sydow (2.708420)
8. Michael Caine (I) (2.720621)
9. Martin Sheen (2.721361)
10. Anthony Quinn (2.722720)
11. Charlton Heston (2.722904)
12. Gene Hackman (2.725215)
13. Sean Connery (2.730801)
14. Harry Dean Stanton (2.737575)
15. Orson Welles (2.744593)
16. Robert Mitchum (2.745206)
17. Elliott Gould (2.746082)
18. Christopher Plummer (2.746427)
19. James Coburn (2.746822)
20. Ernest Borgnine (2.747229)
21. Karen Black (2.750952)

The complete list of the top 1,000 can be viewed at the Oracle of Bacon Web site, hosted by the University of Virginia. It's a great place to play Six Degrees of Kevin Bacon the easy way, by letting your computer do all the work.

Dustin Hoffman and Gene Hackman were roommates early in their careers.

ED WOOD'S
MASTERPIECE

In "The Worst Filmmaker of All Time" (page 55) we told all about Ed Wood's career. Just to back up our case, we thought we'd include a few comments from critics about Plan 9 from Outer Space.

O**NLY HUBCAPS**
"Some say [*Plan 9 from Outer Space*] is the worst movie anyone ever made. Certainly it's the worst movie Ed Wood ever made. And nobody but Wood could have made it. The lunacy begins with a portentous introduction from our old friend Criswell, the clairvoyant. 'Greetings my friends,' Criswell reads from his cue card. 'We are all interested in the future because that's where you and I are going to spend the rest of our lives.' While we're still mulling over the meaning of that statement, Wood hits us with the heavy-duty special effects—UFOs flying over Hollywood Boulevard. Actually, they're only hubcaps, super-imposed on a pseudo-sky."
—*The Worst Movies of All Time*, by Michael Sauter

ATTACK OF THE UNDEAD
"God knows what the first eight "Plans" were, but *Plan 9* is a doozy. . . . Aliens Dudley Manlove and Joanna Lee (today a successful scriptwriter) were sent by The Ruler to raise the dead so that they'd attack the living. That's just about what Wood tried to do with his dead friend Bela Lugosi, billed as the star of the film although he died *prior* to production. Wood had a couple of minutes of footage of Lugosi from an aborted project, so he simply inserted the snippets into this film and repeated them over and over so that Lugosi had adequate screen time. Lugosi's character— The Ghoul Man—was played in the rest of the movie by a chiro-practor, an extremely tall fellow who spends his screen time with a cape covering his face so we won't know he's an impostor. The ruse doesn't work, but I don't think Wood really cared."
—*Guide for the Film Fanatic*, by Danny Peary

Hoffman was also roomies with Robert De Niro.

BEYOND RIDICULE
"Words such as amateurish, crude, tedious and aaarrrggghhhh can't begin to describe this Edward D. Wood film with Bela Lugosi in graveyard scenes made shortly before his death. . . . The unplotted plot by Wood has San Fernando Valley residents troubled by UFOs of the worst encounter. Humanoid aliens Dudley Manlove and Joanna Lee land their cardboard ship with a ninth plan to conquer the world (the first eight failed, you see). They resurrect corpses, including Vampira, Tor Johnson and Lugosi's double. The results are unviewable except for masochists who enjoy a good laugh derived from watching folks making fools of themselves."

—*Creature Features Movie Guide Strikes Again*,
by John Stanley

MASTERFUL SPECIAL EFFECTS
"The graveyard set provides the film with many of its eerie moments, thanks to a number of dead tree branches and cardboard tombstones; in one scene a policeman accidentally kicks over one of the featherweight grave markers.

"Despite the resourcefulness of the director, there are slight technical shortcomings in the final version of *Plan 9*. Even Wood's staunchest defenders will admit that the Old Master seemed to have a tough time with lighting. In one scene, as Mona McKinnon runs in horror from Bela Lugosi's double, she goes directly from a graveyard at midnight to a nearby highway at high noon. This same confusion between night and day occurs several times in the course of the film."

—*The Golden Turkey Awards*, by Harry and Michael Medved

CHEAP, CHEAP, CHEAP
"Money was always a problem for Wood. Budgets were routinely non-existent, forcing him to film on the cheap, scrimping . . . as best he could. . . . How cheap was *Plan 9*? The flying saucers are hubcaps suspended by wires. In several scenes the movie jumps from daylight to nighttime and back. And outdoor lawn furniture doubles as bedroom furniture. . . . In all of the literature about *Plan 9* (and there's reams of the stuff) one question about the movie has never been answered. If *Plan 9* was to revive the dead, what were the other eight plans?

—*Why the People of Earth Are "Stupid,"* by Tom Mason

"She might have fooled me. But she didn't fool my mother."

A SIGN BY ANY OTHER NAME

*How a gigantic advertisement became a movieland
icon (after a little cosmetic surgery).*

The Hollywood sign began its life as part of another California dream: making it big in real estate. In 1923 a group of investors (including Harry Chandler, publisher of the *Los Angeles Times*, and movie director Mack Sennett) prepared to develop a new, posh, residential neighborhood in the Hollywood Hills. They called it Hollywoodland.

To promote it, Chandler and company put together a big promotional campaign. Their biggest ad was going to be the world's largest sign, mounted on the side of Mount Lee, overlooking the new neighborhood. Chandler hired contractor George Roche to create the Hollywoodland sign. The 13 white letters, each 50 feet high and 30 feet wide, were made of metal barn roofing and telephone poles; holes were poked in each letter to help them withstand the winds on the hill. Like a movie marquee, the sign was lit up: 4,000 20-watt lightbulbs flashed sequentially—first *HOLLY*, then *WOOD*, then *LAND*. A caretaker lived in a shed behind one of the *L*s and had a full-time job just changing the burned-out bulbs. The sign was visible for miles and became one of the most famous sights in Los Angeles.

REAL ESTATE AND THE SIGN CRASH

Although it was only intended to stand for two years, the sign outlived the investment company that built it. The stock market crash and the Great Depression forced Chandler's real estate syndicate into bankruptcy. Maintenance on the sign ceased, and by 1939 all the lightbulbs had been stolen or broken. Residents of the area complained that the decrepit sign would bring down their property values and lobbied for its removal (their rallying cry: "Loose signs sink neighborhoods"). Finally, in 1944, the Hollywood Chamber of Commerce took over the sign and the land surrounding it. But maintenance was still lacking, and the tin sign deteriorated. When

—Norman Bates (Anthony Perkins), *Psycho* (1960)

the *H* blew over in 1949, leaving OLLYWOODLAND alone on the hill, things were bleak.

Later that same year, the Hollywood Chamber of Commerce decided to restore the old sign. They removed the *LAND* and repaired and replaced the remaining letters: from that point on, the sign just read HOLLYWOOD. As the entertainment industry expanded in the 1950s and 1960s, the sign became one of the most famous symbols of the movie business.

I'D LIKE TO BUY A VOWEL
In honor of the sign's historic status, the Los Angeles Cultural Heritage Board declared it Cultural Historical Monument #111 in 1973. Gloria Swanson presided at a rededication ceremony. But it turned out the sign was in need of more than cultural status. By the early 1970s, time had taken its toll on the original letters. Termites, vandals, and exposure to the elements had weakened the sign so much that the letters were deteriorating past the point of repair. By 1978 one *O* had fallen over, and another *O* outright collapsed. The top of the letter *D* fell apart, and arson scorched the bottom of the first *L*. Again, residents complained that the broken-down sign had to be torn down.

But the Hollywood sign, like so many actors, was due for a comeback. In 1978 the Hollywood Sign Trust was formed and it started their "Save the Sign" campaign. Entertainers signed up to help restore the hillside icon. An auction held at the Playboy Mansion raised money by "selling" letters to celebrities. Each letter cost $28,000. Gene Autry bought an *L*. Hugh Hefner, the *Y*. Alice Cooper bought an *O* in honor of Groucho Marx. The auction and other successful campaigns raised $250,000 that went to the creation of a stronger, more durable Hollywood sign.

The old tin letters were torn down, and brand-new steel ones rose in their place on Mount Lee. The new Hollywood letters, from the sign's restoration in the 1970s, stand as tall as the old ones, but now they are thicker and stronger; the entire sign weighs 450,000 pounds.

STILL SEEING THE SIGN
Today the chamber of commerce, the Hollywood Sign Trust, and the City of Los Angeles are the official caretakers of the sign, making sure it continues to be the most photographed attraction in

Hollywood. The sign has been trademarked, and although the chamber of commerce is mum on exactly how much money the trademark earns, it's enough to make sure that the sign will be in top shape for years to come.

- The sign is not lit up every night, the way it used to be. Since the restoration in 1978, it has been lit only three times at night: in 1978, to inaugurate the new sign; in 1984, for the Los Angeles Summer Olympics; and in 1999, for the Los Angeles centennial celebration.

- Harvey and Daeida Wilcox first purchased the tract that became Hollywood in 1886. Since it was covered with fig trees, Harvey wanted to name it Figwood, but Daeida didn't like the name. They agreed to call it Hollywood instead.

- Residents of Hollywoodland included actor Boris Karloff and English novelist Aldous Huxley. The latter wrote the screenplays for *Pride and Prejudice* (1940) and *Jane Eyre* (1944).

- In 1995, the letters got a fresh coat of white paint, but it was too foggy to see them at the unveiling ceremony.

* * *

A FEW ALTERATIONS
The Hollywood sign is one of the most famous icons of the entertainment business. It's also a prime target for practical jokers.

On New Year's Day, 1976, residents of Los Angeles woke up to see something different on the side of Mount Lee. Instead of the familiar HOLLYWOOD sign, they saw the HOLLYWEED sign. A group of local pranksters scaled the hills during the night and changed the last two Os into lowercase Es. Ringleader Steve Brown and his buddies wanted to do something special to commemorate the status change of marijuana possession from a felony to a misdemeanor. He also said, "I thought it would be a lot of fun."

Other sign alterations have followed over the years, like HOLY-WOOD when the Pope held an Easter Sunday service at the Hollywood Bowl and OLLYWOOD when Colonel Oliver "Olly" North testified during the Iran-Contra Hearings in the late 1980s. But today security is much tighter at the sign, so practical jokers have a much harder time getting their messages across.

VAMPIRES ON
BIKINI BEACH

*With the single possible exception of Sherlock Holmes, film
historian David Skal writes, "Dracula, has been depicted in
film more times than almost any fictional being." Here's a look at
some of the more unusual vampire movies that have been made.*

Dracula Blows His Cool (1982) "Three voluptuous models and
their photographer restore an ancient castle and open a disco in it.
The vampire lurking about the castle welcomes the party with his
fangs."

—*Video Hound's Golden Movie Retriever 2001*

**Little Red Riding Hood and Tom Thumb vs. the Monsters
(1960)** "Little Red Riding Hood and Tom Thumb fight a vampire
and a witch in a haunted forest! One of three Hood movies made
the same year in Mexico and shipped up here like clockwork in the
mid-60s to warp the minds of little kids whose parents wanted to
go Christmas shopping."

—*The Psychotronic Encyclopedia of Film*

Planet of the Vampires (1965) "Some astronauts crash land on a
strange planet where the undead kill the living, only to discover
that the alien-possessed vampiric survivors are preparing to land on
another alien world—Earth!"

—*The Essential Monster Movie Guide*

The Devil Bat (1940) "Bela Lugosi plays a crazed scientist who
trains bats to kill at the scent of a certain perfume."

—*Halliwell's Film and Video Guide*

Haunted Cop Shop (1984) "When vampires invade a meat-packing
plant, the elite Monster Police Squad is brought in to stop them.
When the squad botches the job, the Police Commissioner bumps
them down to foot patrol until the vampires attack the county hospital. Impressive special effects."

—*The Illustrated Vampire Movie Guide*

"Throw that junk in," is the last line of what celebrated movie?

Samson vs. the Vampire Women (1961) "Sexy vampire women keep muscular male slaves on slabs in their atmospheric crypt. Santo the silver-masked Mexican wrestling hero (called Samson in the dubbed version) defeats them all."
—The Psychotronic Encyclopedia of Film

Vampires on Bikini Beach (1988) "Californians save their beach from undesirable vampires." (Is there some other kind?)
—The Illustrated Vampire Movie Guide

Billy the Kid vs. Dracula (1965) "The title says it all. Dracula travels to the Old West, anxious to put the bite on a pretty lady ranch owner. Her fiancé, the legendary Billy the Kid, steps in to save his girl from becoming a vampire herself. A classic."
—Video Hound's Golden Movie Retriever 2001

The Return of the Vampire (1943) "Bela Lugosi plays Armand Tesla (basically Dracula under another name), who returns to claim a girl after 'marking' her when she was a child. But his assistant, the werewolf-with-a-heart, turns on him and drags him out into the sunlight, where he melts in spectacular fashion."
—Amazon Reviews

Atom Age Vampire (1960) "Badly dubbed Italian timewaster with cheese-ball special effects and a tired premise. A mad professor restores the face of a scarred accident victim."
—Video Movie Guide

Haunted Cop Shop II (1986) "This improved sequel to the 1984 original features non-stop action. The vampire creature is destroyed by the hero relieving himself into a swimming pool and completing an electrical circuit!"
—The Illustrated Vampire Movie Guide

Blacula (1972) "In 1815 in Transylvania, an African prince falls victim to Dracula. A hundred and fifty years later, his body is shipped to L.A. and accidentally revived. Jaded semi-spoof notable chiefly as the first black horror film. The star's performance is as stately as could be wished under the circumstances."
—Halliwell's Film Guide

Answer: *Citizen Kane* (1941). The pile of "junk" includes the Rosebud sled.

POPCORN PARTNERSHIP

*Fresh, hot, salty, buttery popcorn. Just
the smell of it makes you think of the movies.
But when did the movie-time popping begin?*

POPPING UP EVERYWHERE
From the late 1800s on, Americans popped corn for celebrations. They strung popcorn garlands for decorating trees, mantles, and staircases. They covered their corn in caramel, buttered it, salted it, or used candied sugar syrup to glue it into popcorn balls. But it all had to be made at home on the stove—that is, until 1893.

That's when popcorn moved out of the kitchen thanks to the Charles Cretors Company. They built the first mobile popcorn machine and exhibited it at the 1893 World's Columbian Exposition in Chicago. The machine weighed "only" between 400 to 500 pounds and, according to *Scientific American*, could be easily pulled by a boy—or a small pony—to political rallies, fairs, picnic grounds, and other places where popcorn would be popular.

TO THE MOVIES
In the early 1920s, popcorn vendors set up shop outside movie theaters and sold the snack to people on their way in. Wrede Smith, whose family has been making Jolly Time popcorn since 1914, worked at a corner popcorn and hamburger stand. He carried popcorn boxes up and down the aisles in the local movie theater, selling them for a small commission—or sometimes just working for free popcorn. At first some theater owners weren't too thrilled about the snack's presence in theaters; buttery popcorn flew in the face of the sophisticated atmosphere they were trying to cultivate. Plus, they weren't very excited about sweeping it up after the shows ended. But the cinema owners who welcomed popcorn to their theaters won more business, so the snack's contribution to the bottom line began to win over theater owners nationwide.

Rod Steiger chewed 263 packs of gum during the shooting of *In the Heat of the Night.*

The popcorn partnership took another giant leap forward in 1925, when Charles T. Manly of Butte, Montana, invented the first electric popcorn machine. It eliminated the smelly (and dangerous) gas fumes created by the engines of earlier machines, which also made it safe to pop corn indoors. From then on, theater lobbies were destined to smell like warm popcorn and butter evermore.

IT'S ELECTRIC

During the 1930s popcorn's popularity grew and grew. It was cheap to make and easy to share, so audiences gobbled it up. According to Hollywood rumors, movie stars were fans themselves; Claudette Colbert loved popcorn so much that she brought it to theater screenings for herself and friends. She even worked it into the romantic comedy *The Gilded Lily* (1935).

During the Depression, popcorn's low price (a bag cost from five to ten cents) made it an even bigger hit and demand for the kernels rose. Between 1934 and 1940, the popcorn harvest jumped from 5 million pounds to 100 million. The reason? People's budgets were tight, so the low price was just right—especially when movie houses were packed with people eager to escape their worries. And the theaters benefited from the popcorn munching as well: high sales of the "audible edibles" helped to keep many of them afloat.

During World War II, sugar was rationed and sent to the troops: candy was scarce, but popcorn was plentiful and cheap, and farmers were annually harvesting about four pounds of corn per American during wartime. As the years passed, having fun at the movies and eating popcorn were forever paired in American hearts and minds. And the pairing has paid off: Today, movie theaters still rely on the power of popcorn to make money. Popcorn sales can make up a significant portion of a movie theater's annual profits.

* * *

POPCORN VARIETY

Minihybrid 250, the first hybrid corn developed especially for popping, was released in 1934. There are now two major popcorn types: Snowflake, invented by Orville Redenbacher, is the large popcorn sold in theaters and at sports events. Mushroom, a smaller, more rounded variety, is used in candies and sweet snacks such as Cracker Jack and popcorn balls.

Stagecoach was the first of nine films that John Ford filmed in Monument Valley, Utah.

THE MAN WHO CAME TO HOLLYWOOD

*He was only 5 feet 2 inches, but Carl Laemmle was a giant
in the movie industry. He's the man who invented movie
stars, publicity stunts, and a lot of other Hollywood
shenanigans we couldn't live without.*

Born in Germany in 1867, Carl Laemmle immigrated to New York to seek his fortune when he was just 17. Ten years later, he was in Chicago, working at a department store and earning $18 a week. Always ambitious, and now with a family to support, Laemmle decided to open his own store. After an extensive search, he found the perfect building. It was long—just right for the long counters needed to hold his dry goods, and perfect for his night job.

After hours, Laemmle hung a large white sheet at one end of his long store and put a projector at the other end. He charged five cents admission and showed the latest "flickers"—what movies were called back then. Before long he was drawing a standing room–only crowd, but they thoughtlessly leaned on his merchandise, which irritated him no end. So Laemmle found another long store, put in some seats and—voilá!—he had a movie theater, or, in the parlance of the day, a "nickelodeon."

THE TRUST
The logical, and more lucrative, next step was to rent movies to other theaters. As the flickers increased in popularity, Laemmle Film Service became the country's largest film distributor. This ticked off the early production companies—including Edison, Vitagraph, and Biograph—known as "The Trust," or the Motion Picture Patents Company. The conglomerate monopolized the early film industry by buying up "film exchanges" (distribution companies that bought short films and rented them to exhibitors at lower rates). Laemmle refused to kowtow to The Trust—he not only held on to his exchange, but he started making his own movies, which ticked The Trust off even more. The big guns took him to court, but ended up losing their case after a three-year feud.

In the Heat of the Night (1967) is set in the Deep South state of Mississippi.

THE LITTLE IMP

By then, Laemmle's first film company, The Independent Moving Pictures Company of America—or, as he affectionately called it, IMP—was firmly entrenched in New York, where he'd moved with his family in 1912. Always the clever businessman, Laemmle listened as his patrons raved over their favorite actors. He realized that a successful movie company needed a "star."

THE FIRST MOVIE STAR

At the time, Biograph Films featured a 20-year-old actress who was dazzling audiences. Fans of the Biograph Girl demanded to know her name, but Biograph, believing unidentified actors meant low-paid actors, refused to tell. Laemmle knew better. He not only hatched a plan to bring young Florence Lawrence (the Biograph Girl) to IMP, he did it with theatrical flair. In one of the world's first publicity stunts, Laemmle leaked a story to the press. A streetcar had killed the Biograph Girl! The shocked public flew into a frenzy, but was relieved when Laemmle announced that it was all a hoax. He swore that jealous competitors made up the whole thing. To prove she had not yet met her maker, Miss Lawrence appeared in St. Louis, Missouri, where Laemmle hired "fans" to mob her and tear off her clothes. Florence Lawrence became a household name. Her movies made big box office. A star was born. That same year, Laemmle also lured future superstar Mary Pickford away from Biograph, advertising his coup as "Little Mary is an IMP now."

THE MASTER OF THE UNIVERSAL

As IMP grew, Laemmle decided it was time for a new corporate name—something big. When he saw a truck with the name "Universal Pipe Fittings," he found what he was looking for. The Independent Moving Pictures Company of America was replaced by the Universal Film Manufacturing Company, the precursor of Universal Pictures. Soon after, Laemmle purchased one of the first film studios in California. A studio was a fine thing, but a city would be even better—a city with one sole purpose: to make movies. So, in 1914, Laemmle paid $165,000 for a 230-acre site in the San Fernando Valley, just 10 miles from Los Angeles. A year later, in front of thousands of movie fans, 48-year-old Laemmle presided over the opening of Universal City.

It was actually filmed mostly in Sparta, Illinois. No scenes were shot in Mississippi.

In addition to its six-mile-long main street, Universal City boasted its own police department, fire brigade, and school. Two restaurants served 1,000 customers daily. Blacksmiths, tailors, and mechanics coexisted with leather shops, mills, and apothecaries. Buildings varied from English colonials to Italian villas, with French provincials and Japanese teahouses in between. Laemmle knew that people were curious about the making of motion pictures, so he opened the gates and charged the curious 25 cents to take a tour. Sometimes a lucky few even got cast as extras!

A REAL HORROR SHOW
Over the next 20 years, Universal built its success on classics like *Phantom of the Opera* (1925), *Dracula* (1931), *Frankenstein* (1931), *The Mummy* (1932), *The Invisible Man* (1933), and *The Bride of Frankenstein* (1935).

BEHIND THE SCENERY
Laemmle was a soft touch. In addition to the 70 relatives he'd given jobs to, Laemmle put his son, Carl Laemmle Jr., in charge of production when he turned 21. The kid wasn't up to it; he was too extravagant during the Depression years, so by March 1935, the studio was in debt and Laemmle was forced to sell his city to a group of financiers for a little more than $5 million. The new owners were in for a surprise. They found two dead men still on the payroll, employees who showed up just to collect paychecks, and others who came to work every day, but had no real jobs. Some of Laemmle's relatives even lived on the lot. They were all evicted. The last to leave were Laemmle's widowed sister-in-law and her daughter; the ladies had been living in one of Universal City's three-bedroom bungalows—their furniture compliments of the prop department.

UNIVERSAL SUCCESS
Carl Laemmle died in 1939, but not before he saw his former company bounce back to financial health thanks to the acquisition in 1936 of singing teenage superstar Deanna Durbin. Today Universal is still one of the most successful studios in Hollywood and has produced two of the highest-grossing movies of all time, *E.T. The Extra-Terrestrial* and *Jurassic Park*.

ODD NAMES, IMPORTANT JOBS

*When you watch a film's closing credits, some of the job
titles—like key grip and best boy—can make you laugh. But
what do the people holding these jobs actually do?*

BEST BOY: This can be the assistant to the head of either a film's
lighting department or rigging department. The position's range of
responsibilities depends upon the size of the crew, but they can
include everything from making sure all lighting or rigging is satis-
factorily placed, to hiring crew and handling negotiations. Best
boys are not always boys (or men), although the position is usually
credited as "Best Boy" regardless of gender.

CLAPPER LOADER: You know that thing they clap together at
the beginning of a scene, with the number and take of the scene
on it? That's a clapper (also known as a slate). The clapper loader
is the person who snaps it together to make the clapping sound. He
or she is also responsible for putting film stock into camera magazines. As digital film cameras become more commonplace, this task
will probably change or be phased out.

DOLLY GRIP: The film camera used in making a movie is usually
stationed on a movable rig called a dolly. The guy who moves the
dolly around (and does the things required to make it move, like
laying down track) is the dolly grip. Pushing a film camera around
on a dolly is more complicated than it sounds, in no small part
because the camera is actually running and filming scenes while
the dolly is being pushed around the set. Before the shoot, the
dolly grip has to confer with the camera crew to coordinate efforts
so everything stays in focus and moves when and where it's supposed to.

FOCUS PULLER: Anyone who's fiddled with a camcorder knows
how hard it is to keep everything in focus. Well, keeping all the
shots clear is the focus puller's job on a film set. When the camera

Answer: Steven Spielberg's Holocaust film, *Schindler's List* (1993).

moves on a set, the focus puller will make tiny adjustments to the camera's focus with a device called a follow focus. The focus puller does this without actually looking through the camera lens (because the cameraperson is doing that). As you might expect, doing this with any measure of competence takes a fair amount of skill (and practice).

FOLEY ARTIST: Most of the common sounds you hear in movies—glass breaking, leaves rustling, and doors opening—are actually added in later by people working in a room filled with special noise makers. These people are the Foley artists (named after Jack Foley, one of the earliest sound effects masters). Their noise-making implements don't often resemble what's supposed to be making noise on-screen: For example, clopping horses hooves are often imitated with coconut shells, which is parodied in the film *Monty Python and the Holy Grail*. In Hitchcock's 1960 film *Psycho*, Janet Leigh's demise was sonically replicated by a Foley artist stabbing a melon. Blaster fire in *Star Wars* (1977) was actually the sound of a hammer striking antenna tower wire.

GAFFER: The gaffer, sometimes credited as the chief lighting technician, is the head of a movie's electrical department, and it's his or her job to make sure all the lights are correctly placed for whatever scene is being shot. The gaffer works with the director of photography and the key grip (see below) to cover the scene and (if it's a big movie) has a staff of electricians to boss around. The name *gaffer* comes from an old English term meaning any man who is in charge of a group of hired hands.

KEY GRIP: In movies, grips are rigging technicians, the people who build the structures upon which lights are hung (but they don't touch the lights themselves—that's someone else's job). They are also the folks responsible for moving major set pieces. The key grip runs the crew of other grips, works with the director of photography, and coordinates with the gaffer to set up the scenes to be shot. A key grip sometimes acts as safety officer on a film set, making sure nothing explodes that's not supposed to, that stunts are safely performed, and that props are in working order.

In short, they're all real jobs—just real jobs with funny names.

Gene Kelly had a 103° fever when he danced to the title song in *Singin' in the Rain.*

MOVIE FIRSTS

Ever wonder what's considered the very first movie?
How about the first movie theater?

FIRST MOTION PICTURE CAMERA—1889
The Kinetograph was commissioned by Thomas Edison and built
by William Kennedy Laurie Dickson.

FIRST MOTION PICTURE STUDIO—1894
Established by the Edison Corporation, in West Orange, New
Jersey. It was nicknamed "The Black Maria," which was a slang
term for a police van, because that's what the building looked like.

FIRST MOVIE—1903
The Great Train Robbery. A 12-minute short, composed of 14 "shots,"
it was also the first Western (but it was shot in New Jersey).

FIRST MOVIE THEATER—1905
The Nickelodeon, located at 441 Smithfield Street in Pittsburgh,
was the first building designed just to show movies. (The first
movie shown was *The Great Train Robbery*.) Three years earlier in
Los Angeles, audiences could catch movies at the Electric, a venue
dedicated only to movies; but the Electric was a tent, so technically it wasn't a theater.

FIRST FEATURE-LENGTH FILM—1911
Two reels of D. W. Griffith's *Enoch Arden* shown together, making
it the first feature-length film. It clocked in at a whopping 20 minutes, almost twice the length of most commercial releases. Studio
heads refused to show two reels for the price of one, so they initially released the film as two separate movies, but audiences figured out that the two parts belonged to the same movie. They
demanded that they be screened as one. Studios complied but
charged twice as much admission anyway.

Burt Reynolds and James Caan both turned down the role of Han Solo in *Star Wars*.

FIRST FANZINE—1912

Photoplay, the first magazine for movie fans, debuted. The magazine's popularity soared (and spawned a lot of competitors) as it fed audiences the inside scoop on their favorite stars.

FIRST MILLION-DOLLAR CONTRACT—1921

Comedian Roscoe "Fatty" Arbuckle was the first movie star to sign a million-dollar contract. Paramount Studios paid him $1 million a year for three years. His three-day celebration over Labor Day weekend would lead to the scandalous death of starlet Virginia Rappe and a murder accusation levied at Arbuckle.

FIRST IN-FLIGHT MOVIE—1925

The Lost World was shown on a 1925 British Imperial Airways flight. Movies didn't become a regular attraction on planes until 1961, when TWA featured movies as a part of scheduled commercial flights. The first one shown was *By Love Possessed,* starring Lana Turner and Efrem Zimbalist Jr.

FIRST MOVIE HOUSE WITH AIR CONDITIONING—1925

The Rivoli in New York City was the first theater to use air conditioning to cool off its customers. Its marquee boasted, "Cooled By Refrigeration: Always 69 Degrees."

FIRST "TALKIE"—1927

The Jazz Singer had the first spoken dialogue. Its star, Al Jolson, ad-libbed, "Wait a minute! Wait a minute! You ain't heard nothin' yet."

FIRST BEST PICTURE AT THE FIRST ACADEMY AWARDS—1928

Wings—the first (and only) silent movie ever to win best picture.

FIRST FILM IN TECHNICOLOR—1935

Becky Sharp was the first movie to use the three-color process, and Hollywood was thrilled with the results. Director Rouben Mamoulian described the improvement: "Up to now, the moving picture industry has been like an artist allowed to use only pencil. Technicolor has given us paints."

"Father, you're living in the past. This is the 14th century."

FIRST 3-D MOVIE—1952

Although *House of Wax* (1953) is the first 3-D movie from a major studio, *Bwana Devil* (1952) was the very first movie to use the in-your-face effect. (An interesting side note: *House of Wax* director Andre De Toth had only one eye, so he couldn't experience the 3-D effects.)

FIRST FEATURE-LENGTH MOVIE SHOWN ON TELEVISION—1956

RKO Studios opened up its film vaults to television, and *King Kong* (1933) was the first movie shown on TV in the United States. The broadcast was such a success that other horror movies from the 1930s quickly found their way onto the small screen.

FIRST USE OF LETTER RATINGS FOR MOVIES—1968

Rating system, using G, GP (later changed to PG), R, and X to indicate the suitability of movies for different audiences.

FIRST X-RATED MOVIE—1968

Directed by Brian DePalma, *Greetings*, an antiwar comedy about draft dodging, was the first to be rated X. (It was also Robert De Niro's first movie.)

FIRST (AND ONLY) X-RATED MOVIE TO WIN AN OSCAR—1969

Midnight Cowboy, directed by John Schlesinger. (It has since been downgraded to R.)

DEBUT OF HOME BOX OFFICE (HBO) ON CABLE TV—1972

First movie shown? *Sometimes a Great Notion* (1971) starring Paul Newman, Henry Fonda, and Lee Remick. It told the story about logging in a small Oregon town.

FIRST USE OF THX SOUND SYSTEM IN THEATERS—1983

George Lucas debuted his theater sound system (named after his first film *THX 1138*) in two theaters showing *Return of the Jedi*. THX was the first system designed to reproduce exactly what the

—Prince Philip (Bill Shirley), *Sleeping Beauty* (1959)

filmmaker recorded, so audiences had a full sound experience. It would become the industry standard in theaters and today is even used in home and car stereos.

FIRST COMPUTER-ANIMATED FEATURE FILM—1995
Toy Story was the first cartoon to be drawn entirely by computer.

FIRST FILM SHOT ENTIRELY WITH DIGITAL TECHNOLOGY—2002
For *Star Wars Episode II: Attack of the Clones*, George Lucas worked with Sony for six years to design the perfect cameras to shoot this movie. The entire project was shot, processed, edited, distributed (by satellite download), and projected digitally.

* * *

LOST LETTERS

When the Hollywood sign was refurbished in the late 1970s, the original letters were torn down and thrown away. Or so everybody thought. Hank Berger, a 28-year-old nightclub promoter decided that he wanted the old sign. "The hell with the new one—the old one's the real one." After buying the original tin letters from the Hollywood Chamber of Commerce and paying $10,000 for licensing fees, he hauled off the old sign. In 1980 Berger started selling souvenir plaques with pieces of the original sign glued to them for $29.95. His company sold about 14,000 of them before business started to flag. So he moved east and left the letters with a friend of his business partner. They sat in the corner of a tool-and-die company for 22 years.

Then in 2005, Cleveland native Dan Bliss ran into Berger and learned about the tin letters from the old sign. Bliss was fascinated and bought the sign from Berger. He moved out to L.A. and picked up the sign. Now he too is selling pieces of the sign embedded in limited-edition necklaces. (Available on his Web site, the Hollywood sign jewelry costs just $43.99 plus shipping.)

NOTHING NEW UNDER THE SUN, PART 1

It seems that someone in Hollywood was listening when they were told, "If at first you don't succeed, try, try again." It's a good thing they did, too, or else we wouldn't have these excellent remakes to enjoy.

THE MALTESE FALCON (1941)
Remake of: *The Maltese Falcon* (1931)
Many people don't realize that the most famous version of this film, starring Humphrey Bogart, was a remake. And it was the third time that Dashiell Hammett's novel had been filmed. The second version, *Satan Met a Lady* (1936), is more comedic and stars Bette Davis. The first version of the *Falcon*—renamed *Dangerous Female* when shown on TV, so as to avoid confusion with the Bogie pic—was racier than the remake (Spade is more of a ladies' man in this version). But that didn't save *Dangerous Female* from the loud, over-dramatic performances that limited its appeal.

John Huston's remake became the definitive version because of its cast and the exceptional way they played off one another. Bogart, Sydney Greenstreet, Peter Lorre, and Mary Astor are perfectly cast as adversaries in the race to find the valuable jeweled bird. Huston also punched up the dialogue—adapting much of it directly from Hammett's book. Leonard Maltin calls it an "outstanding detective drama that improves with each viewing."

OCEAN'S ELEVEN (2001)
Remake of: *Ocean's Eleven* (1960)
According to movie critic James Berardinelli, "The 2001 version of *Ocean's Eleven* represents one of the rarest of Hollywood rarities: a remake that is actually better than the original."

The original 1960 caper movie starred members of the Rat Pack: Frank Sinatra, Dean Martin, Peter Lawford, Sammy Davis Jr., and Joey Bishop. These real-life friends had a palpable chemistry on-screen. The plot of the original *Ocean's Eleven*—11 friends from

World War II work together to rob five Las Vegas casinos simultaneously—is largely unimportant. It is primarily a chance to get the Rat Pack on film together—a formula that made the movie a success.

The new version has George Clooney as Danny Ocean, who, on the very day he is released from prison, plans a major heist against three Las Vegas casinos. He enlists 10 master criminals—characters played by Brad Pitt, Don Cheadle, and Matt Damon, among others—to help him pull off his plan. The movie is shot beautifully—Las Vegas has never looked better, especially the lovely dancing fountains of the Bellagio. The screenplay, written by David Mamet, is brisk and clever, with all the plot twists and turns expected in films of this type. Movie critic Philip Wuntch wrote, "Maybe the secret is to remake a bad movie. The new *Ocean's Eleven* improves on all aspects of the original . . . it's better written, better paced, and infinitely better directed."

YOU'VE GOT MAIL (1998)
Remake of: *The Shop Around the Corner* (1940)
In the older film, Margaret Sullivan and Jimmy Stewart play coworkers in a small gift shop, who despise each other. In their spare time, however, they are anonymous pen pals falling in love with one another.

The remake brings this concept into the computer age. Tom Hanks plays the millionaire owner of a megabookstore who, by opening a branch nearby, is threatening to obliterate Meg Ryan's mom-and-pop neighborhood bookstore called The Shop Around the Corner. Unbeknownst to both, they are also e-mail correspondents who are falling in love with one another. The contrast between their stormy in-person relationship and their warmly supportive Internet dialogue provides the film's dramatic tension. With Nora Ephron's snappy dialogue (she directed and cowrote the screenplay), and the stars' extreme likability, this romantic comedy is a treat.

HIS GIRL FRIDAY (1940)
Remake of: *The Front Page* (1931)
This remake of 1931's *The Front Page* stars Cary Grant and Rosalind Russell. She is Hildy Johnson, an ace newspaper reporter who is about to abandon her career to marry a dull-as-dishwater insurance agent. Grant is her boss as well as her ex-husband, determined to foil her plan and keep her working (and win her back). Their sassy repartee and the comedy's brisk pacing, as well as the

---

An actual barn was built for the barn-raising scene in *Witness* (1985) . . .

leads' on-screen chemistry, keep the film sparkling. It's true what they say: they just don't make movies like this anymore.

In *The Front Page*, the protagonists are both male, which seems dull when compared to the fireworks between Grant and Russell. The male Hildy Johnson wants to leave his newspaper job, and to move away and marry the woman he loves, but his boss is determined to keep him at work. Though many of the plot elements are the same in both films, having the lead characters of different sexes in the remake—and ex-spouses at that—was a stroke of genius. It lends texture and intriguing possibilities to the story, which are absent in the earlier film.

THE MAGNIFICENT SEVEN (1960)
Remake of: *Seven Samurai (Shichinin No Samurai)* (1954)
Some critics have called this remake the first of the vigilante movies, wherein civilians take matters into their own hands when the law lets them down. The plot revolves around a charismatic leader (Yul Brynner) who gathers together seven misfits. He whips them into shape to rescue an isolated Mexican village from a bunch of bad guys who terrorize the inhabitants and steal their livelihoods. These "good guys" are not your average white-hatted, upstanding citizens to the rescue; they are men with somewhat shady pasts. Though their cause is just, their means are unorthodox.

As prototypically American as this movie is—in spirit as well as in subject—it was based on a film about feudal Japan. Directed by Akira Kurosawa, 1954's *Seven Samurai* tells the tale of a group of unemployed samurai warriors who defend a small farming village against bandits in the 1600s. In the Japanese film, dramatic tension arises not only as a result of the battles, but also because the samurai, the villagers, and the bandits all belong to differing social castes and have difficulty interacting with each other.

The Magnificent Seven launched the careers of a couple of iconic tough guys: James Coburn and Steve McQueen. But the movie succeeds not only because it's tough, but also because it's an in-depth character study that works on many levels—much more than your average shoot-'em-up. When Kurosawa saw *The Magnificent Seven*, he was so pleased that he sent its director, John Sturges, a gift of a katana sword.

But not all remakes are classics to enjoy. Turn to page 230 for some flicks that don't live up to the originals.

... but it was torn down shortly afterward.

WRETCHED REVIEWS

Doesn't it bother you when a movie you love gets a
thumbs-down from those two bozos on TV? Us, too. The
Critics Were Wrong, by Ardis Sillick and Michael McCormick,
compiles hundreds of misguided movie reviews like these.

FRANKENSTEIN (1931)
"I regret to report that it is just another movie, so thoroughly
mixed with water as to have a horror content of about .0001 percent. . . . The film . . . soon turns into sort of comic opera with a
range of cardboard mountains over which extras in French
Revolution costumes dash about with flaming torches."
—*Outlook & Independent*

THE GRADUATE (1967) *Nomination for best actor*
"*The Graduate* is a genuinely funny comedy which succeeds despite
an uninteresting and untalented actor (Dustin Hoffman) in the
title role."
—*Films in Review*

LETHAL WEAPON (1987)
"As a thriller, it lacks logic. As a cop film, it throws standard police
procedures, and with them any hope of authenticity, to the wind.
As a showcase for the martial arts, it's a disappointment. . . . And
as action-adventure, it's pointlessly puerile."
—Johanna Steinmetz, *Chicago Tribune*

M*A*S*H (1970)
"At the end, the film simply runs out of steam, says goodbye to its
major characters, and calls final attention to itself as a movie—
surely the saddest and most overworked of cop-out devices in the
comic film repertory."
—Roger Greenspun, *New York Times*

ROCKY (1976) *Top box-office hit / Oscar winner for best picture and*
director / Nomination for best actor and screenplay
"An overly grandiose script, performed with relentless

grandiloquence . . . Up to a point I'm willing to overlook the egg on a guy's face, but, really, there's such a thing as too much—especially when they're promoting this bloated, pseudo-epic as a low-budget Oscar-bound winner.

—*Washington Star*

2001: A SPACE ODYSSEY (1968)
"Not a cinematic landmark. It compares with, but does not best, previous efforts at filmed science-fiction. . . . It actually belongs to the technically slick group previously dominated by . . . the Japanese."

—*Variety*

ANNIE HALL (1977) *Oscar winner for best picture and director*
"Woody Allen has truly underreached himself. . . . His new film is painful in three separate ways: an unfunny comedy, poor moviemaking and embarrassing self-revelation . . . It is a film so shapeless, sprawling, repetitive and aimless as to seem to beg for oblivion."

—John Simon, *New York*

PSYCHO (1960) *Oscar nomination for best director*
"Hitchcock seems to have been more interested in shocking his audience with the bloodiest bathtub murder in screen history, and in photographing Janet Leigh in various stages of undress, than in observing the ordinary rules for good film construction. This is a dangerous corner for a gifted moviemaker to place himself in."

—Moira Walsh, *America*

SATURDAY NIGHT FEVER (1977)
"Nothing more than an updated '70s version of the . . . rock music cheapies of the '50s. That is to say . . . more shrill, more vulgar, more trifling, more superficial and more pretentious than an exploitation film . . . A major disappointment."

—*Variety*

. . . but the Coen brothers, the film's creators, admitted later that it wasn't.

FATAL FALLOUT

It was a sad day when Hollywood lost John "the Duke"
Wayne. He passed away on June 11, 1979, after battling
cancer for 15 years. Most blamed smoking for his sickness,
but others say that Wayne's ailments came from something else—
radiation exposure on the set of the 1956 movie The Conqueror.

T*he Conqueror* was a flop of a movie, coproduced by Howard
Hughes.It starred John Wayne as a young Genghis Khan,
who lusted for an empire and the beautiful Tartar princess
Bortai (Susan Hayward). From the very beginning the production
was troubled. Wayne wasn't the director's first choice for Khan:
director-coproducer Dick Powell wanted Marlon Brando. But
Wayne read the script first and told financier Hughes that he
wanted the part. Over Powell's objections, Hughes made sure that
Wayne would play the Mongolian.

It was a legendary casting mistake. Sizing up the role, the Duke
said, "The way the screenplay reads, it is a cowboy picture, and
that is how I am going to portray Genghis Khan. I see him as a
gunfighter." He turned Khan into a cowboy, and the critics hated
it. One called it the "most improbable piece of casting unless
Mickey Rooney were to play Jesus in *The King of Kings*." Wayne
himself later regretted taking the part; he once said that the moral
of *The Conqueror* was "not to make an ass of yourself trying to play
parts you're not suited for."

EXPOSURE

But *The Conqueror*'s miscasting didn't make it notorious. It
became infamous for the high mortality rate of those who worked
on the set. The movie was shot near St. George, Utah, a perfect
visual stand-in for the Gobi desert. But St. George was also
downwind from an atomic weapons testing site. In 1953 the U.S.
government detonated 11 atomic bombs at Yucca Flat, Nevada,
about 150 miles away; winds carried pink radioactive clouds and
dust over Utah, much of it settling on St. George and other
downwind communities. Today experts estimate that in Utah
alone, 40,000 citizens were exposed to high dosages of radiation
from the toxic fallout.

Bill Murray was considered for the role of Forrest Gump.

Just two years after the testing, *The Conqueror* cast and crew showed up to shoot the film just outside St. George. On-site filming lasted for 13 weeks, exposing everyone to a great deal of contaminated soil and dust. Although the harmful effects of radiation exposure were not as well documented back then, the cast and crew were aware of the presence of nuclear radiation. But no one seemed to view the contamination as a deadly threat. Publicity pictures even showed John Wayne holding a Geiger counter.

To make matters worse, when production returned to Hollywood, Hughes shipped 60 tons of the Utah soil back to the studios; he wanted to use it in interior shots and retakes so the dirt would match the location shots. So the stars continued to work with the radioactive soil after they returned to California.

THE NUMBERS

Four years after filming wrapped, director Dick Powell, admittedly a heavy smoker, died in 1963 of lymphatic cancer. That same year, actor Pedro Armendáriz developed kidney cancer; he shot himself when he learned his condition was terminal. Before fellow cast member Agnes Moorehead died in 1974 from uterine cancer, she loudly and publicly claimed that the radiation exposure on the set of *The Conqueror* had caused her illness. Susan Hayward succumbed in 1975 to brain and skin cancer. In 1964 Wayne was diagnosed with lung cancer (at the time, most blamed his three-pack-a-day cigarette habit). He had his left lung removed and proclaimed that he had beaten the Big C. But Wayne continued to struggle with cancer for 15 more years. Finally, in January 1979, doctors diagnosed him with stomach and lymphatic cancer. The Duke died six months later.

By 1980 of the 220 people who worked on the movie, 91 were diagnosed with cancer and 46 had died from it. Statistically, only about 13 percent of a group that size would have cancer under ordinary circumstances; but 41 percent of *The Conqueror* cast and crew were stricken. One expert's take on the number of cancer diagnoses was that "radiation contributes to the risk of cancer. With these numbers, it is highly probable that *The Conqueror* group was affected by that additive effect."

But for years, the studios and U.S. government denied the connection between the nuclear testing and *The Conqueror* cast's cancer; heavy smoking was blamed for the illnesses. That explanation,

---

Over 40 horses are featured in *Seabiscuit* (2003), with 10 sharing the title role.

however, didn't account for high incidences of cancer in St. George: over half of its 5,000 citizens fell ill. St. George residents and other "downwinders" from other Southwest communities fought for almost 40 years to make the U.S. government formally recognize the harm it had done. In 1990 the Radiation Exposure Compensation Act was passed; downwinders and others exposed to the radioactive dust in the 1950s were awarded $50,000 each.

* * *

LOONEY TUNE DEBUTS

Porky Pig
First Appeared in: *I Haven't Got a Hat*
Debuted on: March 2, 1935
Fact: Joe Dougherty, a stutterer in real life, first provided Porky's pipes. In 1937 Mel Blanc started voicing the pig—in *Picador Porky*—after he joined Warner Bros.

Daffy Duck
First Appeared in: *Porky's Duck Hunt*
Debuted on: April 17, 1937
Fact: Mel Blanc patterned Daffy's voice after Warner Bros. producer Leon Schlesinger.

Elmer Fudd
First Appeared in: *Elmer's Candid Camera*
Debuted on: March 2, 1940
Fact: An earlier Warner Bros. character, Egghead identified himself as Elmer Fudd in *A Feud There Was* (1938), but *Elmer's Candid Camera* is the first official Fudd appearance.

* * *

AMAZING ANIMATION

It took four months to synchronize the three-minute scene between live actors and animated skeletons in *Jason and the Argonauts*.

HOLLYWOOD SCANDAL: 1921, PART 2

A woman is found dead . . . a well-known celebrity is charged with murder . . . the whole world follows the trial. O. J. Simpson? Nope—Fatty Arbuckle. In its day, the Arbuckle trial was as big as the Simpson trial. Here's the rest of the story (continued from page 40).

GOING TO COURT

As Brady prepared his case, one of the first things he did was see to it that Maude Delmont would not be able to testify. He knew that the other witnesses would prove she had lied in her police statement. Furthermore, Delmont had changed her story so many times that Brady knew she would be caught in her own lies during cross-examination. Rather than let that happen, Brady had her arrested on an outstanding charge of bigamy. Delmont—the only person who claimed that Arbuckle had committed a crime—spent the next several months in jail, where Arbuckle's attorneys could not get at her.

THE TRIAL

The People v. Arbuckle lasted from November 14 to December 4, 1921. More than 60 witnesses were called to the stand, including 18 doctors. According to Bernard Ryan in Great American Trials: Through defense witnesses, lawyer Gavin McNab revealed Virginia Rappè's moral as well as medical history: As a young teenager, she had had five abortions in three years, at 16, she had borne an illegitimate child; since 1907, she had had a series of bladder inflammations and chronic cystitis; she liked to strip naked when she drank; the doctor who attended her in the several days before she died concluded that she had gonorrhea; when she met Arbuckle for the first time on Monday, she was pregnant and that afternoon had asked him to pay for an abortion; on Wednesday, she had asked her nurse to find an abortionist. . . . Medical testimony proved that Virginia Rappè's bladder was cystic—one of the causes of rupture of the bladder.

Harrison Ford turned down the male lead in *Jurassic Park* (1993).

Arbuckle Takes the Stand. The climax of the trial came on Monday, November 28, when Arbuckle testified in his own defense. He recounted how he had found Rappè in his bathroom vomiting into the toilet, and how he had helped her into the next room when she asked to lie down. Arbuckle testified that he spent less than 10 minutes alone with Rappè before summoning Maude Delmont, who took over and asked him to leave the room. He stood up well under cross-examination; and the final testimony, in which expert witnesses testified that the rupture of Ms. Rappè's bladder was not caused by external force, seemed to cinch the case for Arbuckle.

THE VERDICT

As the case went to the jury, both sides appeared confident of victory. But on December 4th, after 44 hours of deliberation, the jury announced that it was hopelessly deadlocked, and the judge declared a mistrial.

One juror, a woman named Helen Hubbard—whose husband was a lawyer who did business with the D.A.'s office—held out for a conviction throughout the entire deliberations.

The Second Trial. The case went to trial a second time, beginning on January 11 and lasting until February 3. The second trial was much like the first, only this time the defense introduced even more evidence concerning Ms. Rappè's shady past. But Arbuckle's lawyers, confident they would win handily, did not have Arbuckle take the stand in his defense. That was a huge mistake—this time the jury deadlocked 9-3 in favor of conviction.

The Third Trial. The case went to trial a third time on March 13. This time, Arbuckle's defense left nothing to chance: it provided still more evidence questioning both Rappè's physical health and her moral character, and it brought Arbuckle back to the stand to testify on his own behalf.

FINAL VERDICT

The case went to the jury on April 12, 1922. They deliberated for less than 5 minutes, then returned to court and read the following statement:

We the jury find Roscoe Arbuckle not guilty of manslaughter.

Acquittal is not enough for Roscoe Arbuckle. We feel that a great injustice has been done him. We feel also that it was only our plain duty to give him this exoneration, under the evidence, for there was not the slightest proof adduced to connect him in any way with the commission of a crime.

He was manly throughout the case, and told a straightforward story on the witness stand, which we all believed.

The happening at the hotel was an unfortunate affair for which Arbuckle, so the evidence shows, was in no way responsible.

We wish him success. . . . Roscoe Arbuckle is entirely innocent and free from all blame.

THE AFTERMATH

Roscoe Arbuckle was a free man, but his life was in tatters. The trials had cost him more than $750,000, wiping out nearly his entire life savings (the $3 million Paramount contract had fallen through when the scandal broke). As if that wasn't bad enough, the IRS went after him a few months later, when it seized the remainder of his estate to collect more than $100,000 in back taxes. It also obtained a court order to attach whatever wages he earned in the future until the entire tax debt was paid back.

THE HAYS OFFICE

Things got even worse for Arbuckle. Largely because of the scandal, 12 of Hollywood's top studio moguls hired William Hays, chairman of the Republican National Committee and a former postmaster general, to become America's "movie czar." His job: keep Hollywood's image clean. His first task: deal with Arbuckle.

Hatchet Job. Six days after Arbuckle was acquitted, the "Hays Office" (as it came to be known) banned him from the screen. The public was led to believe it was a moral issue. Actually, Hays was doing the bidding of Paramount heads Adolph Zukor and Jesse Lasky, who no longer wanted to work with Arbuckle, out of fear that he was box office poison. But they didn't take any chances; rather than risk losing Arbuckle to a competing studio, they lobbied the Hays Office to ban him from the film industry entirely.

—Princess Leia (Carrie Fisher), *Star Wars* (1977)

COMEBACK

The ban was lifted eight months later, but the taint remained and Arbuckle had trouble finding work. He began work on a short subject film called Handy Andy, but was so hounded by reporters that he gave up on the project.

Over the next decade he appeared in stage shows, ran a Hollywood nightclub, and directed a number of films under the pseudonym William B. Goodrich (Will B. Good). But it wasn't until 1932—more than 10 years after the trials—that he had a chance to return to the screen. Studio head Jack Warner hired him to act in a film called *Hey, Pop!* It was a box office success, and Arbuckle was signed for six more films. He only completed three—*Buzzin' Around, Tamalio,* and *In the Dough.* The evening *In the Dough* finished shooting, Arbuckle celebrated at dinner with his wife and went home to bed. He died in his sleep at about 2:30 a.m., leaving an estate valued at less than $2,000.

* * *

BELLY UP TO THE BAR

GARBO DRINKS
The Order: "Give me a visky, ginger ale on the side, and don't be stingy, baby."
The Drink: Whiskey Mac—whiskey with ginger ale.
The Customer: Anna (Greta Garbo), *Anna Christie* (1930)

BOTTOM'S UP, BLUE EYES
The Order: "Preacher! Go on down and get me some bourbon. J. T. S. Brown. No ice, no glass."
The Drink: Bourbon, in the bottle
The Customer: Fast Eddie Felsen (Paul Newman), *The Hustler* (1961)

FROM YOUR BARTENDER, WITH LOVE
The Order: "One medium dry vodka martini, mixed like you said, sir, and not stirred."
The Drink: Vodka martini—vodka, vermouth, and an olive
The Customer: James Bond (Sean Connery), *Dr. No* (1962)

THE MONSTER LIVES!

*When Universal Pictures coined the term "horror movie" in
1931, it was because of this film . . . and Boris Karloff, the actor
who brought the monster to life. As one critic puts it: "Just as the
monster of the story was stitched together from pieces of the dead,
Universal's cinematic Monster was stitched together from the
genius of Jack Pierce's makeup, James Whale's direction, and
Boris Karloff's performance. The results were so perfect that
the image of the Frankenstein monster, as seen in this classic
film, has become ingrained into the fabric of our culture."*

LUCKY BREAK

L Have you ever heard of William Henry Pratt? Most people
haven't. In the late 1920s he was an unemployed actor, making ends meet by driving a truck for a lumber yard. In 1931 he
landed a small part playing a gangster in a movie called *The
Criminal Code*. It happened to premiere just as director James
Whale began his search for someone to play the monster in
Frankenstein.

A friend of Whale's saw the film, noticed Pratt, and suggested
that the director take a look at him. So Whale went to see *The
Criminal Code*. He was impressed with Pratt's work . . . but more
important, he recognized that Pratt's gaunt features, exaggerated
with lots of makeup, would make an excellent monster-face.

Whale drew some preliminary sketches of Pratt as the monster
and showed them to Jack Pierce, head of Universal's makeup
department. Then he approached Pratt about playing the part.
Years later, Pratt recalled how he learned about the role:

I'd spent 10 years in Hollywood without causing the slightest
stir. Then one day I was sitting in the commissary at
Universal, having lunch, and looking rather well turned out, I
thought, when a man sent a note over to my table, asking if
I'd like to audition for the part of a monster.

THE NAME GAME

Pratt took a screen test and got the job on the spot. But he didn't
get public acknowledgment for the role until much later. He wasn't

. . . an unlimited supply of hand-rolled Monte Cristo cigars.

considered an important member of the cast, so the studio didn't even bother to list his name in the credits. Only a question mark appears next to the words "The Monster."

Within a year, however, Pratt's name would become a household word. . . . Or at least his stage name would: Universal Pictures thought that "William Henry Pratt" sounded too ordinary for such an exotic monster and asked him to change it to something a little more unusual. Pratt picked a name that would be synonymous with horror for over 35 years—Boris Karloff.

MAKEUP
Universal put Jack Pierce, head of the studio's makeup department, in charge of creating Karloff's makeup. He prepared for the job by studying anatomy, surgery, electrodynamics, and criminology. It was this research that led to the monster's unusual flat-topped skull, as Pierce later related to *The New York Times*:

> My anatomical studies taught me that there are six ways a surgeon can cut the skull in order to take out or put in a brain. I figured that Frankenstein, who was a scientist but no practicing surgeon, would take the simplest surgical way. He would cut the top of the skull off straight across like a pot-lid, hinge it, pop the brain in, and then clamp it on tight. That is the reason I decided to make the Monster's head square and flat like a shoe box and dig that big scar across his forehead with the metal clamps holding it together.

Pierce also added a caveman-like protruding brow to suggest de-evolution, and Karoly Grosz, a Universal poster illustrator, came up with the idea of putting steel bolts in the monster's neck.

FACE FACTS
Karloff had several false teeth on the right side of his mouth; these were removed to give his already gaunt face an even more hollow appearance. This look was further accentuated when Karloff himself suggested to Pierce that his eyelids be heavily puttied with embalmers' wax, which gave the monster a sense of pathos.
The rest of the facial makeup was applied to accent rather than cover up Karloff's natural features, so that his face would retain its expressiveness. "We were all fascinated by the development of Karloff's face and head," Mae Clarke, who played Elizabeth, Dr. Frankenstein's fiancée in the film, later recalled. "White putty on the face was toned

down to a corpse-like gray. Then there was a sudden inspiration to give the face a green tint. It awed us and gave Boris and the rest of us a different feeling about the whole concept." The movie was filmed entirely in black and white (that's all there was back then), but in some prints of the film, Universal had Karloff's face tinted green by hand before they were distributed to theaters.

BODY LANGUAGE

"Karloff's face fascinated me," James Whale would recall years later. "His physique was weaker than I could wish, but that queer, penetrating personality of his, I felt, was more important than his shape, which could be easily altered." And alter it they did:

- Karloff's frame was stiffened by a five-pound spinal brace that ran up his back and steel struts in his legs.

- He also wore platform asphalt spreader's boots, which weighed twelve and a half pounds apiece.

- On top of the braces, Karloff wore padding and on top of that a thick, double-quilted suit that added tremendous bulk to his frame; its sleeves were cut short to make his arms appear longer than they really were. All in all, the braces, struts, boots, and costume weighed more than forty-eight pounds.

TEST RUN

Even after Karloff was fully made up, he wasn't sure whether the makeup was truly scary or not—would it frighten people, or just make them laugh? As he recounted years later,

I was thinking this while practicing my walk, as I rounded a bend in the corridor and came face-to-face with this prop man. He was the first man to see the monster—I watched to study his reaction. It was quick to come. He turned white— gurgled and lunged out of sight down the corridor. Never saw him again. Poor chap, I would have liked to thank him—he was the audience that first made me feel like the monster.

IN THE THEATER

When Universal previewed *Frankenstein* before test audiences in Santa Monica, they noticed two important things:

1. It was Karloff's monster, not the other characters, who made the film work. This was real horror for panicked Universal execs.

He was 37 before he learned the truth about his illegitimate birth.

They'd considered Karloff unimportant and neglected to put him under contract. They quickly called his agent and signed him up. Karloff's response: "After more than 20 years of acting, for once I'll know where my next breakfast is coming from."

2. The film made people fidgety and squeamish. Rather than downplay the response, the studio decided to publicize it. They added a prologue, warning filmgoers what they were in for. Edward Van Sloan, who played Dr. Frankenstein's mentor, Dr. Waldman, told audiences:

> Mr. Carl Laemmle [head of Universal] feels it would be a little unkind to present this picture without a word of friendly warning. . . . [Frankenstein] is one of the strangest stories ever told. . . . It will thrill you . . . It may shock you. It might even—horrify you! So, then, if you feel that you do not care to subject your nerves to such a strain, now is your chance to—well, we've warned you!

Theaters around the country added to the hype by posting nurses in the lobby, making free "nerve tonic" available to those who needed it, and other gimmicks. One movie house in Texas even hired a woman to sit in the empty theater and watch the film alone. But the publicity wasn't necessary—*Frankenstein* was one of the biggest hits of 1931 and went on to become one of the all-time classic Hollywood films. To this day, Boris Karloff's sensitive portrayal of the monster is the performance by which all other monster movies are measured.

GONE TO PIECES
By the late 1930s it seemed like Frankenstein might finally be dying. Boris Karloff, who'd played the monster in *Frankenstein* (1931), *Bride of Frankenstein* (1935), and *Son of Frankenstein* (1939), hammered the first nail in the creature's coffin when he announced that he'd grown weary of the role. As David Skal writes in *The Monster Show*, Karloff "suspected that the monster would be increasingly relegated to the role of prop or buffoon" and didn't want to be part of it. It didn't take long for Karloff's prediction to come true. With each new film Universal released—*Frankenstein Meets the Wolf Man* (1943), *The House of Frankenstein* (1944), and *The House of Dracula* (1945), the monster became less frightening. The studio finished the job in 1948, when it ended its Frankenstein series with *Abbott and Costello Meet Frankenstein*.

Actor George Sanders's last words: "Dear World, I am leaving you because . . .

Karloff agreed to help promote that film . . . as long as he didn't have to watch it.

KID STUFF
But even as familiarity worked against Frankenstein films, demographics were working in their favor. Thanks to the post–World War II baby boom, younger viewers were making up an increasingly large share of the movie audience. By 1958 72 percent of all moviegoers were between the ages of 12 and 25.

Hollywood started making movies especially for teenagers—and they quickly found out that teenagers loved horror films. Sticking a monster, vampire, or werewolf into a film became an easy way to increase ticket sales.

Low-budget studios like American International Pictures (*I Was a Teenage Werewolf*) couldn't use Karloff's familiar monster because Universal Studios owned a copyright on that Frankenstein "look." But they could use the name Frankenstein because it was in the public domain (which means no one owns it).

And they did use it—hundreds of times. "Frankenstein" became a generic term for any manmade monster. He showed up in theaters as an alien, a sex fiend, a "demon of the atomic age," a resurrected teenage auto wreck victim, and so on; 65 years later the Frankenstein movies keep on coming. As *The Videohound's Complete Guide to Trash Pics and Cult Flicks* says:

> Frankenstein lives in the movies better than anywhere else. With dozens of films based directly on characters from the novel, not to mention the hundreds with at least a tenuous connection to it, it may be the single most adapted work in all of cinema. No other name draws audiences so well.

Boris Karloff, the man who made Frankenstein—and horror films—a part of our culture, died in 1969. But he's been granted a weird kind of immortality. Every time a mad scientist builds a monster onscreen, it's an homage to Karloff's genius.

* * *

ROAR!
The MGM mascot, Leo the Lion, made his first audible roar on screen in 1928 for the debut of the otherwise silent movie *White Shadows in the South Seas*.

SILVER SCREEN CEO QUIZ

Harvard MBA? Dale Carnegie books? Hah!
Who needs 'em? Everything you need to know about big
business is right there on the big screen. Try matching the
pro-business proverbs on the following page with
the people who said them, listed below.

1. Charles Foster Kane (Orson Welles), *Citizen Kane*
2. Willy Wonka (Gene Wilder), *Willy Wonka & the Chocolate Factory*
3. Auric Goldfinger (Gert Fröbe), *Goldfinger*
4. Joel Goodsen (Tom Cruise), *Risky Business*
5. Cruella De Vil (Glenn Close), *101 Dalmations*
6. Blake (Alec Baldwin), *Glengarry Glen Ross*
7. Lawrence Garfield (Danny DeVito), *Other People's Money*
8. Jim Young (Ben Affleck), *Boiler Room*
9. Gordon Gekko (Michael Douglas), *Wall Street*
10. Joan Crawford (Faye Dunaway), *Mommie Dearest*

* * *

BIG-BIZ MOVIE TRIVIA

- Writer and director Ben Younger got the idea for *Boiler Room* when he went on a job interview at a trading firm much like the one depicted in the film.

- *Wall Street* director Oliver Stone's father was a stock broker, inspiring Stone's work on this film. His father died a year before the movie was released, and one of the characters in the film, an avuncular old-timer named Lou, is named for him.

- When Orson Welles was shooting *Citizen Kane*, he had to get up six hours before shooting began at 9 a.m. to have his "Kane as an old man" makeup applied.

At 46, in *Live and Let Die*, Roger Moore became the oldest actor to play James Bond.

A. "The point is, ladies and gentlemen, that greed, for lack of a better word, is good. Greed is right. Greed works."
B. "A-B-C. A—Always, B—Be, C—Closing. Always be closing."
C. "A sale is made on every call you make. Either you sell the client some stock, or he sells you a reason he can't. Either way a sale is made, the only question is who is gonna close?"
D. "Once is happenstance. Twice is coincidence. Three times is enemy action."
E. "Invention, my dear friends, is 93 percent perspiration, 6 percent electricity, 4 percent evaporation, and 2 percent butterscotch ripple."
F. "I did lose a million dollars last year. I expect to lose a million dollars this year. I expect to lose a million dollars next year. You know, Mr. Thatcher, at the rate of a million dollars a year, I'll have to close this place in 60 years."
G. "Don't worry—I've got a perfectly good idiot to take the fall for it."
H. "Porsche. There is no substitute."
I. "Don't f*** with me fellas. This ain't my first time at the rodeo."
J. "Make as much as you can for as long as you can. Whoever has the most when he dies is the winner."

Turn to page 485 for the answers.

* * *

MORE BIG-BIZ MOVIE TRIVIA

- To make Tom Cruise look more like a teenager when *Risky Business* was filmed, he was told to lose lots of weight by working out and then gorge on junk food to get that baby-faced look. He was 22 during his role as Joel, the teenage entrepreneur.
- In 1959 Joan Crawford joined the ranks of the business world when she was elected to the board of directors at PepsiCo.

The mansion in *Hannibal* (2001) is the Biltmore estate in Asheville, North Carolina.

LONG LASTING

"Why fool around with hamburger when you have steak at home?"
—Paul Newman

*"Sexiness wears thin after a while and beauty fades, but to be married to
a man who makes you laugh every day, ah, now that's a real treat."*
—Joanne Woodward

In Hollywood the marriages are many, but the successesful ones
are few. So many glam couples go their separate ways, but there
is a pair of cinematic icons that beat the odds to stay married
for nearly half a century—Paul Newman and Joanne Woodward.
The Newman-Woodward union isn't unique just for its longevity,
but also for its many accomplishments. The two movie legends
have managed illustrious acting careers, raised children, worked for
political causes, and contributed over $175 million to charity.

But how did Hollywood's longest true love story begin? Not
the way you might expect. They've been together so long, few
folks remember that this golden couple wasn't always a symbol of
family values.

BOY MEETS GIRL
Newman and Woodward were raised in very different circumstances. Paul Newman grew up in the well-to-do suburb of Shaker
Heights in Cleveland, Ohio. Joanne Woodward grew up in small-
town Georgia. From childhood on, Woodward wanted to be an
actress; she enrolled in Louisiana State University as a drama
major. Newman's father owned a successful sporting-goods store, so
his son was expected to join the family business. Newman fell into
acting; he only began to study drama after an arrest for a drunken
brawl got him kicked off the Kenyon College football team. After
graduation, Newman studied acting at the Yale School of Drama
and at the Actors' Studio.

After college Woodward moved to New York City in the early
1950s, lived in a roach-infested flat (with no hot water), and auditioned for acting jobs. In 1952 Newman was also in New York,
hoping for a break that would lead to a chance to perform—and
some decent money because he had a family to support. Newman

was married to Jacqueline "Jackie" Witte, and they had a two-year-old son, Scott.

As he made the rounds of casting agents, Newman noticed tall, blond Joanne in the offices of a theatrical agency and decided that she was "extraordinarily pretty." The two were introduced, but it was not love at first sight. Woodward disliked Newman right away. She looked into those blue eyes and wrote him off because he was too pretty, "like an Arrow collar ad."

BOY AND GIRL FALL IN LOVE

The pretty pair got a chance to know each other much better when they each were cast in the hit play *Picnic*, which opened on Broadway in 1953. Newman won a supporting role: Alan Benson, a rich kid who loses his fiancée Madge to a handsome drifter, Hal. In addition to playing Alan onstage, Newman was the understudy for the starring role of Hal. As for Woodward, she was Madge's understudy. As understudies, Newman and Woodward had to rehearse falling in love. Cast members noted that they were extremely convincing.

Newman's good looks and charisma made him the "hot" kid to watch on Broadway, and one of those watching him was Woodward. She had picked Paul out of the cast and said, "I'm going to get that one." Along with physical chemistry, the pair had much in common. Newman was drawn to Woodward's smarts and love of literature; the two bonded over their dedication to quality acting. Woodward would later say that ever since *Picnic*, Paul Newman had been her closest friend. But it was a troubled friendship—Newman was a married man . . . and a new father. He and his wife had a daughter during the play's long run. But backstage it was common knowledge that the Hal and Madge understudies were in love.

BOY AND GIRL MUST PART

When *Picnic* closed, Newman's career took off. He appeared in television dramas, won a contract with Warner Bros. Studios, and starred in a biblical epic, *The Silver Chalice*. He also earned rave reviews when he starred on Broadway as a psychopathic killer in *The Desperate Hours*. Woodward, too, was finding success. She performed in television plays as well as on Broadway. And in her first movie, the Civil War drama *Count Three and Pray*,

Woodward's humorous portrayal of a rambunctious tomboy made her a talent to watch.

In the busy four years that followed *Picnic*, the two budding movie stars were also, according to Woodward, running away from each other. Woodward became serially engaged to three other men, including the novelist and playwright Gore Vidal. Paul Newman and his wife had another daughter, but their marriage was far from happy. Newman was drinking heavily and troubled by the guilt he felt over being in love with another woman. In July 1956, Newman was arrested on Long Island, New York, and charged with leaving the scene of an accident and resisting arrest. He finally realized that he needed to put an end to this situation and asked his wife for a divorce. She refused, but Paul moved out anyway.

BOY AND GIRL REUNITE

In 1956 Newman and Woodward moved in together in Southern California, becoming an official Hollywood couple—even though Newman remained married. He continued to see his children and to seek a divorce. After two years his wife relented; the split was not friendly, but both Newman and Witte kept the matter private to protect their kids.

Gossip began to spread about how soon Newman and Woodward would make it official, but the pair kept silent. Then in January 1958, shortly after Newman's divorce became final, the pair had a quickie wedding at the El Rancho Hotel in Las Vegas. On their honeymoon in London they posed for cameras in their hotel bed (clothed, of course—this was the fifties!). It was a typically showbiz beginning to a marriage that would never be typical again.

BOY AND GIRL LIVE HAPPILY EVER AFTER

Forty-seven years later, the Newmans are still married. They have three daughters, Elinor (Nell), Melissa, and Claire (Clea). Based in Westport, Connecticut, they've kept their marriage and family life very private, but they've also become prominent public figures. They promote many causes including Newman's Own salad dressings and food products, whose profits are all donated to charity. And the couple is still rehearsing and acting together. In 2005, they each garnered Emmy nominations for their performances in the television miniseries *Empire Falls*.

BATHROOMS ON THE BIG SCREEN, PART 2

A few more powder room quotations from the movies—in honor of our favorite room in the house.

Oscar Madison (Walter Matthau): Where are you going?
Felix Ungar (Jack Lemmon): To the john.
Oscar: Alone?
Felix: I always go alone. Why?
Oscar: No reason. You going to be in there long?
Felix: As long as it takes.

—*The Odd Couple* (1968)

Congressman (Roger Corman): How do you go to the bathroom in space?
Jim Lovell (Tom Hanks): Well, um . . . I tell you it's a very complicated procedure that involves cranking down the window and looking for a gas station.

—*Apollo 13* (1995)

"I pee really fast. I live with five brothers, three cousins, and only one bathroom. Believe me—I can pee faster than anyone in the world."

—Isabel Fuentes (Salma Hayek), *Fools Rush In* (1997)

"I was nursing a director of General Motors. 'Kidney ailment,' they said. 'Nerves,' I said. And I asked myself, 'What's General Motors got to be nervous about? Overproduction,' I says. 'Collapse. When General Motors has to go to the bathroom ten times a day, the whole country's ready to let go.'"

—Stella (Thelma Ritter), *Rear Window* (1954)

"Sometimes the only way I know you're alive is when I hear you flush the toilet."

—Ev Kester (Leslie Parrish), *The Giant Spider Invasion* (1975)

FRANKENSTEIN MEETS THE SPACE MONSTER

Some of these Frankenstein films are pretty watchable. Others are so bad, only a dedicated fan could even consider sitting through them. These are real movies—we didn't make them up!

Frankenstein Meets the Space Monster (1965) NASA builds a robot named Frank and sends it into space, where it meets a space monster and goes berserk.

Assignment Terror (1971) An alien lands on Earth, brings Frankenstein, Dracula, the Mummy, and other monsters to life, "but is thwarted by the socially aware Wolf Man."

Jesse James Meets Frankenstein's Daughter (1965) Frankenstein's granddaughter, Maria, tries to capture Jesse James and his sidekick to turn them into monsters.

I Was a Teenage Frankenstein (1957) A descendant of Dr. Frankenstein moves to America, where he sets up a lab and begins building monsters out of the bodies of hot rod racers killed in car accidents.

Frankenhooker (1980) After a woman dies in a freak lawnmower accident, her mad-scientist boyfriend brings her back to life by sewing her head onto body parts taken from prostitutes on New York's 42nd Street.

Frankenstein General Hospital (1988) Frankenstein's 12th grand-son tries his experiments in the basement of a modern hospital.

Frankenstein Conquers the World (1964) "A boy eats the radioactive heart of the Frankenstein monster and begins to grow into an ugly giant that watches Japanese teenagers do the Twist" (*The Frankenstein Movie Guide*). Japanese title: *Frankenstein vs. the Giant Crab Monster.*

Frankenstein Campus (1970) A college student plots to turn his fellow-students into monsters. "If you can sit through this tripe, go to the head of the class." (*Creature Features Movie Guide*)

Humphrey Bogart appeared in only one horror film . . .

Frankenstein Island (1981) "A group of balloonists crash on a mysterious island populated by bikini-clad warrior-women descended from aliens. . . . Frankenstein's great-great granddaughter Sheila is around . . . experimenting on captives." (*The Frankenstein Movie Guide*)

Frankenstein Created Woman (1966) "Male spirit is transplanted into the body of a beautiful woman with a heaving bosom, who then goes around stabbing respectable folks with a knife." (*Creature Features Movie Guide*)

Frankenstein 1970 (1958) A descendant of Dr. Frankenstein sells the TV rights to his famous ancestor's story and uses the money to build an atomic-powered Frankenstein monster. The studio thought a futuristic-sounding title would help at the box office.

Frankenstein's Daughter (1958) Frankenstein's grandson tests a drug called degeneral on a teenage girl, and it "degenerates her into a bikini-clad creature running through the streets."

Frankenstein '80 (1979) Dr. Otto Frankenstein puts together a sex-crazed monster who goes on a killing spree. Lots of blood, including real surgical footage.

Frankenstein's Castle of Freaks (1973) Using his "Electric Accumulator," Count Frankenstein brings back Goliath the caveman, Kreegin the Hunchback, and Ook the Neanderthal Man! *South Pacific* star Rossano Brazzi—"sounding like a cross between Chico Marx and Bela Lugosi"—plays the Count.

Frankenstein's Great-Aunt Tillie (1983) Victor Jr. and his 109-year-old aunt "search for the family fortune and become involved with women's emancipation." (*The Frankenstein Movie Guide*)

* * *

HOLLYWOOD IRONY

Hellcats of the Navy, a 1957 film starring Ronald Reagan and Nancy Davis (the future Mrs. Reagan), was cowritten by screenwriter Bernard Gordon. Gordon used the name Raymond T. Marcus because he'd been blacklisted during the McCarthy era, during which Reagan had served as government informant.

. . . The Return of Dr. X (1939). Bogart played a zombie.

FILM FESTIVALS

For new talents, film festivals are the place to be discovered—just
like directors Quentin Tarantino and Steven Soderbergh were at the
Sundance festival. Once a small, local event, Sundance is now an
A-list happening where outsiders can show their work to Hollywood
insiders. Uncle John has the inside scoop on the ins and outs of
film festivals, for the mainstream and the fiercely independent.

By the 1980s Hollywood studios had become money
machines, churning out blockbusters with big stars, big budgets, and safe stories with broad appeal. Much to the frustration of independent filmmakers, there weren't a lot of executives
willing to take a chance on smaller, riskier films. But thanks to
Robert Redford and a group of cinema pioneers in Utah, the
Sundance Film Festival came to be the venue for Hollywood outsiders. Sundance has grown tremendously since 1978, when its first
festival screened eight independent films (called regional cinema
back then); in 2005 the festival screened 61 new films, chosen
from thousands of entries from the United States and all over the
world. For better or worse, the Sundance Film Festival has become
the epicenter of American independent films.

HUMBLE BEGINNINGS
Sundance's origins go back to Salt Lake City in September 1978. A
group of local movie enthusiasts—John Earle (head of the Utah
Film Commission), Sterling van Wagenen (film professor), and
Lawrence Smith (local filmmaker)—were inspired by a movie festival held two years earlier for the bicentennial. They decided to
hold a similar annual festival with an Americana theme and to call
it the Utah/U.S. Film Festival. The main attraction would be 65
classic movies about America, all shown during one week at the
Trolley Corners theater; almost as an afterthought, they added a
competition for independent filmmakers and put out a nationwide
call for submissions. Only 25 movies came in, and the organizers
picked eight of them for the contest. Much to the surprise of the
organizers, the screenings of those eight films had the highest
ticket sales of all the movies shown. The founders knew they were
onto something.

For the next two years, they held the festival in Salt Lake City and expanded the independent film contest. In January 1981 the festival relocated to Park City, Utah, a quiet mountain town and ski resort just 50 miles from Salt Lake City. Park City was also home to the Sundance Institute, newly founded by Robert Redford. Redford had been associated with the Utah/U.S. Film Festival since its beginning; his movie *Jeremiah Johnson* had been shown at the first festival, where he also participated in a panel discussion on Westerns. Always interested in outsider films, he founded the Sundance Institute and poured millions of dollars into it to help independent films develop and prosper. Three years later, Redford's institute—a burgeoning learning ground for young filmmakers—took over artistic direction and funding of the whole festival. It was something unique: a national venue for new and promising independent films produced outside the Hollywood system.

Within a few years, Hollywood began noticing Sundance Institute grads—directors and actors alike. Sundance's first breakout hit was Steven Soderbergh's first film, *Sex, Lies, and Videotape* in 1989; it won the newly created Audience Award and a distribution deal with Miramax. Made for just $1.2 million, it grossed more than $24 million in the United States alone. It was one of the first films out of Sundance to prove that outsiders could make money too. Hollywood took notice.

SUNDANCE GOES MAINSTREAM

In 1991 the Park City film festival was renamed the Sundance Film Festival. Redford's institute had already solidified its reputation as *the* place for young, talented filmmakers to learn their craft and step into the spotlight. And that spotlight only got brighter.

Over time, so many Sundance films became successful that bigname actors were increasingly willing to work with talented, unknown directors. Every year the entries became more polished, higher budget efforts. And the prizes became less accessible to first-time—and more experimental—filmmakers. In 2005, its 14th year, the Sundance festival drew crowds of 36,000 people to Park City, Utah—which had reported only 7,300 residents in the 2000 census. Narrow streets were jammed with cars and people. At first restaurants and hotels were overwhelmed. Then the town grew to accommodate the yearly event—and the additional increased tourism as Sundance attendees returned to ski.

During the festival the town still swarms with people—many of them Hollywood film industry professionals on the prowl for talent. With thousand-dollar sunglasses, lines of limos, 500 press badges, and myriad clicking cameras, Hollywood annually comes to Utah. Sundance films have landed big distribution deals and have been bought outright, making millions for their creators. Many are nearly as well known as anything Hollywood has ever produced. *Sideways*, a touching comedy set in California's wine country, was nominated for five Oscars (and won one of them) in 2004.

The artistic revolutionaries seem to have won the war. But what about the visionaries whose talent doesn't fit the mold, whose films are still on the edge, far out of the mainstream? Where do they go now?

SLAMDANCE

Thousands of independent original films are submitted to the Sundance committee each year, but only 18 make it in. Slamdance, its founders say, was born of that rejection. Three directors—Dan Mirvish, *Omaha (The Movie)*; Shane Kuhne, *Redneck*; and Jon Fitzgerald, *Self Portrait*—didn't make the cut in 1994. So, during the Sundance festival in 1995, they brought their films to Park City anyway and managed to find venues for showings—and thus a second revolution began. With a cadre of devoted advocates armed with more than 10,000 leaflets, stickers, and posters, Slamdance announced its presence. Approaching Sundance attendees, these advocates attempted to attract filmmakers for their own festival the following year.

Since 1995 Slamdance has provided screenings in Park City during the Sundance festival. It has created awards, parties, and a renewed sense of revolution. Its contest categories reflect a new age of storytelling. Unlike Sundance, which focuses on filmmaking, Slamdance has an interactive Web presence and includes awards for video game designers, teleplay writers, and online short films of 10 minutes or less, in a category called the Anarchy Competition. That competition is run year-round; the films shown and judged online. Finalists compete for an award that includes a showing at Slamdance in Park City the following year.

What was the Disney-owned Touchstone studio's first R-rated film?

THEY WON'T DANCE

Nodance, founded in 1999 by James Boyd, emphasized giving screenings to first-time and digital filmmakers. It lays claim to being the world's first DVD-projected festival. Where? Park City, of course, during the Sundance festival. Mindful that the screening and selection process is daunting to many first-time directors, Nodance offered a sign-up screening that would show any film submitted. In tune with the digital generation, it recognized music videos as an art form, and its discussion forums included alternative rock musicians as well as successful screenplay writers and actors. The festival is on hiatus, but fans expect it to come back as digital filming continues to gain popularity.

But if you have a film about base-jumping or extreme skiing, is there a festival for you? You bet! X-Dance was launched in 2001 to celebrate adrenaline culture and action sports filmmakers. Its 2005 award winners included a surfing film, a mountain-biking film, and a biopic of a skateboarding and snowboarding master athlete. With cutting-edge bands, extreme sports celebs, film screenings, and panel discussions, the X-Dance festival is home to films that seem as far removed from traditional Hollywood fare as they could be. But as the X-Dances, Nodances, and Slamdances become mainstream, you can bet there will be more outsiders looking to take their places on the filmmaking fringes.

* * *

SUNDANCE BREAKOUT HITS

Blood Simple (1984)

sex, lies, and videotape (1989)

Reservoir Dogs (1992)

The Brothers McMullen (1995)

Memento (2000)

In the Bedroom (2001)

Donnie Darko (2001)

American Splendor (2003)

Garden State (2004)

Napoleon Dynamite (2004)

Down and Out in Beverly Hills, with Richard Dreyfuss, Bette Midler, and Nick Nolte.

THE HOLLYWOOD BLACKLIST, PART 2

The House Un-American Activities Committee reconvened in 1951, this time led by Joseph McCarthy, the notorious senator who would later be censured by Congress for "conduct contrary to Senatorial tradition." Part 1 is on page 73.

Between the first and second rounds of the House Un-American Activities Committee (HUAC) hearings, Edward Dmytryk, one of the Hollywood Ten, took advantage of an "escape clause": he was released early from prison when he admitted past membership in the Communist Party and agreed to cooperate with the committee. He directed three films in England while waiting to appear as a "friendly" witness. On his return in 1951, he helped incriminate several of his former colleagues.

But the "friendliest" witness of them all was director Elia Kazan, cofounder of the Actors Studio in New York City, who had been named as a Communist during round one by studio boss Jack Warner.

THE COMMITTEE'S BEST FRIEND
When Kazan first testified in January 1952, he admitted former membership in the party in the 1930s but refused to name anyone else who had belonged. A few months later—after he lost the Oscar for Best Director (for *A Streetcar Named Desire*) and learned that he was facing the blacklist—he voluntarily testified before Congress; he then named eight people who had been in his cell, i.e., his group within the party. And talk about *chutzpah*—the group included two men he himself had recruited.

Kazan's controversial decision still splits Hollywood to this day. When he received a Lifetime Achievement Award at the Oscars in 1999, he was given a standing ovation—but it was far from unanimous; a noticeable portion of the audience refused to applaud, much less stand up.

THE HOLLYWOOD HUNDREDS
The Hollywood Ten were the most famous members of the blacklist,

but historians estimate that between 325 and 500 entertainers, directors, and screenwriters found themselves either out of work or generally unwelcome in Hollywood. Among them were entertainers John Garfield, Lee Grant, Sterling Hayden, Judy Holliday, Burgess Meredith, Zero Mostel, Paul Robeson, and Pete Seeger; writers Dashiell Hammett, Lillian Hellman, Arthur Miller, Clifford Odets, Dorothy Parker, Leo Penn (father of Sean and Chris), and Irwin Shaw; and directors Jules Dassin and Martin Ritt.

WHAT LIST?

Some of the blacklisted artists managed to succeed elsewhere. Arthur Miller's commentary on anti-communist hysteria, his 1953 play *The Crucible*, won two Tony Awards. Miller was called to testify in 1956 but refused to name anyone, earning a contempt charge that was dismissed—which may have had something to do with his marriage to Marilyn Monroe that same year.

Writer Irwin Shaw decamped to Europe and wrote a few best-selling books (including *Rich Man, Poor Man*, which became a hit TV miniseries in 1976). He would later declare that the blacklist "only glancingly bruised" his career.

Director Jules Dassin moved to France and made a series of films in Europe, including *Never on Sunday*, which he wrote, directed, and starred in with Melina Mercouri, his wife of 28 years. (His first postblacklist American film was 1964's *Topkapi*, which was the inspiration for the *Mission: Impossible* TV series.)

SCREENPLAY BY JOHN DOE

Some writers got around the blacklist by using pseudonyms, or fronts—fellow writers who agreed to pretend the work was theirs. Dalton Trumbo of the Hollywood Ten wrote more than a dozen screenplays between 1949 and 1958, two of which won Academy Awards: 1953's *Roman Holiday* (for which Trumbo used screenwriter Ian McLellan Hunter as a front) and 1956's *The Brave One* (for which he used the pseudonym Robert Rich).

LIGHTENING UP

Trumbo, with a little help from friends and admirers, was the first writer to break through the blacklist, with two 1960 productions: director Otto Preminger hired Trumbo to write the screenplay for *Exodus* and producer-star Kirk Douglas hired him to write *Spartacus*.

Ring Lardner Jr. had kept writing, too, using fronts or writing uncredited screenplays. His first postblacklist credit was for *The Cincinnati Kid;* from there he would go on to win his second screenwriting Oscar, for 1970's M*A*S*H.

Martin Ritt got back in the director's chair in the late 1950s. And in 1976 he produced and directed blacklisted writer Walter Bernstein's screenplay *The Front,* in which Woody Allen stars as a restaurant cashier who fronts for blacklisted writers—and eventually finds himself blacklisted, too. The movie included a few blacklisted actors, too, Zero Mostel and Herschel Bernardi among them. Bernstein got an Oscar nomination for the screenplay.

AFTERMATH

The cold war continued into the 1980s, but the Red Scare had died down and the stigma of the blacklist slipped away with it. But it had claimed its victims, among them actor John Garfield, who died of a heart attack at age 39, attributed at least in part to the blacklist. Actor Sterling Hayden was another: he had named names and regretted it for the rest of his life. The best thing that can be said of it was that the blacklisting was finally over.

* * *

"Kazan is one of those for whom I had contempt, because he carried down men much less capable of defending themselves than he."

—Dalton Trumbo

"I'd rather not talk about [Kazan]. He was once my friend, my teacher. I've never been able to look [him] in the eye, nor he me. Because he knows that I know."

—Martin Ritt

"You look for forgiveness, you try to understand, but I can't manage it with Kazan. What he did was diabolical. And what he did afterward was diabolical—to try and reach and offer work to blacklisted people. He tried to corrupt them by giving them work and by doing so making them accept him."

—Jules Dassin

"She tried to sit in my lap while I was standing up."

THE POISON PEN: BOX OFFICE BOMBS

Remember when your parents said that if you can't say something nice then don't say anything at all? Overall, it's pretty good advice—unless you grow up to be a movie critic and you're faced with cinematic sludge like these flicks.

HEAVEN'S GATE (1980)
"Mr. Cimino's approach to his subject is so predictable that watching the film is like a forced, four-hour walking tour of one's own living room."
—Vincent Canby, *The New York Times*

ISHTAR (1987)
"This movie is a long, dry slog. It's not funny, it's not smart and it's interesting only in the way a traffic accident is interesting."
—Roger Ebert, *Chicago Sun-Times*

JOHNNY BE GOOD (1988)
"The people who made this movie should be ashamed of themselves."
—Roger Ebert, *Chicago Sun-Times*

GHOST DAD (1990)
"Almost makes you forget how funny Bill Cosby can be."
—Scott Weinberg, *eFilmcritic.com*

HUDSON HAWK (1991)
"It's hard to imagine a major, big-budget movie that could come along this year and be worse than this one, a solid contender for the longest 95 minutes in movie history."
—Chris Hicks, *Deseret News* (Salt Lake City, Utah)

COOL WORLD (1992)
"Mommy! Mommy! Make the bad man stop!"
—Rob Vaux, *Flipside Movie Emporium*

—Philip Marlowe (Humphrey Bogart), *The Big Sleep* (1946)

SHOWGIRLS (1995)
"A film of thunderous oafishness that gives adult subject matter the kind of bad name it does not need or deserve."
—Kenneth Turan, *Los Angeles Times*

WATERWORLD (1995)
"It's one of those marginal pictures you're not unhappy to have seen, but can't quite recommend."
—Roger Ebert, *Chicago Sun-Times*

THE POSTMAN (1997)
"Fails to deliver"
—Jack Garner, *Democrat and Chronicle* (Rochester, New York)

BATTLEFIELD EARTH (2000)
"Battlefield Earth should be shown only at maximum-security prisons when a prisoner is tossed in solitary for bad behavior."
—Max Messier, *FilmCritic.com*

ROLLERBALL (2002)
"Say this for the soundtrack, it drowns out the lousy dialogue."
—Peter Travers, *Rolling Stone*

GIGLI (2003)
"Such an utter wreck of a movie you expect to see it lying on its side somewhere in rural Pennsylvania, with a small gang of engineers circling and a wisp of smoke rising from the caboose."
—Stephen Whitty, *The Star-Ledger* (Newark, New Jersey)

CATWOMAN (2004)
"Catwoman doesn't belong on the big screen. It belongs in the litter box or to be scraped off the bottom of our shoes as we head quickly for another theater."
—Connie Ogle, *Miami Herald*

THE DUKES OF HAZZARD (2005)
"The latest evidence that, for Hollywood studios at least, there can never be too much of a mediocre thing."
—A. O. Scott, *The New York Times*

Jayne Mansfield's home on Sunset Boulevard was known as the Pink Palace.

YOU'RE IN
THE ARMY NOW

There were reel heroes . . . and then there were real heroes.
Here are some stories of stars who served in the U.S. Army.

JIMMY STEWART

As a young boy Jimmy Stewart was fascinated with airplanes and aviation. He spent hours studying planes, building models, and once saved enough money so he could ride in a Curtiss biplane with a barnstorming pilot. After moving to California for his movie career, he fulfilled a lifelong dream and took flying lessons.

As the United States moved closer to entering World War II, Stewart volunteered for army duty, even though studio boss Louis B. Mayer tried to talk him out of it. Stewart's mind was made up, and in March 1941, Private James Stewart reported to duty at Fort MacArthur, California. He was assigned to the U.S. Army Air Corps (which later became the U.S. Army Air Force). After repeated requests for combat assignments, Stewart went to England in 1943 as the commanding officer of the 703rd Bomb Squadron of B-24s. Stewart flew 20 missions, was promoted to colonel before the war's end, and was awarded six battle stars.

But Jimmy Stewart didn't stop serving when World War II was over. In later years, he joined the Air Force Reserves and flew several missions over Vietnam. He was awarded the Presidential Medal of Freedom in 1985. When he died, Brigadier General James Stewart was buried with full military honors.

CLARK GABLE

When World War II broke out, Clark Gable was already one of America's most popular stars. He had job security, a healthy salary of $30,000 a month, and a happy marriage to Carole Lombard.

Soon after the attack on Pearl Harbor, Gable and Lombard contacted the White House to offer their services to the American government. Even though the White House encouraged them to keep making movies, Lombard went to work with the war bond effort, and Gable talked about enlisting, even though at 41 he was much older than draft age.

It even had a pink, heart-shaped swimming pool.

Tragedy struck when Lombard died in a plane crash following a war bond tour. Gable was inconsolable. He lost interest in making movies and decided to enlist. Despite some initial resistance, Gable's studio, MGM, eventually saw an opportunity to score some good publicity and supported the star's enlistment plans. They even sent along a publicist when Clark Gable became a private in the U.S. Army Air Corps on August 12, 1942. He had his sights set on becoming a gunner.

Although Gable was a movie star, those who served with him said he was a "regular guy." Gable made the same amount of money as any other buck private and took the same tests as the other men on his squad. He did the same drills and attended the same classes. He also saw real action, eventually receiving the Distinguished Flying Cross and the Air Medal. Hitler reportedly even placed a $5,000 bounty on him. Clark Gable completed combat in September 1944 but continued to appear in recruiting films.

GLENN MILLER

It's entirely possible that Glenn Miller was one of America's most popular musicians at the beginning of World War II. Miller and his band had been touring the United States for years; Miller was earning an estimated $20,000 a week when he decided to offer his services to the army.

Commissioned as a captain for the U.S. Army Air Corps, Miller became commander of the 418th Army Air Forces Band. This group of talented musicians would entertain Allied troops overseas. In two years the band played more than 800 performances, including concerts and dances. Five hundred of them were broadcast to millions of listeners. Miller's work was so successful that he was promoted to major in 1944.

In December 1944 the band was scheduled to play a Christmas concert in Paris. Miller needed to make advance arrangements for the group and decided to fly ahead separately. On December 15, 1944, despite less-than-perfect weather, Miller jumped aboard a single-engine Royal Air Force plane. He was never seen again. Official reports state that the plane went down in the British Channel due to engine failure or iced-over wings, but no wreckage or bodies were ever recovered—which led to an abundance of conspiracy theories. Some speculate that the Germans captured Miller.

What song did the computer in *2001: A Space Odyssey* (1968), learn to sing?

Others think he was a victim of friendly fire. No one knows for sure. It is likely to indefinitely remain one of Hollywood's biggest mysteries.

* * *

MORE STARS WHO SERVED IN THE ARMY DURING WORLD WAR II

Gene Autry: Served as flight officer for Air Transport Command

Art Carney: Was manning a machine gun when he was injured by a German mortar shell, injuring his right leg

Jackie Coogan: Flew as an air commando behind the lines in Burma

Sammy Davis Jr.: Served in the army's first integrated unit

Charles Durning: Drafted in 1943, he fought at Normandy and in the Battle of the Bulge

Charlton Heston: Served in the U.S. Army Air Force as a radioman and gunner

William Holden: Although he asked repeatedly for combat duty, Holden spent his war years assigned to public relations for the army

Audie Murphy: Was credited with capturing, wounding, or killing more than 200 Germans. Due to his bravery, Murphy was America's most decorated war hero of World War II and became a film star after the war

Ronald Reagan: Was serving as an Army Reserve officer when the Japanese bombed Pearl Harbor. He served as a liaison officer and was eventually assigned to make training films for the army

Mickey Rooney: Rooney was slated to start training in chemical warfare, but before he could start, he was assigned to Special Services, to entertain the troops

Turn to page 269 for more on actors at war.

BOX OFFICE BLOOPERS

*Here are a few mistakes to look for in popular movies. You can find
more in a series of books called* Film Flubs, *by Bill Gibbons.*

MOVIE: *Gone With the Wind* (1939)
SCENE: Scarlett is running on the street in Atlanta.
BLOOPER: She passes an electric light as she is running, years
before the invention of the incandescent bulb.

MOVIE: *Foul Play* (1978)
SCENE: Goldie Hawn is sitting on a park bench, eating a
sandwich.
BLOOPER: As she eats her lunch, "the sandwich is whole, then
half-eaten, then uneaten again, then half-eaten, then it has just
one bite out of it, then it disappears completely."

MOVIE: *Driving Miss Daisy* (1989)
SCENE: Hoke and Daisy cross the state line from Georgia into
Alabama. He comments that they're in Alabama . . . then two
state troopers pull them over.
BLOOPER: They forgot to change uniforms. They're dressed as
Georgia cops.

MOVIE: *Star Wars* (1976)
SCENE: Luke returns safely after blowing up the Death Star.
BLOOPER: He accidentally calls out "Carrie!" to Princess Leia.
(She's played by Carrie Fisher.) Note: It's in the re-released ver-
sion, too.

MOVIE: *Maverick* (1994)
SCENE: Mel Gibson is talking with a clerk at the railway station
in the Old West.
BLOOPER: You can see a white truck driving across the screen.

MOVIE: *Batman* (1989)
SCENE: The Joker (Jack Nicholson) and his gang are defacing
artwork in a museum.
BLOOPER: One of the gang splatters a portrait with pink paint.
In the next shot, the work is back to its original state.

Country star and actress Dolly Parton has an appropriate CB handle. What is it?

MOVIE: *Indiana Jones and the Last Crusade* (1989)
SCENE: Hitler signs an autograph for Jones.
BLOOPER: He spells his name wrong. He signs it *Adolph*, with a "ph"—the American spelling—instead of the German *Adolf*. And he signs it with his right hand; Hitler was a lefty.

MOVIE: *First Knight* (1996)
SCENE: King Arthur's knights are charging into battle on horseback.
BLOOPER: There are tire tracks in the foreground.

MOVIE: *Psycho* (1960)
SCENE: Janet Leigh is lying dead in the shower, after the famous "shower scene."
BLOOPER: The corpse swallows.

MOVIE: *48 Hours* (1982)
SCENE: Eddie Murphy escapes from jail, with Nick Nolte's aid.
BLOOPER: Nolte puts Murphy in his car handcuffed. Then Murphy's hands are free—he stretches one arm over the back of the seat. Next scene: He's handcuffed again.

MOVIE: *Funny Farm* (1988)
SCENE: Chevy Chase jumps into a lake with his clothes on. He gets out of the water and gets into his car.
BLOOPER: Next scene, his clothes have miraculously become dry.

MOVIE: *North to Alaska* (1960)
SCENE: John Wayne gets into a fight in a bar.
BLOOPER: He loses his toupee. Then in the next scene, he's hairy again.

MOVIE: *Presumed Innocent* (1990)
SCENE: Harrison Ford is besieged by journalists outside the courtroom. A reporter holds a cassette tape recorder up to Ford's face for a comment.
BLOOPER: It has no tape in it.

On the road, Dolly is "endowed" with the handle Booby Trap.

THEY CAME FROM THE INKWELL

Today it's a billion dollar business. Meet Gertie, Koko, Felix, and the drunken drawing that started it all.

They began, just over a hundred years ago, as lines, blobs, and squiggles. They became some of the most beloved—and highest-grossing—stars on film. From the little lost fish in *Finding Nemo* to the majesty of *The Lion King*, animated cartoon characters, or "toons," today can earn over $300 million a flick. Hard to believe such serious funny business all started with one cartoonist's wacky artwork—oh, and a bottle of vino, too.

PUT ON A HAPPY FACE

Before he became interested in films, James Stuart Blackton worked in vaudeville as the Komikal Kartoonist, entertaining audiences with humorous "lightning sketches" drawn at top speed. In 1895 Blackton met Thomas Edison, whose laboratory was working on an interesting invention—single-viewer moving-picture machines called Kinescopes.

Blackton took an interest in moving pictures and cofounded the Vitagraph Company, one of the first film studios. Using stop-motion technique (where the camera stopped, and the scene was changed before the camera started again), Blackton created the first animated drawing in 1900, called *The Enchanted Drawing*.

The film, which lasts only about a minute and a half, blends live action with an animated face on an easel. It shows Blackton at an easel drawing a large face. He then draws a wine bottle, glass, cigar, and hat—each one becoming real when Blackton reaches for them. The face's expressions also change each time Blackton reaches for something. It seems happy enough—until Blackton removes the wine bottle from the page, but Blackton makes it smile again by giving it some wine to drink. Those animated expressions make *The Enchanted Drawing* the forerunner of animated films.

"You can't show your bosom 'fore three o'clock." Who said it to whom, in what film?

Six years later Blackton created another silent short, *Humorous Phases of Funny Faces*, which featured even more animated action. This time an artist's hand draws simple figures on a chalkboard; they suddenly come to life—until the hand erases them. Blackton painstakingly created *Funny Faces* with thousands of drawings on a chalkboard and some clever photography. Cameras filmed his hand drawing the subject and then stopped while Blackton erased the old drawing and made a new one, with the subject in a slightly different position. Each single chalk drawing of his subject was photographed onto a single frame of movie film. When the film was run through a projector, it seemed as if the drawings, and the subjects on the chalkboard, were moving. Simple animated cartoons had begun.

When *Humorous Phases of Funny Faces* was produced in 1906, storefront theaters, known as nickelodeons, were springing up all over the country. In a nickelodeon, a patron paid a nickel to view a film program through a one-person peepshow-type viewer. Nickelodeons offered programs between 10 minutes and one hour in length. Shown as part of the program in many nickelodeons, *Funny Faces* became the first animated short film ever exhibited in theaters.

BEFORE MICKEY THERE WAS GERTIE

Following Blackton's lead, other American cartoonists turned to the new medium. Winsor McCay, author of a popular comic strip called *Little Nemo in Slumberland*, began filming his drawings. One of his firsts, Gertie the Dinosaur, became the original cartoon star.

In early 1914 McCay exhibited Gertie as part of his vaudeville act. Holding a whip, McCay stood near a movie screen and gave a short lecture on animation. Then he cracked his whip and, to the shock of his audience, Gertie, a huge dinosaur, lumbered on-screen. Gertie followed McCay's commands (when she wasn't crying, dancing with happiness, eating trees, or grabbing a woolly mammoth by the tail and tossing him in the lake).

By late 1914 McCay had created a theatrical release version of the cartoon. By then movies had moved from nickelodeons to big theaters where large audiences could watch Gertie's antics projected on a screen. The film's advertisement called it the "Greatest Animal Act in the World," and the public agreed. They loved her personality, and Gertie became the country's first animated star.

Mammy (Hattie McDaniel) to Scarlett (Vivien Leigh), in *Gone With the Wind.*

REVOLUTIONS IN TOONTOWN

Though Gertie caused a sensation, McCay's great cartoon wasn't quickly imitated. It had taken 10,000 drawings to produce Gertie the Dinosaur—animation seemed just too labor intensive (and costly) to ever become widely produced entertainment. Still, pioneering cartoon studios kept looking for ways to make animation better and cheaper.

One of them was Bray Studios in New York. In 1914 John Bray's chief animator, Earl Hurd, introduced cels—drawings of characters on clear celluloid. The celluloid was then photographed overlaying a painted background, and images could be used and reused without drawing the background over again for every shot. Thanks to cels, teams of animators could mass-produce cartoons. A new art form could now become a new industry. The studio used this technology in their cartoon series *Colonel Heeza Liar* (directed by Walter Lantz who went on to fame as the director of *Woody Woodpecker*). Although the series has largely faded from memory, the Bray Studios' contribution to animation has not.

Two more great cartoon innovators were the Fleischer brothers, Max and Dave. The brothers had mechanical as well as artistic talent; they invented another new way to speed up animation production called rotoscoping. The Fleischers filmed live actors and then, with a device called the rotoscope, traced each single frame of film, making the movement in their cartoons more lifelike than any cartoon that had gone before. In 1915 Dave capered in front of the camera in a clown suit and became the model for Koko the Clown, who performed in an imaginative series called *Out of the Inkwell*. In the series, cartoon characters performed in real-life locales; it was so successful that its reruns entertained audiences years after the Fleischer studio was disbanded. (For more on the Fleischers see page 106.)

THAT DARN CAT

Thanks to all these innovations, cartoons really took off in the 1920s with the arrival of the first international cartoon star, Felix the Cat. Created by Otto Messmer and Pat Sullivan, Felix's antics and demeanor resembled that of the great Charlie Chaplin. But thanks to the magic of animation, Felix could go where the Little Tramp did not. He had wild flying adventures on a magic carpet to Egypt, and outer-space encounters on a visit to Mars. Another plus: only the

Roy Rogers said his favorite of his nearly 100 movies was *My Pal Trigger* (1946).

irrepressible Felix could get out of a jam by taking off his tail and turning it into a handy object like a telescope or canoe paddle!

Like Gertie the Dinosaur, Felix was popular with audiences and made them laugh. Felix was the first cartoon megastar. In 1923 *Felix in Hollywood* showed the kitty mingling with Douglas Fairbanks Sr., Cecil B. DeMille, Charlie Chaplin, and even censor Will Hays. Felix the Cat merchandise flew off the shelves; watches, dolls, Christmas ornaments, anything with the cat's face on it was a must-have. Charles Lindbergh even took a Felix doll with him on his famous transatlantic flight in 1927. Felix was so big that he became the first giant balloon made for the Macy's Thanksgiving Day Parade that same year.

Felix the Cat's success showed Hollywood that toons could mean big money. Thanks to improved animation techniques and charismatic characters, the cartoon had secured its place in movie history.

* * *

WILLIAM RANDOLPH HEARST, CARTOON KING
In the early 20th century, a short cartoon was as much a part of the moviegoing experience as popcorn. But how did it get that way? It's thanks to newspaper magnate William Randolph Hearst, a huge fan of the comic strips that ran in his papers.

In 1915 Hearst's company was producing newsreels for the movies. He had the great idea to turn his comic strips into "living comic strips" and then add the short pieces onto the end of his newsreels (all in an effort to sell more papers). Hearst's cartoons didn't generate any famous cartoon characters (like Felix or Koko the Clown), but audiences came to expect an animated film when they went to a movie theater.

* * *

FORWARD THINKER
Louis Lumiére, the man who opened the world's first movie theater in Paris, had this to say: "The cinema is an invention without any commercial future."

THE WOLFMAN AT THE MOVIES, PART 1

The werewolf is one of the most recognized movie monsters in history, thanks in large part to the 1941 film The Wolf Man, *starring Lon Chaney Jr. Here's a behind-the-scenes look at the making of that classic film.*

FRIGHT FACTORY

The early 1930s was the golden age of movie monsters. In 1930 Universal released the classic *Dracula*, starring Bela Lugosi; a year later it had another huge hit with Boris Karloff's *Frankenstein*. Inspired by their success, Universal decided to make a movie about a werewolf. In 1931 they handed writer/director Robert Florey a title—*The Wolf Man*—and told him to come up with an outline.

A few months later, Florey submitted notes for a story about a Frenchman who has suffered for 400 years under a witch's curse that turns him into a werewolf during every full moon . . . unless he wears a garland of wolf-bane around his neck.

The studio approved the idea and scheduled the movie as a Boris Karloff vehicle for 1933. A shooting script was written . . . and rewritten . . . and rewritten several more times. By the time it was finished, the script was about an English doctor who is bitten by a werewolf in Tibet, then turns into one himself on his return to London. Universal renamed the picture *Werewolf of London.*

BAT MAN

By now, however, Boris Karloff was too busy to take the part so it went to a Broadway actor named Henry Hull. *Werewolf of London* hit theatres in 1935. The movie wasn't very good: One critic has called it "full of fog, atmosphere, and laboratory shots, but short on chills and horror." That was largely because Hull didn't look scary. He refused to cover his face with werewolf hair, complaining that it obscured his features. Makeup man Jack Pierce—already a legend for creating Bela Lugosi's Dracula and Boris Karloff's Frankenstein—had no choice but to remove most of the facial hair, leaving Hull look-

Italian producer Carlo Ponti was considered for the Don Corleone role in *The Godfather.*

ing like a demonic forest elf. *Werewolf of London* was a box office disappointment. It was also Hull's last werewolf film.

SECOND TRY

In the early 1940s Universal launched a second wave of horror films featuring Dracula, Frankenstein, and other classic monsters. They decided to give the werewolf another try, too.

This second werewolf film started the same way the first one did: with the title *The Wolf Man*. This time the scriptwriter was Curt Siodmak. He started from scratch, researched werewolf legends himself, and used what he learned to write the script. The story he concocted was about an American named Lawrence Talbot who travels to his ancestral home in Wales and is bitten while rescuing a young woman from a werewolf attack.

Once again, the studio wanted to cast Karloff in the lead, and once again, he was too busy to take it. They considered Bela Lugosi, but he was too old for the part. So they gave it to newcomer Lon Chaney Jr., son and namesake of the greatest horror star of the silent movie era. Chaney Sr. was known all over the world as "the Man of 1000 Faces," for his roles in *The Phantom of the Opera* and *The Hunchback of Notre Dame*. Chaney Jr. had recently starred in *Man Made Monster*, and Universal thought he had potential in horror films.

THE MAKEUP

Jack Pierce was still the makeup artist at Universal, and he welcomed the chance to use his original design: a hairy face complete with fangs and a wolfish nose, plus hairy hands and feet. The makeup took a total of four hours to apply, most of which was spent applying tufts of fur—authentic yak hair imported from Asia—one by one, and then singeing them to create a wild look. Chaney's wolfman didn't talk—all it did was grunt, growl, and howl—and that was no accident: when Chaney was fully made up, he couldn't talk and could only eat through a straw. As he recounted years later, the only thing worse than wearing the makeup was taking it off:

> What gets me is when it's after work and I'm all hot and itchy and tired, and I've got to sit in that chair for forty-five minutes more while Pierce just about kills me ripping off the stuff

Artist Salvador Dalí created the dream sequences for Alfred Hitchcock's *Spellbound*.

he put on in the morning! Sometimes we take an hour and leave some of the skin on my face!

THANKS, DAD
Most actors would probably have refused to wear such difficult makeup, but Chaney (whose real first name was Creighton) had no choice: he was desperate to make it in the film business.

While he was alive, Lon Chaney Sr. had fought Creighton's attempts to become an actor. He even forced his son out of Hollywood High and into a plumbing school when he asked to take acting lessons. As Chaney Sr.'s career soared to its heights in the late 1920s, Chaney Jr. was working as a boilermaker.

The elder Chaney died of throat cancer in 1930; Creighton Chaney signed with RKO studios two years later. After moving from bit part to bit part for more than two years, he reluctantly changed his name to Lon Chaney Jr. to cash in on his father's fame. "They had to starve me to make me take his name," he groused years later.

Finally, in 1939—only days after his car and furniture were repossessed by a furniture company—Chaney scored a hit in a stage version of *Of Mice and Men*. That led to a starring role in the movie version, and in 1940, a contract with Universal.

Continued on page 263.

* * *

MORE LOONEY TUNE DEBUTS
Bugs Bunny
First Appeared in: *A Wild Hare*
Debuted on: June 27, 1940
Fact: A Bugs-like character had appeared in four previous cartoons, but *A Wild Hare* is widely accepted as the first to feature his true personality.

The Road Runner & Wile E. Coyote
First Appeared in: *The Fast and the Furry-ous*
Debuted on: September 16, 1949
Fact: In the first cartoon, animators froze the initial chase scene to give the Latin names for the Road Runner and Coyote. Respectively, they were: *Accelleratti Incredibus* and *Carnivorous Vulgaris*.

Overstatement: "I don't care if people think I'm an overactor. . . ."

HOW DO THEY DO THAT?

Hollywood tough guys know how to take a beating. Whether they're being shot at, being thrown through a window, or being strangled, all the action looks real—and painful. How does Hollywood do it? We've got the scoop.

THE RIDDLED WITH BULLETS RIDDLE

Ever see a movie where something (usually a car) is riddled with bullets? One after another, multiple bullet holes appear in the sides of cars as they're shot at in a hail of gunfire. How do they get the bullet holes to appear one by one? Do they use real guns?

Heck, no. The bullet holes are already there before the scene is shot. Each hole is pre-drilled in the side of the car, and a small exploding device (called a squib), which can be remotely detonated, is inserted in the hole. The rest of the hole is plugged with bits of clay that are painted to match the car. At the appropriate moment, a technician sets off the squibs in rapid succession. And presto, instant gunfire.

Squibs are handy devices. When packed with fake blood, they're placed under clothing to simulate someone being shot; the actor is wired with a firing system that he controls by a button hidden somewhere on his person.

TIMING IS EVERYTHING

Another movie trick involves safety glass that's designed to break into small pieces with rounded rather than sharp edges—like your car's windshield. The problem with safety glass is that it takes a lot more force to break than ordinary glass. So if a stunt player was supposed to fly through a glass window—and the window would necessarily be made of safety glass—he or she would be more likely to bounce off it than go through it.

Here's the secret: The stunt technicians use explosives to detonate the glass just before the stunt person crashes into it. The timing, of course, is critical. Some movies, like *True Lies* (1994), feature a few scenes where you can spot the early explosion: if you use the freeze-frame function on your VCR or DVD player you'll be able to see the window shatter one or two frames before the actor goes through it.

LUCA BRASI SLEEPS WITH THE FISHES
The murder of Luca Brasi in *The Godfather* (1972) is a stunningly graphic screen moment. While sitting at a bar, he is garroted (strangled) from behind. As he struggles—first to free himself, then for breath—his face turns a deep, dark purple. Want to know how they made it look so real? Before the scene, the actor (Lenny Montana) had his face dusted with a translucent powder that turns black on contact with water. As the scene played out, it was a simple matter to spray a very fine mist (undetectable by the camera) onto Montana's face for a realistic-looking death scene.

* * *

QUOTES OF EVIL
Some favorite lines from our favorite villains.

"Ah, Kirk, my old friend. Do you know the Klingon proverb that tells us revenge is a dish that is best served cold? It is very cold in space."
—Khan (Ricardo Montalban),
Star Trek 2: The Wrath of Khan (1982)

"Just try and stay out of my way. Just try! I'll get you, my pretty and your little dog too!"
—The Wicked Witch of the West (Margaret Hamilton),
The Wizard of Oz (1939)

"It's Dr. Evil. I didn't spend six years in Evil Medical School to be called 'mister,' thank you very much."
—Dr. Evil (Mike Myers),
Austin Powers: International Man of Mystery (1997)

SCRIPT WRITING: PART 1, THE BASICS

So you've got a story to tell—one loaded with high concept (what Hollywood types call a hook, meant to catch and keep audience attention). Before you fire up the computer and get typing, there are a few things you should know. Hollywood's got some pretty strict rules on how to put a script together, but Uncle John's here to help.

PAPER
Type your script on one side of white letter-size paper (never use paper larger than 8.5 by 11 inches). Then, use a three-hole punch so your paper can be easily bound.

TITLE PAGE
On the title page, center your name and the script's title. Put your contact information in the lower right corner. If you registered your script with the Writers Guild of America (WGA), include that number in the lower left-hand corner.

MARGINS
Margins are extremely important, so don't fudge them. For the basic layout, the top, bottom, and right margins are one inch. But the left margin should be 1.5 inches. Why? So the pages can be easily punched with holes and fastened together.

Different elements of the script need special margins. Dialogue should be set 2.5 inches from the left. Slug lines, or scene descriptions, are set 3.7 inches from the left. They should also be capitalized, include the location of the scene, describe the action, and be as brief as possible.

If you're wondering where to put the directorial cues (the directions that tell the camera people to use a close-up or wide shot), don't. Modern screenplays don't include this stuff anymore because the script is easier to read without it. It makes it easier to follow the story line without having to know any special language.

—Mickey (Burgess Meredith), *Rocky* (1976)

BINDING
Scripts are fastened together by #5 brass brads. (Those buttonlike fasteners with two pins that look like little legs doing a split.) Only put a brad in the top and bottom holes; leave the middle hole brad free.

FONT
Scripts are written in Courier 12. Why? Because one page in this font equals about one minute of film time, which means you can judge the length of a movie just by the number of pages in the script. Most movies are 90 to 120 minutes long. So if one page equals one minute, well, you do the math!

PAGE NUMBERS
Page numbers are in the upper right-hand corner. Every page, except the first, gets a number.

SPACING
You should single-space: paragraphs, inside dialogue, before dialogue, and after a character's name.

Double-space: before and after all action prompts, scene or action dynamics, and all paragraphs describing scenes, actions, or characters. Double-space before a character's name and after all dialogue.

To learn the lingo of the biz, turn to page 300.

* * *

BIGGEST STAR WARS COLLECTION
Jason Joiner may just be the biggest *Star Wars* fan ever. Why? This native of London owns every piece of *Star Wars* merchandise ever made. He's been certified by the *Guinness Book of World Records* as the owner of the largest *Star Wars* collection, composed of more than 20,000 toys, books, and dolls. Joiner is also a special-effects expert and has even worked on the *Star Wars* films.

When a journalist asked Marilyn Monroe what she wore to bed, she replied . . .

THE BUZZ ON
BUSBY BERKELEY

What has 300 legs, is covered in feathers, and sounds like a large flock of woodpeckers? A Busby Berkeley dance line.

B usby Berkeley's private life was as flamboyant as his musical extravaganzas. He preferred to drink his martinis in the bathtub, married six times, and made the front page of the Hollywood scandal sheets more than once.

MAMA'S BOY
William Berkeley Enos had show business in his blood; he was born in Los Angeles in 1895 to theatrical director Francis Enos and actress Gertrude Berkeley. William was nicknamed "Busby" after Amy Busby, a popular Broadway star who had toured with his parents. After Busby's father died, he and his mother were inseparable; they lived together—even through the first four of his six marriages—until her death.

HUT, TWO, THREE, FOUR!
Berkeley spent his teen years at the Mohegan Lake Military Academy near Peekskill, New York, and served as a field artillery lieutenant in World War I. After the war he got his future on-the-job training conducting U.S. Army parades and stage shows—directing battalions of as many as 5,000 drill troops at a time.

A MAN IN DEMAND
He dabbled in stage acting but found his niche in choreography. His first job was in a 1925 production called *Holka Polka*, which lasted two weeks on Broadway. But his knack for staging elaborate dance routines didn't go unnoticed: the famous impresario Florenz Ziegfeld hired him next to direct the dance numbers for Rodgers and Hart's *A Connecticut Yankee* (1927).

In 1930 Samuel Goldwyn (the G in MGM) brought Berkeley to Hollywood to choreograph a couple of Eddie Cantor movies and Mary Pickford's only musical, *Kiki*.

Darryl F. Zanuck then lured him away from Goldwyn to choreograph *42nd Street* (1933) for Warner Bros. The head of the studio, Jack Warner, had nixed the idea of choreography in the movie because there was a glut of ex-Broadway musicals in production at the time. So Zanuck had Berkeley covertly shoot all the dance numbers at night and then tacked most of them onto the end of the film. In spite of his initial objections to the dancing, Jack Warner liked the finished product—as did the public—and Zanuck set Berkeley to shooting extra dance scenes for the already finished *Gold Diggers of 1933*.

WHAT'S NEW?
What Berkeley was doing was completely original. If you study his work you'll notice that in some cases there isn't a whole lot of dancing going on—what you get instead is the military precision of flocks of pretty girls and handsome guys on revolving platforms or enormous flights of stairs, all of which are shot from every angle Busby Berkeley could think of: from the front, the back, the sides, the top, and the bottom. The movies gave him the freedom to direct dance routines that couldn't possibly be contained on a stage.

GOING THROUGH THE ROOF
The "Berkeley top shot" was his trademark: he'd film his dancers from directly above while they formed intricate and ever-shifting geometric shapes by moving their legs, arms, and whatever else in perfect unison. The result was like looking into a kaleidoscope. And if he couldn't get the distance he wanted, he would cut through the roof and install his camera up there. He used his camera for close-ups, too: "We've got all these beautiful girls in the picture, why not let the public see them?"

QUIET—GENIUS AT WORK
His numbers could usually be shot in one take because he'd plan every move in advance. He drove more than one producer crazy by giving the order to build a set and then sitting in front of it for a few days plotting and planning every move and angle, while the dancers and crew, who were being paid, sat around doing nothing.

What were Frank Sinatra's last words, according to his daughter Nancy and a columnist?

FAR FROM ROUTINE

Berkeley's most memorable routines include *42nd Street's* "Shuffle
Off to Buffalo" and the two production numbers from *Gold Diggers
of 1935*, his directorial debut. The movie is a bit of fluff that con-
trasts sharply with the beauty and drama of its two show-stopping
numbers:

- In "The Words Are in My Heart," 56 pretty girls in long white
  dresses sit at 56 white baby grand pianos that spin and glide
  across the shiny black floor as if on air; at the end, the pianos
  morph into one huge platform on which a lone dancer swirls
  like a ballerina in a music box.

- The 13-plus minutes of "Lullaby of Broadway" may be
  Berkeley's best arrangement. It's a hypnotic film-within-a-film
  (including more than 150 chorus boys and girls who perform a
  perfectly synchronized tap dance) that chronicles the daily routine of a Broadway "babe" (who sleeps all day and carouses all
  night) and ends—surprisingly—in tragedy.

Which may not have been surprising to the people who knew
him personally.

HERE COMES TROUBLE

Berkeley drank heavily, a habit that led to a real-life tragedy in
1935 when, driving home from a party one night, Berkeley's car hit
two other cars, killing three people. After three trials he was
acquitted, largely because he was his mother's sole support. But he
never got over the incident, and it darkened his life from then on.

MARCHING ORDERS

On the set, Berkeley operated like a field marshal—in tempera-
ment as well as technique—but found rapport with most of the
musical stars he worked with: Ginger Rogers, Mickey Rooney, Dick
Powell, Eleanor Powell, Gene Kelly, and Carmen Miranda (for
whom he created "The Lady with the Tutti-Frutti Hat" in 1943's
The Gang's All Here).

Esther Williams, the star of MGM's aqua-musicals, got along
well enough with him but tells of Berkeley's "nasty habit" of calling
her at three o'clock in the morning—from his bathtub. "I can't get
ideas for you unless I'm wet," he told her. The martini in his hand

was also "necessary for [him] to get these ideas." But the increasingly irresponsible Berkeley pushed her to do more and more dangerous feats, one of which almost got her killed while filming the water-skiing sequence in *Easy to Love* (1953).

He pushed Judy Garland, too, who bristled at having to shoot sequences over and over. Her complaints got him fired from *Girl Crazy* (1943). The two locked horns again when MGM hired Berkeley to direct *Annie Get Your Gun* (1950). Garland had become increasingly difficult to work with, so the studio thought they needed a disciplinarian like Berkeley to stand up to her. The plan backfired, and MGM ended up firing them both. *Annie* was the last movie Berkeley was hired to direct.

THE COMEBACK KID

Busby Berkeley was rediscovered during the "camp" craze of the 1960s and hailed by film historians for the genius that he was. He became a popular guest speaker at universities and on TV talk shows and served as production supervisor for the smash 1971 Broadway revival of *No, No, Nanette*, starring Ruby Keeler, whom he'd worked with in *42nd Street* way back when.

And through it all, the great choreographer carried a deep dark secret: he'd never learned how to dance.He died in Palm Springs on March 14, 1976, at the age of 80.

* * *

JULIA GETS SATISFACTION

Remember a 1988 movie called *Satisfaction*? No? It was about an all-girl rock band on tour in Europe and starred Justine Bateman at the height of her *Family Ties* fame. The movie was supposed to transition Bateman's career to the big screen, but it flopped. her career didn't really take off, but one of her co-star's did. The forgotten movie was Julia Roberts's first credited performance, which helped her to land her breakout roles in *Mystic Pizza* and *Steel Magnolias* and to launch her on her way to superstardom.

Burt Reynolds's house in Jupiter, Florida, was once a hideaway for gangster Al Capone.

THE SECOND
SNOW WHITE

*Walt Disney had a vision for a full-length feature, but he knew
it needed to be different from other cartoons of the day. Instead
of relying on gags and jokes, he would tell a story with strong
characters, great music, and superb animation. It was labeled
Walt's Folly, but it was really Walt's Triumph.*

When Walt Disney decided to make the Snow White
story into a movie—he had wanted to since age 15,
when he saw a silent, live-action version—everyone,
including his wife and his brother, thought he was being just plain
foolish. He struggled to find financing for the movie, but it was no
surprise that few believed in Disney's idea. Animators warned him
that cartoons were supposed to be short; there was no way an audience would be interested in 90 minutes of animation.

DISNEY DIRECTS
Disney persevered. He had set a budget of $250,000 and quickly
overran it. But it was vital that no corners be cut. Disney had hired
a huge staff: 32 animators, 102 assistants, 167 "in-betweeners" (also
known as assistant animators), 20 layout artists, 25 artists doing
watercolor backgrounds, 65 effects animators, and 158 inkers and
painters. There were 2,000,000 illustrations made using more than
1,500 shades of paint.

The writers invested a lot of time developing the personalities of
all the characters—especially the seven dwarfs: Happy, Grumpy,
Sleepy, Sneezy, Bashful, Dopey, and Doc. Other names were considered (and rejected) like Awful, Biggy, Blabby, Dirty, Gabby,
Gaspy, Gloomy, Hoppy, Hotsy, Jaunty, Jumpy, Nifty, and Shifty.
Sneezy was a last minute replacement for Jumpy. In the original
proposal, Dopey, the last dwarf to be developed, was supposed to
talk; he became a mute because no suitable voice actor could be
found.

From the beginning, every scene in the movie was heavily scru-
tinized. Each sequence had to advance the story in addition to

having to be perfectly animated. Walt Disney himself made sure that everything was done right, no matter how long it took or how much it cost. Months and months of story meetings were held just to discuss the dramatic moment when the Huntsman tries to murder Snow White; transcripts from the story meetings show the arguments over big things (like the length of the scene) to small details (like how shiny the dagger would be as it was raised). Even after a sequence had been fully developed and animated, Walt was still ruthless with his edits. A lengthy sequence animated by Ward Kimball wound up on the cutting room floor because Disney felt it slowed the story down. Kimball called it "one of the early tragedies" of his life.

MONEY MATTERS

As costs continued to mount, Disney would joke that the bankers were losing more sleep than he was. When expenses climbed to roughly $1.5 million (very expensive for the 1930s), Walt remarked that "Roy (Disney) didn't even bat an eye. He couldn't; he was paralyzed." Everything was riding on this movie, and everyone at Disney Studios knew it. When Disney still needed more money to finish, he reluctantly agreed to an advance screening for a Bank of America executive, Joseph Rosenberg. The film was still pretty rough—with just pencil sketches and storyboards in some places. But the story goes that Rosenberg, who remained silent during the screening, later observed that Snow White would "make a hatful of money."

Rosenberg's remarks were right on the money. Disney's folly transformed into Disney's success almost immediately. It was released on December 21, 1937, and went on to make more money than any other film in 1938; more than 20 million Americans went to see it. At the end of its original run, the movie grossed over $8.5 million—a nice take in those days. Since its release (after you adjust for inflation), Snow White and the Seven Dwarfs has made more than $697 million dollars in the United States alone. It's the tenth-highest-earning motion picture of all time. A critical success as well as a financial one, Snow White and the Seven Dwarfs received an honorary Oscar statuette (and seven miniature ones) for being "a significant screen innovation which has charmed millions and pioneered a great new entertainment field for the motion picture cartoon." More than 50 years later the

U.S. government would honor Disney's *Snow White* by placing it into the National Film Registry. Walt Disney's vision paid off, and animated features are now blockbusters in their own right.

* * *

SNOW WHITE ORIGINS

The Brothers Grimm are often credited with writing the Snow White fairy tale, but they really collected it from two sisters in Hesse, Germany. The tale had been handed down for generations in sisters Jeannette and Amalie Hassenpflug's family. But the tale wasn't even original to the Hassenpflug family. Records show that similar stories have been told for centuries throughout Europe, Asia Minor, and central Africa.

* * *

ON ACTRESSES

"Evil people . . . you never forget them. And that's the aim of any actress—never to be forgotten."
—Bette Davis

"For an actress to be a success, she must have the face of Venus, the brains of a Minerva, the grace of Terpsichore, the memory of a Macaulay, the figure of Juno, and the hide of a rhinoceros."
—Ethel Barrymore

"The average Hollywood film star's ambition is to be admired by an American, courted by an Italian, married to an Englishman, and have a French boyfriend."
—Katharine Hepburn

"People often become actresses because of something they dislike about themselves: they pretend they are someone else."
—Bette Davis

"In Hollywood, the women are all peaches. It makes one long for an apple occasionally."
—Somerset Maugham, writer

In *Rain Man* (1988), "Boy at Pancake Counter" is Jake Hoffman, Dustin Hoffman's son.

AUDREY HEPBURN: BY THE NUMBERS

*Fashionable and elegant, doe-eyed and gamine, this delightful
actress epitomized Hollywood chic in the 1950s and 1960s.
Twenty years later, she would begin the work she was
most proud of as a goodwill ambassador for UNICEF.*

1
Number of American films she made before receiving a Best
Actress Oscar for *Roman Holiday* (1953).

2
Before discovering the 21-year-old Hepburn, the number of years
that Broadway producers searched for an actress to star in *Gigi*.
Audrey was such a smash in her first role that her name was placed
above the title the day after the opening. (Her success was no
fluke. She would go on to win a Tony for best actress in her second
starring role, in *Ondine*.)

3
Her rank in the American Film Institute's list of Greatest
American (Female) Screen Legends.

4
Number of times Cary Grant was offered the chance to star opposite Hepburn. He turned down *Roman Holiday*, *Sabrina* (1954), and
Love in the Afternoon (1957) because he thought he was too old for
her. Finally he agreed to *Charade* (1963) when she was in her mid-
30s and he was closing in on 60.

6
Number of languages Hepburn could speak fluently: English,
French, Dutch, Flemish, Spanish, and Italian.

At $3.9 million, *Ben-Hur* (1925) was the most expensive silent film ever made.

10
Ms. Hepburn's shoe size. She told *People* magazine that she was self-conscious about the size of her feet. (She thought they were too big.)

12
In inches, the length of Holly Golightly's cigarette holder in *Breakfast at Tiffany's* (1961).

15
Age at which high schooler Hepburn began working as a courier for the Dutch Resistance in World War II. She delivered forged identity papers and counterfeit ration cards in her book bag or lunch box.

22
Average age difference, in years, between Audrey and her leading men in her first five motion pictures. There's a tie for the biggest gap: both Humphrey Bogart and Fred Astaire were 30 years older than their costar.

30
Age of Audrey's second husband, Andrea Dotti, when they met. Her age: 39.

32-20-35
In inches, her measurements. Hepburn thought her hips were too big and dressed accordingly.

46
Age of President John F. Kennedy when Hepburn sang "Happy Birthday, Mr. President" to him at his Waldorf-Astoria birthday party, one year after Marilyn Monroe delivered her famous rendition.

58
Age at which Hepburn began her work with UNICEF as an ambassador and trainer. Her annual salary was one dollar per year.

63
Age at her death from cancer, diagnosed after her return from a UNICEF relief mission to famine-stricken Somalia just three and a half months before.

67
In inches, her height, which kept her from her first chosen vocation: ballerina.

250
Number of francs a lovesick fan was fined in 1962 after breaking into Hepburn's Switzerland home and stealing the Oscar she won for *Roman Holiday*. The sympathetic judge ruled that "love is not a crime."

365
Packs of cigarettes per year that Hepburn smoked through most of her adult life.

1929
The year of Audrey's birth. She was born on May 4 in Brussels, Belgium.

1954
The year Hubert de Givenchy began his fashionable collaboration with Hepburn over the film *Sabrina*. Givenchy designed Sabrina's evening wear; Edith Head designed the daytime clothing. When Head won the Oscar for Costume Design that year, she didn't even mention Givenchy.

35,000
In dollars, husband Mel Ferrer's fee for a featured role in *Sex and the Single Girl*—while Hepburn was earning $1 million plus for *My Fair Lady* (1964). This frequent disparity in their incomes eventually led to their divorce in 1968.

1,000,000
As of 2004, how many dollars the Audrey Hepburn Memorial Fund at UNICEF has raised for educational programs in Eritrea, Ethiopia, Rwanda, Sudan, and Somalia.

The first choices for the leads in *The African Queen* were John Mills and Bette Davis.

ACTING LIKE ANIMALS

Ever wonder about those noncanine animal stars in the movies? Well, here's a bit of trivia on some of them.

BART THE BEAR
Called the John Wayne of Bear Actors, 9-foot-tall Bart was a star. Usually cast as "The Bear" (talk about typecasting), Bart appeared in 16 films; his best-known role was the bear who mauls Brad Pitt's character in the 1994 drama *Legends of the Fall*. He's costarred with well-known actors like John Candy, Dan Aykroyd, Steven Seagal, Anthony Hopkins, and Alec Baldwin. Bart has even been a presenter at the Oscars: in 1999, he helped Mike Myers present the award for best sound effects. Bart, who at 1,700 pounds was huge for his subspecies of Kodiak bear, died of natural causes in 2000 at the ripe old age (in bear years) of 23. But his legacy lives on in his son (also named Bart), who appeared in *Dr. Dolittle 2* (2001) and *Without a Paddle* (2004).

BANDIT THE RACCOON
This feisty critter starred with Marilyn Monroe is the 1954 Western *River of No Return*. During a shoot in a giant indoor studio featuring 200 pine trees, Bandit became frightened and hid somewhere in the maze of the fake forest. Monroe helped Bandit's trainer look for him by crawling on her knees through the spiderwebs, dust, and wooden struts of the set's support structure. Bandit was found safe and sound.

CASS OLÉ
The star of *The Black Stallion* and *The Black Stallion Returns* was found after an extensive worldwide search. Producers found Cass Olé, an Arabian stallion, in San Antonio, Texas. The horse learned to act—pulling back his ears to show anger and pulling back his lips to show affection. But for the climatic rescue scene at sea, Cass Olé didn't learn to swim; it was too dangerous for him. So a swimming horse, a breed specifically developed to swim in the ocean, was imported from France for that scene. Regardless, Cass Olé became a big star, met presidents Carter and Reagan, and sired more than 130 foals before his death in 1993.

Pulp Fiction cost $8 million to make, of which $5 million was for actors' salaries.

CANDY-MAKING SQUIRRELS

Charlie and the Chocolate Factory (2005) faithfully adapted the famous "nut scene" from Roald Dahl's original book: the movie shows a room full of squirrels who crack nuts and sort them on a conveyor belt. What viewers might not know is that those big-screen squirrels are real. Director Tim Burton founded a "school for squirrels" where 200 of the rodents spent 19 weeks learning to sit on stools, and to crack and sort nuts—just for that short scene.

PENGUIN ARMY

Tim Burton had another group of animals trained for 1992's *Batman Returns*, where the supervillian Penguin uses a flock of armed penguins to try to take over Gotham City. Burton went to every extreme to make sure the birds were comfortable on the set; they had their own refrigerated trailer, their own swimming pool, and fresh fish every day. The set was kept at freezing temperatures just to keep the birds comfortable (and the actors very chilly). The live penguins were joined on set by robotic look-alikes, some of which looked so real that genuine penguins snuggled up to them and fell asleep.

HERBIE THE DUCK

The lead duck in the 1961 comedy *Everything's Ducky*, Herbie, was known to defecate every time he quacked. When Herbie was on the set, the frustrated crew members had to watch where they stepped to avoid constantly slipping and sliding. But luckily for them, Herbie had three doubles for *Everything's Ducky*. They all looked like him: pure white with yellow-orange bills. There was Burp Adenoids, who hiccuped a lot. And Duster, whose tail never stopped wagging. And Flops, who always fell down.

FREDDIE THE LION

Star of the 1965 movie *Clarence, the Cross-Eyed Lion*, Freddie was actually cross-eyed in real life. And, for a time, his wranglers tried their best to fix his eye problem. They even got him a giant pair of prescription sunglasses! Freddie was known for his mild-mannered personality and was really good with children. He was so calm that he let his animal costar, Judy the chimpanzee, climb on his back and grab a free ride whenever she wanted. And because he didn't have a mean bone in his body, producers had to get another lion to act as his double for the snarling scenes of the movie.

KEIKO THE KILLER WHALE

Fans of the sleeper hit movie *Free Willy* (1993) remember Keiko's portrayal of the killer whale freed with the help of a young boy. Born in 1976, Keiko was pulled from Icelandic waters when he was two and sent to Marineland in Canada. From there he was sold to a Reino Aventura, a Mexican theme park. Keiko became a star attraction there, and when Hollywood needed a whale for *Free Willy*, he got the part. After the movie wrapped, Keiko returned to Mexico, but fans of the movie lobbied hard for his release. The Free Willy Foundation was formed and raised enough money to rescue Keiko, who was relocated back to the frigid waters off Iceland in 1998. There trainers worked to prepare him for his return to the wild. In 2002 Keiko was set free. He settled down off the coast of Helsa, Norway, where the friendly whale became a favorite of the locals until his death in 2003.

* * *

ANIMAL-ACTOR TRIVIA

- Bear actors are on top of the animal-actor pay scale. They make as much as to $20,000 per day.
- Jinx, the cat from *Meet the Parents* (2000) and *Meet the Fockers* (2004), is a gray Himalayan whose real name is Meesha.
- Forty-eight Yorkshire pigs were needed for consistency in the filming of *Babe* (1995) because baby pigs grow so fast.
- The chimps in *Dr. Dolittle* (1998) were computer animated.

* * *

LONG LASTING

Joanne Woodward and Paul Newman are the only husband and wife to have their handprints in the same block of concrete in the forecourt of Grauman's Chinese Theatre.

In 1969 gossip began to spread that the Newmans' marriage was collapsing. To combat the rumors, they took out a $2,000 full-page ad in the *Los Angeles Times* that simply said: "We Are Not Breaking Up."

—Johnny Castle (Patrick Swayze), *Dirty Dancing* (1987)

BEFORE HIS TIME: VALENTINO

*Rudolph Valentino's smoldering stare, sleek body, and
dancer's grace made him the first cinematic sex symbol,
adored by legions of women and envied by just as many men.
But it was his untimely death at age 31 that made him a legend.*

Born in Italy to an Italian father and French mother in 1895,
Rodolfo Alfonso Raffaello Piero Filiberto Guglielmi di
Valentina d'Antonguolla emigrated to New York when he
was 18. He found work first as a gardener and waiter, then as a taxi
dancer (a professional dance partner who's paid by the dance). He
joined a touring operetta company that disbanded in Utah, so he
continued on to San Francisco, where he took up dancing again.
Next stop Hollywood, on the advice of a friend. He shortened his
name to Rudolph Valentino and started to land a few extra and bit
parts in silent films, usually as a shifty-eyed villain.

A STAR IS BORN
Valentino's big chance came in 1921, when a screenwriter (female,
of course) convinced the studio to star him in the upcoming *Four
Horseman of the Apocalypse*. Director Rex Ingram added a tango
scene for Valentino—and talk about being catapulted into stardom. The movie was hugely successful, as was its new star. But it
was *The Sheik*, released later that year, that turned the 26-year-old
movie star into a phenomenon.

Male audiences snickered at his acting and found his character
effeminate. But tell that to the ladies: showings of the film—in
which a passionate Valentino plays an Arab chieftain who carries
off a young British heiress to be ravished in his tent—had the
females in the audience fainting in the aisles. Women fell in love
with him because, as one movie magazine put it, "He does not look
like your husband. He is not in the least like your brother. He does
not resemble the man your mother thinks you ought to marry." He
was dangerous, he was intense, he was exotic, and the ladies couldn't
get enough of him.

Uma Thurman originally turned down the role of Mia in *Pulp Fiction* (1994).

Five years later, Valentino was in Manhattan to promote *The Son of the Sheik* (his fourteenth film), when he collapsed on the sidewalk. Rushed to the hospital, he died after surgery for a perforated gastric ulcer. He was only 31.

POSTMORTEM
Valentino's death caused mass hysteria: two women attempted suicide outside the hospital, and at least two others succeeded in killing themselves. Rumors abounded that a jealous mistress (or cuckolded husband) had killed him, or that he wasn't really dead. Riots broke out as 100,000 fans flocked to the New York funeral home to view his body. Actress Pola Negri, who swore she'd been engaged to Valentino and who'd sent a floral arrangement of 4,000 red roses, collapsed in hysteria while hovering over his coffin. Thousands of people across the country lined the railroad tracks to pay homage as a train carried Valentino's body to its final resting place in Hollywood.

THE LEGEND
The year after Valentino's death, a mysterious veiled lady in black began appearing every August 23 at 12:10 p.m., the date and time of Valentino's death, to lay red roses at his crypt in the Hollywood Forever Cemetery. Several women confessed to being the lady in black—including Pola Negri, who died in 1987, and a terminally ill woman whom Valentino had visited in the hospital; they supposedly made a pact that the grave of the first to die would be visited by the other every year. This woman claimed to have passed on the honor to her daughter. Today, some 80 years after his death, a well-meaning group gathers at the cemetery to carry on the tradition.

* * *

"Women are not in love with me but with the picture of me on the screen. I am merely the canvas on which women paint their dreams."

—Rudolph Valentino

Director Quentin Tarantino changed her mind by reading the script to her over the phone.

GETTING SERIES-OUS

People like to complain that Hollywood just recycles old ideas and characters with movie series and sequels. But here's a little secret: the film series of yesteryear, which—if they had numbered them that way—would have reached into the 10s, 20s . . . and even the 30s. Once you've had a look at these series, you might never look at sequels the same way again.

44 FILMS: CHARLIE CHAN
The cunning Chinese detective Charlie Chan began as the literary creation of author Earl Derr Biggers. But the character's lasting fame came from a series of movies that began with 1931's *Charlie Chan Carries On* (a title that sounds like it belongs on a sequel— possibly because it was adapted from the fifth Charlie Chan book). Chan was played by actor Warner Oland, who was Swedish, for 16 films (through 1937's *Charlie Chan at Monte Carlo*). After Oland's death in 1938, Sidney Toler (a white man from Missouri) took the role through another 11 films. When he died in 1947, Roland Winters (another white guy, from Boston) took over through the final film in the series, 1949's *The Sky Dragon*. By that time the film series had been transferred from Twentieth Century Fox to the low-budget studio Monogram Pictures, and it began looking a bit frayed around the edges.

Interestingly, the first time a Chinese actor actually played Charlie Chan was in the 1970s when Keye Luke (who had appeared in several Charlie Chan movies as #1 Son, Lee Chan) voiced the character for a Saturday morning cartoon show.

28 FILMS: BLONDIE
This series was based on Chic Young's popular comic strip of the same name—the one that's still running in newspapers today (more than 30 years after Young himself expired). The series began in 1938 with *Blondie* and would last through 1950's *Beware of Blondie*. During those dozen years and 28 films, most of the cast remained the same, with Penny Singleton as Blondie and Arthur Lake as Dagwood. Even Daisy was played by the same canine for the entire run. After the series ended, Lake would reprise his role as Dagwood in a 1957 television series, which lasted only a single season.

James Earl Jones made his film debut in *Dr. Strangelove* (1964) as "Lt. Lothar Zogg."

21 FILMS: JAMES BOND
The Bond series of spy films has the distinction of being both the longest-running film series in Hollywood—going strong for more than 40 years now, dating back to 1962's *Dr. No*—and the highest number of films in a series still in production—*Casino Royale*, scheduled for 2006, will be the twenty-first (not to be confused with the 1967 film of the same name, which was a spoof of the popular Bond series). Sean Connery was the first, and for many the definitive James Bond; few know that Bond author Ian Fleming originally chose Roger Moore for the role but he couldn't sign on because he was busy with the TV series *The Saint*. After George Lazenby took a crack at the role, Moore inherited the part, followed by Timothy Dalton, Pierce Brosnan, and Daniel Craig.

15 FILMS: THE ANDY HARDY SERIES
Diminutive actor Mickey Rooney was already a popular child film star (having starred in a long-running comedy-short series as Mickey McGuire) when, at age 17, he was cast as the spunky Andy Hardy in 1937's *A Family Affair*. The role and Rooney were made for each other, and Rooney became so popular he was awarded a special juvenile Oscar in 1938. Thirteen other Andy Hardy films would follow, through 1947—Judy Garland appeared in two, and Esther Williams made her studio debut in another. More than a decade after 1946's *Love Laughs at Andy Hardy*, MGM resurrected the character in *Andy Hardy Comes Home* (with Rooney as a grown-up Hardy) to see if the series could be restarted. It couldn't.

14 FILMS: SHERLOCK HOLMES
There have been Sherlock Holmes films almost as long as there have been films (his first confirmed appearance on film was in 1900). But the definitive screen Holmes is the one portrayed by British actor Basil Rathbone, who played Holmes in a series of movies from 1939 to 1946. He first appeared as the character in 1939's *The Hound of the Baskervilles*, followed shortly thereafter by *The Adventures of Sherlock Holmes*. Those two films had Holmes in his traditional Victorian setting, but beginning with 1942's *Sherlock Holmes and the Voice of Terror*, Rathbone's Holmes was transported to contemporary times, to battle Nazis and other 20th-century thugs. In all, Rathbone played Holmes 14 times in the film series, ending with 1946's *Dressed to Kill*. He then went on to play the

sleuth in more than 200 radio performances, one of which was rumored to have been sampled in Disney's 1986 animated film tribute to Holmes, *The Great Mouse Detective*—whose hero, Basil, was named after the actor.

* * *

DEAD MEN WEAR NOIR

Clips from these movies were seamlessly edited into Steve Martin/ Carl Reiner's 1982 private eye spoof *Dead Men Don't Wear Plaid*:

Johnny Eager (1941)

Suspicion (1941)

This Gun for Hire (1942)

The Glass Key (1942)

Double Indemnity (1944)

The Lost Weekend (1945)

Deception (1946)

Humoresque (1946)

The Big Sleep (1946)

The Killers (1946)

Notorious (1946)

The Postman Always Rings Twice (1946)

Dark Passage (1947)

I Walk Alone (1947)

Sorry, Wrong Number (1948)

The Bribe (1949)

White Heat (1949)

In a Lonely Place (1950)

EVEN MORE "I SPY" AT THE MOVIES

*Here are a few more of the little in-jokes and gags that
moviemakers throw into films for their own amusement.
The info comes from* Reel Gags, *by Bill Givens, and*
Film and Television In-Jokes, *by Bill van Heerden.*

THE BLUES BROTHERS (1980)
I Spy . . . Steven Spielberg
Where to Find Him: He plays the Cook County small-claims
clerk. (Note: Spielberg returned the favor to co-star Dan Aykroyd
by giving him a cameo role in *Indiana Jones and the Temple of
Doom.* He played the English ticket agent at the airport.)

MAVERICK (1994)
I Spy . . . Actor Danny Glover
Where to Find Him: Glover, who appeared with *Maverick* star Mel
Gibson in the *Lethal Weapon* series, shows up in a cameo as a bank
robber. He and Gibson seem to recognize each other, then shake
their heads and say, "Nah." Clover even uses his line from the
Lethal Weapon films, "I'm too old for this s***."

RESERVOIR DOGS (1992)
I Spy . . . A real-life act of revenge
Where to Find It: The scene in which actor Tim Roth shoots a
woman. The actress was his dialogue coach, who had apparently
made life difficult for him during the filming. He insisted that she
be cast in the role so he could "shoot" her.

TWISTER (1996)
I Spy . . . A tribute to Stanley Kubrick (Jan de Bont, *Twister's*
director, is a big Kubrick fan)
Where to Find It: In the characters' names; one is Stanley,
another is called Kubrick. And when a drive-in theater is hit by a
twister, the movie playing onscreen is Kubrick's *The Shining.*

BACK TO THE FUTURE (1985)
I Spy . . . A nod to "The Rocky and Bullwinkle Show"
Where to Find It: The scene in which Michael J. Fox crashes into the farmer's barn. The farmer's name is Peabody; his son is Sherman. Peabody and Sherman were the brilliant time-traveling dog and his boy in the Jay Ward cartoon show.

WHEN HARRY MET SALLY . . . (1989)
I Spy . . . Estelle Reiner, director Rob Reiner's mother
Where to Find Her: She's the woman who tells the waiter: "I'll have what she's having," when Meg Ryan fakes an orgasm in a restaurant.

TRADING PLACES (1983), TWILIGHT ZONE—THE MOVIE (1983), COMING TO AMERICA (1988), and other films directed by John Landis
I Spy . . . The phrase "See You Next Wednesday"
Where to Find It: Landis says it was the title of his first screenplay and he always tries get it into a film somewhere. In *Trading Places* and *Coming to America*, for example, it's on a subway poster. In *The Blues Brothers*, it's on a billboard. In *The Stupids*, it's on the back of a bus. In *Twilight Zone*, someone says it aloud . . . in German.

RAIN MAN (1988)
I Spy . . . A reference to Dustin Hoffman's family
Where to Find It: When Hoffman recites names from the phone book. Two of them—Marsha and William Gottsegen—are his real-life in-laws.

NATIONAL LAMPOON'S ANIMAL HOUSE (1978)
I Spy . . . A way to get into Universal Studios free
Where to Find It: In the final credits, it says "Ask for Babs"— referring to a character in the film who supposedly became a tour guide there. For many years, if someone really did ask for Babs, they'd get free or discounted admission to the tour. Bad news: Universal doesn't honor the promotion anymore.

Luke Skywalker in *Star Wars* (1977) was originally written as a girl.

RECORD SETTING

Sometimes they just don't have awards for what Hollywood does best. In honor of the biggest, the smallest, the most explosive, and the most expensive, here are a few feats that deserve a little recognition.

MOST BAD WORDS USED IN A MOVIE

Clocking in at 81 minutes, *South Park: Bigger Longer and Uncut* (1999) manages to pack in 399 curse words and 128 offensive gestures.

MOST ACTING APPEARANCES IN THE MOVIES

John Wayne still holds the record for most leading roles, starring in 142 movies. But the person with the most performances is Mel Blanc, with 709 films.

HIGHEST MOVIE STUNT JUMP WITHOUT A PARACHUTE

A. J. Bakunas (standing in for Burt Reynolds) in the 1978 film *Hooper* jumped off a 232-foot-tall building. He landed safely on an air mattress and broke nothing but the world record. (Ironically, Reynolds was playing a stuntman in the movie.)

LONGEST LEAP IN AN OCCUPIED CAR

Stunt driver Gary Davis drove a stripped-down Plymouth in *Smokey and the Bandit II* (1980). The car raced up a ramp at 80 mph and sailed through the air for 163 feet before landing safely.

MOST EXPENSIVE EXPLOSIONS

The final explosion sequence in the film *Pearl Harbor* (2001) destroyed six ships (each measured between 400 and 600 feet long). The explosions took 30 days to rig and required 700 sticks of dynamite, 2,000 feet of cord, and 4,000 gallons of gasoline. The price tag? $5.5 million.

MOST EXPENSIVE STUNT

Performed at an altitude of 15,000 feet, stuntman Simon Crane jumped between two jet planes in *Cliffhanger* (1993). Because it was so dangerous, the stunt could be performed only once and cost $1 million. Sylvester Stallone, the film's star, was so determined to have the stunt performed that he offered to reduce his salary by $1 million to pay for it.

BIGGEST BOX OFFICE EARNER

Harrison Ford: he's been in three *Star Wars* movies, three *Indiana Jones* movies, and seven more films that made $200 million each. When you add it all up, Ford has appeared in more than 25 films that generated total box office earnings of $3,010,111,472.

SHORTEST ACTOR TO APPEAR IN A MOVIE

At 2 feet 8 inches, Verne Troyer (best known as Mini-Me in the *Austin Powers* movies) first broke into movies as a stunt double . . . for a nine-month-old baby in *Baby's Day Out* (1994).

TALLEST ACTOR TO APPEAR IN A MOVIE

Towering at 7 feet 2 inches, Richard Kiel found fame as Jaws, the steel-toothed henchman in *The Spy Who Loved Me* (1977) and *Moonraker* (1979). Before he became an actor, he sold cemetery plots and worked as a nightclub bouncer.

TALLEST TO PLAY COUNT DRACULA

British actor Christopher Lee (6 feet 5 inches) is the tallest man to ever play the bloodsucker. He's also the tallest person to play Frankenstein's monster.

* * *

THE FIRST GANGSTER MOVIE

In 1912 the very first gangster movie opened. Directed by D. W. Griffith and co-written by Anita Loos, *The Musketeers of Pig Alley* were led by the Snapper Kid, whose gang robbed the honest citizens of a New York tenement.

SEEN AROUND HOLLYWOOD

*A close-up on places around town that have
been the settings for real-life Hollywood events.*

The Lasky-DeMille Barn, 2100 North Highland Avenue
Now all spiffed up and renamed the Hollywood Heritage Museum,
this small frame building was a barn that Cecil B. DeMille rented
for $250 a month with his partners, producers Sam Goldwyn and
Jesse Lasky. It served as the very first film studio in Hollywood and
in it DeMille filmed his first movie, 1913's *The Squaw Man* (which
was also the first feature-length movie shot in Hollywood). It now
houses a museum devoted to silent films.

The Hollywood Roosevelt Hotel, 7000 Hollywood Boulevard
It's said that Shirley Temple got her first tap-dancing lesson from
Bill "Bojangles" Robinson on the hotel's tile staircase. David Niven
lived in the servants' quarters when he first came to Hollywood,
Mary Martin performed at the hotel's nightclub for $35 a week,
and Marilyn Monroe posed on the diving board for an ad for sun-
tan lotion. The hotel's Blossom Room was the site of the very first
Academy Awards banquet on May 16, 1929.

The Hollywood Bowl, 2301 North Highland Avenue
"The Bowl" was designed by Lloyd Wright (son of Frank Lloyd
Wright), and opened for business in July 1922. Among the listed
box holders for the 1928 season were: C. Chaplin (#117), Mr.
and Mrs. Cecil B. De Mille (#641), and Fay Wray (#861).
Seating just under 18,000, the Bowl is the largest natural
amphitheater in the U.S. Headliners over the years have
included Abbott and Costello, Simon and Garfunkel, Margot
Fonteyn and Rudolph Nureyev, and the Beatles, who were the
first rock-and-roll band to perform there.

Actress Mia Farrow is the biological or adoptive mother of 15 children.

The Polo Lounge at the Beverly Hills Hotel, 9641 Sunset Boulevard

Anyone who is anyone has dined at the Polo Lounge. Legend has it that the Lounge was so-named because Will Rogers and his movie star friends Douglas Fairbanks and Spencer Tracy used to cool off there after a weekend polo game up at Rogers's ranch. Now you'd be more likely to see Nicole Kidman or Tom Cruise—but not together, of course. The Lounge has been the scene of countless movie and studio deals (like when Paramount was bought out by Gulf & Western) and parties (Elton John's 55th birthday). Today the hotel is owned by the Sultan of Brunei.

The Cocoanut Grove at the Ambassador Hotel, 3400 Wilshire Boulevard

The hotel's Cocoanut Grove nightclub was *the* place to party for three decades in Hollywood. Bing Crosby was discovered at the Grove, Joan Crawford won scads of the club's dance contests, and the décor included palm trees from the set of Rudolph Valentino's *The Sheik*. In 1968 the hotel was the site of an American tragedy, when Bobby Kennedy was assassinated in the hotel's pantry.

The Ambassador has been closed since 1989, but the building still stands—for now. In October 2001 the Los Angeles Unified School District announced plans to buy the property. Despite protests by preservationists, most of the hotel will be demolished—but at this time the plan is to make the Cocoanut Grove into a school auditorium.

The Church of the Good Shepherd, 505 N. Bedford Drive

This local parish church of the stars stands just around the corner from Rodeo Drive. Rudolph Valentino and Bing Crosby were regulars at Sunday mass, and Elizabeth Taylor (at age 17) was married here for the first time while 3,000 fans crowded the street outside. But it's the funerals, not the weddings, that put Good Shepherd on the map of the stars: Valentino, Gary Cooper, Rita Hayworth, Alfred Hitchcock, Danny Thomas, Carmen Miranda, and Frank Sinatra all took their last bow at the church.

Chateau Marmont, 8221 Sunset Boulevard

The castlelike hotel has served as the place to be if you don't want anyone but insiders to know where you are. James Dean and

---

Will Ferrell's father was a longtime keyboard player for the Righteous Brothers.

Natalie Wood first met at the Marmont at a script rehearsal of *Rebel Without a Cause*. When actor Montgomery Clift was almost killed in a 1956 auto accident near her home, Elizabeth Taylor leased the penthouse as a place for him to recuperate. But it hasn't been all quiet on the Marmont front. The hotel has been the site of many a wild party—Jim Morrison once dangled from a balcony here. And it is also the site of a well-known tragedy—John Belushi died here in 1982 of a drug overdose.

The Hollywood Canteen, 1006 Seward Street
The Hollywood Canteen was founded in 1942 by Bette Davis and John Garfield, modeled after New York's Stage Door Canteen. Like the original, it served as a home away from home for World War II servicemen. Plenty of Hollywood's biggest names jitterbugged with the GI's while Judy Garland sang, Mickey Rooney played the drums, and Rosalind Russell washed the dishes. It inspired the 1944 movie *Hollywood Canteen*, starring Davis, Garfield, and a star-studded cast, the proceeds of which went to the local USO. Sixty years later, the Hollywood Canteen is still open for business, serving a mostly Italian menu amid 1940s memorabilia.

Shrine Auditorium, 649 W. Jefferson Boulevard
Where the stars appear in bulk. Built in 1906 and rebuilt in 1920 after a fire, the Shrine is the largest theater in all of North America, and the sheer size of it (6,300 seats) is what has made it one of the preferred venues for Hollywood's most important awards shows. The auditorium hosted the Academy Awards show on and off since 1947, usually alternating with the Music Center at the Dorothy Chandler Pavilion (which has a paltry 2,500 seats).

* * *

THE FIRST DRIVE-IN
Inventor Richard Hollingshead, opened the first American drive-in movie theater in Camden, New Jersey, on June 6, 1933. Four hundred cars could fit on the 10-acre lot. By the mid-1950s there were more than 4,000 drive-ins in the United States. Today there are only about 400 left.

Actress Jodie Foster has two children but has never publicly identified the father(s).

DIRECTORS' SIGNATURES

From Hollywood's earliest days, directors have sought to leave
their individual marks on their films. Some have devised
small signatures that identify a film as their work.

T he French have a word for it: *auteur* (author). It's the name for a theory of filmmaking—the idea that a film director is like a book's author and is responsible for a film's vision, form, and content. Many directors do make films that are easily recognizable as theirs, based on the themes and style that they use in their movies. But there are also small signature touches that some directors add to their films that, if you recognize them, increase the enjoyment of these movies.

SIGNATURE HITCHCOCK
Probably the most well known of all director signatures—it's the director himself! With his unmistakable profile, Alfred Hitchcock appears in a cameo in 37 out of 54 of his films. To help you out, we've sniffed out Hitchcock sightings in some of his best-known films.

Psycho: About four minutes into the film, Marion (Janet Leigh) returns to her office. You can glimpse Hitchcock, wearing a cowboy hat, through the window. Don't blink or you'll miss him—he's only on-screen for a few seconds.

Rear Window: About 30 minutes into the film, Hitchcock is winding a clock in the songwriter's apartment.

Dial M for Murder: This is one of Sir Alfred's trickier cameos. About 13 minutes into the film, a class reunion photo is shown. That's him on the left of the picture.

Strangers on a Train: Right at the start of the movie, Hitchcock can be seen boarding the train, carrying a double bass.

Lifeboat: Hitchcock appears briefly as the "Before" and "After" pictures in a newspaper ad for a weight-loss program. Around the time of this movie's filming, Hitchcock had crash dieted and dropped 100 pounds.

SIGNATURE CAPRA

Frank Capra had a pet raven named Jimmy and found a place for him in his movies, starting with *You Can't Take It With You* (1938). In the heartwarming Christmas classic, *It's a Wonderful Life* (1946), Jimmy the raven sits on Uncle Billy's desk in the Bailey Building and Loan. (Billy was played by Thomas Mitchell.)

SIGNATURE FRANCIS FORD COPPOLA

Francis Ford Coppola has made many pictures, but *The Godfather* trilogy is probably the most well known. In all the *Godfather* movies, oranges (the fruit, and also the color) play a significant role: they signify death and violence. There is a kind of orange, called a blood orange, which was developed in Sicily, the island from which the movies' family emigrated. Coppola described the orange as "a symbol of foreboding and death, as well as memories— good and bad—from the old country." For instance, just before he is shot in the first film, Don Corleone buys two oranges. When he falls to the ground, he overturns a basket of the fruit, and we see them roll on the ground.

There is a bowl of oranges on the table when Tom Hagen eats dinner with Jack Woltz, the Hollywood director who refuses to cast Corleone crony Johnny Fontane in his film. It didn't mean death for Woltz, but for his prized racehorse, Khartoum. At the big pow-wow held by the Five Families, there are bowls of oranges in front of Corleone, Tattaglia, and Barzini—all three men are dead by the end of the film.

And speaking of Corleone's death, what does he have in his mouth as he staggers among the tomato plants in his death throes? Yup—he's got an orange wedge in front of his teeth, intended to amuse his grandson (even though he winds up scaring the boy). This scene, as it happens, was ad-libbed by Marlon Brando. The boy playing his grandson was having difficulty with the scene, so Brando played a trick he liked to play with his own grandchildren. The fright registering on the child's face was not acting: he was not expecting the way Brando looked, and it startled him.

SIGNATURE TARANTINO
Quentin Tarantino is best known for violent films with a healthy dose of black humor. And there are several signatures to watch for: Each movie contains a "trunk shot" during which the camera is set deep in the trunk of a car so it can capture the actors as they lean in and over it. Each also has an ad for Red Apple cigarettes (a fictional brand). Tarantino almost always has one or more of his characters barefoot—it's Uma Thurman in *Pulp Fiction* and the *Kill Bill* movies.

SIGNATURE SCORSESE
Taking a leaf from Alfred Hitchcock's book, Martin Scorsese appears in cameos in almost all his films. Going Hitchcock one better, Scorsese also puts many members of his family in small roles.

Cape Fear: Scorsese's mother plays a customer at the fruit stand.

The Color of Money: Scorsese is walking a dog in the casino scene. The dog was actually the director's dog and received a credit as Dog Walkby.

Goodfellas: Scorsese's mother plays Tommy's mother. The director let her ad-lib her entire scene. His father plays the prisoner who put too many onions in the "gravy" (tomato sauce).

Raging Bull: Scorsese can be seen asking Jack to go onstage. Also in *Raging Bull*, Scorsese's father is part of a mob at the Copa nightclub.

Taxi Driver: Scorsese is sitting in the background of the campaign headquarters as Cybill Shepherd walks in. He also plays the irate husband in the taxi.

* * *

KICKING THE WINE AND ROSES
Director Blake Edwards (*The Pink Panther*) was so haunted by the story behind *The Days of Wine and Roses*, which he directed in 1962, that he went into recovery one month after the movie wrapped and has stayed clean and sober ever since.

Andy Garcia proposed to his wife, Maria (called Marvi), on the first night he met her.

DARK SIDE OF THE RAINBOW

*When we think of the 1939 classic The Wizard of Oz,
usually we start humming "Somewhere Over the Rainbow,"
or "Ding-Dong! The Witch Is Dead." But maybe we could
also hum "Money" and "Brain Damage" by Pink Floyd. Why?
Because some say their album, Dark Side of the Moon
(1973), was recorded as an alternate soundtrack for the film.*

D id Pink Floyd record *Dark Side of the Moon* to be played
along with the MGM musical *The Wizard of Oz?* Of course,
the similarities between the two are obvious: one's about
life, death, work, war, time, and insanity, and the other is about
witches, wizards, Munchkins, a talking scarecrow, and Kansas.
Okay, maybe the subject matter isn't so similar. But fans of "Dark
Side of the Rainbow," as the conglomeration is called, insist that
the synchronicities between the album and the movie are too
strong to be a coincidence.

THE RUMOR MILL
No one's quite sure how this rumor got started: there were Web
sites dedicated to the Dark Side of the Rainbow as early as 1994.
George Taylor Morris, a DJ at WZLX, a classic rock station in
Boston, mentioned Dark Side of the Rainbow on his show in the
spring of 1997. "The phones just blew off the wall," he says. "That
first weekend you couldn't get a copy of *The Wizard of Oz* anywhere in Boston." The Dark Side of the Rainbow was out of the
closet; soon the mainstream press was picking up the story. Even
MTV brought on the members of the band to address the rumor
that they had written the album to accompany the movie.

SEE FOR YOURSELF
What great mysteries are revealed by listening to Pink Floyd while
watching Judy Garland? To find out, just pop *The Dark Side of the
Moon* into your CD player and *The Wizard of Oz* into your VCR or
DVD player. Turn the TV sound way down, the stereo way up, and

start the movie. When the MGM lion roars for the third time at the beginning of *The Wizard of Oz*, start the album. You'll know you've done it correctly when transition from Track 1a ("Speak to Me") to Track 1b ("Breathe") occurs just as the words Produced by Mervyn LeRoy appears on the screen. Then sit back, relax, and look for the synchronicities.

THE EVIDENCE

What You See	What You Hear
Dorothy balances on a fence at the farm.	"Balanced on the biggest wave" is sung from the song "Breathe."
Dorothy falls into the pigsty, and the panicked farmhands rush to save her.	As "Breathe" ends, the frenetic "On the Run" starts.
Miss Gulch, the villain, makes her first appearance on screen on her bicycle.	Jarring alarms and clanging bells sound as "Time" begins.
Dorothy runs away from home.	"No one told you when to run . . ." is sung.
The Tornado: 1. The tornado sways on the horizon. 2. Dorothy frantically tries to enter the cellar and then takes refuge in the house. 3. Dorothy is knocked out by a flying door and falls on the bed.	"The Great Gig in the Sky" 1. A slide guitar swells along with the tornado. 2. Wailing vocals sound anxious and frightened. 3. The vocals calm and become gentle as Dorothy falls.
Dorothy opens the farmhouse door to reveal brightly colored Munchkinland.	The cash register "cha-ching" starts "Money."
The black-clad Wicked Witch of the West appears in Munchkinland.	The words "black, black, black" are sung in "Us and Them."

Richard Gere's first three big film roles were all turned down by John Travolta.

The Wicked Witch of the West looks at the Wicked Witch of the East's remains.

The lyrics "and who knows which is which" (witch is witch?) from "Us and Them" are sung.

The scarecrow begins dancing and singing "If I Only Had a Brain."

"The lunatic is on the grass" from the song "Brain Damage" is sung.

Dorothy presses her ear to the Tin Man's chest.

A pulsating heartbeat finishes the album.

But for every amazing coincidence there are long stretches of unrelated sounds and images. Listening to chaotic "On the Run" while Dorothy plaintively mouths the words "Somewhere Over the Rainbow," is just one of the juxtapositions that doesn't really line up.

The album itself lasts only 43 minutes, while the film is about an hour and 45 minutes long. Fans have different theories as to what to do after *Dark Side* has finished its first run-through. There are those that say the authentic Dark Side of the Rainbow experience ends with the first play through. Others say that the way to go is to put *Dark Side of the Moon* on repeat and listen to it two and a half more times through the rest of the movie. And still others think other Floyd albums, like *Meddle* and *Wish You Were Here*, should be played next.

THE STRAIGHT POOP

So did Pink Floyd intentionally create a new soundtrack for Oz? EMI-Capitol, the record company that distributes the album, isn't fighting the rumor—probably because in the weeks following the story's publication, sales of *Dark Side of the Moon* doubled. Band member Roger Waters, the main creative force behind the album, has also stayed silent on the subject. Other band members have piped up, however. Guitarist David Gilmour said that he tried the synch himself but it didn't seem to work. Alan Parsons, the producer, pointed out that there was no way the band could have written the album for the movie. In 1972, when most of the recording was completed, they didn't have the technology to play the movie in the studio. Nick Mason, the band's drummer, quipped, "It's absolute nonsense, it has nothing to do with *The Wizard of Oz*. It was all based on *The Sound of Music*."

They were *Days of Heaven*, *American Gigolo*, and *An Officer and a Gentleman*.

NOTHING NEW UNDER THE SUN, PART 2

The question all critics must ask themselves when reviewing a remake of an earlier movie is, "Was this remake really necessary?" More often than not, the answer is negative. Here are five films that the Hollywood "powers that be" should have thought twice about remaking. Continued from page 149.

PSYCHO (1998)
Remake of: Psycho (1960)
Many critics consider Alfred Hitchcock's 1960 film, *Psycho*, the perfect example of a suspenseful slasher film. So if it is perfect, why did director Gus Van Sant feel it needed to be remade in 1998? And then why did he proceed to use Hitchcock's exact script, camera angles, and the same musical score? That makes it shot-for-shot the same movie . . . but then again, strangely, it's not exactly the same. Not anywhere close.

One major difference is that the 1998 version is in color, and the original was shot in black-and-white. Many critics, however, feel that color only detracts from the overall visual impact of the cinematography. Knowing that protagonist Marion Crane's dress is orange (critic Roger Ebert was reminded of his grandmother's wing chair) didn't add much to the story.

Another difference (and, we suspect, the chief reason for remaking the movie) is that Hollywood's strict censorship code was no longer in effect. Though Hitchcock could only suggest the sexual overtones of his *Psycho*, Van Sant was free to spell them out explicitly. The remake shows a lot more of Marion's flesh than was possible in the original film, and nothing is left to the imagination concerning the nature of Norman Bates's interest in Marion. But, ironically, the suspense is dulled by the decision to spell everything out—Bates's hidden sexual attraction is creepier when left to the viewer's imagination. The changes that Van Sant did make seem to drain much of the tension from the film, leading critics to call it "a lot less scary," "banal," and "bland."

Heather Graham on herself: "I see myself as this nerdy geek that people find attractive."

PLANET OF THE APES (2001)
Remake of: *Planet of the Apes* (1968)

Critics have used words such as "plodding" and "manipulative" to characterize this remake. David Edelstein of *Slate* calls it a "monkey see old hit, monkey do remake."

Imagine a planet where evolution has run amok and primates are the masters while humans are slaves. That is the basic concept of the *Planet of the Apes* franchise. The original 1968 film spawned four sequels in the 1970s and became a phenomenon as one of the first modern blockbuster science fiction/action-adventure series. In the original film, Charlton Heston's character crash-lands on a strange planet ruled by simians. They have developed language and culture, while mute humans are hunted down to the point of extinction. The stage is set for a clash of the civilizations. The original film had much to say—and without much subtlety—about social issues of the day: racism, acceptance, and the horrors of war.

The 2001 remake (or "re-imagining," as director Tim Burton insists) looks great, with spectacular visual effects and expressive ape makeup, but there are big problems with the screenplay and the acting that can't be overlooked. Scriptwriters made changes from the original movie—including its trademark ending (don't worry, we won't give it away)—that befuddled viewers. Instead of dealing with issues of race and discrimination, the 2001 version is largely composed of interminable chase scenes and chaotic fight sequences. Mark Wahlberg plays the lead who falls through a time-space warp and crash-lands on an ape-ruled planet. But Wahlberg is wooden and stiff, making it difficult to empathize with his character: one critic described the performance as "so square that he makes Charlton Heston . . . seem like Jack Kerouac."

THE TRUTH ABOUT CHARLIE (2002)
Remake of: *Charade* (1963)

Charade is considered one of the best films of all time by the Internet Movie Database. It is a gem of a movie starring a resplendent Audrey Hepburn as Regina Lampert, the soon-to-be-divorced wife of a secretive man who, early in the film, turns up dead. Revelations follow in rapid succession, as Hepburn learns that her husband was really a thief who absconded with the large spoils of his illegal activities. Furthermore, she is being pursued by a trio of his double-crossed accomplices. They believe that they are entitled to the money and that Hepburn must have it in her possession. She is befriended by Peter Joshua (Cary Grant), a mysterious stranger, whose motivation and background are also suspect. As romantic sparks fly between the two (even though, at 59, Grant was 25 years older than his costar), the mystery and adventure thicken.

Again, it's not altogether clear why any director—including Oscar-winner Jonathan Demme (*Silence of the Lambs*)—would decide to update such a classic and universally acclaimed film. One critic described *The Truth About Charlie* as "one bad idea after another." Critics gave Thandie Newton relatively high marks for her performance in the Audrey Hepburn role. But Mark Wahlberg in Cary Grant's role (whose name was inexplicably changed from Peter Joshua to Joshua Peters) was called "all wrong" and dubbed "no Cary Grant." The chemistry between the two leads, so apparent in the original, was sorely lacking in the remake. As film critic Paul Newman wrote, "With Walhberg and Newton, instead of surging, hot hormones, you get slow-dripping, lukewarm tap water." (We promise, we're not picking on Mark Wahlberg, but he should think about reconsidering the next time he's offered a part in a remake!)

THE LONGEST YARD (2005)
Remake of: *The Longest Yard* (1974)

The New York Times called *The Longest Yard* "the crummy remake of the 1974 film of the same title." That pretty much says it all! In this remake Adam Sandler plays former NFL quarterback Paul "Wrecking" Crewe, who finds himself in prison for a number of infractions. There he becomes a pawn in the scheming prison warden's efforts to field a championship team of prison guards. In the grand tradition of sports-themed movies, Crewe assembles a motley crew of inmates and whips them into shape to take on the warden's team of sadistic guards. He is assisted by Chris Rock as Caretaker, his right-hand man, and Burt Reynolds (who played Paul Crewe in the original film) as the team's coach.

Although critics had mostly high praise for the original film, and Reynolds's performance in particular, they almost unanimously panned the remake. Adam Sandler just didn't physically resemble anybody's idea of a professional quarterback. Whereas Burt Reynolds, once a pro prospect himself, had the physique, the

Elizabeth Taylor and Sophia Loren have cameos as extras in *Quo Vadis* (1951).

charm, and the gravitas to portray a washed-up athlete seeking redemption, Sandler just seems, well, silly by comparison. If sports movies are your thing, rent the original.

THE TEXAS CHAINSAW MASSACRE (2003)
Remake of: *The Chain Saw Massacre* (1974)
We've saved the *worst* for last!

OK, so you like horror flicks. You love the ones where a bunch of teenagers find themselves trapped somewhere, chased by an evil force, and picked off one by one, until the last one left standing must escape to warn the rest of civilization. Chances are you've seen the original *Texas Chain Saw Massacre*, where a group of teenagers on their way to visit a grave site find themselves in a claustrophobic house inhabited by a deranged family. Predictably, mayhem ensues—with chain saws (but of course) whirring, assorted cutlery flying, and cannibalism thrown in for good measure. This movie was so terrifying that it was banned from British theaters for 25 years.

As chaotic as the original sounds, the first *Chain Saw* is restrained when compared to the remake. Some of the horror in the earlier film was implied, not shown. The remake shows no such self-discipline and revels in lots and lots of gore. And then some more gore. It ends up having a mind-numbing rather than a horrifying effect. The story line of the remake is largely the same, which also aroused much criticism; one critic panned it as "so utterly unimaginative it doesn't even count as *hommage*; it's just a smudgy copy of a still chilling original."

Movie critic Roger Ebert called the 2003 remake, "a contemptible film: vile, ugly and brutal. There is not a shred of a reason to see it." Ouch. As if that weren't devastating enough, he added, "Don't let this movie kill 98 minutes of your life." Double ouch.

Now, armed with Uncle John's suggestions and warnings, you know a few movies to avoid on your next trip to the video store.

Martin Scorsese plays Robert De Niro's homicidal passenger in *Taxi Driver* (1976).

TAGLINES OF TERROR

The goal of the Hollywood marketing machine is to put viewers in seats, and the tagline is one of its favorite tools. It would be no exaggeration to say that horror movies have some of the most effective taglines ever written. But can you match the movie with the slogan? Take our quiz and then check page 485 for the answers.

THE MOVIES

A. *Dracula* (1931)

B. *Frankenstein* (1931)

C. *The Mummy* (1932)

D. *The Invisible Man* (1933)

E. *Bride of Frankenstein* (1935)

F. *Cat People* (1942)

G. *House of Wax* (1953)

H. *The Blob* (1958)

I. *House on Haunted Hill* (1959)

J. *Blacula* (1972)

K. *Halloween* (1978)

L. *Prom Night* (1980)

M. *Child's Play* (1988)

N. *Scream* (1996)

THE LINES

1. "It crawls . . . It creeps . . . It eats you alive!"
2. "The Trick is to Stay Alive"
3. "It Comes to Life!"
4. "The Monster Demands a Mate!"
5. "If you're not back by midnight . . . you won't be coming home"
6. "Kiss Me and I'll Claw You to Death."
7. "You've never been scared until you've been scared in 3-D."
8. "The story of the strangest passion the world has ever known."
9. "Catch Me If You Can!"
10. "His bite was outta sight!"
11. "The Man Who Made a Monster"
12. "Consult your doctor! Bring your seat belts!"
13. "You'll only wish it was make-believe"
14. "Someone has taken their love of scary movies one step too far."

"I need him like the axe needs the turkey."

VARIETY: THE SPICE OF LIFE

Every producer, wannabe actor, starving screenwriter, and each
agent—everyone who's anyone in show business—reads Variety.
It's the magazine that covers the entertainment industry from the
inside: who's in charge, who's making deals, what's making money,
and what's not. And it's required reading for those in the biz.

BROADWAY BABY
Variety got its start covering the Great White Way
(Broadway) in New York City in the 1900s. Publisher Simon
"Sime" Silverman came from a well-to-do family (his father was a
banker), and adored Broadway and vaudeville, despite his family's
objections. Back then, the rich snubbed flashy Broadway shows
and their emphasis on modern clothes, fast talk, and frank sexuality. But young Silverman fell in love with Broadway anyway and,
while working for his father, moonlighted as a vaudeville reviewer.
Finally, after being denied a partnership in the banking business,
Silverman decided to found his own newspaper dedicated to the
entertainment he loved. He borrowed $2,500 from his dad and set
to work on the new venture: he called it *Variety*. The first issue
came out on December 16, 1905, cost a nickel, and was only 16
pages long.

Variety's beat was the Broadway stage. And soon the publication
became an integral part of the show business culture. It reveled in
the lower-class sensibility of the scene and thumbed its nose at
gentility. The staff journalists were former vaudevillians; a disrep-
utable group, they called themselves "mugs." Each one had his own
nickname that appeared in his byline too: Sime for Silverman, Ibee
for theatrical reporter Jack Pulaski, and Skigie for Silverman's son,
Syd, to name a few. (At age 13, Skigie would make *Variety* history
by writing its very first movie review for *The Great Train Robbery*.)

In the early years, Sime wasn't sold on the future of motion pictures as adult entertainment (which is why he had his teenage son
review them). Movie reviews appeared sporadically, even though

—Jean Harrington (Barbara Stanwyck), *The Lady Eve* (1941)

reviews of New York movie houses were a regular feature. (Then, movies were sandwiched in between vaudeville acts, so they weren't part of the main attraction.)

MOVING TO MOVIES

Things changed in 1914 when *Variety* got involved in a labor dispute. The powerful manager of a circuit of vaudeville houses, E. F. Albee (grandfather of the Pulitzer Prize–winning Edward Albee) was fighting unionization efforts of performers and was infuriated by *Variety*'s pro-union stance. He made it clear that anyone who advertised in Silverman's rag would be fired from his productions.

Variety's advertising revenue plummeted, and Silverman needed to find other ways to make money. Since Albee had no influence in the movie biz, Silverman turned to it. He approached silent screen stars to see if they were interested in buying some ad space. Lucky for him, they were. And the first movie star to purchase an ad on the front cover was America's Sweetheart, Mary Pickford. After that, movie reviews and ads began to appear regularly and soon became a major source of revenue. As movies began to dominate the entertainment business in the 1920s, the importance of vaudeville and Broadway began to wane. Keeping pace with the times, *Variety* slowly morphed into the trade paper of the film industry and finally opened a Los Angeles bureau in 1933.

But Silverman would not live to see the ultimate Hollywood success of his newspaper. He died the same year the Los Angeles office opened. The New York office remained open and still publishes a New York edition today, called the *Daily Variety Gotham*. The paper remained family-owned and operated until 1987. Then Silverman's grandson Syd—who took over from his dad, Skigie, in the 1950s—sold the paper to a media conglomerate and retired. Today *Variety* still shapes and reflects the movie business. It remains a must-read for those in the know (and those who want to be in the know). In the words of editor Peter Bart, "We are the connective tissue between the world's media centers."

SPEAKING THE SLANGUAGE

One of the things *Variety* became best known for was its inventive use of language, or "slanguage" as the original mugs called it. Words like *socko* (great), *boffo* (greater), and *whammo* (greatest) were added to the theatrical lexicon by the staff. People didn't quit their jobs, they *ankled*. Legs became *gams*. Projects didn't fail, they *flopped*. Other contributions: *scram, bimbo, smash, whodunit,* and even *movies.*

A VARIETY OF HEADLINES
In addition to the slanguage, *Variety* has a legacy of creating catchy headlines. They pack a punch, but often need translation. Take some of these favorites, for instance:

Dancer Stagers; Fiends on Gams. Chorines Sifted by Stems
This 1929 headline was another way of saying that female dancers had to have shapely legs to get jobs.

Wall Street Lays an Egg
The stock market crash of 1929.

Sticks Nix Hick Pix
From 1935, this is one of *Variety's* most famous. It meant that Midwestern movie-goers preferred films set in Europe or New York City to movies about farmers.

Peace in Pieces: No Salve for BO Aches
Pix Hardest Hit Through 2-Day Peace Whoopee
When World War II ended, the BO (box office) in local theaters was terrible. Everyone was out celebrating victory, which led to these rather ungracious headlines.

Greatest Show Off Earth
The moon landing in 1969.

***Helena* Costs Kim an Arm and a Leg**
In 1993, when movie star Kim Basinger pulled out of a verbal agreement to star in *Boxing Helena* (a movie where her character's limbs are amputated), the producers sued her. She lost her case and was fined $8.92 million, prompting this headline.

Lizards Eat Arnold's Lunch
Jurassic Park and *Last Action Hero* (starring Arnold Schwarzenegger) were released on the same weekend in 1993. *Last Action Hero* lost out big time to the dinosaurs.

Pooh Gets Flushed
In March 2004 a long-standing civil lawsuit against Disney was settled. A family had sued for royalties from Disney's many *Winnie the Pooh* cartoons and lost.

WANNA BE
IN PICTURES?

Think you have what it takes to become a big movie star? Do
you have the talent? The drive? The ambition? Even with all
that, Hollywood can still be a tough place. Uncle John
has 10 tips to help you on your way to stardom.

1. Go where the jobs are. If you're looking to make any money working as a movie actor, we hear they make lots of films in Los Angeles.

2. Practice. Practice. Practice. Formal acting training can be a big help when "polishing your craft."

3. A picture is worth a thousand words—and so is a really good headshot. Spend the money and get it professionally done. Make it black-and-white and 8x10.

4. Create an acting résumé, and update it regularly.

5. Find out who is hiring. Read trade magazines regularly, since that's where casting ads are placed.

6. Audition. Audition. Audition. The more you do it, the less scary it is.

7. Be on time. Never miss, or be late to, an audition.

8. Develop a thick skin. Criticism and rejection are par for the course. Don't take it personally, and don't be discouraged.

9. Beware of scams and unscrupulous people who want to take money from unsuspecting, budding actors. (This means you never pay for an audition.)

10. Don't give up your day job. Most of Hollywood's working actors make about $5,000 a year from acting jobs. Living comfortably requires a side job. So here are a few suggested temporary gigs while you climb your ladder to the stars: waitperson, delivery driver, babysitter, or dog walker.

Robert De Niro accidentally broke Joe Pesci's rib in a sparring scene in *Raging Bull.*

CLARK GABLE, CHICKEN FARMER?

Clark Gable won an Oscar for his work in It Happened One Night *(1934). He almost gained a daughter from it, too.*

In 1934 in Essex, England, a British housewife named Violet Norton went to the movies and was surprised to see her old boyfriend Frank Billings there. A chicken farmer, Billings used to live next door to Norton before running out on her and their baby girl, Gwendolyn, born in September 1922. Twelve years later, there he was, in front of Norton's eyes—up on the silver screen, starring in *It Happened One Night* and using a new name, Clark Gable. Norton was convinced that she'd finally discovered the elusive Billings, now masquerading as an actor and living in Hollywood, California.

LOTS OF LETTERS
Norton wasn't afraid to let Gable/Billings know that she was on to him. She wrote letter after letter to Clark Gable detailing their affair and insisting that he take responsibility for their daughter. But Gable ignored her. Violet and Gwendolyn decided to move from England to America, but only made it to Canada in 1935. But even from Canada, Violet never ceased her efforts. She ran ads in a movie magazine: still no response. Then she tried writing to movie stars like Mae West, but that didn't work either. She contacted the British consul in Los Angeles, as well as the U.S. Attorney General, but still nothing. Finally her efforts caught the attention of a retired Canadian businessman who felt sorry for her and paid her way to California; mother and daughter arrived to confront Gable in Hollywood in December 1936.

CALIFORNIA, HERE WE COME
Once in California, Norton hired private investigator Jack L. Smith who, on his client's behalf, contacted the Motion Picture Producers Association and the publicity department at MGM, Gable's studio. Smith demanded blood tests and money, in the

High Noon has been screened more often at the White House than any other film.

form of a $150,000 trust for Gwendolyn, and threatened to go public with the story if Gable didn't pay. But Smith made a big mistake when he contacted the MGM publicity staff. They contacted the U.S. attorney's office, which was very interested in Norton's use of the U.S. mail to make her demands. So interested, in fact, that they put her on trial for mail fraud several months later.

But Norton still insisted that Gable was the English chicken farmer who had fathered her child. She confidently told reporters that Gable was a "fraud" and that he really was the British chicken farmer, Frank Billings. How could she be so sure? She told reporters, "I can tell by the way he makes love to that Joan Crawford—just the same as he did to me."

THE BEST OFFENSE . . .

Gable's team put up a good defense against Norton's claims. Jack Powell, an assistant U.S. attorney, testified that Gable couldn't have been in England when Gwendolyn was conceived; Gable, a U.S. citizen, didn't have a passport until 1930. Gable's pre-Hollywood employers produced payroll records showing that he was stateside during the early 1920s. Probably the most damaging testimony came from Harry Billings, Frank's own brother, who swore under oath that Gable was in no way related to him.

Gable even called on old flames to testify on his behalf. Franz Dorfler was Gable's fiancée long before he came to Hollywood from Oregon. The two were engaged in 1922, waiting to marry when they could support themselves. But they eventually broke up when Gable went to Hollywood. The two hadn't seen each other in years, but she agreed to help him. (Oddly enough, Gable had to search for Dorfler and found her working in, of all places, his agent's kitchen.) She testified that Gable had been at her family's ranch in September 1922, making his presence in England impossible.

Norton didn't make a very strong case for herself. Her "strongest" piece of evidence to show the court that Billings and Gable were the same man was a picture of Frank Billings wearing a British army uniform. The weak resemblance convinced no one of anything (except that maybe what Norton really needed was an eye exam).

THE VERDICT

It was obvious to the jury that Gable was neither Frank Billings nor Gwendolyn's father. They convicted Norton of mail fraud, and she was ultimately deported. Gable's star continued to shine brightly in Hollywood, and he even began exploring new business ventures, including chicken farming. A few years later, the King of Hollywood and his new wife, Carole Lombard, bought 600 birds to start "The King's Eggs." But their enterprise failed, proving conclusively both that Gable was not Frank Billings and that he wasn't a very good chicken farmer.

* * *

THE KING COMPLAINS

Clark Gable complained that he had more costume changes than any other actor in Gone With the Wind (he had 36 costumes). Many of his costumes were so tight that he couldn't sit down in them.

* * *

"FRANKLY, MY DEAR . . ."

On June 27, 1939, cameras rolled on Rhett Butler saying good-bye to Scarlett O'Hara in one of the most famous parting scenes ever shot. But two versions of the scene had to be shot—in case censors wouldn't allow the original line, "Frankly, my dear, I don't give a damn." In the second version, Butler says, "Frankly, my dear, I just don't care."

* * *

MISTAKEN IDENTITY

Actor Leslie Howard was probably best known for playing Ashley Wilkes in Gone With the Wind (1939). He tragically died in a plane crash in 1943 while traveling from Lisbon to London on business related to World War II. The Germans shot down his plane because they believed Winston Churchill was on board.

BATHROOMS ON THE BIG SCREEN, PART 3

*This collection of quotations shows that sometimes
a lot of movie action can happen off screen.*

"I may have to go to the bathroom every 45 minutes, but at least I get to pee in a gold toilet."
—Sidney Wernick
(Jon Lovitz),
*Dickie Roberts: Former
Child Star* (2003)

"Brilliant gold taps, virginal white marble, a seat carved from ebony, a cistern full of Chanel Number Five, and a flunky handing me pieces of raw silk toilet roll. But under the circumstances I'll settle for anywhere."
—Mark "Rent-boy" Renton
(Ewan McGregor),
Trainspotting (1996)

"Don't you just love it when you come back from the bathroom and find your food waiting for you?"
—Mia (Uma Thurman),
in a restaurant in
Pulp Fiction (1994)

"Well I want a solid gold toilet, but it's just not in the cards, baby."
—Austin (Mike Myers),
*Austin Powers: The Spy
Who Shagged Me* (1999)

"What? What do you say to a man who's crying in your bathroom?"
—Oscar Madison
(Walter Mattheau),
The Odd Couple (1968)

"It is physically impossible to French-kiss a man who leaves the new roll of toilet paper resting on top of the empty cardboard roll. Does he not see it? Does he not see it?"
—Rachel (Rita Wilson),
The Story of Us (1999)

"What if I'm looking for a bathroom, I can't find one . . . and my bladder explodes?"
—Bob Wiley (Bill Murray),
What About Bob? (1991)

Midnight Cowboy was the only X-rated movie shown to a U.S. president in office.

GREAT STORY . . . JUST CHANGE THE ENDING

It might surprise you to learn that some of your favorite movies were changed from the originals to "improve" them. Did it work? Here are a few examples. You be the judge.

A FISH CALLED WANDA (1988)
Original Ending: More in line with the dark and deceitful nature of the characters, Otto (Kevin Kline) gets killed by the steamroller. And Wanda (Jamie Lee Curtis) ditches Archie (John Cleese) at the airport, keeping all of the stolen jewels for herself.
But Wait: Test audiences didn't approve. Two more endings were filmed before viewers were satisfied—Otto lives, and Wanda and Archie go to South America together. The result: *A Fish Called Wanda* was a box office smash, bringing in nearly $200 million.

BLADE RUNNER (1982)
Original Ending: Director Ridley Scott's original existential ending confused test audiences, leaving many questions unanswered, most notably Deckard's (Harrison Ford) identity. Was he a replicant or not?
But Wait: Warner Brothers had invested a lot in the film and ordered Scott to "fix it." Reluctantly, he added narration by Ford and filmed a more typically violent Hollywood ending in which Deckard is indeed a replicant. Ten years later, in one of the first "director's cut" videos, Scott restored the film to his original vision. Which one is better? Both are available, so you can decide for yourself.

THE SCARLET LETTER (1995)
Original Ending: Hollywood is notorious for altering novels but it outdid itself with this one. In Nathaniel Hawthorne's classic tale, Hester Prynne is judged an adulteress and sentenced to wear the letter "A" for the remainder of her days. After her secret lover confesses to the people, he dies in Hester's arms—an ending that echoed the sentiment of the times.

But Wait: Demi Moore's Hester is a bit more "modern"—she gets revenge on her oppressors and the reunited family lives happily ever after. Defending the new ending, Moore attested that "not many people have read the book anyway." Even fewer people saw the movie.

FATAL ATTRACTION (1987)
Original Ending: Dan (Michael Douglas) is charged with murder as we hear a voice-over of Alex's (Glenn Close) suicidal confession. Test audiences yawned their disapproval.
But Wait: Months after filming was completed, the cast was called back to film the more climactic ending in which Dan's wife (Anne Archer) murders Alex in the bathtub.

BUTCH CASSIDY AND THE SUNDANCE KID (1969)
Original Ending: Paul Newman's and Robert Redford's characters are shot by soldiers in a gruesome death scene.
But Wait: The version released to the public ends with a freeze-frame of the two stars making their final charge, thereby immortalizing them instead of killing them.

THELMA AND LOUISE (1991)
Original Ending: Similar to *Butch Cassidy and the Sundance Kid*, Geena Davis and Susan Sarandon's car falls all the way to the canyon floor, presumably smashing them to bits.
But Wait: Fearing a negative reaction to killing off the film's stars, the theatrical release shows their car sailing off the cliff, but leaves their fates up in the air, so to speak. The DVD includes the alternate ending.

THE PRINCESS DIARIES (2001)
Original Ending: The original finale had Mia (Anne Hathaway) simply agreeing to fly off to the fabled European kingdom of Genovia to become a princess.
But Wait: Director Garry Marshall's five-year-old granddaughter felt shortchanged; she wanted to see the castle. Marshall acquiesced and had Disney buy stock footage of a European castle and digitally add the flag of Genovia to it. "It cost us a penny or two," explained Marshall, "but it made my granddaughter happy."

Director David Lean wanted Albert Finney for the lead in *Lawrence of Arabia* . . .

TAKE THIS JOB AND SHOVE IT

It's a good thing some screenwriters are aware of—and sympathetic to—the plight of the working man and woman. Here are a few gems that capture the hardships of the nine-to-five lifestyle.

"You can bend the rules plenty once you get to the top, but not while you're trying to get there. And if you're someone like me, you can't get there without bending the rules."
    —Tess McGill (Melanie Griffith), *Working Girl* (1988)

"You see, Bob, it's not that I'm lazy. I just don't care. . . . I have eight different bosses right now. . . . Eight, Bob. So that means when I make a mistake, I have eight different people coming by to tell me about it. That's my only real motivation—not to be hassled, that, and the fear of losing my job. But you know, Bob, that will only make someone work just hard enough not to get fired."
    —Peter Gibbons (Ron Livingston), *Office Space* (1999)

"I'm not suited to this job. Where do I come off testing products? Machines hate me. I should be working at a job I have some aptitude for, like donating sperm to an artificial insemination lab."
    —Fielding Mellish (Woody Allen), *Bananas* (1971)

"You like to think that the weight of the world rests on Dante's shoulders. Like this place would fall apart if Dante wasn't here . . . you overcompensate for what's basically a monkey's job. . . . You're so obsessed with making it seem so much more epic and important than it really is. You work at a convenience store, Dante! And badly, I might add."
    —Randall Graves (Jeff Anderson), *Clerks* (1994)

"Oh yeah, I started out mopping the floor just like you guys. Then I moved up to washing lettuces. Now, I'm working the fat fryer. Pretty soon I'll make assistant manager, and that's when the big bucks start rolling in."
    —Maurice (Louie Anderson), *Coming to America* (1988)

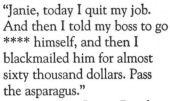

"Janie, today I quit my job. And then I told my boss to go **** himself, and then I blackmailed him for almost sixty thousand dollars. Pass the asparagus."
—Lester Burnham
(Kevin Spacey),
American Beauty (1999)

"Just remember this, Mr. Potter: that this rabble you're talking about, they do most of the working and paying and living and dying in this community. Well, is it too much to have them work and pay and live and die in a couple of decent rooms and a bath?"
—George Bailey
(Jimmy Stewart),
It's a Wonderful Life (1946)

"I've put up with all of your pinching, poking, staring and chasing me around the desk because I need this job. But this is the last straw. I've got a gun out there in my purse. Up until now I've been forgiving and forgetting . . . , but I'll tell you one thing. If you say another word about me or make another indecent proposal, I'm gonna get that gun of mine, and I'm gonna change you from a rooster to a hen with one shot."
—Doralee Rhodes (Dolly Parton), *Nine to Five* (1980)

"I realize that I'm the president of this company, the man that's responsible for everything that goes on here. So, I want to state, right now, that anything that happened is not my fault. "
—J. B. Biggley (Rudy Vallee),
How to Succeed in Business Without Really Trying (1967)

"If Higbee thinks I'm working one minute past 9:00, he can kiss my foot. Ho ho ho."
—Santa Claus (Jeff Gillen),
A Christmas Story (1983)

"You think I am brave because I carry a gun; well, your fathers are much braver because they carry responsibility for you. . . . And this responsibility is like a big rock that weighs a ton. It bends and it twists them until finally it buries them under the ground. And there's nobody says they have to do this. They do it because they love you, and because they want to. I have never had this kind of courage. Running a farm, working like a mule every day with no guarantee anything will ever come of it. This is bravery."
—Bernardo O'Reilly
(Charles Bronson),
The Magnificent Seven (1960)

HOLLYWOOD HAUNTS

*Some stars can't get enough of the spotlight—even
after they're dead. Their ghosts are still on the scene to
make some personal, and spooky, appearances.*

THE BAD SIGN

Who's That Ghost? Peg Entwistle
Haunted Hangout: The Hollywood sign
Spooky Sights: A beautiful yet sad blonde woman dressed in 1930s
clothing, accompanied by the scent of gardenias
Spectral Scoop: Lillian Millicent Entwistle (nicknamed Peg) was
born in the United Kingdom in 1908 and came to New York at a
young age with her father. Peg made it on Broadway and landed
parts in several shows. In 1932 she decided to pack her bags for
Hollywood, where she hoped to make it in the movies.

At first it seemed that Peg had found success. RKO studios gave
her a contract and a meaty role in the mystery *Thirteen Women*
(1932). When the film was edited, most of Peg's scenes landed on
the cutting-room floor. Then RKO dropped her contract. Peg made
the rounds of auditions hoping to find more work but found nothing but rejection.

On September 18, 1932, Peg couldn't take it anymore. She
wrote a farewell note: "I am afraid I am a coward. I am sorry for
everything. If I had done this a long time ago, it would have saved
a lot of pain." Then she put the note in her purse, hiked up the
slopes of the canyon to the Hollywood sign (which at that time
spelled out Hollywoodland), climbed a workman's ladder to the top
of the letter *H*, and took her fatal dive.

Today hikers and park rangers have reported seeing Peg's ghost
lingering around the Hollywood sign. She appears then suddenly
disappears, leaving behind the scent of gardenias, her favorite
perfume.

THE HOT TODDY

Who's That Ghost? Thelma Todd
Haunted Hangout: The former site of Todd's home and supper
club—a three-story building at 17575 Pacific Coast Highway

—**Nefretiri (Anne Baxter),** *The Ten Commandments* **(1956)**

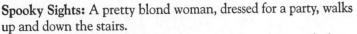

Spooky Sights: A pretty blond woman, dressed for a party, walks up and down the stairs.

Spectral Scoop: Thelma Todd grew up in Massachusetts, before moving to California to become a successful actress. Known to her friends as Hot Toddy, the blonde comedienne capitalized on her fame to open Thelma Todd's Sidewalk Café on the ground floor of a three-story building near Malibu. She helped run an exclusive nightclub, located on one half of the second floor, and lived in an ocean view apartment on the other half of the floor.

Todd died mysteriously on December 16, 1935. Her dead body slumped behind the wheel of her convertible, she was still wearing her jewels, her mink, and her party clothes from the previous night. An inquest ruled the death accidental, but the press and public weren't buying. Some said it was suicide. Others said it was murder. (For more on the story of Todd's death, see page 50.)

New owners of the property have reported seeing a pretty blonde walking up and down the stairs—still dressed in a gown and and high-heeled shoes. After a production company inherited the site, some of their staff members had frightening encounters with her moaning spirit in the hallways.

THE PHANTOM'S PHANTOM

Who's That Ghost? Lon Chaney

Haunted Hangouts: A bench at Hollywood and Vine; Universal Studios soundstage

Spooky Sights: A sad man sitting on a bench; a man climbing the catwalks

Spectral Scoop: One of the greatest actors of the silent-film era, Lon Chaney Sr., who was born in 1883 to deaf-mute parents, learned from an early age how to communicate emotion without using his voice. Chaney's legendary skills with makeup and pantomime allowed him to create a multitude of characters, which earned him the nickname the Man of a Thousand Faces. He appeared in over 150 films and is probably best remembered for his moving portrayals of tormented outcasts in *The Hunchback of Notre Dame* (1923) and *The Phantom of the Opera* (1925).

Chaney swore he would never do a talking picture: "I have a thousand faces but only one voice." But he did eventually come around to sound, and he appeared in one talkie, *The Unholy Three* (1930). He created several different character voices in his role as

---

Some Like It Hot (1959) was originally banned from being shown in Kansas.

a dishonest ventriloquist. Seven weeks after its release, Chaney died of a throat hemorrhage from bronchial cancer.

Soon after Chaney's death, people began seeing his ghost sitting on a bench at the Hollywood and Vine bus stop. The bench was eventually removed, and with it went Chaney's ghost. But others claim that Chaney's phantom haunts Stage 28 at Universal Studios, where he filmed *The Phantom of the Opera*. Technicians and visitors there claim to have seen the great Lon Chaney abruptly appearing, climbing the catwalk, then disappearing.

*For more on Hollywood haunts,
turn to page 348.*

* * *

ANITA LOOS

*One of Hollywood's first (and best) screenwriters, Anita Loos
was a keen observer in the early years of motion pictures.*

"Show business is the best possible therapy for remorse."

"In the past, as now, Hollywood was a stomping ground for tasteless-ness, violence, and hyperbole, but once upon a time it turned out a product which sweetened the flavor of life all over the world."

"When I was very young and first worked in Hollywood, the films had bred in me one sole ambition: to get away from them."

"If we have to tell Hollywood good-bye, it may be with one of those tender, old-fashioned, seven-second kisses exchanged between two people of the opposite sex, with all their clothes on."

The reason given was that cross-dressing was "too disturbing for Kansans."

WHERE ARE THEY NOW?

Not every deceased Hollywood star lies in California. Here's the final resting place of a few of your favorite celebrities.

PAUL LYNDE (1927–1982)
The original center square on *Hollywood Squares*, Paul Lynde is buried in Amity Cemetery in Mount Vernon, Ohio.

KATHARINE HEPBURN (1907–2003)
One of Hollywood's biggest stars ever, Hepburn rests in a family plot at Cedar Hill Cemetery in Hartford, Connecticut.

JACKIE GLEASON (1916–1987)
The Great One is buried at Our Lady of Mercy Catholic Cemetery in Miami, Florida. A white marble gazebo stands over his grave.

BURL IVES (1909–1995)
Burl Ives is buried in Mound Cemetery in Jasper County, Illinois. His lengthy epitaph includes a quotation from Carl Sandburg, who called him, "The mightiest ballad singer of this or any other century."

FRANCES FARMER (1913–1970)
Controversial star of the 1930s and 1940s, Frances Farmer now finds peace in Oaklawn Memorial Gardens Cemetery in Fishers, Indiana.

SIR LAWRENCE OLIVIER (1907–1989)
One of the greatest Shakespearean actors of his generation, Olivier is one of the few actors interred at Westminster Abbey in London, England.

HOWARD ASHMAN (1950–1991)
The composer of favorite songs from Disney's *The Little Mermaid*, *Beauty and the Beast*, and *Aladdin*, Howard Ashman now lies in Oheb Shalom Memorial Park in Baltimore, Maryland.

Marilyn Monroe stars in what film in which she's listed in credits only as "The Girl"?

DIVINE (1945–1988)

The drag queen made famous in John Waters's films, Divine is buried at Prospect Hill Cemetery in Towson, Maryland. His tombstone also bears his less glamorous real name, Harris Glenn Milstead.

COLONEL TIM MCCOY (1891–1978)

One of the first big cowboy stars in the 1930s and 1940s, McCoy now cools his heels in Mount Olivet Cemetery in Saginaw, Michigan.

INGRID BERGMAN (1915–1982)

Bergman's ashes are interred next to her parents in Northern Cemetery in Stockholm, Sweden.

GORDON MACRAE (1921–1986)

Star of *Oklahoma* (1955) and *Carousel* (1956), Gordon MacRae lies in Wyuka Cemetery in Lincoln, Nebraska. President Ronald Reagan is quoted on his tombstone: "Gordon will always be remembered wherever beautiful music is heard."

MYRNA LOY (1905–1993)

The beautiful star of *The Thin Man* series is buried in Forest Vale Cemetery in Helena, Montana.

DUDLEY MOORE (1935–2002)

This British comedian, piano player, and actor is interred at Hillside Cemetery in Scotch Plains, New Jersey. A picture of him at the piano is engraved on his headstone.

GRETA GARBO (1905–1990)

Garbo's simple marker in the Woodland Cemetery in Stockholm, Sweden, just bears her name, a reproduction of her autograph engraved in gold script.

JIM HENSON (1936–1990)

Creator of Kermit the Frog and other Muppets, Jim Henson had his ashes scattered at his ranch outside Santa Fe, New Mexico.

DANNY KAYE (1913–1987)
Kaye's and his wife's ashes are buried underneath a memorial bench in Kensico Cemetery in Valhalla, New York. Their names are not featured prominently on the memorial, which has a bronze relief that includes images of significance from their lives.

GARY COOPER (1901–1961)
Originally buried in California, Cooper's wife relocated to New York and took his body with her. He is now buried at Sacred Hearts of Jesus and Mary Cemetery on Long Island, New York. His grave is marked with a bronze plaque and a three-ton boulder.

JOAN CRAWFORD (1908–1977)
At the Ferncliffe Cemetery and Mausoleum in Hartsdale, New York, Crawford is interred next to her last husband, Alfred Steele.

WILL ROGERS (1879–1935)
On the grounds of his museum in Claremore, Oklahoma, Will Rogers is buried beneath his own memorial, which features a quotation of his: "If You Live Life Right, Death is a Joke as Far as Fear is Concerned."

HEDDA HOPPER (1880–1966)
A woman who wrote much in life, this gossip maven's simple headstone just bears her name and years of birth and death. She lies at Rose Hill Cemetery in Altoona, Pennsylvania.

CHARLES BRONSON (1921–2003)
Charles Bronson is buried in Brownsville Cemetery in West Windsor, Vermont. His marker features the Mary Elizabeth Frye poem "Do Not Stand at my Grave and Weep."

LEE MARVIN (1924–1987)
A descendant of Robert E. Lee, Marvin is buried in Arlington National Cemetery in Virginia.

LEO THE LION (d. 1938)
In Gilette, New Jersey, a large evergreen tree has grown over the burial spot of the MGM mascot. He's buried on the grounds of his trainer's former home.

The word Beatles is never mentioned in the Beatles flick *A Hard Day's Night.*

BREAKING THE CODE

*In its early days, Hollywood didn't have much content regulation; there
were no ratings and few rules about what could be on the big screen—
that was until the establishment of the Hays Code in the 1930s.*

Maybe it was Fatty Arbuckle's scandalous trial in 1921 or
the explicit drug use portrayed in *Human Wreckage*
(1923). Or maybe it was the nudity in the original full-
length *Ben-Hur* (1925) and in *Bright Lights* (1925). No one movie
or event can be blamed for the general public's and the government's growing unease with some of the things depicted on the silver screen. In the late 1920s, movies and movie stars were increasingly seen as immoral, something from which the public needed
protection.

To circumvent possible legislation—and to assure an uneasy
public—the studios turned to a body they had created back in
1922, the Motion Picture Producers and Distributors of America
(MPPDA). This association was set up so the studios could police
themselves and avoid any government intrusion on their business.
Politician Will Hays had been put in charge, although the position
didn't have much real power. But he did have some impressive cre-
dentials—he was postmaster general for President Harding as well
as former Republican National Committee chairman—which probably helped to justify his $100,000 MPPDA salary.

CODE? WHAT CODE?
Even though a "code" was written by 1930, the organization had
no real authority. And that's the way Hollywood wanted it: They
could pay lip service to conservative groups, while keeping their
movies profitable—and filled with sex and violence. The 1932 film
Red-Headed Woman caused much controversy: it featured a sultry
Jean Harlow having an affair with a married man, shooting her
own husband and getting away with it, and then gambling with
another lover. Religious organizations and women's groups were
horrified at the movie's overt sexuality, disregard for class distinc-
tions, and unpunished immorality.

Released in 1965, *Doctor Zhivago* was not shown in Russia until 1994.

Other films, such as 1933's *Mayor of Hell*, challenged racial prejudice and class oppression: James Cagney's character leads a "socialist revolution" in a boy's reform school by overthrowing the warden, during which a young African American boy comforts a terrified white schoolmate. Another controversial film, 1932's *Freaks*, was cast with members of real sideshow acts and tried to shed light on shunned elements of society and their community. The movie had a healthy dose of what was then considered "deviant" sexuality: a woman tries to seduce a midget, a Siamese twin "feels" a kiss given to her sister, and a transvestite makes a pass at the Strong Man. (The movie still rubs some viewers the wrong way today.)

CRACKING DOWN

But Hollywood would learn it couldn't ignore its rules forever. A powerful Catholic group, the Legion of Decency, finally threatened to stage massive boycotts of films that failed to meet the Hays Code, which would have severely hurt Hollywood's bottom line. So, in 1934, the major studios shrewdly decided that every film they paid for would adhere to the code, and they finally gave Will Hays the power to make sure everyone else followed suit. The studios had a monopoly on the movie theaters, and without Hays's approval, a movie couldn't open in any of them.

WHAT WERE THE RULES?

Noting in the preamble that movies "may be directly responsible for spiritual or moral progress, for higher types of social life, and for much correct thinking," the code stressed that the audience should never sympathize with "crime, wrongdoing, evil, or sin." Certain sinful elements, such as adultery and seduction, could be suggested only when necessary for the plot; other things were strictly forbidden. On the list of sexual no-no's were:

excessive and lustful kissing
suggestive postures and gestures
sex perversion (homosexuality)
white slavery (prostitution of white women)
miscegenation (interracial romances)
sex hygiene and venereal diseases
scenes of actual childbirth
complete nudity

The rules for violence were a little more lax, requiring that killings and murders simply not "inspire imitation," and that crimes such as "safe-cracking" and the "dynamiting of trains" not be shown in detail (in case anyone was taking notes!). According to the "principle of compensating values," villains could commit crimes as long as they got theirs in the end.

Yet Hays didn't stop with just sex and violence—the code had a series of regulations on a wide range of other topics. No bad words or religious profanity were allowed; costumes that might have over-exposed dancers' bodies were not allowed; ministers could not be villains or even "comic characters"; and the flag always had to be treated respectfully. But there were a few odd things that the code did allow, as long as they were done in "good taste": "branding of people or animals," "actual hangings," and the "sale of women."

CHIPPING AWAY AT THE CODE

Filmmakers naturally bristled under the regulations, and skirmishes often broke out. One of the most famous battles was in 1938, between David O. Selznick and the Hays office, over Rhett Butler's classic line in Gone With the Wind, "Frankly my dear, I don't give a damn." The problem was that it was already in the best-selling book, and the public expected it to be in the film. Selznick finally compromised—he used the line and paid a fine of $5,000.

Howard Hughes defied the Hays Code in 1943 with his movie The Outlaw, which featured the well-endowed newcomer Jane Russell. Having completed the film in 1941, Hughes battled the censors for two years over its sexual content, finally premiering it in a San Francisco theater in 1943 without the Hays stamp of approval. (At the end of each screening, Hughes angrily had Jane Russell and a costar act out a 20-minute scene that had been cut at the request of the Hays office.) The movie had been banned in New York, causing Hughes to shelve it until 1946. When it was rereleased in 1946, the owner of the theater was arrested; Hughes filed, and lost, a $1 million suit against the Motion Picture Association of America (the new name of the MPPDA). But the movie was taken on the road and shown throughout the country as Hughes continued to fight. His persistence finally paid off: by 1947, The Outlaw was no longer banned.

Yet it wouldn't be until the 1950s that the code would really begin to crack. Battles over content actually became an important marketing tool: Otto Preminger directed several films, such as 1953's *The Moon Is Blue*, that were hits partly because of his publicized skirmishes with the code. Yet in the end, the code was just no match for the liberal 1960s, with its influx of unregulated, popular foreign films and loosening of obscenity laws. Instead of trying to regulate what went into movies, a rating system was created in 1968 that warned people what was already in them. The Production Code of 1930 was finally dead.

* * *

ON TALENT

"Success is a great deodorant. It takes away all your past smells."
—Elizabeth Taylor

"The word *genius* was whispered into my ear, the first thing I ever heard, while I was still mewling in my crib. So it never occurred to me that I wasn't until middle age."
—Orson Welles

"I believe that God felt sorry for actors so he created Hollywood to give them a place in the sun and a swimming pool. The price they had to pay was to surrender their talent."
—Cedric Hardwicke

"In Europe an actor is an artist. In Hollywood, if he isn't working, he's a bum."
—Anthony Quinn

* * *

"I work to please myself. I'm still not sure if movies are an art form. And if they're not, then let them inscribe on my tombstone what they could about any craftsman who loves his job: 'Here lies Vincente Minnelli. He died of hard work.'"
—Vincente Minnelli, director

RETURN OF THE POISON PEN: SCARY STUFF

We know that scary movies aren't for everyone. Some people love the thrills of slashers, psychos, monsters, and ghosts, but movies like these make everyone—especially the critics—turn away.

The Angry Red Planet (1960)
"They don't make 'em like this anymore. It's easy to see why."
—Ken Hanke, *Mountain Express*
(Asheville, North Carolina)

Orca (1977)
"If it were medically possible to overdose on claptrap, Orca . . . would be compelled to carry a warning from the Surgeon General."
—Staff, *The New York Times*

Kingdom of the Spiders (1977)
"A hammy [William] Shatner battles yucky spiders. Too bad the spiders don't win."
—Bob Bloom, *Journal and Courier* (Lafayette, Indiana)

The Swarm (1978)
"The bees don't look as if they'd hurt a fly. Mr. Allen might just as well have devoted his talents to man-eating goldfish, poodles on the rampage, or carniverous canaries."
—Janet Maslin, *The New York Times*

Halloween III: The Season of the Witch (1982)
"One of those Identikit movies, assembled out of familiar parts from other, better movies."
—Roger Ebert, *Chicago Sun Times*

. . . in order to make *Wild Wild West* (1999), which tanked.

Jaws: The Revenge (1987)
"And thrillseekers, this one's pretty dismal. There's more suspense in *On Golden Pond*."
—Desson Howe, *Washington Post*

Children of the Corn (1987)
"Plenty of corn, for sure, but no chills."
—James Sanford, *Kalamazoo Gazette*

The Phantom of the Opera (1989)
"The newest adaptation is the *Freddy Krueger* version, a concept that results in all the terror and suspense of Charlie Brown in Macbeth."
—Caryn James, *The New York Times*

Mary Shelley's Frankenstein (1994)
"Although it wouldn't be fair to say that this horror is entirely absent, you could miss it if you blink."
—Jay Boyar, *Orlando Sentinel*

I Still Know What You Did Last Summer (1998)
"*When Bad Things Happen to Stupid People* might have been a better title."
—Bob Graham, *San Francisco Chronicle*

Thirteen Ghosts (2001)
"For a movie called *Thirteen Ghosts*, this movie is surprisingly soulless."
—John Monaghan, *Detroit Free Press*

The Amityville Horror (2005)
"About as scary as a Toyota commercial."
—William Arnold, *Seattle Post Intelligencer*

House of Wax (2005)
"Midway through, the heroine falls face first into a stinking pit of animal guts. The experience of watching this movie feels a lot like that."
—Soren Anderson, *The News Tribune*
(Tacoma, Washington)

THE RIGHT DIRECTION, PART 1

*They started in the pioneering days of silent films and
during Hollywood's golden age, from 1929 to 1949, making
movies that are still revered as classics and that still
influence filmmakers around the world.*

THE BIG DADDY—D. W. Griffith (1875–1948)
THE MAN: Born on a La Grange, Kentucky, farm and
raised in Louisville, David (Lewelyn) Wark Griffith was the
son of a Confederate war hero who died when the boy was only 10.
Griffith was bitten by the acting bug after seeing a local amateur
production. He joined a local theater troupe in his early 20s, then
went on the road with a series of touring companies. He frequently
found himself penniless and, when he wasn't hawking encyclope-
dias or magazines door-to-door, he tried his hand at writing plays.
He sold his first stage play when he was in his early 30s. But when
it didn't make him enough money to live on, Griffith turned his
sights to the less respectable—but what he hoped would be more
lucrative—business of making movies, which was then centered in
New York.

There Griffith was offered a starring role in the 1908 Edison
Company film *Rescued From an Eagle's Nest*. But he soon found a
better audience for his talents at Edison's biggest competitor,
Biograph. That company not only bought his stories and starred
him in quite a few of them, but people there also recognized his
abilities as a producer and director. In less than four years at
Biograph—and while operating as Biograph's production chief at
the same time—Griffith personally directed an astounding total of
450 short films (each about 12 minutes long.

He left Biograph in 1913 to make feature-length movies. He did
that at the Reliance-Majestic studio, where he made *Birth of a
Nation*, the three-hour Civil War epic that film historians think of
as the most influential movie ever made. It was the first movie epic

---

—Gollum (Andy Serkis), *The Lord of the Rings: The Two Towers* (2002) and the movie business's first blockbuster, too, eventually earning millions.

Griffith went on to cofound United Artists studio and to direct more movies (with mixed success) for the next 16 years. The financial troubles that forced him to work within the ever-growing, restrictive studio system stifled his creativity. His last film, an independent cheapie called *The Struggle* (1931), was supposed to be his comeback. But the critics thought it too old-fashioned; Griffith's career in movies was virtually over. He supposedly directed a few scenes in Hal Roach's 1940 film *One Million B.C.*, but if he did, he received no credit for it. Some business investments kept him afloat until his death—nearly alone and nearly forgotten—at age 73.

THE MOVIES: *Birth of a Nation* mesmerized viewers with its advances in filmmaking—not to mention its costumes, suspense, and tense, violent scenes. But the film's portrayal of black Americans as villains and the Ku Klux Klan as heroes brought protests, riots, and calls for censorship. A defensive Griffith, who was reportedly bewildered and hurt by the charges against his movie, went on to make an even bigger epic, *Intolerance* (1916), which wove together four stories illustrating the inhumanity of prejudice. Ironically, his well-meant film was a flop, even though quite a few critics consider it his greatest film.

Griffith continued to tell big stories on-screen and his works were often firsts. *Hearts of the World* (1918) was a propaganda/romance film that incorporated actual footage of World War I; *The Greatest Thing in Life* (1918) featured a then-shocking kiss between a white soldier and a dying black soldier; *Way Down East* (1920), often called the first feminist film, was an artistic triumph and a box-office hit, second only to *Birth of a Nation* in receipts. And Griffith's large-scale epic *Orphans of the Storm* (1921) featured spectacular crowd scenes of the French Revolution (all shot on 14 acres in Mamaroneck, a suburb of Manhattan).

THE LEGACY: In making *Birth of a Nation*, Griffith gave birth to modern filmmaking. He innovated techniques that we now take for granted—changing camera angles, close-ups, dramatic lighting, rhythmic editing, crosscutting (switching shots back and forth between characters)—and that changed moviemaking forever. His talent for storytelling coupled with an understanding of the need for a new and subtle style of acting was also revolutionary.

Another important innovation introduced by Griffith was his extension of the shooting season; he took his troupe of actors (Mary Pickford, Dorothy and Lillian Gish, and Mabel Normand, among them) to California during the winter, thus setting in motion the eventual shift in locale from the East Coast to Hollywood.

THE FRENCH DIRECTION—Howard Hawks (1896–1977)

THE MAN: Howard Hawks's wealthy Midwest family migrated to Southern California when he was 10. Hawks planned to be an engineer after he graduated from Cornell. But in 1917, after a summer job as prop man with Famous Players–Lasky studio (the forerunner of Paramount) in Hollywood, he became fascinated with films and started his rise through the ranks. After serving in World War I in the Army Air Corps, he worked at an aircraft factory designing and flying planes—and designed and raced cars as well. But the pull of Hollywood was too strong. Back at the studio (now Paramount), Hawks did a little bit of everything: he wrote scripts, and he worked as a casting director, script supervisor, editor, producer, and assistant director. But Paramount wouldn't let him direct. So in 1926 he sold a story to Twentieth Century Fox on the condition that he direct it. The studio accepted his offer—and let him produce the film, too. *The Road to Glory* was a solid feature about the horrors of trench warfare in World War I. Hawks made seven more silent films; and when talkies came in, he came into his own.

He was married three times; his second wife, Nancy Gross, whom he nicknamed Slim, discovered Lauren Bacall after seeing her on the cover of *Harper's Bazaar*. Slim suggested that her husband invite the young woman to Hollywood for a screen test. The result was Bacall's starring role in *To Have and Have Not* opposite her future husband, Humphrey Bogart. Hawks based Bacall's screen persona in the film on Slim, including her glamorous dresses; long, blond hair; smoky voice; and demure yet mysterious demeanor. He was still planning films, including a remake of the 1928 *A Girl in Every Port* (to star John Wayne), at the time of his death after complications from a fall.

THE MOVIES: Howard Hawks could direct any genre: gangster movies like *Scarface* (1932); screwball comedies like *Bringing Up Baby* (1938); wartime romances like *To Have and Have Not* (1944); mysteries like *The Big Sleep* (1946); and even a musical, *Gentlemen Prefer Blondes* (1953), which launched Marilyn Monroe's career. The heroes in Hawks's films are often professionals who always "get the job done," and who often wind up learning that teamwork is the best way of dealing with problems.

THE LEGACY: Howard Hawks was a popular filmmaker, but he was never much discussed until the French "new wave" filmmakers (who were making avant-garde films during the late 1950s and early 1960s) discovered his work. They saw that Hawks, despite making films in different genres, held to a distinctive style in all his movies. The French filmmakers praised Hawks for his emphasis on fast-paced scenes and overlapping dialogue. And they liked his heroes—tough, wisecracking men and women—like the fast-talking newspaperwoman Hildy (Rosalind Russell) in 1940's *His Girl Friday*.

New filmmakers began to study Hawks and they paid him the highest form of flattery by imitating him. In 1972 Peter Bogdanovich did a remake of *Bringing Up Baby* in *What's Up, Doc?* In 1983 Brian De Palma filmed a popular remake of *Scarface* with Al Pacino.

Continued on page 466.

* * *

ON HOLLYWOOD

"Hollywood is wonderful. Anyone who doesn't like it is either crazy or sober."

—Raymond Chandler

"[Hollywood is] the flatulent cave of winds."

—John Barrymore

"I can stay here [Grabtown, North Carolina] and be a secretary, or I can go to Hollywood and breathe the same air that Clark Gable breathes."

—Ava Gardner

Chicago became Miramax's highest-grossing film when it reached $171 million.

THE WOLFMAN AT THE MOVIES, PART 2

Part 1 on page 192 told of early Hollywood werewolf films and the lead-up to Lon Chaney Jr. landing the classic role. Here is more of the story.

ALL THIS AND WORLD WAR II

A The studio had modest hopes for *The Wolf Man*. They scheduled its release for December 11, 1941, right before Christmas. But on December 7, Japan bombed Pearl Harbor and the United States entered World War II. Universal was sure the movie would become a box office disaster. After all, who was going to take time out for the movies when they were going to war?

To their surprise, it was a hit. The film played to packed movie houses all over the country, and was the studio's biggest money-maker of the season. It established the Wolf Man as an important movie monster, along with Dracula and Frankenstein. It almost singlehandedly made werewolves a part of the popular culture, and it turned Lon Chaney Jr. into one of the best known actors in the country.

World War II probably had more to do with making *The Wolf Man* a hit than any other factor. What Universal had failed to realize was that the war fueled a need for the kind of escape that horror films provided. Inside a darkened theater, moviegoers could forget their troubles, at least for a while, as they watched ordinary mortals triumph over seemingly insurmountable evil. As David Skal writes in *The Monster Show: A Cultural History of Horror:*

> Talbot's four-film quest to put to rest his wolf-self is, in a strange way, an unconscious parable of the war effort. The Wolf Man's crusade for eternal peace and his frustrated attempts to control irrational, violent, European forces . . . *The Wolf Man*'s saga was the most consistent and sustained monster myth of the war, beginning with the first year of America's direct involvement in the war, and finishing up just in time for Hiroshima.

In 1994, Whoopi Goldberg became the first woman to host the Academy Awards.

WOLF MAN FACTS
The hardest scene to shoot was the final "metamorphosis" scene, in which Chaney turns from a werewolf to a human as he dies. Chaney describes the process:

> The way we did the transformation was that I came in at 2:00 a.m. When I hit the position, they would take little nails and drive them through the skin at the edge of my fingers, on both hands, so that I wouldn't move them anymore.
>
> While I was in this position, they would take the camera and weigh it down with one ton, so that it wouldn't move when people walked. They had targets for my eyes. Then, they would shoot five or ten frames of film in the camera. They'd take the film out and send it to the lab. While it was there, the make-up man would come and take the whole thing off my face and put on a new one. I'm still immobile. When the film came back from the lab, they'd put it back in the camera and then they'd check me.
>
> They'd say, "Your eyes have moved a little bit, move them to the right. . . ." Then they'd roll it again and shoot another 10 frames. Well, we did 21 changes of make-up and it took 22 hours. I won't discuss about the bathroom. . . .

For the rest of the cast and crew, the worst part of filming *The Wolf Man* was breathing the special effects fog that was used in the outdoor scenes. "The kind of fog they used in those days was nothing like the kind we have today," cameraman Phil Lathrop remembers. "It was greasy stuff made with mineral oil. We worked in it for weeks and the entire cast and crew had sore eyes and intestinal trouble the entire time. Besides that, we were all shivering with cold because it was necessary to keep the temperature below 50 degrees when using the fog." Female lead Evelyn Ankers fainted on the set after inhaling too much fog during a chase sequence.

The Wolf Man made a lot of money for Universal, but not much of it filtered down to the writers and actors who actually brought it to life. "My salary was $400 a week," scriptwriter Curt Siodmak recalls. "When the picture made its first million, the producer got a $10,000 bonus, the director got a diamond ring for his wife, and I got fired, since I wanted $25 more for my next job.

LON CHANEY'S WOLFMAN SEQUELS

Chaney made four wolfman movies for Universal during the war years . . . more than Universal made of Dracula or Frankenstein. The others were:

- *Frankenstein Meets the Wolfman* (1943). Chaney travels to Castle Frankenstein to see if he can find a cure for his wolfman condition in Dr. Frankenstein's notes. All he finds is the Frankenstein monster, played by Bela Lugosi, who had turned down the original *Frankenstein* in 1931 because there wasn't any dialogue. *Movie Note:* Lugosi played a particularly stiff Frankenstein, not just because he was growing old, but also because in the original version of the film, Frankenstein is left blind and mute after a botched brain transplant. In the version released to theaters, all references to blindness, muteness, and the brain transplant were removed, so he just looks old.

- *House of Frankenstein* (1944). Mad scientist Dr. Gustav Niemann (Boris Karloff) escapes from an insane asylum with the help of his hunchback assistant Daniel (J. Carrol Naish) and flees to Castle Frankenstein. There he teams up with Dracula (John Carradine), Frankenstein (Glenn Strange), and the Wolfman (Chaney) to terrorize the countryside until they are finally killed by villagers.

- *House of Dracula* (1945). Dr. Franz Edelman (Onslow Stevens) finds a way to cure Dracula (John Carradine) of his vampirism, but Dracula refuses to submit. Instead, he bites Dr. Edelman and turns him into a vampire; then Edelman raises Frankenstein from the dead, just as the Wolfman arrives on the scene. *Movie Note:* Originally titled *The Wolfman vs. Dracula*, the movie had to be renamed because the Wolfman and Dracula do not actually meet in the film.

- *Abbot and Costello Meet Frankenstein* (1948). Bud Abbott and Lou Costello team up with the Wolfman to prevent Dracula (Lugosi) and a mad female scientist (Lenore Aubert) from transplanting Costello's brain into the Frankenstein monster. Critics say the film is symbolic of the decline of Universal's horror classics in the late 1940s—fans say it is one of the best films Abbot and Costello ever made.

Answer: A star on the Hollywood Walk of Fame (as of late 2005).

THE END

Chaney would reprise the wolfman role in movies and in television for the rest of his life, including appearances on *The Pat Boone Show* and *Route 66*. He also played the Frankenstein monster in *The Ghost of Frankenstein* (1942), Count Dracula in *Son of Dracula* (1943), and the Mummy in three *Mummy* movies. A heavy drinker, by the 1960s he was reduced to appearing in low-budget schlock like *Face of the Screaming Werewolf* (1965), *Hillbillies in a Haunted House* (1967), and *Dracula vs. Frankenstein* (1970). He died of a heart attack in 1973. But the wolfman lives on.

Continued on page 370.

* * *

PRODUCERS SAY THE DARNDEST THINGS

"For god's sake, don't say 'yes' until I'm finished talking."
—Darryl Zanuck

"I don't have ulcers, I give them."
—Harry Cohen

"I would rather take a 50-mile hike than crawl through a book."
—Jack Warner

But the king of the mangled phrase was Sam Goldwyn:

"I'd hire the devil himself if he'd write me a good story."
"I had a great idea this morning, but I didn't like it."
"A verbal contract isn't worth the paper it's printed on."
"You've got to take the bitter with the sour."
"Gentlemen, include me out."

Chris O'Donnell was offered Will Smith's role in *Men in Black*, but turned it down.

MASTERS OF STOP-MOTION

Ray Harryhausen may be the most famous of the
stop-motion animators (for more on him, see page 80),
but there are a few others that are worthy of note.
Here are three more masters of that craft.

WILLIS O'BRIEN

O'Brien's work inspired the young Ray Harryhausen, but he wasn't
the first one impressed by O'Brien's works. This early master of
stop-motion animation began his work in the 1910's by putting
together humorous film shorts of cavemen and dinosaurs. These
impressed Thomas Edison (at the time the biggest film producer in
the United States), who hired him to do more animations. In
1915, O'Brien created *The Dinosaur and the Missing Link.* O'Brien's
effects wizardry is evident in two big silent hits, 1918's *The Ghost of
Slumber Mountain* and 1925's spectacular *The Lost World.* But his
two biggest special-effects triumphs involved gorillas: O'Brien animated King Kong in the landmark 1933 film, and in 1949, his
effect work for *Mighty Joe Young* earned the film the first special
effects Academy Award. O'Brien kept working in effects until his
death in 1962.

HENRY SELICK

As Harryhausen was inspired by O'Brien, so Harryhausen inspired
Selick, who saw *The 7th Voyage of Sinbad* at age 5. "At that age, it
burned something into my consciousness. I totally believed those
skeleton warriors were real," he remembers. Selick demonstrated a
flair for art throughout his childhood and went on to become an
animator at Walt Disney Studios. There he learned from Eric
Larson, one of Disney's legendary "Nine Old Men" (the core team
of animators who created the studio's most famous movies from the
1930s through the 1970s).

When Selick entered the workforce, stop-motion had been
eased out of special effects and animation. Animation had become
a strictly two-dimensional affair. Selick earned a living creating

---

Dumbo is the only Disney animated feature film with a title character who doesn't speak.

Disney cartoons (his first credit is on *The Fox and the Hound* in 1981), but continued to create shorts and commercials in the style of Harryhausen. Then in 1990 Selick's stop-animated, surreal short *Slow Bob in the Lower Dimensions* attracted a lot of attention on the animation film festival circuit. *Slow Bob's* success would lead to Selick's being tapped to direct what would become a masterpiece of stop-motion: 1993's *The Nightmare Before Christmas* (about a spooky Halloween skeleton who decides one year to take Santa's gig at Christmastime with predictably disastrous results). *Nightmare* became a surprise hit in the theaters and later a cult phenomenon on video and DVD, allowing Selick to create more films, *James and the Giant Peach* (1996) and *Monkeybone* (2001).

NICK PARK

British stop-motion animator Park not only found inspiration in the work of Harryhausen but also in the creations of 2-D animators Tex Avery and Chuck Jones. These cartoony influences can be seen in almost all his work. In his early days, Park had a hand in one of the most famous music videos of all time: "Sledgehammer" by Peter Gabriel, in which everything in the video, including Peter Gabriel, is animated in stop-motion.

But Park is better known worldwide for his famous creations Wallace and Gromit, the cheese-loving inventor and his unusually intelligent dog. They first appeared in *A Grand Day Out*, which Park finished while still in college in 1989. Wallace and Gromit's popularity demanded sequels, and their slapstick stop-animated adventures won two Best Animated Short Oscars (for *Wallace & Gromit: The Wrong Trousers* in 1992 and *Wallace & Gromit: A Close Shave* in 1995) and officially launched Park and his compatriots at Aardman Animations. They made their first feature-length film in 2000, the hit *Chicken Run*. That film's commercial success—and a subsequent push to get it considered for Best Picture—encouraged the Academy of Motion Picture Arts and Sciences to create the Best Animated Feature Oscar category. *Chicken Run* was the first of a five-picture arrangement with DreamWorks; Aardman's latest offering, *Wallace & Gromit in the Curse of the Were-Rabbit* (2005), was the second.

THE NAVY AND THE MARINES

The army isn't the only branch of the armed forces to have benefitted from a little star power (see page 183). In World War II these Hollywood stars went to sea to see what they could see. See?

HENRY FONDA

Americans were highly patriotic following the bombing of Pearl Harbor, and Henry Fonda was no exception. Fonda, who had been nominated for an Academy Award for his work in *The Grapes of Wrath* the year prior, was technically exempt from the draft because of his age. Nonetheless, without telling anybody (including Twentieth Century Fox, his studio), he registered for the draft and in 1942 enlisted in the navy. Just like every other sailor, Fonda went through boot camp with the tests and physical demands. He studied hard and, although he wanted to become a gunner, became a quartermaster.

After a brief time as a quartermaster on the USS *Satterlee*, Fonda was sent to New York and then ordered to Washington, DC, to make training films. Disappointed, Fonda convinced the officer in charge that he could serve the government better in combat. His argument was well taken, and Fonda left the set to report to naval training school (Air Combat Intelligence) for training on antisubmarine warfare. Shortly after his classes were over, Fonda was assigned to the *Curtis*, a support ship for seaplanes.

Henry Fonda saw battle near Iwo Jima, Guam, and Saipan, including a near miss by a kamikaze pilot that demolished the part of the ship where Fonda usually slept (luckily, he was on shore at the time). He received the bronze star and a presidential citation in 1945 for his role in the confirmed sinking of a Japanese submarine. Following a brief tour in Navy Public Affairs, Fonda left active duty, although he was with the naval reserves until late 1953. He also worked with the USO during the Vietnam War.

—The Joker (Jack Nicholson), *Batman* (1989)

TYRONE POWER

Not everyone was impressed by celebrity. That was a lesson Tyrone Power learned just after Pearl Harbor. Power decided to help with the war effort and tried to enlist in the naval reserves, but they turned him down. In August 1943 a peeved Power enlisted in the marines.

After boot camp Power went to marine officer's training school and eventually served in the South Pacific. However, according to Roy Hoopes in his book *When the Stars Went to War*, Tyrone Power's biggest enemy was boredom. Power was shipped from base to base and from ship to ship; the marines didn't seem to know where to put him. After the war ended, Power, who had had a relatively quiet stint with the marines, returned to Hollywood, although he maintained his U.S. Marine Reserve status for the rest of his life.

DOUGLAS FAIRBANKS JR.

Who would have thought that a boy surrounded by rich and famous people, a boy whose father was a screen legend, whose mother was a socialite, and whose stepmother was America's Sweetheart, would grow up to join the navy and fight in World War II? After he filmed a few movies and became a screen legend in his own right, that's exactly what Douglas Fairbanks Jr. did.

Following the filming of the classic *Gunga Din* in 1939, Fairbanks became involved in international politics and believed that the United States should support the Allies. Turmoil was breaking out all over Europe by then, and Fairbanks contacted President Franklin Roosevelt and offered to help by doing whatever the White House needed done. In early 1941 Douglas Fairbanks Jr. was commissioned into the U.S. Navy, but President Roosevelt assigned him as a special envoy to Latin America. Two months after his envoy assignment ended, Fairbanks reported for active duty.

Fairbanks's introduction to the navy did not go very smoothly. While he underwent training as a deck officer, he was teased and harassed. But he took it all in stride and eventually, because of his unwillingness to get angry after all that hassling, the other officers decided he was all right. Later, on his first "official" assignment, Fairbanks was fortunate to serve with others who taught him more about his job. While aboard the *Ludlow*, he learned about antisubmarine warfare, including radio and visual communications, gunnery, and navigation; on and off throughout his navy career, those skills were in demand. Fairbanks saw battle aboard the *Wasp* (which was later sunk by a Japanese submarine), as well as aboard the *Wichita* (which was forced to abandon a convoy because of heavy German bombing).

By war's end Fairbanks was promoted to commander and had seen action in several skirmishes. Fairbanks thought about staying with the navy and even volunteered for a short time, until RKO Pictures came calling. Then he left the armed services and went back to moviemaking.

* * *

OTHER STARS WHO SERVED IN THE SEA SERVICES DURING WORLD WAR II

Eddie Albert: Saw action near the Japanese-held island of Betio.

Ernest Borgnine: Left the navy in 1941 and reenlisted after Pearl Harbor. He was a U.S. Navy gunner's mate from 1935 to 1945.

Tony Curtis: Attended signal school and sub school.

Kirk Douglas: Enlisted in the navy and served as communications officer in antisubmarine warfare.

Buddy Ebsen: Rejected repeatedly by the navy, Ebsen joined the U.S. Coast Guard.

John Ford: Saw action at Normandy from a PT boat.

Rock Hudson: Served as an aircraft mechanic in the navy.

Robert Montgomery: Commanded PT boats in the Panama Canal and the South Pacific.

Wayne (Bert) Morris: Joined naval reserves and flew F6F Hellcats, downing seven Japanese planes.

Paul Newman: Served in the navy as a radioman and gunner.

Rod Steiger: Spent four years in the Pacific, including serving in the Iwo Jima and Okinawa campaigns.

I'D LIKE TO THANK THE ACADEMY . . .

The Academy Awards is when Hollywood celebrates its best and brightest. Movie fans everywhere are familiar with the sealed envelopes, the gold statues, and the acceptance speeches. But these little-known facts about the Academy Awards may surprise you.

O scar isn't really called Oscar. It's not even officially called the Academy Award. The award's full title is the Academy Award of Merit; the academy is the Academy of Motion Pictures Arts and Sciences formed in 1927 by film industry employees to arbitrate labor disputes, to provide a forum for sharing techniques and innovations, and to improve the film industry's image. Two years later—almost as an afterthought—it began giving out awards for achievement. Most people know the academy for just the awards, although it also continues its other functions (except that it ended its involvement with labor in 1937).

At the first ceremony, only 14 awards were given out. The original award categories were as follows: Actor, Actress, Art Direction, Cinematography, Directing (Comedy), Directing (Drama), Engineering Effects, Outstanding Picture, Unique and Artistic Picture, Writing (Adaptation), Writing (Original), Writing (Title Writing), plus two special achievement awards. Currently there are 25 awards. The newest category to be added was Best Animated Feature in 2001.

Eligibility dates originally ran from the middle of one year to the middle of the next. This is why, in official records, the earliest six award years are recorded as 1927–28 to 1932–33. After 1933 the academy shifted to a more practical schedule based on the calendar year.

The winners' names were not always closely guarded secrets. The first awards ceremony, held on May 16, 1929, was an unpretentious banquet in the Blossom Room of the Hollywood

---

Linda Fiorentino won her role in *Men in Black* (1997) in a poker game with the director.

Roosevelt Hotel. There was no suspense because everyone already knew who had won; the results had been published nearly three months earlier. After that, the academy continued to give the press the names of the winners ahead of time—on the condition that they didn't print the results until after the ceremony. But in 1939— in one of the tightest academy races ever (among the ten Best Picture nominees were *Dark Victory; Gone With the Wind; Goodbye, Mr. Chips; Mr. Smith Goes to Washington; Of Mice and Men; Stagecoach;* and *The Wizard of Oz*)—the *Los Angeles Times* printed the names of the winners, including Best Picture (*Gone With the Wind*), in their early evening edition. It came out before the actual ceremony, thereby ruining the suspense for everyone. Since then, the winners are revealed *only* at the ceremony.

* * *

PREMIERE'S 10 GREATEST MOVIE STARS
Premiere magazine editors compiled a list of the "50 Greatest Movie Stars." It is not without controversy. Here's who made the top 10.

1. Cary Grant	6. Paul Newman
2. Marilyn Monroe	7. Julia Roberts
3. Tom Cruise	8. Greta Garbo
4. John Wayne	9. James Stewart
5. Ingrid Bergman	10. Henry Fonda

* * *

I'LL HAVE THE CHILI
The original Chasen's—the Spago of its day—has been closed for over ten years, but at one time it was Hollywood's premier restaurant, one of the biggest attractions being its chili. In fact, when Elizabeth Taylor was making *Cleopatra* in Rome, she had Chasen's chili flown in regularly. The building is now home to an upscale food market in which some of the original booths have been preserved. But not the booth where Ronald Reagan proposed to Nancy Davis in 1952; that one has been transferred to the Ronald Reagan Presidential Library in Simi Valley, outside Los Angeles.

Besides the movie part, she also raked in about $1,200.

FROM PRIME TIME TO BIG TIME

You might not know it, but some of today's most successful actors got their first big breaks on television.

The Actor: Johnny Depp
The Character: Officer Tom Hanson
The Show: 21 Jump Street (1987–1991)
Way back in 1987 when the Fox Network was in its infancy, *21 Jump Street* was a breakout hit for the new network—thanks to this attractive star who played one of the young undercover detectives. His good looks made him a teen idol, something the talented actor wasn't too excited about. He left the show after its fourth season to pursue more serious roles . . . and found them in films like *Edward Scissorhands* (1990), *Donnie Brasco* (1997), *Fear and Loathing in Las Vegas* (1998), and *Charlie and the Chocolate Factory* (2005).

The Actor: George Clooney
The Character: Dr. Doug Ross
The Show: ER (1994–present)
Appearing on ER wasn't this actor's first time on TV. He had parts on *The Facts of Life* and *Roseanne* before playing the sexy, but conflicted pediatrician on NBC's fast-paced medical drama. He left the hospital in 1999, and fans of Dr. Ross missed him terribly. Luckily for them, his move to the big screen went well, and fans can catch him in *Three Kings* (1999), *O Brother Where Are Thou?* (2000), and *Ocean's Eleven* (2001).

The Actor: Sally Field
The Character: Frances Elizabeth "Gidget" Lawrence
The Show: Gidget (1965–1966)
Nicknamed Gidget (a combo of *girl* and *midget*), this surfer girl hung out at the beach, lived with her dad (a widowed, college professor), and went through the usual teenage trials with her boyfriend Moon Doggie. The series starred an 18-year-old

---

The mystical, fit-all jeans in *The Sisterhood of the Traveling Pants* (2005) were Levi's.

unknown who would later star as a flying nun on TV before her big-screen career took off. She's won two Oscars, for *Norma Rae* (1979) and *Places in the Heart* (1984). And we like her. We really, really like her.

The Actor: Bruce Willis
The Character: David Addison
The Show: *Moonlighting* **(1985–1989)**
To some, he might be better known as the star of *Die Hard* (1988), *Pulp Fiction* (1994), or *The Sixth Sense* (1999), but to many he will always be the wisecracking Addison from the Blue Moon Detective Agency. This former bartender costarred with Cybil Shepherd, and the two shared some of the snappiest dialogue and most sizzling chemistry to ever grace the small screen. But, according to our sources, that's all they shared. Offscreen, the two did not get along.

The Actor: Morgan Freeman
The Character: Many, including Easy Reader, Count Dracula, Mad Scientist, and Mel Mounds the Disc Jockey
The Show: *The Electric Company* **(1971–1977)**
This talented actor got his start playing parts on a PBS educational show that taught children how to read. Pint-size viewers got to know him as he taught them about punctuation and phonics alongside fellow cast members Rita Moreno and Bill Cosby. But he went on to bigger projects—like *Glory* (1989), *The Shawshank Redemption* (1994), and his Oscar-winning turn in *Million Dollar Baby* (2004).

The Actor: Leonardo DiCaprio
The Character: Luke Brower
The Show: *Growing Pains* **(1985–1992)**
Introduced toward the end of the show's run, this actor played a homeless teenager adopted by the Seaver clan. Producers thought this young, cute cast member would regenerate teenage interest in *Growing Pains*. Unfortunately, the plan didn't work, sending this actor out to find work elsewhere. Luckily for him, *What's Eating Gilbert Grape* (1993), *Titanic* (1997), and *The Aviator* (2004) lay ahead.

The title for *I Am Sam* was inspired by the character in Dr. Seuss's *Green Eggs and Ham*.

KATE'S GREATS

*Thoughts and observations from one
of America's best actors, Katharine Hepburn.*

"If you obey all the rules, you miss all the fun."

"Love has nothing to do with what you are expecting to get—only with what you are expecting to give—which is everything."

"Life can be wildly tragic at times, but whatever happens to you, you have to keep a slightly comic attitude. In the final analysis, you have got not to forget to laugh."

"If you always do what interests you, at least one person is pleased."

"To keep your character intact, you cannot stoop to filthy acts. It makes it easier to stoop the next time."

"It's life isn't it? You plow ahead and make a hit. And you plow on and someone passes you. Then someone passes them. Time levels."

"I never realized, until lately, that women were supposed to be the inferior sex."

"Never complain. Never explain."

"If you don't paddle your own canoe, you don't move."

"Acting is the most minor of gifts. After all, Shirley Temple could do it when she was four."

"Someone asked someone who was about my age: 'How are you?' The answer was, 'Fine. If you don't ask for details.'"

"If you want to sacrifice the admiration of many men for the criticism of one, go ahead, get married."

"Without discipline, there's no life at all."

"I'm an atheist, and that's it. I believe there's nothing we can know except that we should be kind to each other and do what we can for other people."

"Enemies are so stimulating."

"Life is hard. After all, it kills you."

The principal actors in *Shrek* (2001) never met each other. They read their parts separately.

CAST OF CHARACTERS

Ten characters with problems. Ten films with Oscars. Can you match them up? (Extra credit if you can name the actors who played the roles.)

THE CHARACTERS

1. Clarice Starling, an FBI trainee with a hunt for a serial killer
2. Jimmy "Popeye" Doyle, a cop with a heroin-smuggling case
3. William Wallace, a Scotsman with a rebellion
4. Margo Channing, a woman with a two-faced apprentice
5. Pu Yi, a monarch without a throne
6. Phileas Fogg, a reserved Englishman with a bet
7. Frodo Baggins, a hero with a burden
8. Ratso Rizzo, a con artist with a cowboy
9. Richard Blaine, an exiled American with a saloon
10. Randle P. McMurphy, a patient with a tyrannical nurse

APPEARING IN

A. *Casablanca* (1942)

B. *All About Eve* (1950)

C. *Around the World in Eighty Days* (1956)

D. *Midnight Cowboy* (1969)

E. *The French Connection* (1971)

F. *One Flew Over the Cuckoo's Nest* (1975)

G. *The Last Emperor* (1987)

H. *The Silence of the Lambs* (1991)

I. *Braveheart* (1995)

J. *The Lord of the Rings: The Return of the King* (2003)

Turn to page 486 for answers.

Stagecoach was John Wayne's 80th film, but he was paid less than most of his costars.

THE GARDEN OF GHASTLY DELIGHTS

Hollywood has created its share of gore fests—from Friday the 13th (1980), to A Nightmare on Elm Street (1984), to Scream (1996). But all bloody, creepy slasher movies owe a large debt to the shock-theater pioneers in France, courtesy of turn-of-the-century Parisians who got their horror up close and personal at the Grand Guignol.

The Théâtre du Grand Guignol (pronounced with a hard G, like *gross*) was a small 280-seat theater founded in 1897 on the slopes of Montmartre in Paris. Over a century later, the Grand Guignol still means one thing: blood. And lots of it. Movie critics today still use the term Grand Guignol to describe a sort of over-the-top kind of blood and gore—with good reason. Eye gougings, stabbings, flayings, impalements—all were "performed" in front of a live audience.

ON SACRED GROUND

The theater was located in a small building that was originally a convent, a setting that lent itself surprisingly well to the sinister. The seats looked like pews, and two leering wooden angels hung over the stage. The stage, only 20 by 20 feet, was so close to the front row, one critic joked that the audience could shake hands with the actors without leaving their seats. With the addition of dim, red lighting and the abundance of shadows, the theater oozed the macabre even before the curtains opened.

WHAT'S IN A NAME?

Oscar Méténier, a former police secretary, founded the Grand Guignol in April 1897. Named after a popular children's puppet, the Grand Guignol was meant to be a big puppet show for the adult set. It would use live actors instead of puppets and specialize in one-act plays that showed slices of life from the Parisian underworld.

Eventually, Méténier left the Grand Guignol, handing it over to Max Maurey, who continued the one-act plays. But he turned slice-of-life drama into what one critic called "slice of death." In 1901 Maurey discovered the Grand Guignol's signature playwright, André de Lorde, the man who would earn the title Prince of Terror because of his gruesome plays. The son of a physician, Lorde spent his childhood listening to the screams of patients in his father's office, which resulted in a lifelong fascination with pain and death—a fascination he would turn into over a hundred terrifying plays for the Grand Guignol.

IS THERE A DOCTOR IN THE HOUSE?

Maurey, Lorde, and the cast judged the success of each production by the number of audience members that fainted—an average of two an evening. And they fainted with good reason. One popular play featured a young girl imprisoned in a madhouse with three old women who gouged her eyes out with a knitting needle. Horrified at what they had done, the crones turned on one of their own and seared off her face with a hot plate. Another play set a record with 15 faintings. Interestingly, it was mostly men that fainted, probably because they didn't look away at the worst parts.

As a publicity stunt, Maurey hired a physician to be present at all performances, although some accounts say that one doctor was not enough. A Guignoler, attempting to revive his fainting wife, called for the doctor. From the lobby Maurey replied that the doctor had just fainted as well!

A THOUSAND DEATHS TO DIE

Maxa, an actress at the Grand Guignol nicknamed the High Priestess of the Temple of Horror, kept a detailed diary of her career. In it she detailed the more than 10,000 times and 60 different ways that she was murdered on stage: these included being devoured by a puma, cut up into 93 pieces and glued back together, scalped, strangled, disemboweled, guillotined, hung, and burned alive. With four or five plays in one evening, that's a body count even Hollywood would be proud of!

The stage tricks that made the Grand Guignol the most realistic horror in town were closely guarded secrets—some were even patented. This was probably more to disguise the simplicity of the tricks than to keep other theaters from stealing them. The cornerstone was 10 different recipes for fake blood, each congealing at a different rate for different types of spurting and oozing wounds.

—Superman (Christopher Reeve), *Superman* (1978)

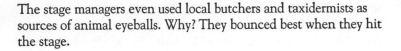

The stage managers even used local butchers and taxidermists as sources of animal eyeballs. Why? They bounced best when they hit the stage.

CROWNED HEADS

The theater hit its peak in popularity after 1915, which some historians attribute to the Guignol's filling a gap left when public executions were discontinued. Society women in particular flocked to the Grand Guignol in the 1920s and 1930s to scream and swoon into the arms of their male companions—or just the stranger in the next seat over. The audience often included royalty, among them the king of Greece, Princess Wilhemina of Holland, and the sultan of Morocco's children.

THE THRILL IS GONE

But after the real-life horrors of World War II, the Grand Guignol fell out of favor and never regained its former popularity. By the 1950s, audiences went to new horror movies (that stole some of their tricks straight from the Grand Guignol), and only curious tourists and college students frequented the theater. The Guignol tried in vain to generate new interest through publicity stunts (like staging the kidnapping of their own scantily clad leading ladies), but it was no use; the crowds didn't come. But the Guignol did go out with a scream. Performed by Maxa, it was so long and loud, that it permanently damaged her vocal chords. The little theater of horrors finally closed its doors forever in November 1962.

GUIGNOL SPLATTERS THE SILVER SCREEN

Though the little theater on the slopes of Montmartre is long gone, its aesthetic lives on. A number of cheap horror films have been set in a Grand Guignol–style theater like *Mad Love* (1935) and *Theatre of Death* (1966). Vincent Price's classic *Theatre of Blood* (1973) uses the Grand Guignol as its template. The blockbuster *Interview with the Vampire* (1994) even set a scene of frenzied vampire feeding on the Grand Guignol's stage.

Even more numerous are the films that owe their gore to the Grand Guignol. Though it is unlikely that movie directors Tobe Hooper (*The Texas Chain Saw Massacre*), John Carpenter (*Halloween*), or Sam Raimi (*The Evil Dead*) ever saw the Grand Guignol in its waning days, many film critics have compared the

---

For *The Lion King*, Disney animators went to Africa to study animal movement up close.

over-the-top bloodbaths in these movies to the Parisian theater. Now, thanks to Uncle John, you too can make astute allusions to the Grand Guignol when you and your friends watch next summer's popcorn thriller. Just remember that revolting as the slasher films of today are, it's all been done before—in front of a live audience, at that.

* * *

RAYMOND CHANDLER

Mystery novelist and screenwriter Raymond Chandler had a love-hate relationship with the movies.

"That's one thing I like about Hollywood. The writer is there revealed in his ultimate corruption. He asks no praise, because his praise comes to him in the form of a salary check."

"If my books had been any worse, I should not have been invited to Hollywood, and . . . if they had been any better, I should not have come."

"The challenge of screenwriting is to say much in little and then take half of that little out."

"Hollywood has all the personality of a paper cup."

"The wise screen writer is he who wears his second-best suit, artistically speaking, and doesn't take things too much to heart. He should have a touch of cynicism, but only a touch. The complete cynic is as useless to Hollywood as he is to himself."

"Hollywood's idea of 'production value' is spending a million dollars dressing up a story that any good writer would throw away."

The lead in *Beverly Hills Cop* (1984) was originally written for Sylvester Stallone.

ELIZABETH TAYLOR: BY THE NUMBERS

*With violet eyes to die for, Elizabeth Taylor collected
Oscars, husbands, and diamonds with ease. Just a few
brief highlights from a life with few dull moments.*

1.63
In meters, Miss Taylor's height. (That's about 5 feet 4 inches.)

2
Number of wedding rings Taylor wore while married to Eddie
Fisher: Fisher's on the ring finger of her left hand, and her recently
deceased husband Mike Todd's on her right.

5
Number of times Taylor was nominated for a Best Actress Oscar:
for *Raintree County; Cat on a Hot Tin Roof; BUtterfield 8; Suddenly,
Last Summer;* and *Who's Afraid of Virginia Woolf?* She won twice
(for *BUtterfield* and *Woolf*), even though she intensely disliked
BUtterfield 8. After winning that year, she told more than one person backstage, "I still think it's a piece of s***."

6
In years, the length of Taylor's marriage to John W. Warner, who
was elected to the U.S. Senate two years into their marriage.
Taylor didn't like the role of senator's wife; she felt she'd been
exiled to "a domestic Siberia."

7
Number of men married to Liz: Conrad "Nicky" Hilton Jr.; Michael
Wilding (two children: Michael Jr. and Christopher); Michael
Todd (one child: Liza Todd); Eddie Fisher (one child adopted:
Maria Taylor, later named Maria Burton); Richard Burton; John W.
Warner; Larry Fortensky.

8
Number of Liz Taylor's marriages. (She married Burton twice.)
Also the size of a typical Taylor-Burton entourage, both on loca-
tion and vacations: four children, two nannies, and two secretaries.

In *Rain Man*, Dustin Hoffman originally wanted Bill Murray to play Charlie.

9
The number of months her first marriage lasted. She married Nicky Hilton at age 18 (some say to escape her overbearing mother), but was disappointed to discover his drinking and gambling problems.

10
Number of minutes a day allotted to arithmetic at the MGM schoolhouse that Taylor attended as a child star. Fifteen minutes of spelling or geography might be crammed between takes. This amounted to virtually no education at all, a circumstance that bothered her for most of her life.

12
Age at which Taylor starred in *National Velvet* and rocketed to stardom.

18.50
In dollars, Larry Fortensky's hourly union wage as a driver for a construction company; he kept the job even after moving in with Taylor in 1989.

19
Age at which Taylor married her second husband, English actor Michael Wilding, 20 years her senior. He became known as Mr. Elizabeth Taylor. She divorced him after meeting Mike Todd, who became her third husband.

20
Number of minutes after their first divorce that Taylor called Burton and asked, "Richard, do you think we did the right thing?"

69.42
Number of carats in the pear-shaped diamond Burton gave to Taylor. It cost him $1.1 million. Taylor sold it in 1978 to fund a hospital in Botswana.

180+
In pounds, the amount of weight that Taylor, at her heaviest in 1980, carried on her small frame.

200
In dollars, the cost of a limited edition, bottled ounce of the perfume Passion, Elizabeth Taylor's first foray into the fragrance

business. Each "Signature" bottle was autographed in gold by Taylor.

414
Number of days Elizabeth Taylor and Mike Todd were married before his plane, *The Liz*, crashed into the Zuni Mountains of New Mexico. Taylor was supposed to fly with him, but she stayed home instead to nurse a bad cold.

1932
The year of Miss Taylor's birth. She was born in England on February 27 to American parents from Arkansas City, Kansas.

2,800
Pounds of luggage that Taylor arrived with in Leningrad when filming for *The Blue Bird* began in 1975.

25,000
In dollars, the cost of a diamond tiara that Mike Todd gave to Taylor to wear to the Academy Awards in 1957. Elizabeth was a presenter that year; Todd won the Oscar as producer of the Best Picture: *Around the World in Eighty Days*.

100,000
In dollars, Taylor's fee for one day's work—playing a madam—in the Civil War TV miniseries *North and South* (1985).

315,000
In dollars, the total worth of four major artworks—by Cézanne, Monet, Cassatt, and Utrillo—that Mike Todd purchased to hang in Taylor's hospital room after an operation on her spine in 1957.

1,000,000
In dollars, the minimum salary that Taylor negotiated for *Cleopatra*, a fee that no actor had ever received before. Her contract included living expenses for herself and her entourage, and 10 percent of the movie's box office receipts. Her total take eventually surpassed $7 million.

88,000,000
In dollars, the amount of money the Taylor-Burtons earned in the 1960s. They spent $65 million of it.

Armageddon (1998) was the first film in which actual NASA space suits were used.

RAMBO, STARRING AL PACINO

You be the judge. Could these actors have filled the roles listed here? Turns out, they were each considered for the parts. Read more on page 32.

GENE HACKMAN AS HANNIBAL LECTER (*The Silence of the Lambs*—1991) Hackman wanted to direct the film and write the screenplay, so Orion Pictures bought the rights to the novel. Then Hackman dropped out. Director Jonathan Demme signed Anthony Hopkins for the part without telling Orion head Mike Medavoy, who was furious that "an Englishman" would play Lecter. Medavoy agreed on one condition: that Jodie Foster be cast as FBI agent Clarice Starling instead of Meg Ryan. Demme agreed; Foster won her second straight Oscar.

GOLDIE HAWN AND MERYL STREEP AS THELMA AND LOUISE (*Thelma and Louise*—1991) Streep wanted to test her comedic talents; Hawn's film *Private Benjamin* had made $100 million at the box office. They seemed perfect for the film, and wanted to work together. But their schedules were full. "We weren't available right then," Hawn says, "and the director, Ridley Scott, wouldn't wait." Michelle Pfeiffer and Jodie Foster turned down the film; so did Cher. So Scott gave the parts to Geena Davis—who had only two films to her credit—and Susan Sarandon.

ELVIS PRESLEY AS THE MIDNIGHT COWBOY (*Midnight Cowboy*—1969) Desperate to be taken seriously as an actor, the King went shopping around for "a more serious movie role." The part of the male prostitute in *Midnight Cowboy* was one of the parts he considered, but he ultimately turned the film down and did one called *A Change of Habit* instead. Reason: "Since it was about a doctor (Elvis) and a nun (Mary Tyler Moore) in the ghetto, that qualified as being more 'serious.'" *A Change of Habit* was Elvis's biggest box office dud; *Midnight Cowboy* won the Oscar for Best Picture and turned Jon Voight into a star.

The Sixth Sense is one of only four horror films to be Oscar nominated for Best Picture.

AL PACINO AS RAMBO (*First Blood*—1982) Pacino wasn't the first major star interested in the part of John Rambo. (Eastwood, De Niro, and Paul Newman turned it down.) He wanted Rambo to be "a little more of a madman," and had the script rewritten. But the new draft made the character too dark and nutty, so Pacino passed on the role. So did John Travolta, Michael Douglas, and Nick Nolte. Then Carolco Pictures bought the script and offered it to Sly Stallone, who rewrote the insane Vietnam vet into a misunderstood American hero, "kind of like a Rocky movie." *First Blood* was Stallone's first non-Rocky film that didn't bomb. It saved his career. The sequel, *Rambo*, established it for good.

DORIS DAY AS MRS. ROBINSON (*The Graduate*—1967) Day's Hollywood image was as "the perennial virgin." "There was something about taking that All-American housewife image and turning it all around," says producer Larry Turman. "I sent the script to her, but we never heard a thing." Day later explained that she read the script, but just couldn't see herself playing the role. So it was offered to Anne Bancroft, who could.

BURT REYNOLDS AS RANDALL P. McMURPHY (*One Flew Over the Cuckoo's Nest*—1975) When Marlon Brando turned down the part, director Milos Forman had breakfast with Burt Reynolds and told him he was one of two actors being considered for the part. Reynolds was thrilled. "If the other guy isn't Jack Nicholson," he replied, "I've got the part." When Forman stopped eating dead in his tracks, Reynolds knew he wasn't going to get the part. Nicholson got the role, and won the Oscar for best actor.

BURT REYNOLDS AS GARRETT BREEDLOVE (*Terms of Endearment*—1983) About ten years after Reynolds was turned down for *Cuckoo's Nest*, director James L. Brooks sent him the script for *Terms of Endearment*. The lead had been created especially for him, but Reynolds rejected it. "I'd promised . . . that I'd star in *Stroker Ace*," Burt explained later. So Brooks offered the part to Jack Nicholson, who jumped at it. "How many scripts make you cry?" he said. "I read hundreds of screenplays every year and this one made me think, 'Yeah, I know just how this guy feels.' It was terrific." *Stroker Ace* was one of the forgettable films of the year; *Terms of Endearment* won Nicholson his second Oscar.

BOX OFFICE BLOOPERS

Here are some more great bloopers
from the silver screen.

MOVIE: *The Bridge on the River Kwai* (1957)
SCENE: The film's opening credits.
BLOOPER: This blockbuster won seven Oscars, but no awards for spelling. They misspelled the star's name, Alec Guinness, as "Guiness."

MOVIE: *Clueless* (1995)
SCENE: A close-up shot of Cher's (Alicia Silverstone) report card.
BLOOPER: The name on the report card is Cher Hamilton, not the character's name, Cher Horowitz.

MOVIE: *Vanilla Sky* (2001)
SCENE: Julie (Cameron Diaz) and David (Tom Cruise) are in the car. Julie goes crazy and drives it off a bridge.
BLOOPER: The exterior shot reveals there's no one in the car.

MOVIE: *Die Hard* (1989)
SCENE: When Sgt. Al Powell (Reginald Veljohnson) crashes his squad car, his forehead is bleeding pretty badly.
BLOOPER: Throughout the remainder of the film, no evidence of the wound is present.

MOVIE: *Double Indemnity* (1944)
SCENE: Fred MacMurray plays a bachelor.
BLOOPER: Then why is he wearing a wedding ring?

MOVIE: *North by Northwest* (1959)
SCENE: In a restaurant, Eve (Eva Marie Saint) pulls a gun on Thornhill (Cary Grant).
BLOOPER: Just before the shot is fired, a boy sitting at a table in the background puts his fingers in his ears to muffle the sound of a gun he has no way of seeing . . . but obviously knows is there.

MOVIE: *Twister* (1996)
SCENE: The story chronicles one of the biggest tornadoes in Oklahoma's history.
BLOOPER: Most of the road signs are from Texas.

MOVIE: *Shrek* (2001)
SCENE: Shrek (Mike Myers) and Fiona (Cameron Diaz) blow up some balloons and let them go.
BLOOPER: The balloons fly up in the air. (Okay, we know they're fairy tale characters, but that doesn't explain how they could exhale helium.)

MOVIE: *Independence Day* (1996)
SCENE: Inside a tunnel, Jasmine (Vivica A. Fox) and her son, Dylan (Ross Bagley), escape through a service door just before they're overtaken by a wall of fire. Then Jasmine calls the dog.
BLOOPER: Even allowing Hollywood its usual "artistic license," the fact that Jasmine and Dylan make it out is barely plausible. But the dog? A shockwave is tossing cars like toys, yet somehow super-dog manages to jump out of the way barely a few feet in front of it.

MOVIE: *Kate & Leopold* (2001)
SCENE: Spectators on a bridge are waving American flags.
BLOOPER: The flags have all 50 stars . . . in 1876.

MOVIE: *Pulp Fiction* (1994)
SCENE: Vincent (John Travolta) and Jules (Samuel L. Jackson) are in an apartment when someone bursts out of the bathroom and starts shooting at them.
BLOOPER: The bullet holes are in the wall before the gunman starts shooting.

MOVIE: *Cocktail* (1988)
SCENE: Tom Cruise goes into the Regency Theatre in Manhattan and gets into a fight.
BLOOPER: It must have been a long fight—when he went into the theater, *Barfly* appears on the marquee. When he exits, it says *Casablanca*.

Marie Osmond turned down the female lead (Sandy) in *Grease* (1978).

FROM B MOVIE
TO THE BIG TIME

Sam Raimi got his start directing B movie horror flicks, but today he directs Hollywood blockbusters, like the big budget Spider-Man (2002). So how did Raimi get from B movie to big time? It's all thanks to his first movie, the cult classic unrated, ultra-low-budget horror flick Evil Dead *(1981).*

Sam Raimi was like thousands of American teenagers—he wanted to work in movies when he grew up. Unlike most, he actually made it. It wasn't easy; in the beginning, no one in Hollywood would give him a chance. So he and his friends decided to make their own break.

THE MICHIGAN MAFIA
Sam Raimi was a geek in high school in Detroit. And like many such teenage outcasts, he spent his weekends with other geeks. He had an 8 mm camera, and with his friends Bruce Campbell and Scott Spiegel, his older brother Ivan, his tag-along younger brother Ted, and a few others, he made movies. This group, who called themselves the Michigan Mafia, drew their inspiration largely from the Three Stooges. They created Super 8 films, and their work continued through college, during which time another film fanatic, Sam's roommate Rob Tapert, joined the crew. (If you're really curious, you can still find bootlegs of Raimi's first films on eBay.)

After college Sam Raimi and his friends decided they wanted to make their own feature film. Unfortunately, no one in Hollywood was in the market for inexperienced filmmakers. Undeterred, Raimi and company decided to do it themselves. Though most of their Super 8 films had been comic schlock, when it came to low-budget movies, there was only one choice: horror. Suspense and gore were cheap, and they sold big. Low-budget horror films, like *The Texas Chain Saw Massacre*, had gone on to mainstream success; the Michigan Mafia thought a film of theirs could do the same. To get started they only needed one thing: money.

Jurassic Park briefly held the all-time box office record, until it was overtaken by *Titanic*.

DEATH OF THE DEAD

By banging on the doors of all their friends, their friends' relatives, and their relatives' business partners, Raimi and company managed to scrounge up just enough money for their magnum opus: *Evil Dead*. They hired a cast—with Bruce Campbell playing the lead—and drove to Tennessee, a location the group thought would be warmer than Michigan, for their six weeks of shooting in November. Most of the action took place in the woods surrounding an abandoned cabin, so warmer weather would be easier on everybody. Too bad the fall of 1979 in Tennessee was one of the coldest on record! By the end of the shoot—which dragged to more than 12 weeks—the cast and crew were living in their cabin/set with no heat, no electricity, and no running water. But more than half the cast had bailed out before then. For the second half of filming, Raimi had to use stand-ins for the actors who quit, or Fake Shemps as they came to be called (in honor of the body doubles used by the Three Stooges after Shemp Howard's death in the middle of one of their films).

NECESSITY IS THE MOTHER OF INVENTION

With no money for fancy cameras, Raimi improvised. There was the Vas-o-Cam: a camera placed on a two-by-four slicked with vaseline so that it could move smoothly, with no dolly required. There was the Shaky-Cam: a camera bolted to a two-by-four; when two cameramen held either end of the board, they could run with the camera and execute wild maneuvers not possible even with more expensive setups. And there was the Ram-o-Cam: the camera that Raimi used to burst through glass windows. These rigs were so effective that Raimi has continued to use them, even on his higher-budget films.

HE LIKES TO TORTURE ACTORS

Bruce Campbell still warns actors about to work with Raimi that Sam "likes to torture actors." For *Evil Dead*, one actress had to run screaming, half-naked through the cold woods, in the middle of the night, for hours on end. To get a shot of a dismembered body with its limbs still jiggling on the floor, Raimi nailed floorboards over the actors, who were trapped in uncomfortable positions and covered in bugs. But members of the cast weren't the only ones suffering on this shoot. With such a tight budget, filming would often

In Pixar films, the end credits list babies born to crew members during the production.

continue for more than 24 hours without a break. Once, after shooting for 50 hours straight, Sam Raimi fell so deeply asleep on the set that the crew members couldn't wake him—and had to finally call it a night.

KID TESTED, KING APPROVED

With filming, special effects, postproduction, and marketing all included, the budget for *Evil Dead* rang in at $350,000. The principal photography cost only $90,000. With the help of legendary Hollywood promoter Irvin Shapiro, *Evil Dead* made it into the Cannes film festival in 1982. There it might have been forgotten, if not for the raves of one audience member. Stephen King wrote a review in praise of the film, calling it "the most ferociously original horror film of the year." With that seal of approval, *Evil Dead* was well on its way to becoming a cult classic.

Because of its gore, *Evil Dead* was released unrated, so it couldn't be shown in major theaters. Nevertheless, word of mouth and video cassettes ensured its success. In 1998, on its 15th anniversary, *Evil Dead* was in the top three of *Billboard's* video sales chart. The film spawned two sequels, *Evil Dead II* (1987) and *Army of Darkness* (1993), sometimes called *Medieval Dead* by fans. There's even been a musical version.

THE CLASSIC

Sam Raimi has gone on to direct big-budget films for major studios, a long way from his low-budget roots. But throughout it all he's retained a few visual signatures that started back in his super 8 days.

- **The Classic**—Sam Raimi's car, a cream-colored 1973 Oldsmobile Delta 88, nicknamed the Classic, has appeared in all of Raimi's films, except for *The Quick and the Dead*, which was a Western. As Bruce Campbell has pointed out, that car's been in more films than he has.

- **Fake Shemps**—Raimi still inserts stand-ins for other actors, only now he uses a few of his friends and relatives for the arms, legs, or backs of other actors. Raimi fans can usually spot the body parts of Bruce Campbell or Ted Raimi making cameos.

- **The POV Shot**—Raimi loves using point-of-view (POV) shots in his films, but he twists the convention by taking the point of view of an inanimate object: the evil spirits in *Evil Dead*, bullets in *Darkman*, and a flying eyeball in *Evil Dead II*.

That tradition started with *Toy Story* (1995).

BEATTY, BONNIE, AND CLYDE

"They're young . . . they're in love . . . and they kill people."
It's the story behind the movie Bonnie and Clyde.

THE FILM
Bonnie and Clyde (1967)

THE STORY
In the 1930s during the Great Depression, Clyde Barrow and Bonnie Parker meet, fall in love, start a gang, and rob banks. As their crime spree spreads from Oklahoma to Texas, they progress from amateur thieves to legendary outlaws—becoming folk heroes to the victims of the Depression, but public enemies to the authorities who hunt them down.

THE BACKSTORY
Obsessed from the moment he read the script, 28-year-old Warren Beatty was determined to produce and star in *Bonnie and Clyde*. But in 1966 Beatty was still fairly new to the motion picture business and had yet to make a big, commercial hit. If he wasn't going to rob a bank himself, Beatty had to find $1.8 million in financing from Warner Bros. Studios. But studio head Jack Warner was furious at the young star for his refusal to play President Kennedy in *PT 109* (the president himself wanted Beatty for the part!) and was reluctant to greenlight the film.

Beatty wanted Arthur Penn to direct, but Penn and Beatty had just lost money for the studio on a film called *Mickey One*. Warner's initial opinion of *Bonnie and Clyde* and Beatty: "What does Warren Beatty think he's doing? . . . This gangster stuff went out with Cagney."

Other actors might crumble before such opposition, but Beatty was willing to get on his knees to beg an executive for the money. One witness swears that Beatty even kissed the shoes of Warner himself and wouldn't get up until the studio head agreed to make the film. However it happened, Warner Bros. ultimately agreed to make the film.

"I am the Supreme Being. I'm not entirely dim."

ON LOCATION
Though Warner wanted the film made on the studio back lot, Beatty took the cast and crew to rural Texas. There, dust storms and withered fields could evoke the failed farms of Depression-era America. In the Texas boonies they'd be far from Warner and his likely objections to the violence that would become a hallmark of the film—in which more than 30,000 rounds of (blank) ammunition were fired.

THE DISH ON THE STARS
After the lead female role was rejected by Natalie Wood, Jane Fonda, Tuesday Weld, Sharon Tate, and other actresses, little-known Faye Dunaway was cast as Bonnie. The film made her a star and did the same for Gene Hackman, who played Clyde's brother Buck. Gene Wilder also made his first appearance on film (he played the hostage, Eugene Grizzard).

For the film's now-famous ending, small squibs (dynamite charges) were placed on Beatty's and Dunaway's bodies. The signal for detonation was Beatty squeezing a pear in his hand; he wanted to squeeze a juicy peach, but those were out of season, so the crew injected the pear with water. When Beatty squeezed, the squibs exploded, and Beatty and Dunaway appeared riddled with bullets. The notorious death scene was done in one take.

THE LEGACY
After the advance screening, Jack Warner did not enjoy *Bonnie and Clyde* at all; during the movie, he left three times to go to the bathroom, not a good sign. He told Beatty and Penn that he just didn't understand the movie. Warner Bros. gave the film a limited release with little marketing support in August 1967; by mid-fall, it was out of the major theaters. But the film's stylish cinematography, unsentimental violence, and romanticized antiheroes had won some great reviews—ammunition for Beatty to use in his fight for a rerelease. Warner Bros. put the movie back in theaters, and it became a cultural phenomenon, made the cover of *TIME*, and was nominated for 10 Oscars including Best Picture. It made $23 million for the studio, its second biggest moneymaker ever at the time (*My Fair Lady* was the first).

Bonnie and Clyde was the first of several small, edgy films from "new Hollywood" to bring a young generation and big profits back

—Supreme Being (Ralph Richardson), *Time Bandits* (1981)

to studios; others included *The Graduate, Easy Rider,* and *Chinatown.* As Jack Warner later told Beatty, "Hey kid . . . if you listened to me, you'd make nothing but flops."

* * *

- Faye Dunaway's stand-in was a student from Lake Highlands High School. Her name? Morgan Fairchild.
- In an early draft of the script, Bonnie was a nymphomaniac, Clyde was bisexual, and both were in love with C. W. Moss (Michael J. Pollard). The explicit subplot was dropped, although hints of it remain.
- Mabel Cavitt of Red Oak, Texas, was getting $12 a scene as an extra before she was picked to play Bonnie's mom in the picnic scene when Bonnie bids farewell to her family.

* * *

STRAIGHT FROM THE WRITER'S MOUTH

"The honors Hollywood has for the writer are as dubious as tissue-paper cuff links."
—Ben Hecht, screenwriter

"In a movie . . . the hero, as well as the heroine, has to be a virgin. The villain can lay anybody he wants, have as much fun as he wants cheating and stealing, getting rich and whipping the servants. But you have to shoot him in the end."
—Herbert Mankiewicz, screenwriter

"Hollywood, to hear some writers tell it, is the place where they take an author's steak tartare and make cheeseburger out of it."
—Fletcher Knebel, author

In the "brain scene" in *Hannibal* (2001), the brain is dark chicken meat.

CHINESE KITSCH

Nothing says Hollywood like Sid Grauman's overgrown Asian temple, aka Grauman's Chinese Theatre. In fact, someone once said that "to visit Los Angeles and not see 'the Chinese' is like visiting China and not seeing the Great Wall." So let's pay a visit, Uncle John–style.

- Home to a conglomeration of Oriental styles—murals, neon dragons, upsweeping columns topped with doves, and the two stone Heaven Dogs that still stand guard outside the entrance—the Chinese theatre cost $2 million to build and decorate in 1927.

- Sid Grauman was managing director until he died, but he never owned more than a third of the business; his partners included Hollywood power couple Douglas Fairbanks and Mary Pickford. Grauman sold his percentage to Fox West Coast Theatres in 1929.

- Silent film star Norma Talmadge turned over the first spadeful of dirt, and actress Anna May Wong—born in Los Angeles's Chinatown—drove in the first rivet.

- Stories vary, but it may have been Grauman himself who first left his footprints in wet cement out front, but purely by accident. This gave him the idea to invite Pickford and Fairbanks to leave their foot- and handprints in the cement also. And so began the tradition.

- The courtyard of the theater includes the imprints of Betty Grable's leg, John Wayne's fist, Jimmy Durante's nose, Al Jolson's knees, Harold Lloyd's eyeglasses, Sonja Henie's ice skates, Harpo Marx's harp, and cigars belonging to Groucho Marx and George Burns. Not to mention Whoopi Goldberg's dreadlocks and R2D2's wheels.

- Roy Rogers's horse Trigger and Gene Autry's Champion put their hoofprints in cement, but the first equine honoree was Tom Mix's horse Tony.

- A tunnel (now sealed up) led from the theater to the Hollywood Roosevelt Hotel across the street, so that after big events stars could depart without being gawked at.

Johnny Depp made his film debut in *Nightmare on Elm Street* (1984).

- The theater opened with the premiere of Cecil B. DeMille's *The King of Kings*. More recently, *The Aviator*, a movie that recreates the 1930 premiere of *Hell's Angels* at Grauman's Chinese Theatre, premiered there.

- Grauman's Chinese Theatre has appeared in the movies, too: *What Price Hollywood?*, *Singin' in the Rain*, *A Star Is Born* (both the 1937 and 1954 versions), *Blazing Saddles*, *Rush Hour*, and *Speed*.

- Mann Theatres bought the Chinese in 1973 and still owns it. They changed the name for a while, but in 2001 switched back to the original: Grauman's Chinese Theatre.

* * *

A GALA AFFAIR

Grauman introduced the concept of the gala movie premiere in 1922, when the world's first was held at another one of his theaters—the Egyptian. The movie: *Robin Hood*, starring Douglas Fairbanks.

* * *

FAIR WARNING

Frankenstein premiered on November 21, 1931. Before the opening credits rolled, *Frankenstein* began with a warning: "We are about to unfold the story of Frankenstein . . . It is one of the strangest tales ever told . . . I think it will thrill you. It may shock you. It might even horrify you. So if any of you feel that you do not care to subject your nerves to such a strain, now's your chance to—well, we warned you."

* * *

BIG MOVIE, SMALL SCREEN

On November 3, 1956, *The Wizard of Oz* was shown on TV for the first time and captured an audience of an estimated 45 million viewers. The annual airing would become a tradition and win it legions of fans for years to come.

Dave Chappelle turned down the role of Bubba in *Forrest Gump* (1994) . . .

THE PIXAR STORY

*Before Pixar began making movies about toys and fish, the computer
animation giant began as just another one of George Lucas's ideas. In
the early 1980s Lucas wanted to create a computer-focused group to
complement his special effects house, Industrial Light & Magic. This
new division would grow and eventually become Pixar. Here's the story
of how they brought computers to the world of cartoons.*

FROM COMPUTERS TO CARTOONS
In 1986 Lucas decided to spin off his computer-effects division, and
Steve Jobs (the once and future head of Apple computers) decided
to buy it. Jobs purchased it for roughly $10 million and turned it
into a company named Pixar. Originally, Pixar focused on making
and selling computer software and hardware. Its star item would be
the cutting-edge Pixar Image Computer, a high-priced item
($135,000) that turned code into 3-D images, and the $60,000
worth of additional software and accessories businesses had to buy
to use it.

During this time, Pixar also maintained a small animation
department—mostly to create short pieces to show off the capabili-
ties of the expensive supercomputer. In addition to being shown at
computer trade shows and conferences, Pixar animators' work
began to attract attention in the movie world. One of Pixar's first
cartoon shorts, *Luxo Jr.* (which starred a hopping desk lamp who
would later become part of the Pixar logo) was nominated for a
Best Animated Short Film Oscar in 1987. It didn't win. But two
years later, another Pixar short, *Tin Toy*, would capture the award
(and also inspire the Pixar team's first feature film a few years
later).

FROM ADS TO MOVIES
Due to all the praise the cartoons were receiving, the Pixar animation division thrived and grew. In addition to its award-winning
cartoon shorts, the department started creating memorable television commercials in the late 1980s and early 1990s, like the
LifeSavers conga line and the vine-swinging bottles of Listerine
mouthwash. The smooth, seamless animation looked three-
dimensional but still retained a fun cartoony look.

. . . and has admitted to deeply regretting it. He thought the movie would bomb.

Advances in Pixar's software allowed the animation department to expand into feature films. In the 1980s Pixar collaborated with Disney to create the Computer Animation Production System (CAPS), software that allowed animators to mix the traditional process of cel animation (characters and backgrounds are hand-painted for every frame before being filmed) with a new process that created and compiled animation on a computer. Disney used CAPS to combine the two cartoon styles in its smash hits of the early 1990s: the ballroom scene in *Beauty & the Beast*, the magic carpet ride through the cave of wonders in *Aladdin*, and the wilde-beest stampede in *The Lion King*. Audiences were thrilled with the breathtaking results. So Pixar and Disney decided to take the next step and create feature-length films using only computers. The two inked a deal in 1991: the Pixar team would create movies, and Disney would distribute (and own) them.

SUCCESS STORY

After changing their name to Pixar Animation Studios, everyone got to work on the first project, *Toy Story*. But before anyone began animating, the plot had to be set, and it had to be good. Director John Lasseter (who had been with the company since its begin-ning; Lucas had hired him away from Disney back in the 1980s) likened the story development to editing the film before anything had been shot. The writers spent six months alone on perfecting it and ultimately decided on the story of two toys competing to be a boy's favorite (the short *Tin Toy* was an inspiration). Then the 110-member team began creating the movie on their computer screens. A cluster of 117 computers "rendered" the movie; render-ing is the process where the code is transferred to images, and lighting, texture, and shading are added to each shot. A time-intensive process, it would take one average computer 43 years to do the job. These computers got it done in four.

The results were worth all the careful planning and hard work. Released in November 1995, *Toy Story* was a smash, making $192 million in the United States and Canada, and another $358 mil-lion worldwide. It nabbed director John Lasseter a special Academy Award "for the development and inspired application of techniques that have made possible the first feature-length computer-animated film." Since then Pixar's films and short subjects have been both financial and critical successes, making lots of money and captur-

Robin Williams has sometimes been credited as Sudy Nim.

ing many awards, including two Best Animated Feature awards for *Finding Nemo* (2003) and *The Incredibles* (2004).

Because of Pixar's runaway success, other movie studios have created their own computer animation divisions to compete. But so far, none have matched the record of Pixar, the pioneers of computer animation.

For more on Pixar's movies, turn to page 305.

* * *

"The main reason to do *Toy Story* was so during work hours, I could go to the store and buy toys on the company credit card."
— John Lasseter, director

* * *

THE ACADEMY GIVETH,
AND THE ACADEMY TAKETH AWAY

After Orson Welles's death in 1985, nobody knew where his Oscar for *Citizen Kane* was. His daughter (and heir) Beatrice requested a duplicate in 1988 from the Academy, which gave her one. But in 1994 Welles's original Oscar resurfaced. Gary Graver, a cinematographer, claimed the late Welles had given it to him years before. Financially strapped, Graver sold the statue for $50,000 to an auction house, which was going to auction it off. When Welles's daughter heard about the upcoming sale, she sued to stop it and reclaimed the Oscar for the estate.

Fast forward to 2003. Beatrice Welles was in dire financial straits and decided to sell her father's original Oscar at a Christie's auction. This time the Academy was the one to sue to block the sale. The Academy claimed that, according to a policy adopted by the Academy in 1950, Beatrice had to offer to sell the statue to it first (for $1) before it could be offered to the public. Beatrice fought back and sued the Academy, arguing that the agreement only applied to the duplicate Oscar created in 1988, not the original 1941 statue. A California court agreed with her, saying that the Academy's policy did not retroactively apply. Welles still has her father's Oscar and still has plans to sell it. She thinks it may fetch as much as $1 million.

SCRIPT WRITING: PART 2, THE LINGO

The Hollywood moviemaking industry has a lingo all its own. Here are a few words that will help you understand what the heck is going on!

Against: A term describing the potential payday for a screenwriter. Let's say you've hit the jackpot and get a contract for $800,000. You'll get 50 percent up front. This $400,000 is against the $800,000, which means you'll be paid $400,000 when the script revisions are finished.

Beat Sheet: When the descriptions of the main events in a screenplay are shortened.

Bump: A bad part, or poorly written section, of a movie that will take the viewer's attention away from the story.

Cheat a Script: A script where the margins and spacing on a page are fudged to try to fool the reader (agent or producer) into thinking the script is shorter than it really is.

Complication: This is where a story peaks. Often the second act of a three-act script.

Development Hell: When the movie development process lasts way too long—sometimes months and even years. It usually happens when there are changes at the top and new executives raise objections to projects. The longer development hell lasts, the more likely the movie will be abandoned or canceled.

EXT.: Short for *exterior*. It means an outside scene.

Freeze-frame: When the image on the screen stops and becomes a still shot.

Hip Pocket: A casual relationship between a writer and an established agent. It's used instead of a signed agreement or contract.

Line Reading: When a director tells an actor a how to perform a line of dialogue.

Logline: A movie description of 25 or fewer words.

Package: The basic elements necessary to get financing for a film.

Production Script: A script that doesn't need major changes or rewrites. It can be used daily for filming on a movie set.

SFX: Abbreviation for *sound effects*.

V.O.: Abbreviation for *voice-over*. Voice-over means that a speaker is narrating action on-screen, instead of the characters or actors actually onscreen.

SOLD!

*Once a movie becomes a hit, things that were once just props quickly
become valuable collectors' items. It's hard to believe how much money
people will shell out for a piece of movie history. Just take a look.*

PRECIOUS PROPS
Item: Bamboo cane used by Charlie Chaplin in *Modern Times*
Price Tag: $91,919

Item: Sled desired by Orson Welles in *Citizen Kane* (There were
four prop sleds: one made of pine and three made of balsa wood.)
Price Tag #1: $60,500 (a balsa wood sled bought by Steven
Spielberg in 1982)
Price Tag #2: $233,500 (the lone pine sled purchased in 1996)

Item: Piano played in the Paris scenes in *Casablanca*
Price Tag: $154,000

Item: Inscribed fiberglass tablets carried by Charlton Heston in
The Ten Commandments.
Price Tag: $81,700

Item: Aston Martin DB5 driven by Sean Connery in *Goldfinger*
Price Tag: $275,000

Item: Rubber shark teeth from *Jaws*
Price Tag: $3,000

Item: Luke Skywalker's lightsaber from *The Empire Strikes Back*
Price Tag: $200,600 (It was expected to sell for $60,000.)

Item: Wilson, the volleyball that kept Tom Hanks company in
Cast Away
Price Tag: $21,000 (An ordinary volleyball costs about $20.)

. . . La Traviata, **which is about a prostitute who falls in love with a wealthy man.**

COLLECTABLE COSTUMES
Item: Santa Claus suit worn by Edmund Gwenn in 1947's *Miracle on 34th Street*
Price Tag: $41,000

Item: Fedora worn by Al Pacino in *The Godfather*
Price Tag: $16,100

Item: White suit worn by John Travolta in *Saturday Night Fever*
Price Tag: $145,000 (purchased by movie critic and fan Gene Siskel)

Item: Darth Vader's helmet from *The Empire Strikes Back*
Price Tag: $115,000

Item: The leather jacket worn by Harrison Ford in *Indiana Jones and the Last Crusade*
Price Tag: $94,400

Item: Loud yellow suit worn by Jim Carrey in *The Mask*
Price Tag: $16,001

RECORD SETTERS
Most Valuable Shoes. In May 2000 one pair of ruby slippers from *The Wizard of Oz* fetched $666,000 at a Christie's auction.

Most Valuable Movie Poster. In 1997 a poster for *The Mummy* (1932) starring Boris Karloff sold for $453,500 at auction. It broke the record held by another Karloff classic, *Frankenstein* (1931), whose poster sold for $198,000.

Most Valuable Prop. It turns out that the Maltese Falcon is the stuff that dreams are made of. The statuette used in the 1941 film sold for $398,500 at a 1994 Christie's auction.

Most Valuable Script. A good script can bring in a lot of money, even after the movie is made. Marlon Brando's Annotated Script from *The Godfather* sold for $312,800 in 2005, setting the world record for a film script. The former record was held by Clark Gable's annotated script for *Gone With the Wind*, which sold for $244,500 in 1996.

The buffalo Mick Dundee pacifies in *Crocodile Dundee* (1986) was drugged.

AKA

*Making a name for yourself as a movie star can take a
lifetime—and usually it's not even your real name. But you
can learn a lot about the stars if you understand how they got their
nicknames. Test your celebrity nickname knowledge with this quiz!*

1. John Wayne, whose real name was Marion, was known as the
   Duke because of his:
   a. Status as movie star royalty
   b. Ability to duke it out—on-screen and off
   c. Respect for Her Majesty the Queen of England
   d. Dog named Duke
   e. Fondness for R & B great Gene Chandler

2. What modern-day tough guy once went by the nickname
   Bobby Milk?
   a. Robert Duvall
   b. Robert De Niro
   c. Billy Bob Thornton
   d. Robert Blake
   e. Robert Downey Junior

3. What Hollywood legend nicknamed his wife Sluggy because of
   her penchant for hitting the bottle—then hitting him?
   a. Humphrey Bogart
   b. W. C. Fields
   c. Orson Welles
   d. David Spade
   e. Quentin Tarantino

4. Which Hollywood action star earned the nickname The Wall
   playing ice hockey in high school?
   a. Vin Diesel
   b. Jesse Ventura
   c. Jean Claude Van Damme
   d. Jim Carrey
   e. Keanu Reeves

There are no opening credits or titles in *Apocalypse Now* (1979).

5. Born Caryn Elaine Johnson, actress Whoopi Goldberg derived her stage name by taking *Goldberg* from the Jewish side of her family and *Whoopi* because:
   a. When she landed her first stand-up gig, she took to the streets yelling "Whoopee! Whoopee!"
   b. She was famous for "making whoopee" in high school
   c. Her favorite song is "Makin' Whoopee," as sung by Ray Charles
   d. She had a gas problem and sounded like a whoopee cushion
   e. She grew up on Whoopee Island in the Florida Keys

6. Superstar Will Smith got his nickname the Fresh Prince through his:
   a. Charm and ability to talk his way out of trouble
   b. Famous Prince tennis racket he used to qualify for state championships
   c. Real life claim to Moroccan nobility
   d. Luck at gambling
   e. Passion for Machiavelli

7. Chevy Chase, born Cornelius Crane Chase, changed his screen name to Chevy because:
   a. His family owned a vacation home in Chevy Chase, Maryland
   b. His grandmother used to call him that
   c. He used to fix Chevys while working his way through school
   d. His wife is a descendant of Chevrolet
   e. *Saturday Night Live* gave him a Corvette as a signing bonus

8. Demi Moore is known in some circles as "Gimme Moore" because:
   a. She always has seconds at dinner
   b. She can successfully negotiate higher salaries and perks
   c. Early in her career, she always angled for more screen time
   d. She wants to have many children
   e. She likes to date younger actors

Turn to page 486 for the answers.

"It's all ball bearings nowadays."

"I SPY":
THE PIXAR EDITION

*Sometimes when you watch a movie the first time, you might miss
stuff—background details, a few jokes, and some cameos. Pixar's
movies are so loaded with in-jokes, puns, and hidden references,
we've put this guide together so you can catch them next time.*

PIXAR CARTOONS
In *Toy Story* (1995), the titles of the books in Andy's room are also
titles of short cartoons that Pixar produced: *Red's Dream, Knick
Knack,* and *Tin Toy.*

In *Toy Story 2* (1999), the old man who restores Woody is the
chess player from the cartoon short *Geri's Game.* When he searches
for his glasses, you can see chess pieces in his drawer.

Also in *Toy Story 2,* when Hamm the piggy bank is channel surfing, shots from *Tin Toy* and *Geri's Game* can be seen.

PIXAR MOVIES
In *Toy Story 2,* Andy has *A Bug's Life* (1998) calendar in his room.
In another nod to *A Bug's Life,* Heimlich the caterpillar can be
seen crawling on a branch.

In 2001's *Monsters, Inc.,* audiences got a sneak peek at a new character, Marlin, the clownfish of *Finding Nemo* (2003).

Watch closely in *Finding Nemo:* A Buzz Lightyear toy lies on the
floor of the dentist's waiting room, and Mike from *Monsters, Inc.*
can also be seen deep-sea diving during the credits. Mr.
Incredible from *The Incredibles* (2004) makes an advance appearance in the dentist's office, where a patient is reading a *Mr.
Incredible* comic book.

—Irwin "Fletch" Fletcher (Chevy Chase), *Fletch* (1985)

HOMAGES

The carpet in the neighbor's house in *Toy Story* (where Sid the evil toy torturer lives) was "borrowed" from *The Shining* (1980).

Boxes of Casey Jr. Cookies from the J. Grant bakery in *A Bug's Life* are P. T. Flea's circus wagons. They're also references to Disney's *Dumbo*; in that movie, Casey Jr. is the name of the circus train, and Joe Grant is the artist who designed the big-eared elephant.

In *Monsters, Inc.*, Pixar honored special effects pioneer Ray Harryhausen by naming the sushi restaurant after him. A six-legged octopus also appears in a nod to Harryhausen's work on *It Came from Beneath the Sea* (1955), which featured a six-legged sea monster.

After *The Incredibles* save the city, two old men talk about how "there's no school like the old school." They're caricatures of Frank Thomas and Ollie Johnson (who also provided the voices), two of Walt Disney's "Nine Old Men," the old school of classic animation.

JOKES

Toy Story: The company on the "For Sale" sign on Andy's front lawn is "Virtual Realty."

A Bug's Life: The sleazy bar in Bug City is in an empty can of "Papa Rivera's Lo-Fat Lard."

Monsters, Inc.: On their way to work, the monsters Mike and Sulley pass "Tony's Grossery."

ROOM A113

A113 is the room number of the animation department at the California Institute for the Arts. Many Pixar staff members, including director John Lasseter, are alums.

In *Toy Story*, A113 appears on the license plate of Andy's mom's car.

My Dinner with Andre was filmed at an abandoned hotel in Richmond, Virginia.

In the airport of *Toy Story 2*, an announcement is made for: "Lasset Air, Flight A113."

In *The Incredibles*, Mr. Incredible is briefed for his mission in room A113.

THE PIZZA PLANET TRUCK

Pizza Planet, a fictional franchise first seen in *Toy Story*, has appeared in all of Pixar's movies, but some appearances are easier to spot than others:

A Bug' Life: There are two Pizza Planet appearances. A Pizza Planet cup sits on top of the sleezy bar in the bug city, which is located next to a trailer in a field. The Pizza Planet truck is parked next to it.

Monsters, Inc.: Mike and Sulley toss the villian through a door and into a trailer, which is parked in a field next to the Pizza Planet truck. (It's the same trailer seen in *A Bug's Life*.)

Finding Nemo: Near the end of the movie, the truck zips by, just outside the dentist's office.

SPOT THE CLAVIN

Another Pixar tradition is to include a part for actor John Ratzenberger (better known as Cliff Clavin on *Cheers*), who has performed in the first six animated features. Sometimes it's easy to hear him, like in *Toy Story* and *Toy Story 2*, where he plays Hamm the piggy bank. In *Finding Nemo*, he plays an entire school of fish. His part in *The Incredibles* might be the toughest to locate. He doesn't "appear" until the end of the movie, as the evil Underminer.

* * *

THEORY OF RELATIVES

When Albert Einstein visited the Warner Bros. studio in the 1930s, Jack Warner shared some thoughts with him: "I have a theory of relatives, too. Don't hire 'em."

The dinner consisted of potato soup, fish pâté, and roast quail.

SCORE!

Alan Parker, director of Angela's Ashes, *wrote that getting John Williams to score your movie is "for a filmmaker . . . akin to winning the lottery." Williams, who has composed some of the most recognizable scores in film history (Star Wars, Indiana Jones, and Superman, to name a few), has scored more than 80 films, and his career is far from over.*

FLUSHING TO JULLIARD

John Towner Williams was born in Flushing, Queens, in New York City, on February 8, 1932. From an early age Williams devoted himself to music. He studied piano from the age of seven and later learned to play the trombone, trumpet, and clarinet. When John was 16, his father, a drummer with the CBS Radio Orchestra, moved the family to Los Angeles. There John first began to work with film studio orchestras. He studied at UCLA before being drafted in 1952 and spending part of his military service conducting the air force band. After his discharge in 1954, he studied piano at the preeminent Juilliard School.

Williams returned to Hollywood as an orchestra pianist, playing for the greats of film music: Bernard Herrmann, Franz Waxman, and Alfred Newman. His first few composing jobs were for TV shows—he would eventually win two Emmys for his TV work in the 1960s. His first film score was for *Daddy-O* in 1958 (a movie so putrid it has been featured on *Mystery Science Theater 3000*).

LITTLE JOHNNY

Starting in 1960, Williams began turning out at least one score a year, mostly for unremarkable films like *John Goldfarb, Please Come Home* (1965) and *Not With My Wife You Don't!* (1966). But his versatility helped his popularity in Hollywood to grow. Williams got his first Oscar nod for the score to *Valley of the Dolls* in 1967. In 1969 he got two more, for *The Reivers* and *Goodbye, Mr. Chips*. By the early 1970s, Johnny, as he was called, became the Master of Disaster Scores. He wrote the sound tracks to *The Poseidon Adventure* and *The Towering Inferno*—both of which are a far cry from the grand symphonic style he became known for.

Army Archerd wrote a column for 52 years for what Hollywood "trade"?

THE LITTLE OSTENATO THAT COULD

But Williams's really big break wouldn't come until 1974, when he worked on a film called *The Sugarland Express*. That film's director, a young Steven Spielberg, came to Williams after hearing his score for *The Reivers*. Spielberg was so pleased with Williams's score for *The Sugarland Express* that he hired Williams for his next movie: *Jaws*.

When Williams invited Spielberg over to listen to what he had been working on, Spielberg expected something melodic and eerie. Instead, Williams sat down at the piano and played the theme with two fingers: Da-duh. Da-duh. Spielberg laughed at him at first, thinking it was a joke—and asked him what the theme *really* was. Despite his initial surprise at the simplicity of the *Jaws* theme (the two bass notes are as primal as the shark), Spielberg came to credit the score for at least half the success of the film. Williams won an Oscar for his composition, Spielberg had a runaway success with the film, and both men experienced the beginning of a beautiful friendship. As of 2005, they have collaborated on 21 films—one of the longest-running and most successful teams in Hollywood.

STAR WARS OF THE THIRD KIND

When George Lucas was looking for a composer for his 1977 space opera, his friend Steven Spielberg recommended John Williams. Although the trend for science fiction scores at the time was for modern sounds, rock beats, and electronic touches, Lucas wanted a traditional, almost Wagnerian classical score, with grand fanfares and themes for each of the characters. Williams delivered in spades, and the *Star Wars* album became the most popular sound track of all time. It even became a hit outside the theater: a disco version of the *Star Wars* main theme, by Meco, hit #1 on the pop charts.

The same year, Spielberg was working on his own space story, *Close Encounters of the Third Kind*. Unlike the creation of scores for most films, when the composer is given as few as four weeks to compose the score long after the film has been shot and edited, Williams started working on the *Close Encounters* score two years before the movie was released. The five-note theme that the humans in the movie use to make first contact with the aliens proved the most difficult to compose. Williams wrote more than 150 variations before he and Spielberg found one they both liked.

And, as with the *Star Wars* main theme, you can listen to a disco version of the *Close Encounters* theme, too. NASA also has taken an interest in the music and uses it as one of the welcoming messages broadcast into space for the real aliens to find.

LORD OF THE SEQUEL

John Williams has scored more sequels in different film franchises than anyone else: *Star Wars*, *Indiana Jones*, *Jaws*, *Superman*, *Home Alone*, *Jurassic Park*, *Harry Potter*—even *Gidget Goes to Rome*, in 1963. But not content to rest on his laurels, Williams wrote some of his most memorable music for the new installments in these movies—giving them their own distinct sounds instead of rehashing the original sound tracks. His approach has yielded unforgettable tracks, like Darth Vader's theme ("The Imperial March") from *The Empire Strikes Back* (1980), now a favorite of college marching bands in football stadiums everywhere. Williams explains this phenomenon by noting that the music is "military in an ominous and aggressive sense. That's probably why they use it."

LITTLE GOLD STATUES

During his long Hollywood career, Williams has garnered a little recognition for his work: 16 Grammys, 14 honorary degrees, 3 Golden Globes, and 5 Oscars. Since his *Jaws* score won the Oscar for Best Original Score in 1975, there have only been seven years that Williams has *not* been nominated for an Academy Award. Many years, he's been competing against himself. As of 2005, he has 43 total nominations, the most of any living person. (This also means he has the most Oscar losses, a whopping 38.) But he doesn't hold the all-time record. That belongs to Williams's old boss, Alfred Newman, who currently holds the record for Oscar nominations with 45.

* * *

When Williams tackled the *Star Wars* prequel scores, he found a few members of the original *Star Wars* orchestra back in the studio with him, more than 20 years later.

What words are printed on Frank Sinatra's tombstone in Desert Memorial Park?

TARZAN OF THE MOVIES, PART 1

Elsewhere in this book, we tell the story of Dracula, the creature who couldn't die. In a way, that's Tarzan's story, too. Nothing could kill him—not inept filmmaking . . . or bad scripts . . . or terrible acting. No matter how poor the movie, he kept getting more popular. And ultimately, it was his success in these films that turned him into a pop icon. Here are highlights of his career as a star of the silent screen.

ON-SCREEN

At about the same time he signed his first Tarzan book deal, Edgar Rice Burroughs became fascinated with the idea of putting Tarzan on the silver screen, too. He hired an agent and tried to sell the idea to several different film studios, but nobody was interested. "The problem with *Tarzan of the Apes* was that it was considered too difficult to film," John Taliaferro writes in *Tarzan Forever*. "No one had ever made a successful movie featuring wild animals. And how to depict a nearly naked man? Even more problematic, how to depict a nearly naked man wrestling and killing a lion? The task was daunting."

LARGER THAN LIFE

Back then, the film industry was brand new, wide open and full of fly-by-night operators out to make a quick buck. When Burroughs finally sold the film rights to *Tarzan of the Apes* in 1916, it was to a Chicago insurance salesman named Bill Parsons . . . who didn't even have a movie company yet. Parsons scraped together the money to form National Pictures, and then hired an actor to play Tarzan. His choice: a hulk named Elmo Lincoln, a former train engineer whose biggest film attribute (some said it was his only attribute) was his massive barrel chest. He was "everything Burroughs had wished Tarzan *wouldn't* be. . . . His beefy build belied the grace, suppleness, and refinement of the literary Tarzan."

Burroughs was so furious with the choice that he sent a letter to his agent instructing him not to sell the film rights to any more books. In fact, Burroughs was so upset that he boycotted the film's opening at the Broadway Theater on January 27, 1918. He even tried to have his name—and Tarzan's—taken off the film.

SUCCESS!
But even though the first movie Tarzan was little more than a caveman who lived in a tree, audiences loved him. In fact, so many people turned out to see the film that many theaters had to schedule additional screenings, some starting as early as 9:00 a.m.

Film critics were impressed, too. "Remember how you sat up most of the night to finish your first adventure story?" The *Chicago Tribune* asked its readers. "Well, it's better than that! And do you remember your first love story? Well, it's better than that!"

Tarzan of the Apes went on to become one of the most popular movies of the year and one of the first silent movies to gross more than $1 million. The film's popularity introduced the Tarzan character to legions of new fans, and helped drive book and magazine sales to new heights. Burroughs, who was on his way to becoming a national figure, earned a fortune. But success had come at a huge price, Taliaferro writes: "In expanding his domain from printed page to motion picture, Burroughs lost custody of Tarzan. . . . He could do little more than sit by as the image of Tarzan was appropriated by directors, actors, and the public imagination. In fact as well as fiction, Tarzan was on his own."

THE NEXT FILM
Money notwithstanding, Burroughs hated the film. But at least, he figured, he wouldn't have to deal with Parsons again.

Wrong. One day Burroughs happened to read in a newspaper gossip column that Parsons was already at work on a sequel—*The Romance of Tarzan*. Burroughs angrily called his lawyer . . . and found out that while he'd sold Parsons the film rights to only one Tarzan novel, there was nothing in the contract that limited Parsons to making only one film.

This time Parsons expected to really cash in. While *Tarzan of the Apes* cost him $300,000 to make, he spent less than $25,000 on *The Romance of Tarzan*. And it showed. A lot of the "action" took place in California, not in the jungles of Africa. And Elmo Lincoln wore a tuxedo in much of the film. *Romance* premiered at the Strand Theater on October 14, 1918, and ran for only seven days. Nobody went to see it. Parsons took a financial bath . . . but it didn't hurt Tarzan.

CHANGE OF HEART
Once again, Burroughs swore he'd never sell the film rights to another story . . . and then a few months later he changed his mind. And who did he choose to pilot Tarzan's comeback? Numa Pictures, a New York film company with a reputation for "shoddy and cheap products."

For *The Return of Tarzan* (later changed to *Revenge of Tarzan*), Numa needed a new star. The smart thing would have been to audition actors. But for some reason, the company's execs decided to visit local firehouses instead.

A 25-year-old fireman named Gene Pollar happened to be working that day. "I slid down the pole," he recounted years later, "and I heard one of the men say, 'That's our man.'" Numa hired him . . . but Pollar simply could not act.

Numa pictures lived up to its reputation for cheesiness in *Revenge of Tarzan*, but the film still did a decent box office business. If nothing else, this proved that Tarzan would bring in audiences, no matter what the vehicle. Pollar, on the other hand, went back to his old firefighting job and never made another film.

SON OF TARZAN
In September 1919, Burroughs tried again. He sold the film rights to his new book, *The Son of Tarzan*, to the new owners of National Pictures. They turned the novel in to a movie serial with 15 chapters, starring P. Dempsey Tabler as Tarzan. Never heard of him? Of course not. Tabler was a 41-year-old has been and hoped the serial would revive his career. It didn't. So he gave up acting, moved to San Francisco, and went into the advertising business.

Meanwhile, Numa Pictures had the right to make one more film based on *The Return of Tarzan*. When they saw how profitable *Son of Tarzan* was, they decided to create a 15-part serial called *The Adventures of Tarzan*. They began looking for someone to play the apeman.

Numa may not have made good films, but they knew how to make money. In the three years since his last *Tarzan* film in 1918, Elmo Lincoln had become a genuine box office star on the strength of two of his own serials, *Elmo the Mighty* and *Elmo the*

Fearless. So when Numa learned he was available again, they signed him up.

Everyone benefitted. Lincoln's final appearance as Tarzan in *Adventures* breathed new life into the franchise, not just in the United States but all over the world. "Within three months," Gabe Essoe writes in *Tarzan of the Movies*, "*Adventures* was completely sold out in the United States, Canada, Australia, Central and Western Europe, Asia, South America, Central America, Mexico, the Indies, Pacific Islands, and the Philippines."

SON-IN-LAW OF TARZAN

Tarzan's movie career hit a lull, and then in the summer of 1926 Burroughs had a chance to prove that he didn't know how to pick the right Tarzan, either. One night he threw a party at his Tarzana ranch. One of the people invited was a former all-American center for Indiana University named Jack "Big Jim" Pierce, who was now coaching high school sports, trying to break into the movie business. As Pierce recalls it, he was minding his own business at the party when he heard a man's voice yell, "There's Tarzan!"

"And then he proceeded to talk me into playing the Apeman," Pierce recalled later. "He said I looked just like what he had always had in mind."

Pierce was already signed to appear as an aviator in the Howard Hughes film *Wings*, but Burroughs talked him out of the role . . . so Paramount gave it to a young actor named Gary Cooper instead, and Pierce signed to star in *Tarzan and the Golden Lion.* During filming Pierce also fell in love with Burroughs's only daughter, Joan, and they later married.

Tarzan and the Golden Lion premiered in February 1927. It was a moderate success, but it was mauled by the critics. "This wins the hand-embroidered toothpick as being the worst picture of the month," *Photoplay Magazine* wrote. Pierce himself became quickly disillusioned. "Because of poor direction, terrible story treatment and putrid acting, the opus was a stinkeroo," he admitted. He went back to coaching high school sports while taking whatever acting jobs he could find. *Wings*, the film he'd backed out of, won the first-ever Academy Award for Best Picture.

TARZAN THE MIGHTY

Burroughs sold *Jungle Tales of Tarzan* to Universal Studios, the first major motion picture studio to make a Tarzan film. They turned it into a 12-chapter serial called *Tarzan the Mighty.*

Universal cast a 30-year-old stuntman and weightlifter named Frank Merrill as Tarzan. A former national gymnastic champ, he had the slender, muscular physique that was perfect for Tarzan ... plus he had the gymnastic skills that made jungle stunts like climbing ropes, swinging through trees, and climbing out of pits and tiger traps a snap. "Wearing an over-the-shoulder leopard skin outfit [and matching headband], he took vine swinging and climbing to a level that shamed all of his predecessors," John Taliaferro writes. "Future Tarzans would scrap Merrill's corny costume, but hereafter each would be expected to live up to his acrobatic standard."

AIII-AHHH-OWWWW

Tarzan the Mighty was a hit (though, as usual, Burroughs hated it), so Universal quickly signed Merrill to a second serial, titled *Tarzan the Tiger.* The last of the silent Tarzan films, it was also the first attempt at making a Tarzan "talkie." Universal distributed a version of the film with a phonograph record, a "soundtrack" that, when played simultaneously with the film, provided a crude musical score and some sound effects that (hopefully) corresponded to the action on the screen. The record also contained the first snippets of lip-synchronized dialog and the very first Tarzan yell ever heard by movie audiences. What did it sound like? As David Fury writes in *Kings of the Jungle,* Merrill's yell "sounded like a man's response to pounding his thumb with a hammer."

As the 1920s ended, Tarzan was stronger than ever. But once again it was the character, not the actor who played him, who survived. After making a few non-Tarzan films, Merrill gave up acting forever and got a job with the City of Los Angeles teaching athletics to kids. He worked with children for the rest of his life.

Turn to page 431 for more.

—Helen Benson (Patricia Neal), *The Day the Earth Stood Still* (1951)

BEFORE HER TIME: JEAN HARLOW

She wasn't a real platinum blonde—but everything else about her was genuine. Left to her own devices she might have had a happy marriage and a houseful of kids. What she got instead was a manipulative, fame-hungry mother who dominated her life until her untimely death.

J ean Harlow was born Harlean Harlow Carpenter in Kansas City, Missouri, in 1911. She was her family's pampered darling, called "the Baby" by everyone. In fact when she first went to school, she was surprised to learn that "the Baby" wasn't her real name. Legend has it that Harlean's ambitious and grasping mother, known in Hollywood as Mother Jean, bleached her little girl's hair from the time she was a toddler. By the time she was a young teenager, the 5 foot 2 inch gorgeous blonde was stopping traffic. Literally. A friend of hers reported that men would just stop their cars and get out and follow Harlean down the street.

When she was sixteen, Harlean married twenty-year-old Chuck McGrew. Mother Jean allowed it because Chuck stood to inherit a nice chunk of change when he turned 21. After the honeymoon Chuck's inheritance came through, and the young couple moved to Beverly Hills.

In the spring of 1928, Harlean was standing outside the Fox studios waiting for her aunt when some Fox execs noticed her. She gave them her phone number and forgot all about it until central casting called. They kept calling, and she kept saying no because she had no interest in being an actress. But when her mother (and ne'er-do-well stepfather) moved to L.A., she no longer had a choice. Mother Jean pushed Harlean to accept the next offer—and renamed her "Jean Harlow."

After a few bit parts, she was discovered by Hal Roach, who third-billed her with Stan Laurel and Oliver Hardy in *Double Whoopee* (1929). But in spite of her professional success, she faced some turmoil in her personal life. Over the next six months, between movies, Harlow had an abortion (arranged by her stepfather) and a divorce (engineered by her mother).

A STAR IS BORN

Harlow's big break came when Howard Hughes noticed her and put her in his production of *Hell's Angels* (1930). The movie opened to tepid reviews in general and terrible reviews of Harlow's acting, but that didn't matter. Audiences loved her. The movie made her an overnight star and the new American sex symbol.

Over the next few years, she made movies like *Platinum Blonde* (1931) and *The Beast of the City* (1932), for which she finally received some good reviews. Her popularity grew with each picture; her personal appearances across the country were always sold out.

An even bigger break came with 1932's *Red-Headed Woman*, a comedy written by Anita Loos (*Gentlemen Prefer Blondes*). Producer Irving Thalberg was dubious about casting Harlow, but was eventually persuaded by MGM and writer-director Paul Bern (who had taken Harlow under his wing and would become her second husband). Harlow was still playing the sex bomb, but she'd finally found her niche—in comedy. And she finally received rave reviews for her work in *Dinner at Eight* and *Bombshell*, both released in 1933. She even made the cover of *TIME* magazine in August 1935.

On the job, she was hard working, even-tempered, and completely professional, as popular among her film crews and fellow actors as she was with the public. Everyone in Hollywood liked her—except for the terminally jealous Joan Crawford, who despised any female star who was younger, prettier, and got better scripts.

Harlow used to say that all she ever wanted was a happy marriage. She went for it three times; her first and last marriages ended in divorce, and her second ended in scandal when Paul Bern died under mysterious circumstances (for more on his death, see page 379). Her third marriage was a "studio wedding" dreamed up by MGM to avert a scandal: Harlow had been seeing a married man, prizefighter Max Baer. So to throw off the gossipmongers, Harlow had to get married—fast. She chose a friend, cinematographer Hal Rosson, and divorced him two years later at the instigation of Mother Jean.

She'd never really been in love with anyone until she met William Powell, who was just as urbane and charming as his *Thin Man* character, Nick Charles. He loved her, too, but he was recently divorced from his wife, Carole Lombard, and reluctant to marry another big star. Powell couldn't stand to be in the same

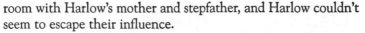

room with Harlow's mother and stepfather, and Harlow couldn't seem to escape their influence.

Harlow rebelled by drinking too much. The heavy drinking, along with a childhood bout of scarlet fever, is what may have eventually done her in. Her friends had been worried about her health for months, but it wasn't until 1937, while filming *Saratoga* with Clark Gable, that she allowed herself to admit that she was sick.

Not wanting to cause a delay on the production, she continued to work until she collapsed on the set. Hoping to hide the fact of Harlow's heavy drinking and to force her to "dry out," Mother Jean kept her at home for several days, until, on June 7, Harlow was taken to the hospital, where she died from uremia, a toxic consequence of kidney failure. She was only 26.

THE LEGEND
The studio had kept Harlow's illness quiet, so the public was shocked when headlines reported the news of her death. Her funeral was a spectacle that attracted an all-star cast of mourners and a mob of onlookers. William Powell, who was seen sobbing and shaking, almost passed out. He had another terrible shock when Harlow's mother announced to the press that the actor was paying for Jean's $30,000 mausoleum and deluxe coffin. The notoriously tightfisted Powell shelled out the money without a word.

To complete *Saratoga*, MGM hired Harlow's stand-in, Mary Dees, as a double, shooting her facing away from the camera and wearing a floppy hat. When *Saratoga* was released, it became the biggest hit of the year; audiences lined up for one last chance to see Harlow. Long after her death she remained Hollywood's ultimate sex goddess, the one that other actresses—including Marilyn Monroe—would emulate.

* * *

NO JIGGLING ALLOWED
Censors forbade any jiggling assets when Jane Russell and Marilyn Monroe sang and danced in *Gentlemen Prefer Blondes*. For their musical number "Two Girls from Little Rock," they had to stretch flesh-colored fabric across their bosoms to "lock them in place."

Daryl Hannah (*Splash*) was once in an all-girl band called Psychotic Kindergarten.

TALES OF DISCOVERY

Hollywood tales of how stars were discovered are always popular.
You never know where the next big star may come from!
Here are some of Uncle John's favorites.

LANA TURNER

The story of Lana Turner, the 1940s Sweater Girl, is one of the most famous. She was discovered while sipping a soda in Schwab's drugstore. It's a story that has been told so many times that it has taken on a life of its own. But how true is it?

Well, it is true that 15-year-old Julia Jean Mildred Frances Turner (Judy for short) was discovered while sipping soda. But it wasn't at Schwab's (why Schwab's has been so ensconced in the popular imagination is somewhat of a mystery). She was actually drinking her soda at the Top Hat Malt Shop, across the street from Hollywood High School. And the truth can now be told—she was actually cutting typing class. She changed her name from Judy to Lana and became a star.

LAUREN BACALL

Betty Joan Perske (who would become the grande dame of the stage and screen known as Lauren Bacall) originally wanted to be a dancer, but changed her mind after trying acting. She studied at the American Academy of Dramatic Arts in New York City and began modeling to pay the bills once she left school. Her face landed on the cover of *Harper's Bazaar*. After seeing the magazine cover, the wife of director Howard Hawkes convinced her husband to give the young model a screen test. Hawkes listened to his wife and was so impressed with Betty that he cast her in *To Have and Have Not* (1944) opposite Humphrey Bogart, her future husband.

JANET LEIGH

Janet Leigh, who is probably best remembered for her unforget-table shower scene in Alfred Hitchcock's *Psycho* (1960), had a storybook discovery story. Janet Leigh (or Jeanette Helen Morrison, as she was then known) was the only child of parents who moved from town to town. She was very bright, skipped

The first film documentary was the Eskimo saga *Nanook of the North* (1922).

several grades in school, and graduated from high school at age 15. After graduation, Janet spent a lot of time going to the movies.

When she was still a teenager, attending the University of the Pacific, her parents were employed at a Northern California ski resort—her father manning the front desk and her mother working as a maid. Jeanette's father kept his daughter's picture on display— anyone who came to check in to the hotel could see it. Actress Norma Shearer, who was staying at the resort, saw the photo and recognized Jeanette's screen potential. Shearer recommended her to Lew Wasserman, a powerful talent agent. A screen test followed, MGM signed her, and Janet's first part was in *The Romance of Rosy Ridge* (1947).

TIPPI HEDREN

Tippi Hedren was discovered by Alfred Hitchcock himself, when he saw her on a TV commercial for diet soda. Hoping to turn her into a second Grace Kelly, Hitchcock immediately cast her in *The Birds* (1963) and followed it up with *Marnie* (1964). Some say Hitchcock was obsessed with Hedren and kept her from working for other filmmakers, hurting her film career.

But who got Hedren into that soda commercial? Tippi herself credits Ella Jane Knott, the woman who spotted the young Hedren exiting a street car in Minneapolis and gave her a job as a model for a department store. Modeling jobs led to small acting jobs, and, ultimately, the part in the fated soft drink commercial.

PETER MAYHEW

His name may not be a household word, and even his face is not that easily recognizable, but the character Peter Mayhew played is. The 7-foot-3-inch tall Mayhew played Chewbacca in the *Star Wars* movies. So how did he land the part? With his large feet.

Mayhew was working as a hospital orderly in London's King's College Hospital when a local newspaper wrote a feature on men with extraordinarily big feet. Mayhew, along with some other large-footed men, appeared in a photo in the newspaper; his tall frame loomed over the rest of the group. Producer Charles Schneer hap- pened to catch the photo, and cast Mayhew in his first film role, the Minoton in *Sinbad and the Eye of the Tiger* (1977). When George Lucas needed a very tall actor to play Chewie in *Star Wars*,

Mel Gibson and Tim Curry both auditioned for the role of Mozart in *Amadeus* (1984).

he approached Mayhew. Delighted to play the giant Wookiee, Mayhew took the part seriously and prepared by visiting zoos and studying the movements of the various animals Chewbacca was based on: bears, apes, and monkeys.

NATALIE PORTMAN

Another *Star Wars* star, Natalie Portman was born in Jerusalem in 1981—she was then known as Natalie Hershlag, a name she still uses outside her Hollywood life. Her father's medical career took the family to Washington, DC, then to Connecticut, then finally to Long Island, New York. It was there that she was discovered at age 11, while eating at a neighborhood pizzeria, by a Revlon modeling scout. Impressed by the young girl's looks, the scout signed her on. After a while, Natalie tired of modeling and decided to try her luck with acting. She made her debut in 1994 when she was 13 in a film called *The Professional*. She appeared in a few more movies before George Lucas knew he had to have her as Queen Padmé Amidala in his next three episodes of the *Star Wars* movies. She was just 14 when she agreed to sign a 10-year contract to appear in all three films.

CHARLIZE THERON

Oscar-winner Charlize Theron grew up an only child on a farm in South Africa. She tried some modeling as a teenager but decided that she'd rather be a ballerina (she studied dance as a child). Theron moved to New York to dance with the Joffrey Ballet Company but suffered a knee injury. Charlize's mother convinced her to move to Los Angeles to try her luck as an actress. She made the rounds of auditions, with no success. Charlize had little money and was at a loss about what to do next.

Supporting her daughter, Charlize's mother sent her a check, and Charlize went to the bank to cash it. As the story goes, Charlize became enraged and began to yell when the bank teller refused to honor the check. It just so happened that an agent was standing in line behind her, and he was very impressed with her "improvisational" performance. He slipped her his card—and the rest is film history. Charlize went on to win an Academy Award for her portrayal of serial killer Aileen Wuornos in *Monster* (2003).

The hit movie *Grease* (1978) was shown in Venezuela as *Vaselina*.

THE CURSED SCRIPT

John Belushi. Sam Kinison. John Candy. Chris Farley.
Four comedians and four untimely deaths—all linked together by the
legend of the cursed script. Each comic read for the part, and each one
died. But what's the real story behind this Hollywood urban legend?

THE STORY

T On the surface, there's nothing sinister about the script itself. The story line comes from a novel called *The Incomparable Atuk*, written by Canadian author Mordecai Richler. In this fish-out-of-water satire, Atuk (pronounced at-TOOK) is an Eskimo who ventures forth from Baffin Island to live in the big city. He becomes an overnight literary success as a poet and quickly adapts to the pretentious, shallow, and greedy society he finds himself in. Filmmakers have described the story as Eskimo Dundee; it seemed perfect for a movie, starring a big, burly comedian as the transplanted Atuk.

THE DEATHS

United Artists first tried to make *Atuk* in the early 1980s and wanted John Belushi to play the lead. The tremendously popular Belushi was a natural choice for the part; his charisma and talent for physical comedy made huge hits out of movies like *Animal House* (1978) and *The Blues Brothers* (1980). Scriptwriter Tom Carroll developed the part with Belushi specifically in mind. When a draft was ready, Belushi read it . . . and then he died of a drug overdose. The project was put on hold.

Atuk was resurrected in 1987, five years after Belshi's death. Alan Metter would direct; he had just finished *Back to School* (1986), starring Rodney Dangerfield and featuring a brash, loud comedian named Sam Kinison. A successful stand-up comic, Kinison signed on to play Atuk as his first leading role. Production began; shooting would take place in New York, Toronto, and Nunavut Territory. Roles were cast: Christopher Walken would play a Donald Trump–type character, Ricki Lake was to be Atuk's Eskimo girlfriend, and a 15-year-old Ben Affleck would be the boy Atuk befriends in the big city. United Artists spent $4.5 million, Metter shot one 30-second scene . . . and then production wrapped.

The legend says Kinison's death caused filming to stop, but a closer look shows that that's not what happened. For reasons that are unclear (some say he demanded a complete script rewrite, while others say he couldn't handle his newfound fame), Kinison refused to show up to film his scenes. His unprofessional behavior caused Metter and the studio to pull the plug on Atuk. Kinison was sued for breach of contract and had to pay a $5 million settlement to the studio. Five years later in 1992, Kinison would be dead in a car crash on a desert highway in rural California.

TWO MORE DEATHS

But Atuk the movie wasn't dead yet. Two more attempts were made to get the film going again. The idea for the main character remained the same: a big, burly guy had to play the Eskimo. Two more large-framed comedians, John Candy and Chris Farley, read the script and expressed interest in the part. But then they died, too: Candy of a heart attack in 1994 and Farley of a drug overdose in 1997. It wasn't long before the urban legend of the cursed script sprung up; Atuk killed any actor interested in the lead role.

But scriptwriter Tom Carroll doesn't believe it. "No matter what anybody's impression was, I think it's either coincidence or a practical explanation." Former director Metter has another explanation: "I wouldn't blame the script. The script called for a big overweight comedian. What are you gonna do?" United Artists still owns the rights to the script and hasn't completely abandoned the project. The trouble might be finding an actor willing . . . and brave enough . . . to take the part.

* * *

"Hollywood keeps before its child audiences a string of glorified young heroes, everyone of whom is an unhesitating and violent Anarchist. His one answer to everything that annoys him or disparages his country or his parents or his young lady or his personal code of manly conduct is to give the offender a 'sock' in the jaw. . . . My observation leads me to believe that it is not the virtuous people who are good at socking jaws."
—George Bernard Shaw

His full name at birth was Antonio Rudolfo Oaxaca Quinn.

SINGING RANGE

*They're mostly all gone now, the singing cowboys and
cowgirls of moving pictures, but if there's a cowboy heaven,
you know they've got a gosh-darn heck of a choir.*

The major studios assumed that the advent of sound would
kill the Western; a lot of the silent stars couldn't make the
transition and crude audio technology made outdoor shoots
difficult. Little did they know that the change to talkies would
propagate a whole new breed of performer: the singing cowboy.

KEN MAYNARD (1895–1973)
The First Singing Cowboy
Born in Vevay, Indiana, Maynard was a professional trick rider for
the Buffalo Bill and Ringling Brothers shows before he hit
Hollywood. He started out in silent films in 1923 (his first was
called *The Man Who Won*). Within a few years he and his horse,
Tarzan, were popular Hollywood stars—amazing their fans with
thrilling horse-and-rider stunts. When talkies arrived, Maynard
easily made the transition. In 1929 he became the first singing
cowboy when he starred in *The Wagon Master*, singing traditional
cowboy songs like "The Lone Star Trail" and "The Cowboy's
Lament." Maynard made scores of Westerns in the 1930s; one in
particular—*In Old Santa Fe*—introduced a young Gene Autry as a
square-dance caller. Autry repaid him years later by secretly supporting the impoverished, alcoholic Maynard until his death at
age 77.

GENE AUTRY (1907–1998)
America's Favorite Singing Cowboy
Growing up in Tioga, Texas, Autry sang wherever he could: in
restaurants, at carny shows, and in the choir of the church where
his father was a minister. Stints on the radio turned into bit film
parts, like the one in *In Old Santa Fe*. That, in turn, led to his first
starring role in the 1935 13-part serial *The Phantom Empire*, in
which Autry and his horse, Champion, battled the Queen of
Murania's underground army, equipped with ray guns, robots, and
missiles. He first starred in a Western, *Tumbling Tumbleweeds*, that

---

Robert Redford turned down *The Graduate* lead because he felt he was too old for it.

same year, which catapulted him into stardom. His movies, like the TV series that followed them, were long on action and short on romance—but his fans didn't care.

Except for a gap during World War II when he served as a flight officer in the Air Transport Command, Autry dominated the Hollywood box office of the 1930s and 1940s, making over 56 Westerns for Republic Pictures. He wrote and recorded hundreds of songs: "Rudolph the Red-Nosed Reindeer," "Here Comes Santa Claus," "Peter Cottontail," and his own theme song, "Back in the Saddle," among them.

Autry was a savvy businessman whose holdings included his own film production company, a radio and TV chain, ranches, oil wells, a flying school, a music publishing company, and the Los Angeles Angels (now the Los Angeles Angels of Anaheim) baseball team, which he bought in 1961. He also funded and built the Autry Museum of Western Heritage in Los Angeles, a world-class museum and research center that celebrates the cowboy in fact and in legend.

TEX RITTER (1905–1974)
First Singing Cowboy Inducted into
Country Music Hall of Fame
Another Texas-born cowboy star, Woodward Maurice "Tex" Ritter dropped out of law school in favor of a singing career on radio and the stage. He landed his first role on Broadway in 1930, and by 1936 he had starred in his first Hollywood Western, *Song of the Gringo*. He was an instant hit with the fans, and for a while rivaled Gene Autry as America's favorite singing cowboy. He starred in 85 Westerns over the course of his career—including *Trouble in Texas*, which featured a little-known starlet named Rita Cansino (who would soon change her last name to Hayworth). He hung up his cinematic spurs in the mid-1940s to continue a successful offscreen career, headlining at the Grand Ole Opry and recording a long string of hit singles, including the #1 hits "I'm Wastin' My Tears on You" (1944), "You Two-Timed Me Once Too Often" (1945), and "You Will Have to Pay" (1946). If you've seen the classic movie *High Noon*, you've heard Tex Ritter sing the Oscar-winning theme song "High Noon (Do Not Forsake Me)."

And fame didn't stop with Tex alone: his son, the late John Ritter, went on to star in movies and the hit TV series *Three's Company*.

Dustin Hoffman, who took the part, was 30—the same age as Redford.

DICK FORAN (1910–1979)
The Matinee Idol of the B Movies
New Jersey–born Foran was a singing cowboy and much more. His beginnings were far from humble: his father was a U.S. senator and Dick went to posh private schools and to Princeton, where he discovered his true calling. His next stop was Hollywood. Soon he was singing in Shirley Temple's 1934 hit *Stand Up and Cheer!* After a string of B movies, he was signed by Warner Bros. to star in *Moonlight on the Prairie*, the first of 12 Westerns he made for the studio. But you can't limit an all-around performer like Foran to Westerns only. In 1940, for instance, he appeared in such diverse films as *The Mummy's Hand*, *The House of the Seven Gables*, *My Little Chickadee*, and *The Fighting 69th*. Foran made a few more Westerns in his long career—even buddying up with Abbott and Costello in 1942's comedy *Ride 'Em Cowboy*—and continued making movies and TV appearances well into the 1950s and 1960s.

SMITH BALLEW (1902–1984)
The Texas Troubador
Although a native Texan, Sykes (Smith) Ballew was decidedly uncowboylike: A dance band conductor in college, he headed off to New York after school, where he crooned for some of the big bands, the Dorseys among them. Eventually he started his own band: the Smith Ballew Orchestra. He continued to record even while starring in Westerns with such unlikely titles as *Roll Along, Cowboy* and *Hawaiian Buckeroo*. His most memorable movie might be 1938's *Rawhide*, costarring Lou Gehrig, (the baseball legend's only film—he died three years later). After *Rawhide*, Ballew starred in only one more movie and then quit Hollywood in 1950 to work for Hughes Aircraft.

But Ballew had one more claim to fame. In 1933 the hunt for singing cowboys was so frenzied that even young John Wayne was encouraged to make a small musical detour on the road to stardom. He appeared in *Riders of Destiny* billed as Singin' Sandy Saunders. In truth, Wayne couldn't sing a lick. It was Smith Ballew's voice; Wayne had merely mouthed the words.

HERB JEFFRIES (1911–)
The Sepia Singing Cowboy

The first African American singing cowboy was born into a
Detroit theater family. Herb's rich baritone voice got him plenty of
work in Chicago clubs, but it was a tour of the segregated South in
his early twenties that instilled in him a mission: to become the
first black singing cowboy. In Hollywood he fortuitously bumped
into Jed Buell, a producer always in search of a good gimmick.
(Later Buell would make *The Terror of Tiny Town*, starring a cast of
little people.) The producer took an old script, *Sunset Under the
Prairie*, renamed it *Harlem on the Prairie*, and cast Jeffries in the
starring role. Jeffries performed his own stunts, wrote the music,
and even edited the picture. He appeared in three more Westerns,
including *The Bronze Buckaroo*, before he went on to singing success with the Duke Ellington Orchestra. His rendition of
"Flamingo" sold over 14 million copies. He was married for a time
to stripper Tempest Storm.

ROY ROGERS (1911–1998) AND DALE EVANS
(1912–2001)
The King of the Cowboys and the Queen of the Cowgirls

Roy Rogers was born Leonard Slye in Cincinnati, Ohio. When he
was 18, he moved to California, where he played and sang with a
variety of country-and-western bands. In 1934 he formed the legendary Sons of the Pioneers, who would become famous for the
songs "Cool Water" and "Tumbling Tumbleweeds" and whose
beautiful harmonies and cowboy yodeling proved to be the perfect
backup for already established singing cowboys of the screen,
including Gene Autry. Rogers went solo in 1937 and appeared in
several Republic features under the name Dick Weston. But it
wasn't until he signed on to do *Under Western Stars* (1938), a
movie that Gene Autry had bowed out of because of a contract
dispute, that he took the name Roy Rogers (the name of his family
dentist back in Ohio: Roy Rodgers).

Rogers's career took off during the years that Gene Autry was
serving in World War II. And in challenging Autry's dominance at
the box office, Rogers would have a loyal partner: his 1944 film
Cowboy and the Senorita featured Dale Evans, who would go on to
costar in 25 more films with him.

—Josey Wales (Clint Eastwood), *The Outlaw Josey Wales* (1976)

Dale Evans was born Frances Octavia Smith in Uvalde, Texas. She was married for the first time at age 14 and divorced at 17, at which point she moved to Memphis to try to jump-start a singing career. After a few jobs singing on local radio shows in Louisville, Dallas, and Chicago, she signed with Fox Pictures. There she appeared in eight movies before being cast as the leading lady opposite Roy Rogers. The two were teamed again and again in movies; and after the death of Rogers's first wife in 1947 and Evans's divorce from her third husband, Roy and Dale married—and stayed married for 51 years. They starred together in a TV series in the 1950s (for which Evans wrote the theme song, "Happy Trails") and a variety show in the 1960s, both of which featured the Sons of the Pioneers.

REX ALLEN (1920–1999)
The Arizona Cowboy

Born in Arizona, Elvie Allen got his nickname early on—his mother named him for her favorite cowboy star, Rex Bell. His father bought him a mail-order guitar from Sears, Roebuck and Co., and Rex's own talent did the rest. He started out in radio and recording, and in 1949 signed with Republic Pictures. Rex did things his own way in his movies: he used his own horse, Koko, and dressed in his own clothes, including a signature white hat. He starred in a total of 19 movies with a string of sidekicks, the most notable of whom were Buddy Ebsen and Slim Pickens. After the release of 1954's *Phantom Stallion*, Rex left Westerns, but not Hollywood. His career continued to flourish—he went on to narrate over 150 nature shows for Disney, and Paramount's animated film *Charlotte's Web* in 1973. But with that last Western movie, *Phantom Stallion*, the singing cowboy era had come to an end.

* * *

SPEED MCQUEEN

Steve McQueen was famous for car chases in the movies, but on March 20, 1970, he won a real-life car chase: the Grand Prix in Florida. McQueen was a member of the winning team despite having a foot in a cast from an earlier motorcycle accident.

When it was shown in China, *Oliver Twist* was called *Lost Child in Foggy City*.

MIXED-UP MOVIES

*Uncle John has a lot of favorite movies—so many that
sometimes he wonders what would happen if they mated.*

The Plot: As she claws her way to the top, a scheming understudy
develops multiple personality disorder.
The Stars: Joanne Woodward and Bette Davis
The Movie: *All About the Three Faces of Eve*

The Plot: Hobbits struggle to destroy an all-powerful magic ring,
while armies of men, led by a giant gorilla, hold off the forces of evil.
The Stars: Elijah Wood, Sean Astin, and an animated ape
The Movie: *The Lord of the Rings: Return of the King Kong*

The Plot: Annie Sullivan and Helen Keller travel to New York
City to learn the true meaning of Christmas from a department
store Santa.
The Stars: Patty Duke, Anne Bancroft, and Edmund Gwenn
The Movie: *The Miracle Worker on 34th Street*

The Plot: A psychotic former child star and her crippled sister
must battle sexism and each other when they enter the rigorous
Navy SEAL training program.
The Stars: Bette Davis, Joan Crawford, and Demi Moore
The Movie: *Whatever Happened to Baby G.I. Jane?*

The Plot: A young lion seeks the aid of a British governess to civi-
lize him and to help him ascend to his rightful place on the throne.
The Stars: Deborah Kerr and Matthew Broderick
The Movie: *The Lion King and I*

The Plot: After a bank robbery, a thief takes a cruise, during
which he falls in love with a former night club singer. They agree
to meet six months later at the top of the Empire State Building,
after she's ditched her fiancé and he's ditched the cops.
The Stars: Steve McQueen and Deborah Kerr
The Movie: *The Thomas Crown Affair to Remember*

"I got into acting so that I could meet girls." —Dustin Hoffman

The Plot: James Bond and Count Dracula team up to fight SPECTRE and romance beautiful women.
The Stars: Sean Connery and George Hamilton
The Movie: *From Russia With Love at First Bite*

The Plot: The American ambassador to Sarkan becomes disenchanted with life, quits his job, and buys a sports car after becoming obsessed with a beautiful high school cheerleader.
The Stars: Marlon Brando and Mena Suvari
The Movie: *The Ugly American Beauty*

The Plot: An air force pilot, Dr. Hackenbush, Tony, and Stuffy join forces to save a horse farm—and the world from hostile alien invaders.
The Stars: The Marx Brothers and Will Smith
The Movie: *Independence Day at the Races*

The Plot: After the end of World War II, a reserved English butler questions his loyalties after aliens arrive on Earth and warn earthlings to live in peace, or else.
The Stars: Patricia Neal and Anthony Hopkins
The Movie: *The Remains of the Day the Earth Stood Still*

* * *

ALL SINGING! ALL DANCING!
MGM's first all-sound movie was *The Broadway Melody* in 1929. It was promoted as "All-Talking, All-Singing, All-Dancing" and encouraged viewers to "hear each throbbing minute of the screen's greatest Achievement!"

* * *

OZZY'S DEBUT
Ozzy Osbourne made his first movie appearance in the 1986 slasher flick *Trick or Treat*. Ozzy's not the killer; in a satirical turn, he is playing a minister who crusades against the evils of heavy metal music.

A NEAR-DEATH EXPERIENCE

Located right behind Paramount Studios, the Hollywood Forever cemetery had its own brush with death. But two brothers from the Midwest saved it from ruin and restored it to one of the hottest Hollywood places to rest in peace.

Hollywood Memorial Park Cemetery had fallen on hard times in 1998. Cracked grave markers and headstones lay on their sides. Broken shards of stained glass lay on the floors of mausoleums. Paths were overgrown and pockmarked with potholes. The shabby cemetery had become an eyesore, and no one had the money to fix it. But once the park had been a beautiful place, where movie stars and movie moguls opted to spend eternity. What had happened to it?

IN THE BEGINNING
Founded in 1899 by Isaac Lankershim and his son-in-law, Isaac Newton Van Nuys, Hollywood Memorial Park originally served the area's small farming community. But once the movie business moved in, it became the cemetery for the stars. Director William Desmond Taylor (who died under mysterious circumstances), actress Barbara La Marr, and heartthrob Rudolph Valentino were all buried there in the 1920s. Their funerals were huge happenings that put Hollywood Memorial Park on the map.

As the movie business got bigger, so did funerals. Studio moguls Jesse Lasky and Harry Cohn were buried at Hollywood Memorial. So was director Cecil B. DeMille. Hollywood's acting legends and pioneers were there too: Douglas Fairbanks, Peter Lorre, Marion Davies, Janet Gaynor, Carl "Alfalfa" Switzer, Tyrone Power, and Edward G. Robinson Jr.

CHEATING DEATH
In 1937 36-year-old Jules Roth, an ex-con who had just finished doing time in San Quentin for grand theft and securities fraud, took a trip to Hollywood Memorial Park. The purpose was probably to

---

Sydney Greenstreet was 62 when he made his film debut in *The Maltese Falcon*.

visit his parents, who were entombed in the Cathedral Mausoleum. (Valentino is right down the hall from them.) He met Alta Phillips, an attractive redhead who was also the daughter of the cemetery's superintendent. Phillips, a trained paralegal, worked at the cemetery and brought in Roth as a "consultant." The pair started a life-long romance (despite the fact that Roth was married), and Phillips taught him about the cemetery business.

The cemetery had hit some rough spots during the Depression, and investors were willing to sell their stock at low prices. In two years, Roth bought out enough investors to secure complete financial control of the cemetery. The park had a new owner, who would run it into the ground over the next 50 years.

It's unclear when and how Roth began stealing from his cemetery business (he also owned two other graveyards in California); serious investigations of his actions didn't begin until the 1980s and weren't completed by the time of his death in 1998. The true extent of his embezzling may never be known, but the damage to Hollywood Memorial was nearly fatal.

In the 1990s business at Hollywood Memorial was lousy: interments had dropped to just 60 people per year. Relatives of the deceased, furious with the condition of the park and stories of vandalism, began to move their loved ones (like makeup artist Max Factor), to other cemeteries. (For the last two years of Roth's ownership, more bodies were moving out than in.) And the movie business had also abandoned Hollywood Memorial. The last big celebrity to be buried there was Mel Blanc in 1989.

State regulators finally seized Hollywood Memorial in 1995. The place was an absolute mess. Earthquake damage had gone unrepaired; toppled tombstones were cracked. Statues had been stolen from the mausoleums, whose roofs leaked and threatened to cave in (Roth hadn't fixed them in 30 years). Broken marble panels were patched with plywood. And one wall of the mausoleum (where Bugsy Siegel is interred) was covered with yellow residue. Rains from El Niño had flooded the lakes and reflecting pools. The property looked terrible, but there were no funds to fix it. It looked like the state would have to shut the cemetery down.

ENTER THE HEROS
Then in 1998 entrepreneurs Tyler and Brent Cassity bought the rundown cemetery for just $375,000 (they were the only bidders).

The two brothers were from St. Louis and were the owners and operators of cemeteries in St. Louis, Chicago, and Kansas City. For Tyler, it was love at first sight: "From the moment I walked in, I knew that it was for me. Cemeteries are libraries of lives, and this library was incredible, one of the most incredible in the country."

The Cassitys quickly got to work on fixing the place up. Tyler (who runs the Hollywood property while Brent manages the Midwest operations) pumped $4 million into the cemetery to spruce it up. Potholes were filled, roofs repaired, and damaged tombstones replaced. A new mausoleum was built, and a historic one, The Abbey of the Psalms, was refurbished and enlarged. The cemetery was given a new name to go with its new look: Hollywood Forever.

Since 1998 Hollywood Forever has come back to life. Business began to boom in the first year with 600 burials. Today there are between one to five interments per day. The Cassitys have upgraded and expanded the facility's capacity and have added new services, like video biographies (called LifeStories), to remember loved ones. In true Hollywood fashion, there is a film studio located in an old Masonic lodge on the grounds where these biographies are created.

The stars have also returned to Hollywood Forever. In 2000 Douglas Fairbanks Jr. was entombed near his father. In 2004 scream queen Fay Wray was buried there, and Don Adams in 2005. Although tour buses are not allowed, Hollywood Forever isn't bashful about pointing out the tombs of the late stars; a map of "Significant Sites" is available in the gift shop.

* * *

CINEMA IN THE CEMETERY

Memorials aren't the only happening at Hollywood Forever. The park has become the place to watch movies in the summertime. Cinespia, a Los Angeles film society, holds their summer outdoor cinema series at Hollywood Forever on Saturday nights. Classic films are shown on the side of one of the huge mausoleums to crowds under the stars. It all began when Cassity showed a Valentino silent on the 75th anniversary of the actor's death; Jack Wyatt, the founder of Cinespia, was looking for a new venue to screen movies. Wyatt loved the idea of showing movies in the celebrity cemetery, and when he approached Cassity with the idea, Cassity agreed.

—Prof. Eustace P. McGargle (W.C. Fields), *Poppy* (1936)

MOVIE BRATS, PART 1

*These maverick directors rode into town in the 1960s
and 1970s and revitalized Hollywood. Once they started
shooting, movies were never the same.*

Hollywood's first "Golden Age" started to wane in the 1950s, and by the end of the 1960s Tinseltown was beginning to feel like a ghost town. Movies weren't only failing to touch the audience's emotions or stir their souls . . . they were also failing to sell popcorn. Television was gaining ground every day, and more and more younger viewers were staying home to watch it. The studios kept churning out movies, but interest (and box office receipts) continued to slump.

The industry found its salvation in a new breed of maverick directors who would come to be labeled "movie brats"—not only for their youth, but also for their fresh and unconventional approach to film. The movies they made reflected the spirit of the times: the questioning of established values and the rising influence of the counterculture.

The movie brats ushered in Hollywood's second Golden Age, which spanned the 1970s. The movement began with Arthur Penn's *Bonnie and Clyde* (1967), and got a couple of nudges from Mike Nichols's *The Graduate* (1967) and Stanley Kubrick's *2001: A Space Odyssey* (1968), but the actual birth began with one unconventional movie and its unconventional director: the brattiest brat of them all.

1969
DENNIS HOPPER—THE REBEL
Dennis Hopper is most famous for his onscreen portrayals of young toughs (*Rebel Without a Cause*) and psycho villains (*Blue Velvet*). Born in 1936 in Dodge City, Kansas, he was voted "most likely to succeed" at his Kansas high school. By his early 20s Hopper seemed destined to fulfill his classmates' prediction, appearing in featured roles in the James Dean movies *Rebel Without a Cause* and *Giant*.

Dustin Hoffman's four-pound silicone breasts in *Tootsie* (1982) cost $175 each . . .

The two actors certainly had rebelliousness in common; the closer Hopper started getting to the top of the bill, the more he became a demanding artiste. An incident on the set of 1958's *From Hell to Texas* (he required 85 retakes for one scene), prompted director Henry Hathaway to yell, "You'll never work in this town again!" Hopper was blackballed; it was ten years before he would land another major role. So in the late 1960s he decided to direct a film of his own.

THE MOVIE Hopper raised $400,000 and enlisted cowriter Terry Southern and actors Peter Fonda and (then unknown) Jack Nicholson to make *Easy Rider*, the story of two bikers who take a motorcycle trip—accompanied by a sound track blasting '60s rock—hoping to discover America. What they find is sex, drugs, and tragedy.

THE LEGACY *Easy Rider* paved the way for a new wave of independent directors who dominated filmmaking for the next decade. The movie pulled young audiences into the theaters, and even if studio moguls scratched their heads over the movie's plot, they understood its box office receipts: $19 million in 1969 alone (nearly twice what Doris Day's last feature film, 1968's *With Six You Get Eggroll*, had grossed).

Hopper directed his next film in an admittedly drugged-out state, and it shows: aptly named *The Last Movie*, it was a bomb and the last movie anyone let him direct for ten years. In 1980, while acting in *Out of the Blue*, a small Canadian film, he was asked to take over as director; the movie came in on schedule and was well received (as was the 1988 Hopper-directed *Colors* starring Sean Penn and Robert Duvall). By 1986 the brat had sobered up. In 1996 he married his fifth wife, to whom he's still married. Today he's one of the busiest actors in Hollywood—and still something of an icon.

1972
FRANCIS FORD COPPOLA—THE GAMBLER
Coppola was one of the first film school graduates to make it big in movies. He was born in 1939 in Detroit and raised in Queens, New York, in the bosom of a creative Italian-American family (his father was a composer-musician and his mother had acted in films in Italy). He contracted polio as a child, and during his convalescence he con-

centrated on puppetry and making home movies. He majored in drama at New York's Hofstra University, got his Masters in film at UCLA, and got his first "Hollywood" job working as an assistant to producer/director Roger Corman, "the king of B movies," for whom he directed *Dementia 13*, a low-budget horror flick.

Coppola's graduate thesis, *You're a Big Boy Now*, was released into theaters in 1966, and won him critical acclaim as well as his masters degree. After graduation he directed *Finian's Rainbow* (1968) for Warner Brothers/Seven Arts, but he was more successful at writing and won a Best Screenplay Oscar in 1971 for *Patton*. That Oscar—and the fact that they could pay the young filmmaker less than a more established director—induced Paramount to ask Coppola to direct and adapt Mario Puzo's best-selling novel about a Mafia family.

THE MOVIES *The Godfather*, the story of the son of a Mafia don whose one wish is to avoid taking over the "family business," was released in 1972. The epic-scale movie painted a three-dimensional portrait of a crime family against a backdrop of family celebrations and sudden, violent death. *The Godfather Part II* (1974), which continued the saga and won six Oscars, was the first movie sequel to win the Oscar for Best Picture.

THE LEGACY If *Easy Rider* made waves in Hollywood, *The Godfather* was a tsunami. Besides being one of the highest-grossing movies in history (winning Oscars for Best Picture and for Coppola's screenplay), *The Godfather* was a cultural event: it became one of the most quoted and imitated movies of all time.

Over the years Coppola's career has teetered between success and disaster, but his contributions can't be overstated. As a producer, he helped develop scores of major young talents—including his friends George Lucas and Steven Spielberg. As a director, he's taken more chances than most. His *Apocalypse Now* (1979), originally scheduled to be shot with a budget of $12 million over six weeks, ended up costing $30 million and taking 16 months—during which star Martin Sheen had a heart attack and a typhoon destroyed the sets—not to mention the additional two years it took to edit the movie. A lesser man might have given up, but Coppola hung in there and the results were Oscar nominations for Best Picture and Best Director, and a Golden Palm for Best Foreign Film at Cannes.

Amadeus (1984) was shot entirely in natural light.

1973
MARTIN SCORSESE—THE SCRAPPER

Like Francis Ford Coppola, Scorsese was often sick as a child; in his case it was asthma that kept him close to home. His youthful pursuit was watching movies—American and European (mostly Italian). Born in 1942, he grew up in New York's Little Italy in a typical Italian-American family; his father was a pants presser, his mother a housewife.

Scorsese joined the seminary in his early teens but dropped out after realizing that his destiny was in the movies, not the priesthood. He enrolled in New York University's film school. In 1969 Scorsese released a student film, *Who's That Knocking at My Door*, an offbeat character study starring then-unknown Harvey Keitel. The movie was seen and praised by a few critics (including a young Roger Ebert). Roger Corman—still on the lookout for young talent—saw it, too, and gave Scorsese his first mainstream job: directing 1972's *Boxcar Bertha*, starring Barbara Hershey and David Carradine.

But Scorsese wanted to make his own movies, to explore the themes that would become his trademark: violence, obsession, confusion over women, and Catholicism.

THE MOVIES *Mean Streets* (1973) was a personal film that drew on Scorsese's own background: his turf in Little Italy, its Mafia presence, and the powerful influence of the Catholic Church. The story of two neighborhood buddies and small-time gangsters, played by De Niro and Keitel, the film's theme is expressed in its first lines, spoken in voice-over: "You don't make up for your sins in church. You do it on the street . . ." Critics raved about *Mean Streets*, not only for its exploration of the conflicting influences of the Church and organized crime, but also for its explicit slice of everyday life. It wasn't until three years later that the general population became aware of Scorsese as a major talent, when they saw *Taxi Driver*—the story of an alienated Vietnam vet (Robert De Niro) who is transformed from cab driver to vigilante assassin.

THE LEGACY *Mean Streets* brought a new combination of documentary realism and cinematic style to American movies. The *New Yorker's* Pauline Kael (the film critic of the day) called it "a true original, and a triumph of personal filmmaking." Scorsese's

---

In Japan, the James Bond film *Dr. No* was released as *We Don't Want a Doctor.*

most haunting films are gritty and violent: *Raging Bull* (1980), starring De Niro as middle-weight boxing champ Jake La Motta is considered a masterpiece. In recent years Scorsese has scored at the box office with big movies like *Gangs of New York* (2002) and *The Aviator* (2004), but his most lasting influence on younger directors—like Spike Lee and Quentin Tarantino—harkens back to his smaller, earlier films.

Want more movie brats? Turn to page 420.

* * *

AMERICA'S GREATEST STARS
The Hollywood Legends Collection from the United States Postal Service honors the following stars:

Edward G. Robinson
Henry Fonda
Cary Grant
Marilyn Monroe
Clark Gable and Vivian Leigh (*Gone With the Wind*)
John Wayne
James Dean
Humphrey Bogart
James Cagney
Bing Crosby
Judy Garland (*Wizard of Oz*)
Douglas Fairbanks
Elvis Presley
Lucille Ball
Gary Cooper (*Beau Geste*)
Ethel Merman
Laurel and Hardy
Will Rogers
Charlie Chaplin
Greta Garbo
Alfred Hitchcock
Boris Karloff (*Frankenstein*)
W.C. Fields
Abbott and Costello

Before becoming an actor, Peter Falk worked at the Connecticut State Budget Bureau.

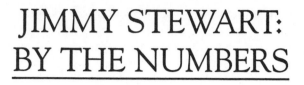

JIMMY STEWART: BY THE NUMBERS

A specialist in roles that needed the touch of the Common Man. Maybe that's why we can call him "Jimmy."

1
Number of Best Actor Oscars won by Jimmy Stewart; it was for his role in *The Philadelphia Story* (1940).

2
Number of TV series Stewart starred in: *The Jimmy Stewart Show*, a sitcom in which he played a professor; and *Hawkins*, a drama in which he played a country lawyer. Both were aired in the 1970s and canceled after a single season.

4
Showing early signs of his future flying career, the age at which little Jimmy tied a box kite to his go-cart and attempted to fly it off the roof of his house.

4
Number of films Stewart appeared in with his best friend, Henry Fonda: *On Our Merry Way* (1948), *How the West Was Won* (1962), *Firecreek* (1968), and *Cheyenne Social Club* (1970).

6
Number of takes it took for Stewart to complete a love scene with bombshell Jean Harlow in *Wife vs. Secretary* (1936). As he said later, "We did it six times. And that dress . . . she didn't seem to wear anything under that dress. Well, I forgot my lines. That's what I did."

17
Number of Western movies in which Stewart rode Pie, his favorite horse. He first chose Pie when he began filming *Winchester '73* (1950), and rode him in every Western he made until the horse,

---

Katharine Hepburn and Spencer Tracy appeared together in nine films.

aged 28, fell ill and died during the filming of *The Cheyenne Social Club* (1970).

20
Number of missions Stewart flew over Germany during World War II, during which he rose from private to full colonel. He retired from the air force reserve in 1968 as a brigadier general, the highest-ranking entertainer in the U.S. military—except, of course, for Ronald Reagan, who would serve as commander-in-chief.

21
In dollars, Stewart's reported monthly income when he first entered military service in 1941. His Hollywood income at the time had been $6,000 a month.

24
Number of hours Stewart, as Mr. Smith, takes to deliver his famous filibuster in *Mr. Smith Goes to Washington*.

41
Age at which Stewart married for the first and only time. His wife, Gloria Hatrick McLean, was a former model and divorcee with two sons. Stewart legally adopted the boys, and the couple had two children of their own—twin girls—in 1951.

48
Age at which Stewart talked director Billy Wilder into letting him play 25-year-old Charles Lindbergh in *The Spirit of St. Louis* (1957).

133
Billboard number Stewart's recording of the song/narration "The Legend of Shenandoah" reached on the charts in 1965.

1932
Year Stewart graduated, with honors, from Princeton University. He studied architecture as an undergraduate.

3,000
Number of mourners who attended Stewart's funeral in 1997.

"I VANT TO BE IN PICTURES," PART 1

Long before Dracula became a pop icon, he was just a character in a not-very-popular novel by Bram Stoker, but everyone's got to start somewhere. Here's the story of how Dracula made his way into pop culture through the stage and screen.

IN THE MAIL

Nosferatu—who cannot die! A million fancies strike you when you hear the name: Nosferatu!

N O S F E R A T U-

does not die!

What do you expect of the first showing of this great work? Aren't you afraid? Men must die. But legend has it that a vampire, Nosferatu, "the undead," lives on men's blood! You want to see a symphony of horror? You may expect more. Be careful. Nosferatu is not just fun, not something to be taken lightly. Once more: beware.

That was the text of a movie advertisement sent to Bram Stoker's 64-year-old widow from Berlin in April 1922. In the ten years since her husband's death, Florence Stoker's financial situation had deteriorated. All of Stoker's books had gone out of print, except for *Dracula*, and sales of that were modest even in the best years. Mrs. Stoker, slowly going blind from cataracts, would have been destitute were it not for help from her son, Noel.

Now, to add insult to injury, came this advertisement in the mail. It was for *Nosferatu, A Symphony of Horrors*, a German film which by its own admission was "freely adapted" from Bram Stoker's *Dracula*. All of Stoker's characters were in the film, only under different names: Dracula was renamed Graf Orlok; Jonathan Harker had become Hutter, his fiancée Mina was renamed Emma, and so on.

Mrs. Stoker was furious. She'd never given the filmmakers, Prana-Film, permission to adapt her husband's work. *Nosferatu* was stolen property, and she wanted it destroyed. So she sued.

Before he played Mr. Spock, Leonard Nimoy owned a pet store during the 1960s.

HONEST MISTAKE?

The makers of *Nosferatu* may not have meant any harm. Filmmaking was still in its infancy in the early 1920s, and Prana-Film, less than a year old, was owned by two businessmen who'd never made films before. But it turned out they were as impractical about making money as they were in obtaining permissions—and two months after Mrs. Stoker filed her lawsuit, the studio went bankrupt.

All existing prints of the film, including the original negative, scattered to the four winds with Prana-Film's dissolution. With no hope left of collecting any financial damages, most people would probably have left it at that. But Mrs. Stoker spent the next ten years hunting down every print of *Nosferatu* she could find . . . and had them all destroyed—including the original negative, which is believed to have been burned in 1925.

"Most 'lost' films have vanished through neglect," David Skal writes in *Hollywood Gothic*. "But in the case of *Nosferatu* we have one of the few instances in film history, and perhaps the only one, in which an obliterating capital punishment is sought for a work of cinematic art, strictly on legalistic grounds, by a person with no knowledge of the work's specific contents or artistic merit." Mrs. Stoker had never even seen the film she worked so hard to destroy.

Despite her dedication, though, she was unsuccessful in destroying every print—a handful survived.

It's fortunate that Mrs. Stoker failed in her attempt to kill *Nosferatu* because the film is not only the first Dracula film ever made, it's also considered by many film historians to be the best. "*Nosferatu*," Skal writes, "would go on to be recognized as a landmark of world cinema, elevating the estimation of Dracula in a way no other dramatic adaptation ever would, or ever could. . . . It had achieved what Florence Stoker herself would never achieve for the book: artistic legitimacy."

DRACULA ON STAGE

In the mid-1920s a British actor named Hamilton Deane licensed the stage rights to *Dracula* from Mrs. Stoker and adapted the novel for the stage, creating a play that could be produced on a shoe-string budget. He also recast the novel's only American character, a Texan named Quincey Morris, as a woman, so that the actresses in his troupe would have more parts.

But the biggest change he made was to clean up Count Dracula. He replaced the vampire's bad breath, hairy palms, and overall bad hygiene with cleanliness, formality, and proper manners. "Gentility and breeding added a new dimension to the character," Skal writes, "and served a theatrical function—he was now able to interact with the characters, rather than merely hang outside their bedroom windows."

COUNT ME OUT

When he set to work adapting *Dracula* for the stage, Deane had himself in mind to play the part of Dracula. But he trimmed the role so much that he decided to play Dr. Van Helsing instead. Perhaps to soothe rocky relations with Mrs. Stoker and her agent, C.A. Bang, Deane cast Bang's brother-in-law, 22-year-old Raymond Huntley, as Dracula. Huntley was paid £8 a week for the part, and was required to provide his own costumes—including lounge suits, full evening tails, a dinner jacket, and a silk hat—all out of his own pocket.

About the only item he didn't have to provide was Dracula's cape, which was considered a stage prop. The cape's huge standup collar completely concealed Huntley's head when he turned his back to the audience, allowing him to "disappear" from the stage by slipping out of the cape and ducking out through a trapdoor in the floor. The trapdoor exit was later removed from the play, but the cape with the standup collar remains a standard part of the Dracula costume to this day.

ON THE ROAD

Hamilton Deane didn't intend his adaptation of *Dracula* to be high art: The play was what was known as a "boob catcher," a play that used gimmickry and sex appeal—and in Dracula's case, death—to draw common people into the theater. For that reason Deane bypassed the London stage (and London theater critics, who would have savaged the production) and took his show on the road, hitting smaller cities and towns all over Britain.

He stayed on the road for more than two years before finally opening at London's Little Theatre on February 14, 1927. As predicted, it was panned by the London critics. The show was at the end of its run . . . or so Deane thought. But as days turned into weeks, and weeks into months, the crowds didn't get smaller—they

—Christine Penmark (Nancy Kelly), *The Bad Seed* (1956)

got bigger. Despite the bad reviews, by the end of summer *Dracula* was playing to capacity crowds and had to move to a larger theater called the Duke of York's. "While glittering productions costing thousands of pounds have wilted and died after a week or so in the West End," the *London Evening News* wrote, "*Dracula* has gone on drinking blood nightly."

COMING TO AMERICA
In early 1927 an American theater promoter named Horace Liveright traveled to London to see *Dracula*. He enjoyed it so much that he saw it again three more times. "Although it was badly produced," he recalled later, "I got a kick out of it each time."

Liveright wanted to bring Dracula to Broadway. But he didn't think Hamilton Deane's adaptation was written well enough for New York audiences. So he got permission from Mrs. Stoker to write another adaptation, one that retained Deane's theatricality but improved his amateurish dialogue.

Liveright offered to take Raymond Huntley to the United States, too, and Huntley agreed to go . . . providing Liveright agreed to raise his pay to $125 a week. No deal. Huntley stayed in London. The part of Dracula went to a Hungarian expatriate actor named Bela Lugosi.

Lugosi, 46, had established himself in Hungary and Germany by playing romantic parts and an occasional villain. But his American career was burdened by the fact that he could speak barely a word of English, and rather than work on his English, he preferred to memorize his lines phonetically.

The result of Lugosi's inability to speak English, Skal writes, "was the oddly inflected and deliberate style of speech now forever associated with the role of Dracula—and a professional albatross that would forever limit the roles offered to him."

VAMPIRE FEVER
Dracula opened at New York's Fulton Theatre on October 5, 1927. It received better reviews than the London version, thanks in large part to the new script and to Lugosi's acting. Lugosi's experience as a romantic lead made his interpretation of Dracula markedly different from Huntley's in London, Skal writes: "The London Dracula was middle-aged and malignant; Lugosi presented quite a different

picture: sexy, continental, with slicked-back patent-leather hair and a weird green cast to his makeup—a Latin lover from beyond the grave, Valentino gone slightly rancid. It was a combination that worked, and audiences—especially female audiences—relished, even wallowed in, the romantic paradoxes."

Dracula was a hit. It played for 31 weeks and 241 performances before closing in 1928. Then Liveright formed a national touring company, and in the process launched America's first vampire craze. By May 1929 Liveright had made more than $1 million on *Dracula*, and would make a million more in less than a year.

A SIGN OF THINGS TO COME
Bela Lugosi was not so lucky: He'd joined the touring company for its west coast swing, but when it moved to the east coast he made the mistake of asking for a substantial raise, one that he felt was commensurate with his ability to draw his fans into the theater. Liveright didn't see it that way, and replaced Lugosi with the man Lugosi had replaced in 1927—Raymond Huntley. Lugosi, not for the last time in his career, was out in the cold.

*Turn to page 388 to find out how
Dracula made it to the movies.*

* * *

HOLLYWOOD SCANDAL
On April 4, 1958, Johnny Stompanato, Lana Turner's gangster boyfriend, was stabbed by Turner's daughter Cheryl Crane. Even though she claimed to be protecting her mother from a vicious beating from an abusive man, Crane had to face an inquest. Her mother testified on her behalf, and a jury found the death a justifiable homicide. Many credit the ruling to Turner's "performance" on the stand.

* * *

INFLATION
In 1973 29-year-old director George Lucas made his first big movie, *American Grafitti*, for only $700,000. His latest release, *The Revenge of the Sith* (2005)? That cost $115 million.

Clint Eastwood has his own beer, Pale Rider Ale, named for his 1985 Western *Pale Rider*.

SWEET SPECIAL EFFECTS

*Ever see an old movie where someone crashes through
a glass window? There's shattered glass everywhere, but
the actors don't have a scratch on them. How do the
Hollywood magicians do it? Uncle John's got the answer.*

J
agged glass is dangerous—especially glass from a broken window. In reality, anyone flying through a glass window risks
severe injury, including severing a limb. So how do actors and
stunt people avoid getting mangled or even scratched up?

The answer lies in the nature of the "glass" itself. The windows
the actors fall through, and even the prop bottles and glasses that
are broken over people's heads, aren't made of glass at all. Today,
innovations in the development of plastics and polymers have put
new, safe glasslike materials at filmmakers' disposal. But until very
recently, stunt coordinators used a much more homey substance for
their glassy feats.

THROUGH A GLASS SWEETLY

In older movies, those windows and bottles are made of candy—
hard, glossy, shiny sugar candy that shatters like glass . . . just without all those sharp, dangerous edges and shards. The similar molec-
ular structures of candy and glass allow them to look alike and
break alike. But glass is harder than candy because it's mostly made
of silica (that's ordinary sand), soda ash, and lime, and has a very
high melting point (1,292 degrees), which makes it sharper and
more dangerous when it breaks. Since candy is softer because it's
made of sugar and water, and has a much lower melting point (367
degrees), its edges aren't as dangerous. And this difference not only
makes the candy safer but also much easier to produce. To make
the candy look like real glass, it is formed exactly the way the glass
would be. It is melted, blown, and then shaped into objects or
panes by a "glass" blower.

He was one of *The Magnificent Seven* and one of *The Dirty Dozen.* Who was he?

HAVE YOUR "GLASS" AND EAT IT, TOO

Interested in making your own stunt glass? Then just follow this recipe for candy glass:

> 7 cups sugar
> 3 cups corn syrup
> 2 cups water

Mix all ingredients together in a clean, metal pot. Gently bring the mixture to a boil (don't stir it) and let it reach 300 degrees on a candy thermometer. While you're waiting for the mixture to heat up (it should take about 40 minutes), line a cookie sheet (or jelly-roll pan) with wax paper. Once the solution has reached 300 degrees, immediately pour it *carefully* onto the cookie sheet. Let the "glass" cool completely before peeling off the wax paper. And voilà, sugar glass.

Note: Always take proper caution when following this recipe. Be very careful while pouring your "glass" onto the cookie sheet.

* * *

THE SECOND TIME AROUND

Bill Haley and the Comets first released "(We're Gonna) Rock Around the Clock" in 1954, but the song didn't go anywhere. When producers decided to use it as the opening music to the juvenile delinquency film *Blackboard Jungle* (1955) one year later, it became a bona fide hit. The re-released song became the first rock-and-roll song to hit #1 and it sold six million copies by the end of the year.

* * *

"It's hard enough to write a good drama; it's much harder to write a good comedy; and it's hardest of all to write a drama with comedy. Which is what life is."

—Jack Lemmon

MORE HOLLYWOOD HAUNTS

Hollywood. A place where so many glamorous lives have come . . . and gone. At least from this flesh-and-blood world.

IT'S A BIRD . . . IT'S A PLANE . . . IT'S A GHOST!
Who's That Ghost? George Reeves, the actor who played Superman on TV
Haunted Hangout: 1579 Benedict Canyon Drive
Spooky Sights: A ghostly man dressed in Superman regalia
Spectral Scoop: Legend says the original Superman still lives, as a shadow of his former self, in the house where he lived—and died. On June 16, 1959, at age 45, Reeves died of gunshot wounds to the head. Although official records say his death was a suicide, there are rumors that the actor was murdered. But any hard evidence proving either theory was destroyed when Reeves's body was cremated.

A year after his death, police officers arrived at the actor's former home when the sound of gunshots was reported. Ten-year-old Jimmy Stein followed them into the star's empty home, where he saw Superman's ghost, standing in the living room behind the officers. The police didn't see a thing.

A few months later, the couple who had bought the home had a run-in with Reeves as well. They claimed to have seen his ghost in the bedroom where he died: Reeves suddenly materialized in front of them, fully decked out in his Superman costume, then slowly faded away. The couple was so scared that they sold the house shortly after the sighting. It has been sold more than a half-dozen times since then with more owners claiming that they encountered Superman's ghost.

VANISHING VALENTINO
Who's That Ghost? Rudolph Valentino, silent-film star
Haunted Hangouts: Paramount Pictures Studios; Falcon's Lair, his last home

---

Cyd Charisse had to be taught to smoke for a dance sequence in *Singin' in the Rain*.

Spooky Sights: A floating, transparent man
Spectral Scoop: A flashy dresser in life, Valentino still likes to hang around clothing in death. He has been known to haunt the wardrobe department of Paramount Pictures, although witnesses say he doesn't bother anyone and seems happy to just float about. Valentino's ghost has also been spotted at the site of his previous home, Falcon's Lair. There he's been seen grooming ghostly horses or playing with the phantom version of his beloved Great Dane, Kabar. Some speculate that the dog was so heartsick after his master's death, that he followed him to the "other side" only days later.

HAUNTED HOTEL
Who Are Those Ghosts? Marilyn Monroe, Montgomery Clift
Haunted Hangout: The Hollywood Roosevelt Hotel
Spooky Sights and Sounds: Monroe's image in a mirror; ghostly bugle playing
Spectral Scoop: Also known as The Spirit's Inn, the Hollywood Roosevelt Hotel is the place to be seen for both current and past stars. For many years the hotel serviced Hollywood's finest, but no ghosts were spotted until after the hotel's restoration in the 1980s. When it reopened in 1985, the past stars' spirits made their appearances, although no one is quite sure why they waited so long. Theories abound, from publicity stunts by the current management to the spirits' anger that the hotel was being renovated (even though in the early 1980s it was so shabby it was almost torn down).

Marilyn Monroe's face has been seen peering from a mirror that belonged in the suite she often occupied. Some claim to have sensed the spirit of Montgomery Clift (*From Here to Eternity*) as ice-cold drafts of air in Room 928 and the nearby hallways where he was known to pace while memorizing his lines. Some have even claimed to hear him practice the bugle, something else he did in the hallways much to the annoyance of other guests.

Staff and management have experienced doors slamming and lights going on and off; they have been pushed and heard eerie piano playing. Which specific ghost can be held responsible for all this activity is unknown, buts psychics claim to have felt the "impressions" of stars such as Humphrey Bogart, Carmen Miranda, Errol Flynn, and Betty Grable.

Number of gallons of blood used by special effects artists for *Scream* (1996): about 50.

I MAKE WESTERNS

When Orson Welles was asked which American film directors appeared to him most, he answered "The old masters . . . by which I mean John Ford, John Ford, and John Ford."

John Ford was one of Hollywood's most demanding and ornery directors. Lots of film people considered him cruel and sadistic and refused to have anything to do with him. But even his worst critics admit that he was the preeminent director of American Westerns, guiding the evolution of the Western from a black-hats-versus-white-hats stereotype into a quintessential American story.

During a career that spanned over 50 years and 200 films, he won seven Oscars; four for directing, one for best picture, and two for best documentary.

HOLLYWOOD NEPOTISM
His real name was Sean Aloysius O'Feeney, and he was born in Maine in 1895, the youngest of 13 children of Irish immigrants. He went to Hollywood at age 16, following after his brother Francis who'd gone 10 years earlier and become a successful actor and director. John began as an assistant to his older brother and later worked as a stuntman and actor before becoming a director.

COWBOYS ARE PEOPLE, TOO
He directed his first feature film for Universal in 1917—a Western called *Straight Shooting*.

Most films of the era used flat lighting and mundane settings, but Ford was heavily influenced by the German style of filmmaking of the 1920s, which pioneered the use of artistic light and shadow. Ford shot most of the exteriors for his Westerns in Monument Valley in Arizona and Utah (known in Hollywood as "Ford country"), the perfect backdrop for his striking visuals. And the characters who moved across his screen had actual personalities, in a genre where one-dimensional characters were the norm.

DON'T THINK YOU'RE SPECIAL
John Ford was tough on all of his actors, often ridiculing them

endlessly—and that was if he liked them. Being ignored by Ford was even worse because that meant he probably wouldn't work with you again. During the filming of *Stagecoach*, Ford constantly ridiculed John Wayne, telling him he was a bad actor and making fun of the way he talked and walked (even though, in his biography of Ford, Peter Bogdanovich insists that Wayne learned his signature walk from Ford himself). Finally the other actors came to Wayne's defense and told Ford to lay off. Later Ford revealed that he'd intentionally created the problem so that the experienced actors on the set, who would normally be jealous of a newcomer in a starring role, would come to Wayne's defense.

Ford's mistreatment of Wayne didn't end with *Stagecoach*. They made 21 films together and Ford taunted Wayne during the filming of all of them. Ford treated all of his favorite actors that way and on several occasions an actor got so fed up he challenged Ford to a fistfight.

THAT'S MISTER ROBERTS, TO YOU, BUDDY!
He made a few propaganda films for the navy during World War II, and retired as a rear admiral.

After the war, Ford's confrontational methods backfired on him during the filming of *Mister Roberts*, which starred Henry Fonda (who'd also starred in the stage version). Fonda had worked with Ford before, most notably on *The Grapes of Wrath*, and had bristled at Ford's mistreatment in the past. This time around, Fonda had more clout with the studio heads and refused to put up with the abuse. Ford wouldn't compromise, so Fonda had Ford replaced by Mervyn LeRoy.

A LITTLE SCARED BY THE RED SCARE
Ford actively participated in the witch-hunting in the entertainment industry during the McCarthy era of the 1950s, when anyone suspected of being a communist was blacklisted.

He took part in an attempted takeover of the Director's Guild of America by legendary director Cecil B. DeMille, who believed that the guild was being run by communists. But Ford somewhat redeemed himself when he became so appalled by De Mille's red-baiting tactics that he publicly broke with him during a guild meeting. First he stood up and introduced himself: "My name's John Ford," he said. "I make Westerns." Then, to DeMille, he said:

... because Kenya forbids using native wild animals in films.

"I don't like you and I don't like what has been happening here tonight." Ford then called for a vote on retaining the current leadership. The vote passed and DeMille's challenge was defeated.

MORE THAN A COWBOY

Ford's Westerns express a deep understanding of America's past and the spirit of the frontier. And though he's best known for them—movies like *My Darling Clementine* and the cavalry trilogy (*Fort Apache*, *She Wore a Yellow Ribbon*, and *Rio Grande*)—Ford won his four directing Oscars for non-Westerns: *The Informer*, *The Grapes of Wrath*, *How Green Was My Valley*, and *The Quiet Man*.

His last feature film was *7 Women* (1966), a critical and box-office disappointment that many critics thought was a throwback to Ford's 1930's techniques. There was talk that he had "lost it" and didn't know how to direct anymore. Stung by the criticism and plagued by ill health, Ford retired. In 1973, he was awarded the American Film Institute's first-ever Life Achievement Award, as well as the Presidential Medal of Freedom a few months before he died of cancer.

* * *

FAVORITE LINES FROM JOHN FORD MOVIES

"Seems like the government's got more interest in a dead man than a live one."

—Tom Joad (Henry Fonda) in
The Grapes of Wrath

"Any man failing to report to duty will be promptly hanged. Amen."

—Reverend Rosenkrantz (Arthur Shields)
in *Drums Along the Mohawk*

"Look, Buster, don't you get overstimulated with me!"

—Eloise Kelly (Ava Gardner) in *Mogambo*

"It's a lousy war, kid . . . but it's the only one we've got."

—Captain Flagg (James Cagney)
in *What Price Glory*

None of the scenes in *Fargo* (1996) were actually filmed in Fargo.

SUBPAR SCI-FI

Now that you've read about some of the best that sci-fi has to offer (see page 102), here are some of the sci-fi flicks that don't quite measure up to our high standards.

N IGHT OF THE LEPUS (1972)

So there are good sci-fi movies with giant ants, giant spiders, and giant apes . . . but giant killer bunnies? Stars Janet Leigh and DeForest Kelley are terrorized after a scientific experiment creates monstrous mutant rabbits who stampede across rural Arizona. The police, the National Guard, and . . . the power company are called in to stop the rampage, which consists largely of poorly filmed rabbits hopping around miniaturized sets in extreme slow motion; the effect was hardly terrorizing. *New York Times* film critic Roger Greenspun lamented the lack of fear inspired by the (allegedly) bloodthirsty bunnies: "Several friends have asked how you can make a rabbit seem scary, and I must confess that *Night of the Lepus* in no way answers their question. It doesn't even reasonably try."

SATURN 3 (1980)

This science fiction film has one of the most unusual pedigrees ever: it was directed by Stanley Donen (best known for directing musicals like *Singin' in the Rain*), written by acclaimed literary novelist Martin Amis, and starred Kirk Douglas and Harvey Keitel. In spite of all that promise, it's a deeply silly and largely incomprehensible film about a team of scientists stationed on the rings of Saturn. The plot: a homicidal robot and his creator have the hots for film costar Farrah Fawcett. "This movie is awesomely stupid," declared Roger Ebert in his review.

HOWARD THE DUCK (1986)

The George Lucas–produced film features a talking duck from another dimension trapped on our world. The movie is so bad it not only killed the careers of its writer and director (Willard Huyck and Gloria Katz), it also bumped off Frank Price, the studio

---

head who greenlighted it. The headline in *Variety*: "'Duck' Cooks Price's Goose." Bottom line: heads rolled at the studio, because it lost them more than $21 million.

BATTLEFIELD EARTH (2000)

This movie stars John Travolta as Terl, the evil leader of an alien race (the Psychlos), who enslave post-apocalyptic humans. A pet project for the actor, *Battlefield Earth* features one of Travolta's most over-the-top performances; he's clearly enjoying himself regardless of the film's fundamental badness. Roger Ebert said, "*Battlefield Earth* is like taking a bus trip with someone who has needed a bath for a long time. It's not merely bad; it's unpleasant in a hostile way." Despite the film's being a massive critical and financial flop, Travolta is on record as considering a sequel.

THE ADVENTURES OF PLUTO NASH (2002)

This comedy features Eddie Murphy as a hustler who lives on the moon in 2087. After angering the local lunar crime boss, Murphy goes on the run while jokes fall flat during confusing scenes and strange visual transitions. The finished movie sat on the shelves at Warner Bros. for two years before finally being released—without screenings for the press, who predictably savaged the film. *Nash* is not only visually one of the worst science fiction films ever made, it is one of the biggest flops in the history of films: it grossed less than $5 million in the theaters but cost more than $100 million to make—losing the studio more than $95 million.

* * *

"The duration of a film should not exceed the capacity of the human bladder."

—Alfred Hitchcock

* * *

SWEET TALK?

In the early days, microphones were so inefficient that performers of tender scenes complained about having to scream their sweet nothings to one another—as if yelling across a football field.

Most wig changes in a movie: 35, by Angela Bassett in *What's Love Got to Do with It?*

ALL ABOUT OSCAR

*Looks can be deceiving: he's just a short, bald guy, but
he's lusted after by every inhabitant of Hollywood.*

The Academy Award statuette, aka Oscar, was designed by
Cedric Gibbons. Gibbons, the art director for Metro-
Goldwyn-Mayer, won 11 Oscars himself between 1930 and
1956.

The statuette—a stylized representation of a knight standing on
a reel of film, holding a sword—was sculpted by George Stanley,
who was paid $500 for the job (a lot of money in Depression-era
America).

CHANGING WITH THE TIMES

The first Oscars were gold-plated bronze on a base of Belgian black
marble. During World War II, when metal was at a premium, the
Oscars were made of plaster (but everyone who received the plaster
statue got a real one when the war was over). Today they're gold-
plated Britannia metal (an alloy made of tin, copper, and antimony)
on a metal base and are slightly taller than the originals. Currently,
Oscar is 13 1/2 inches tall and weighs 8 1/2 pounds.

OTHER OSCARS

A variety of Oscar look-alikes have been given away over the years.
The Honorary Juvenile Award, presented to Shirley Temple in 1934
and to Mickey Rooney and Deanna Durbin in 1938 was a miniature
Oscar. A wooden Oscar with a movable jaw was presented to ventriloquist Edgar Bergen during the 1937 awards, for his creation of
dummy Charlie McCarthy. Walt Disney received an honorary Oscar
and seven miniature statuettes in 1938 when he was honored for
the animated feature *Snow White and the Seven Dwarfs*.

OSCAR WHO?

There are three stories that surface every time someone asks why
the statuette was dubbed Oscar. The most commonly accepted is
that academy librarian Margaret Herrick commented that the statue
looked like her uncle Oscar. Another story has actress Bette Davis
saying the statue looked like her husband Harmon Oscar Nelson.

Dustin Hoffman's salary for *The Graduate* (1967): $17,000.

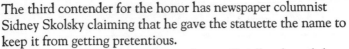

The third contender for the honor has newspaper columnist Sidney Skolsky claiming that he gave the statuette the name to keep it from getting pretentious.

However it came about, the academy officially adopted the nickname for its statue in 1939. As you might expect, Oscar is a registered trademark of the Academy of Motion Picture Arts and Sciences, as are Oscars, Academy Awards, Oscar Night, and A.M.P.A.S. So if you're thinking of naming one of your children any of the above, make sure you get the academy's permission first!

* * *

WAXING PHILOSOPHICAL

"Hollywood's a place where they'll pay you a thousand dollars for a kiss, and fifty cents for your soul. I know, because I turned down the first offer often enough and held out for the fifty cents."
—Marilyn Monroe

"You can take all the sincerity in Hollywood, place it in the navel of a fruit fly and still have room enough for three caraway seeds and a producer's heart."
—Fred Allen, comedian

"Isn't Hollywood a dump—in the human sense of the word. A hideous town, pointed up by the insulting gardens of its rich, full of the human spirit at a new low of debasement."
—F. Scott Fitzgerald

"No one goes Hollywood—they were that way before they came here. Hollywood just exposed it."
—Ronald Reagan

"Where is Hollywood located? Chiefly between the ears. In that part of the American brain lately vacated by God."
—Erica Jong, author

"Hollywood is a place that attracts people with massive holes in their souls."
—Julia Phillips, producer

The battered hat worn by Henry Fonda in *On Golden Pond* was Spencer Tracy's.

A PRODUCT OF SUCCESS

While you might think that putting commercial products in movies is a relatively new practice in Hollywood, it's almost as old as film itself. Here's a brief look at the history of product placement.

Savvy moviegoers know a product placement when they see one. Whether it's the 20 appearances of Marlboro cigarettes in *Superman II* or James Bond's switch from Aston Martins to the BMW Z3 in *Golden Eye*, audiences have become pretty hip to Madison Avenue's presence on the big screen. It's a popular myth that the first big product placement was in *E.T. the Extra-Terrestrial* (1982), when the young hero, Elliott, lures a friendly alien out of hiding by using Reese's Pieces candies—which weren't selling too well at the time. After the candy's big-screen debut, sales shot up 66 percent—and Hollywood noticed. Real products began to show up everywhere in movies; their placement has become a huge industry that takes in more than $3 billion dollars a year. But product placement, like just about anything, isn't really a modern phenomenon. It's been around for about as long as movies have been.

THE EARLY YEARS
The Lumière brothers were pioneers not only of the early cinema but of product placement as well. François-Henri Lavanchy-Clarke, a Lever Brothers representative, was frustrated at not being allowed to exhibit his product, Sunlight Soap, in the 1896 Swiss National Exhibition. Stubbornly, he set up a pavilion next door promoting Lever products. To help draw a crowd, he invited the Lumière brothers to screen their short films. It was the beginning of a beautiful friendship: 70,000 people attended the Lever-Lumière pavilion during its six-month-long exhibition.

Lever and Lumière took their show on the road and gave discounts for the screenings to people with Sunlight Soap coupons. Taking it a step further, Lever Brothers products began to appear in Lumière films, starting with the aptly titled *Laveuses*, or "Washerwomen," in 1897. Lavanchy-Clarke ended up producing

---

John Wayne's silver-and-leather hatband in *True Grit* originally was Gary Cooper's.

many Lumière films, and he even appears in several, with his younger brother Emile serving as cameraman. Moviemakers and advertisers have gotten along quite well ever since.

DRIVING A SMART INVESTMENT

Early Hollywood players were no different. They soon developed a quid pro quo relationship with manufacturers. By the 1920s companies were giving away free product to studios, which helped the movies' bottom lines and gave the companies free advertising. Warner Bros. had a 10-picture deal with Buick that allowed the studio to use the manufacturer's automobiles for free, such as in Busby Berkeley's musical *Gold Diggers* of 1935. And the deal seemed to work out for both Warner Bros. and the car company: the film was one of a string of hits, and Buick went from selling a paltry 47,000 cars in 1933, to more than 220,000 only four years later.

Sometimes movies received free advertising: *Scarface* (1932) benefited from $250,000 worth of free promotion from White Owl cigars, whose ads boasted that the actor Paul Muni smoked them in the film—even though he used a completely different brand on-screen.

Companies were good at coming up with ingenious ways to put their products in front of the public through the use of movie stars: Coca-Cola arranged for stars to swig their soda during downtime on the set. They took pictures and then used the photographs in ads that promoted both Coke and the movies being filmed. Promotional stills of sexy Jean Harlow drinking Coke while filming MGM's 1933 hit *Dinner at Eight* were especially effective. In 1950 Coca-Cola featured ads with Spencer Tracy and promoted his new movie, *Father of the Bride*. In turn, Tracy's character offers his guests the brand-name soda pop at his daughter's on-screen engagement party.

A PRODUCT PLACEMENT IS FOREVER

The De Beers company single-handedly created the market for diamond engagement rings with the unique deal they began to offer the studios in 1939: they would give them a diamond ring to use, but only if the studio gave them script approval. De Beers made sure that the diamonds were always given in a romantic context, that they were given by a man to a woman (rather than the couple buying it together), and that the gift was a surprise. Yet the one thing De Beers couldn't control was how the movie performed at the box office: one of the first films to take them up on the offer was the disappointing *That Uncertain Feeling*, released by United Artists in 1941.

When the Bell System had a telephone they wanted the public to embrace—a so-called French phone that boasted the new design of having both earpiece and microphone in the handset—the company thought the best way to introduce it to the American public was to show Cary Grant using the phone in 1944's *Arsenic and Old Lace*. The French phone quickly caught on with viewers and became the standard phone used in America.

Sometimes a product was created through a movie, such as Black Pony whiskey. The brand was invented for the 1944 film *Laura* and subsequently released as a real product.

BETCHA CAN'T EAT JUST ONE
In the 1950s, the Bell potato chip company was looking to expand. Bell was a regional brand, distributed mainly on the West Coast, so they began sending free cases of their potato chips to movie sets, in the hopes that they could get some screen time. After numerous attempts, the plan finally worked when Billy Wilder needed them for *The Seven Year Itch* (1955). Marilyn Monroe's character eats them after a trip to the grocery store. (But it's tough to say if anyone was looking at a bag of chips when Monroe was on-screen.)

The biggest change in product placement practices over the years is that Hollywood has become less discreet about its relationship with Madison Avenue. The products have always been there—they're just easier to see now. Whole departments and massive budgets are devoted to managing the presence of products on the big screen. In 2004 spending on placements reached nearly $3.5 billion. And experts say there's no end in sight: they estimate that by 2009 spending will reach $6.9 billion.

* * *

AN EXCEPTION
Although audiences complain about the presence of products in movies, not all product placements irritate viewers. In *Home Alone* (1990), John Candy and his polka band give Catherine O'Hara a ride home in a Budget rental truck. After the movie, people actually called Budget to "thank them for getting that poor woman home."

Kevin Smith's comedy *Clerks* (1994) was made on a budget of $26,800.

LIGHTS, CAMERA, EAT!

Because studios aren't big enough to hold some scenes.

Restaurant: Katz's Deli
Location: E. Houston Street, New York City
Movie: *When Harry Met Sally* (1989)
Actors: Meg Ryan, Billy Crystal
Scene: A contender for the most memorable restaurant scene of them all. Sally (Ryan) bets Harry (Crystal) that she can fake an orgasm—and proceeds to do so, to Harry's embarrassment and the amusement of the other diners. When Sally's done, a woman at the next table says to her waiter, "I'll have what she's having." (The woman is director Rob Reiner's mother, Estelle.) The table at which the scene was filmed now has a plaque on it that reads, "Congratulations! You're sitting where Harry met Sally."

Restaurant: Denny's
Location: Eugene, Oregon
Movie: *Five Easy Pieces* (1970)
Actors: Jack Nicholson, Karen Black, Lorna Thayer
Scene: Another contender for most memorable scene. While Rayette (Black) and the two hitchhikers they've picked up look on, Bobby (Nicholson) tries to order a side of toast from the recalcitrant waitress (Thayer). The dialogue goes like this:

> BOBBY: I'd like an omelet, plain, and a chicken salad sandwich on wheat toast, no mayonnaise, no butter, no lettuce. And a cup of coffee.
>
> WAITRESS: A #2, chicken salad sand. Hold the butter, the lettuce, the mayonnaise, and a cup of coffee. Anything else?
>
> BOBBY: Yeah, now all you have to do is hold the chicken, bring me the toast, give me a check for the chicken salad sandwich, and you haven't broken any rules.
>
> WAITRESS: You want me to hold the chicken, huh?
>
> BOBBY: I want you to hold it between your knees.

On his deathbed, director Erich von Stroheim railed against Hollywood.

Restaurant: Hawthorne Grill
Location: Hawthorne, California
Movie: *Pulp Fiction* (1994)
Actors: Tim Roth, Amanda Plummer, John Travolta, Samuel L. Jackson
Scene: Director Quentin Tarantino uses the first and last scenes to hold his circular story together. In the first scene, Pumpkin (Roth) and Honey Bunny (Plummer) decide to hold up the restaurant. In the last scene, hit men Jules (Jackson) and Vincent (Travolta) hold them at bay while born-again Jules gives them his money and quotes from the Bible. The restaurant has since been torn down.

Restaurant: Hawaii Kai (but since renamed)
Location: 49th and Broadway, New York City
Movie: *Goodfellas* (1990)
Actors: Joe Pesci, Ray Liotta
Scene: The restaurant is called the Bamboo Lounge in the movie, and in one unforgettable scene, psycho mobster Tommy (Pesci) teases Henry (Liotta) by seeming to turn on him: "You think I'm funny? Funny how? How am I funny?" Henry and the rest of the table are relieved when they realize it's a joke. Immediately after which, when the restaurant owner asks Tommy to pay the bill, Tommy takes a bottle and smashes it over the owner's head. A few scenes later, Henry and Tommy torch the place so the owner can collect the insurance.

Restaurant: Kate Mantilini
Location: Wilshire Boulevard, Beverly Hills
Movie: *Heat* (1995)
Actors: Al Pacino, Robert De Niro
Scene: LAPD Detective Vincent Hanna (Pacino), has been tailing high-level thief Neil McCauley (De Niro) in his car. Hanna pulls McCauley over and suggests that they call a momentary truce and have a cup of coffee together. Across the table from each other—in the real-life Hollywood hangout—the characters come to understand all the things they have in common, including their troubled personal lives.

Restaurant: Musso and Frank's Grill
Location: Hollywood Boulevard, Hollywood, California
Movie: *Ed Wood* (1994)
Actors: Johnny Depp, Vincent D'Onofrio
Scene: Director Ed Wood (Depp) stomps angrily into Musso and
Frank's (another real Hollywood hangout) in women's clothes and
a wig, where he encounters Orson Welles (D'Onofrio). He turns to
Welles for sympathy—complaining that studios always want to cast
people they know. In an insider's reference to his classic *Touch of
Evil*, the Welles character agrees: "Tell me about it. I'm supposed to
do a thriller for Universal. They want Charlton Heston as a
Mexican."

Restaurant: Carl's Jr.
Location: Saticoy Street, Canoga Park, San Fernando Valley,
California
Movie: *American Beauty* (1999)
Actors: Kevin Spacey, Annette Bening, Peter Gallagher
Scene: The most memorable scene filmed at a drive-in window.
After deciding to change his life, Lester Burnham (Spacey) takes a
job manning the drive-through window at Mr. Smiley's, a fast-food
joint. When his wife, Carolyn (Bening), and her lover, Buddy
Kane (Gallagher), drive up and start snuggling in the front seat,
Lester smirks and says, "Smile! You're at Mr. Smiley's."

* * *

NO OFFENSE . . .
"It's a rather rude gesture, but at least it's clear what you mean."
—Katharine Hepburn, on spitting in the eye
of director Joseph L. Mankiewicz

"Kate Hepburn—God, she's beautiful, God, she plays golf well,
God, she can get anyone in the world on the phone, God, she
knows what to do all the time."
—Joseph L. Mankiewicz, director

DISASTER AND DE NILE, PART 2

Things didn't ease up when Cleopatra moved to Italy.
Here is the second part of the story behind the
movie. The first is on page 44.

CLEOPATRA, TAKE TWO!
The production moved to Italy, to Rome's Cinecittà studios; Alexandria was built again, this time on twenty acres overlooking Anzio Beach. Moving to a new location meant big bucks for Ms. Taylor: now that filming was beginning again in a new location, she was entitled to an additional $1 million.

While the London shoot had its problems, Rome's dilemmas were distinctly its own. First, a group of female extras who played Cleopatra's various servants and slave girls went on strike to demand protection from the amorous Italian extras who went around pinching female derrieres; the studio had to hire a special guard to protect them. But that was the least of it: the Cinecittà employees pilfered props and equipment to the tune of millions.

Fox insisted that production begin in September 1961. The thousand-member cast was outfitted, and Liz was well enough to start shooting, but Mankiewicz felt nowhere near ready. Because he was writing the script as he went along, he had to shoot the movie in sequence, which meant that both the main actors and the thousands of extras were sometimes sitting around for days on end waiting for their scenes to come. Richard Burton and Roddy McDowall (who played Marc Antony's archenemy, Octavian) had so much free time that they were able to offer their services to Darryl F. Zanuck on another movie, The Longest Day, which was shooting in France at the time. (For more on *The Longest Day*, see page 440).

On November 17, 1961, Taylor went into "overtime." Now she was earning $50,000 a week. The studio had to cut corners somewhere, so they fired producer Walter Wanger, who stayed on without pay.

—Herbert H. Heebert (Jerry Lewis), *The Ladies' Man* (1961)

THE SCANDAL

They hadn't liked each other when they'd met years before, but in 1962, once Taylor and Burton had done a love scene or two, they didn't have to act anymore. Within a month they were offscreen lovers, too. Taylor had already scandalized the world by stealing singer Eddie Fisher from his wife, actress and girl-next-door Debbie Reynolds, and their two children. The tabloids went wild with the new story, Liz catching most of the flak. She was denounced on the floor of Congress—and since this was all happening in Rome, the Vatican couldn't resist adding its two cents, accusing Taylor of "erotic vagrancy." Burton was astounded at the scandal's scope: "I've had affairs before," he said. "How was I to know she was so f—ing famous?" His wife, Sybil, went home to London, and Eddie Fisher left for New York.

MEANWHILE, BACK AT THE STUDIO

By this time Fox chairman Skouras was cooking the books so that his board of directors wouldn't know how much money was being spent. Fox was in the worst financial shape in its history. *Cleopatra* was its only film in production. Even the surefire box office success of Zanuck's *The Longest Day* wasn't going to save the studio. When the studio held its next board meeting, Zanuck went on the attack. By the time the meeting was over, he was in as Fox's new chairman and Skouras was out.

THE SHOOT, CONTINUED

Finally, in April 1962, Zanuck put his foot down and told Mankiewicz he had only had three more months to finish *Cleopatra*. And he wasn't getting any more money. By this time Mankiewicz was a physical wreck and had been receiving injections (of exactly what is not known) to keep going. According to his son Tom, "He finally wound up getting an injection in the morning to get him going, sometimes another one after lunch, and a shot at night to get him to sleep." When one of the needles hit his sciatic nerve, the director had to be carried around the set on a stretcher.

THE WRAP

Shooting finally wrapped in August 1962. Fox had spent over $30 million on the production. What did they spend all that money on? Well, aside from salaries, it was the breathtaking costumes:

Patrick Swayze was a professional ballet dancer before he became an actor.

more than 1,000 extras needed more than 26,000 costumes. Taylor had 65 costume changes alone, to the tune of $194,800. The 72 sets were another huge expense. Cleopatra's barge was covered with gold leaf—its gilded rigging alone cost $277,000. And it was the scenes themselves, such as Cleopatra's grand procession into Rome where she's seated on a 30-foot-high replica of the Sphinx, pulled by 300 slaves, and surrounded by thousands of cheering extras (who were actually shouting "Liz! Liz!" instead of "Cleopatra!").

POSTPRODUCTION
Mankiewicz returned to Los Angeles in August to start editing. To skirt bankruptcy, Twentieth Century Fox shut down for four months, forcing 2,000 people out of work. It also sold off its back lot, the land that eventually became Century City. Fox was a ghost town—no movies in the works, commissary closed, and only a few administrative buildings open. In one of them, Mankiewicz was editing. In October, he screened a five-hour-plus version for Zanuck.

The two men argued over the length of the film, and Zanuck fired Mankiewicz. But since the director had written the script, he was the only one who knew how the story fit together. He had to be rehired to complete the project. But even that was not the end.

THE PREMIERES
Fox made one more investment—on publicity for the film—and pretty soon money started coming back in: the New York theater where the film would premiere gave Fox a check for $1.25 million for the privilege; tickets for the first run were sold out four months in advance.

Cleopatra premiered on June 12, 1963. Everyone was there except Elizabeth Taylor, who wanted no part of it. *The New York Times* raved about the picture, but the other reviews were mixed. One thing that everyone agreed on was that the movie, at four hours and three minutes, was too long. Fifty-nine more minutes were cut, and the movie was released into general distribution at its present length: three hours and four minutes.

Liz did go to the London premiere—under pressure from the studio—and later said that everything she'd liked about her role had been cut. She told anyone who would listen that she hated the movie.

Oklahoma! (1955) was shot in Arizona. (Oklahoma was too well developed by 1955.)

THE OSCARS
Cleopatra was nominated for eight Academy Awards and won four: Best Art Direction-Set Decoration, Best Cinematography, Best Costume Design, and Best Effects. A clerical error on the part of the Academy cost Roddy McDowall a nomination for Best Supporting Actor. It was generally agreed that he would have won the Oscar, which instead went to Melvyn Douglas for *Hud*.

THE GROSSES
Including the millions spent on promotion, and the $7 million paid to Taylor in salary, *Cleopatra* cost $44 million to make (over $400 million in today's dollars.) The movie grossed $24 million in its first year of release—not nearly enough to make up for the outlay. In 1966 ABC-TV paid 20th Century Fox a record $5 million for two showings of the film, a deal that finally put the picture into the black. Thanks to a string of hits in the 1960s (*Valley of the Dolls* and *Planet of the Apes* among them), topped by *The Sound of Music*, the studio did recover by 1968. Today, after all these years, *Cleopatra* is still the best-grossing film released in 1963, even if it was the movie that almost sank a studio.

* * *

PANNING THE PRESS
"Her virtue was that she said what she thought, her vice that what she thought didn't amount to much."
—Peter Ustinov, on Hollywood columnist Hedda Hopper

"She was, for all her lifelong love affair with motion pictures, a reporter first. . . . She would skewer her best friend on the greasy spit of scandal if circumstances warranted it."
—Paul O'Neil, on Hollywood columnist Louella Parsons

"All day long, they lie in the sun, and when the sun goes down, they lie some more."
—Frank Sinatra, on Hollywood reporters

In *The Deer Hunter* (1978), Nick (Christopher Walken) urges Michael to drive faster.

BAD BOYS
ON LOCATION

*You can't take them anywhere. Here's what can happen
when bad-boy movie stars leave the safe confines of
Hollywood and go loco on location.*

STEVE MCQUEEN IN GERMANY
(Bullitt, The Blob)
While filming *The Great Escape*, the notoriously lead-footed
McQueen was caught in a Munich speed trap, arrested, and briefly
jailed. Other members of the cast and crew had been caught, too,
but clocked at slower speeds, prompting the local chief of police to
say, "Herr McQueen, we have caught several of your comrades
today, but you have won the prize."

RUSSELL CROWE IN NEW YORK
(Gladiator, A Beautiful Mind)
While in New York City to promote the boxing flick *Cinderella
Man*, Crowe had problems getting a call through to Australia at
his posh hotel. After a few frustrating attempts, he ripped the
phone from the wall, took it down to the lobby, and threw it in the
concierge's direction, where it landed with a crack. The concierge
went to the hospital to be treated for facial injuries. And Crowe
went to jail where he was booked on charges of assault and criminal possession of a weapon—the telephone. After appearing on
Late Night with David Letterman, where the actor admitted that it
had been "possibly the most shameful situation" he'd ever been in,
Crowe made amends by coming to a settlement (for an undisclosed
amount) with the concierge.

JASON PATRIC IN TEXAS
(Sleepers, Speed 2: Cruise Control)
In the Texas capital promoting his 2004 film *The Alamo*, Patric
was standing in the street among a crowd of revelers at about three
in the morning when a policeman asked the group if they would

In real life, Walken has a phobia of driving too fast.

move onto the sidewalk. Patric, who played the hard-drinking roughneck Jim Bowie in the film and may have still been in character, began "mocking" the police officer and assumed "an aggressive stance." A scuffle ensued, and Patric spent the night in jail on charges of public intoxication and resisting arrest.

VINCE VAUGHN IN NORTH CAROLINA
(Dodgeball: A True Underdog Story, Wedding Crashers)
In Wilmington, North Carolina, during the filming of *Domestic Disturbance*, Vaughn allegedly struck up a conversation in a bar with another patron's girlfriend. When Vaughn was challenged to step outside, his costar Steve Buscemi (*Fargo*) intervened—and was knifed for his trouble. An uninjured Vaughn was fined $250 plus court costs, was ordered to undergo alcohol counseling, and was banned from all the bars in Wilmington.

JAMIE FOXX IN LOUISIANA
(Ali, Collateral)
While filming *Ray* in New Orleans, Foxx and his 10-person entourage were asked for IDs at the entrance to Harrah's casino. Foxx refused and headed to one of the tables. The club's security officers called the police. When the star and his sister still refused to leave, Foxx was charged with trespassing, disturbing the peace, battery, and resisting arrest. His sister was charged with all the above and extortion—she had threatened to "cut" one of the guards if he didn't let them in. She also reportedly punched one of the policemen in the face.

EDWARD FURLONG IN KENTUCKY
(American History X, Terminator 2: Judgment Day)
During the filming of *Jimmy and Judy* in Florence, Kentucky, Furlong entered a local grocery store at 11:00 p.m. and "set free" all the live lobsters in its tank. It wasn't just a prank: Furlong is a longtime supporter of People for the Ethical Treatment of Animals (PETA). But he was drunk at the time, so he was arrested and charged with public intoxication.

BRAD RENFRO IN FLORIDA
(The Client, Apt Pupil)
The night before he was scheduled to begin shooting *Bully in Fort*

Lauderdale, 18-year-old Renfro and a buddy entered Holiday Harbor and attempted to set sail on someone else's $175,000 yacht. Renfro cranked up the engines—awakening the people sleeping in adjacent slips—but forgot to untie the boat from its moorings. As he tried to speed away, the neighbors he'd just woken up jumped aboard and held him until police arrived. Renfro had to pay the owner of the yacht $4,200 in damages, and the local police $141 for investigative costs. He was also put on probation—during which he was arrested again, about six months later, for underage drinking.

* * *

QUOTES OF EVIL
More favorite lines from our favorite villains.

"Go ahead. Jump. He never loved you, so why go on living? Jump and it will all be over. . . . "
—Mrs. Danvers (Judith Anderson),
Rebecca (1940)

"If Mr. McMurphy doesn't want to take his medication orally, I'm sure we can arrange that he can have it some other way."
—Nurse Ratched (Louise Fletcher),
One Flew Over the Cuckoo's Nest (1975)

"Dr. Jones. Again we see there is nothing you can possess which I cannot take away."
—Dr. Rene Belloq,
Raiders of the Lost Ark (1981)

"The force is with you, young Skywalker, but you are not a Jedi yet."
—Darth Vader (James Earl Jones),
Star Wars Episode V: The Empire Strikes Back (1980)

Edgar Allan Poe has the most works turned into movies (114) of any American writer.

THE WOLFMAN AT THE MOVIES, PART 3

*Like all classic Hollywood monsters, the werewolf was
spun off into dozens of movies, many of them
low-budget, some just plain unusual.
Take these, for example:*

I Was a Teenage Werewolf (1957)

The original "teenage" horror film, *I Was a Teenage Werewolf,* was filmed in seven days at a cost of $125,000 . . . and made $2 million. It launched an entire genre of low-budget, B-movie films, including *I Was a Teenage Frankenstein, I Was a Teenage Zombie,* and *I Was a Teenage TV Terrorist.*

The movie stars a young Michael Landon (of future *Bonanza* and *Little House on the Prairie* fame) in his first feature-film role. He plays an emotionally disturbed teenager seeking treatment for his problems. A mad scientist hypnotizes him and he "regresses" so far back in time that he becomes a prehistoric werewolf. Landon's girlfriend is not amused, and neither are the police. They gun him down at the end of the film.

The Mad Monster (1942)

Dr. Cameron, a mad scientist, injects a handyman with the blood of a wolf, "turning him into the prototype for an army of wolfmen to battle the Nazis." In the end, however, Dr. Cameron succumbs to pettiness and uses the werewolf "to kill the men he believes responsible for destroying his reputation." The film, banned in the UK until 1952, was finally released with an X rating and a medical disclaimer touting the safety of blood transfusions.

Werewolf in a Girl's Dormitory (1961)

When a series of ghastly murders takes place at a correctional school for wayward girls, investigators discover that Mr. Swift, the school's superintendent, is a werewolf.

Before he made it big in films, Alan Ladd operated a hot dog stand called Tiny's.

Werewolves on Wheels (1971)
"With surfing music blaring on the soundtrack, motorcycle gang members curse, attend impromptu orgies, drink barrels of beer and rough up some monks. In retaliation, cyclists are cursed with lycanthropy [they're turned into werewolves]. What follows is some very unintentional comedy and some very unnecessary nudity."
—*The Creature Feature's Movie Guide*

Leena Meets Frankenstein (1993)
"A hardcore remake of *Abbot and Costello Meet Frankenstein* (1948), which changes from black and white to color for the sex scenes. When their car breaks down, two street-wise babes are stranded at a time-share condo with the classic monsters—the Wolfman, Dracula, his vampire wives, and the Frankenstein monster."
—*The Illustrated Werewolf Movie Guide*

The Rats Are Coming! The Werewolves Are Here! (1972)
"When a newly married man discovers that his inlaws are incestuous werewolves, he and his wife set out to break the family curse. The characters include a 108-year-old family patriarch and the wife's brother Malcolm, who is kept in shackles in a locked room, where he commits unspeakable crimes against chickens and mice. "To pad its short running time, producer Andy Milligan filmed a subplot of man-eating rats in Milligan's hometown of Staten Island. Ads offered: 'Win a live rat for your mother-in-law.'"
—*Cult Flicks and Trash Pics*

Night Stalkers (1995)
A private detective stumbles onto a society of werewolves while investigating the murder of someone who was skinned alive. Probably the world's first all-deaf werewolf film, directed by a deaf director and "shot on video in London and Liverpool with an all-deaf cast for an incredible $600, utilizing sign language, subtitles, and voice-over for the hearing impaired."
—*The Illustrated Werewolf Movie Guide*

Werewolf of Woodstock (1975)
A few days after the Woodstock festival, a beer-drinking, hippie-hating farmer (Tige Andrews from TV's *The Mod Squad*) who lives

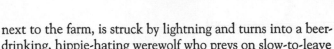

next to the farm, is struck by lightning and turns into a beer-drinking, hippie-hating werewolf who preys on slow-to-leave concert-goers. *The Creature Features Movie Guide* describes it as "undoubtedly one of the dumbest lycanthropy [werewolf] movies ever produced."

Curse of the Queerwolf (1987)

"A straight man is bitten on the butt by a gay werewolf(!) and transforms into the title character. When the moon is full, he finds himself turning into a werewolf—and gay! [Director Michael] Pirro takes advantage of the outrageously funny idea of turning homophobia into a horror movie."

—*Cult Flicks and Trash Pics*

The Werewolf and the Yeti (1975)

A man on a Tibetan expedition in search of the Yeti is bitten by two cannibalistic sisters he finds in a cave. He becomes a werewolf during the next full moon, and battles the abominable snowman.

Full Moon High (1981)

A 1950s high school student (Adam Arkin of TV's *Chicago Hope*) is bitten by a werewolf while on a trip to Armenia with his CIA agent father. Forever young, he returns to Full Moon High twenty years later disguised as his own son.

Blood! (1974)

Dracula's daughter Regina meets the son of Laurence Talbot (the Wolfman) and falls in love. "They get married, move to America, and attempt to raise flesh-eating plants to cure their respective curses."

—*The Illustrated Werewolf Movie Guide*

* * *

THE FANTASY THAT IS JAMES BOND

"Bond smoked like Peter Lorre, drank like Humphrey Bogart, ate like Sydney Greenstreet, used up girls like Errol Flynn . . . then went to a steam bath and came out looking like Clark Gable."

—Harry Reasoner

Joanne Woodward accepted an Academy Award in a gown she made herself for $100.

PHILOSOPHIES ON FILM

*Film characters often espouse their
views on life and how best to live it.*

"Nature is what we are put in this world to rise above."
—Rose Sayer
(Katharine Hepburn),
The African Queen (1951)

"Every man dies, but not every man really lives."
—William Wallace
(Mel Gibson),
Braveheart (1995)

"Old age: It's the only disease you don't look forward to being cured of."
—Mr. Bernstein
(Everett Sloane),
Citizen Kane (1941)

"You didn't come into this life just to sit around on a dugout bench, did ya? Now get your ass out there and do the best you can."
—Coach Morris Buttermaker
(Walter Matthau),
The Bad News Bears (1976)

"Uh, try and be nice to people, avoid eating fat, read a good book every now and then, get some walking in, and try and live together in peace and harmony with people of all creeds and nations."
—Lady Presenter
(Michael Palin),
Monty Python's The Meaning of Life (1983)

"It does not do to dwell on dreams and forget to live."
—Albus Dumbledore
(Richard Harris), *Harry Potter and the Sorcerer's Stone* (2001)

"Life moves pretty fast. If you don't stop and look around every once in a while, you could miss it."
—Ferris Bueller
(Matthew Broderick),
Ferris Bueller's Day Off (1986)

"Hey, hey, hey. Don't be mean. We don't have to be mean because, remember, no matter where you go, there you are."
—Buckaroo Banzai
(Peter Weller), *The Adventures of Buckaroo Banzai Across the 8th Dimension* (1984)

"I feel that life is divided into the horrible and the miserable. That's the two categories. The horrible are like, I don't know, terminal cases, you know, and blind people, crippled. . . . And the miserable is everyone else. So you should be thankful that you're miserable, because that's very lucky, to be miserable."
—Alvy Singer
(Woody Allen),
Annie Hall (1977)

"One man's life touches so many others, when he's not there it leaves an awfully big hole."
—Clarence (Henry Travers),
It's a Wonderful Life (1946)

"Hope is a good thing, maybe the best of things, and no good thing ever dies."
—Red Redding
(Morgan Freeman) reading a note from Andy Dufresne
(Tim Robbins), *The Shawshank Redemption* (1994)

"Fear is the path to the dark side. Fear leads to anger. Anger leads to hate. Hate leads to suffering."
—Yoda (Frank Oz),
Star Wars: The Phantom Menace (1999)

"I would rather have thirty minutes of wonderful than a lifetime of nothing special."
—Shelby Eatenton
Latcherie (Julia Roberts),
Steel Magnolias (1989)

"You wanna know something? Every now and then say, 'What the ****.' It gives you freedom. Freedom brings opportunity. Opportunity makes your future."
—Miles (Curtis Armstrong),
Risky Business (1983)

"Maria, these walls were not meant to shut out problems. You have to face them. You have to live the life you were born to live."
—Mother Abbess
(Peggy Wood),
The Sound of Music (1965)

"Life is a random lottery of meaningless tragedy and a series of near escapes."
—Troy Dyer (Ethan Hawke),
Reality Bites (1994)

"There's a difference between knowing the path and walking the path."
—Morpheus
(Laurence Fishburne),
The Matrix (1999)

VIDEO GAMES GONE HOLLYWOOD, PART 1

These days, video games based on popular movies are everywhere, but the relationship between Hollywood and the gaming industry didn't get off to a very smooth start. Buggy games and clunky graphics made things difficult at first, but the first game marked the beginning of a beautiful friendship.

THE EARLY YEARS

Video games inspired by movies first emerged in the early 1980s, but back then games weren't a part of an original marketing plan. Game production was often rushed into the last-minute phases of the marketing process—along with lunch boxes and T-shirts. While that might have been fine for Thermoses, it wasn't the best approach for computer programming and it nearly sunk the video game industry. But even though the games were a bit clunky, their ability to give fans a whole new way to experience their favorite films was hard to ignore.

Raiders of the Lost Ark

Industry experts consider this the very first movie-based video game. Released in 1982, Raiders of the Lost Ark was played on the Atari 2600 system. While it's not altogether clear what's happening on the screen until someone explains it, the goal of the game is the same as the movie—to get the Ark of the Covenant. Unlike the flick, the crude graphics made Indiana Jones look more like a fire hydrant than a dashing archaeologist. As fun as it was, this game was tough. It took both joysticks to play, bore only a slight resemblance to the film, and the backgrounds were basically a series of polygons.

E.T. The Extra-Terrestrial

While the Raiders game was a smash, the Atari 2600 version of E.T. was a disaster when it came out in 1982. Atari's parent company, Warner Bros., paid Steven Spielberg $20 million for the

---

—Dr. Peter Venkman (Bill Murray), *Ghostbusters* (1984)

licensing rights but rushed the game through development to get it in stores before Christmas. The result? Nobody bought the practically unplayable game. Unlike the movie, E.T. the game suffered from a terrible plot, little action, and poor graphics. Five million games were produced—hardly any were sold (and many that were sold were returned). Warner Bros. had to destroy millions of cartridges and bury them in a New Mexico landfill. Atari's overconfidence led to what is now known as the "Video Game Crash of 1983," when many U.S. manufacturers of video games and home consoles collapsed.

A View to a Kill
Even though the market for home consoles had largely disappeared, the market for less expensive home computers was just beginning to take off in 1985. That's when the first game based on 007's adventures was released. Designed for the Commodore 64, A View to a Kill, based on the Roger Moore, Grace Jones, and Christopher Walken film, let players tear through the streets of Paris, escape a burning City Hall, and navigate a silicon mine . . . when everything worked. Buggy programming could cause Bondmobiles to stick to walls and to crash for no apparent reason. On the plus side, the game's soundtrack came straight from the movie and included a rendition of Duran Duran's movie theme and the classic Bond theme, too.

TIMES CHANGE
Despite the mixed results in the early years, the gaming industry and Hollywood would develop a profitable partnership. It just took a decade to develop. In the 1990s executives began to put a lot more thought into movie-based video games. Instead of rushing them out at the last minute, games began to go into production when a movie script was bought—giving programmers plenty of time to create a game people actually wanted to play. Professional scriptwriters made sure the plot was good, and even the actors from the films had their faces, bodies, and voices digitally worked into play. And the fans? They loved it. The games let them explore the world of the movie for themselves, meet more characters, and go deeper into the stories. So how much did they love it? Enough to earn the gaming industry almost $8 billion a year.

Drew Barrymore wrote her autobiography, *Little Girl Lost*, when she was 14 years old.

Golden Eye 007

More than ten years after the release of the first Bond game, Nintendo profited handsomely from Golden Eye 007, released in 1997. Fans could walk in the shoes, see with the eyes, and wear the tuxedo of James Bond for the first time. Rendered in a 3D environment, everything is shown from 007's perspective (what's called a first-person shooter). Golden Eye's storyline closely followed that of the movie, with the same settings, gadgets, and stunts. Developers and programmers visited the movie sets and used actual blueprints to construct sequences and sets. In its first three years on the market, Golden Eye 007 sold well over 8 million units, showing how much a successful game could bring to a movie franchise. Years after the buzz behind the movie has faded, the Golden Eye game still picks up new fans—even after new, more advanced Bond games were released.

Enter the Matrix

A truly groundbreaking game, Enter the Matrix was released in 2003 and marked one of the first big strategic partnerships between Hollywood and the gaming industry. Creators of *The Matrix* (1999), Larry and Andy Wachowski had a vision: both the game (Enter the Matrix) and the movie (*The Matrix Reloaded*) would continue the story of the original blockbuster. They wrote the game's script, choreographed the action, and involved the same actors from the first film. In addition to the cutting-edge graphics (Atari spent $20 million to develop Enter the Matrix, and it shows), the game's extra features include an hour of movie footage that adds essential plot information—and can only be seen in the video game. Luckily for fans, both the game and the movie sequel were released simultaneously so viewers wouldn't miss out on anything vital.

Finding Nemo

There's no reason the kiddies can't take part in the fun. Nemo's storyline varies little from the Academy Award–winning animated hit: players must reunite Nemo and his father Marlin. This game ties movies and gaming together for the younger crowd—with Pixaresque graphics that look exactly like the original characters. Thanks to the popularity of the movie (and the smart decision to make it available across a number of different platforms), Finding

---

The first actor on the cover of *TIME* magazine (July 6, 1925) was Charlie Chaplin.

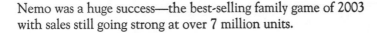

Nemo was a huge success—the best-selling family game of 2003 with sales still going strong at over 7 million units.

Star Wars Episode III: Revenge of the Sith

Released in 2005 just weeks before the movie's premiere, Episode III (the game) gave audiences a sneak peak at the action of *Episode III* (the movie). Players compete on 16 different levels, with smooth and fast-moving graphics. The game lets players be Jedi knights Anakin Skywalker and Obi-Wan Kenobi; they can use light sabers and the Force, just like the big screen. But the game's creators didn't let themselves be limited by what happens in the movie; in fact, they used the game to expand on and add more depth to scenes from the movie, where things had to be edited out.

Video games have now found a comfortable spot in the world of movie merchandising. Blockbusters like *The Hulk, Spider-man, The Lord of the Rings*, and virtually every new Disney release are just a few of the many flicks to have a game developed alongside the motion picture. Now that the bumps were smoothed out between programmers and Hollywood, would new releases remain the only game in town? Producers began to wonder about Hollywood's backlist of tried and true classics. Maybe the next big thing lay somewhere in the past.

Turn to page 444 for more.

* * *

MAE MAKES MONEY

Mae West's movies scandalized the critics, especially 1933's *She Done Him Wrong*. One wrote: "The most flagrant and utterly abandoned morsel of sin ever attempted on the screen, and I must confess that I enjoyed it enormously." In spite of its bawdy reputation, the film made $2 million in less than two months—a hefty take for the Great Depression.

If an actress told you she was born Demetria Guynes, who would you be talking to?

THE BLOND BOMBSHELL MURDER MYSTERY

*It's a Hollywood mystery with a jilted lover, a widowed
blonde, and a man with a bullet in him. The dead man was
a powerful producer, newly wed to Hollywood's hottest starlet.
Some believe he committed suicide. But others say it was murder.*

In the early morning of September 5, 1932, Paul Bern's butler found his employer lying naked on the bedroom floor, dead from a gunshot wound to the head. Paul Bern, a producer at MGM, had recently married Jean Harlow, MGM's blond bombshell and biggest new star; he seemingly had everything to live for. His death seemed inexplicable—until the studio got involved.

THE STUDIO'S VERDICT

Soon after the body was found, MGM executives, including studio head Louis B. Mayer, were on the scene—hours before the police were even called. MGM officials, not the police, would make the announcement that Bern had committed suicide. The producer, they pointed out, had even left a suicide note that read: "Dearest dear, Unfortunately this is the only way to make good the frightful wrong I have done you and wipe out my abject humiliation. Love, Paul. You understand last night was only a comedy."

Howard Strickland, head of MGM's publicity department, put his team into overdrive spreading the news that the Bern's cryptic letter referred to marital failures in the bedroom. Both a physician connected to MGM and Louis B. Mayer confirmed that the husband of the platinum blonde was impotent and that the problem had driven him to suicide. The juicy story spread like wildfire in newspapers across the nation.

On September 8 the coroner's inquest began, and it would also deliver a verdict of suicide—though an exact motive remained undetermined. The producer's family and friends were outraged and refused to believe that Bern killed himself. He had money, a gorgeous wife, and a string of many "successful" past relationships with actresses. Why would such a man commit suicide?

STRIKING HOLLYWOOD GOLD

Paul Bern's rags-to-riches life story sounds like a movie. Born Paul Levy in Germany in 1889, he immigrated to America with his family at the age of nine and grew up poor in the tenements of New York. At 19 Paul entered the American Academy of Dramatic Arts, tried his hand at acting, and changed his last name to Bern. Handicapped by his slight stature and build, Bern abandoned the stage in 1922 and headed out to California to try directing.

By 1925 Bern was a successful director for Paramount studios—famous for coaxing alluring performances from leading ladies such as Pola Negri and Greta Garbo. In 1928 Bern's success led him to MGM, where he advanced to studio producer. His first big job was to work with Irving Thalberg on the star-studded film *Grand Hotel* in 1932, which won the Oscar for Best Picture. Seen from the outside, Bern had it made. He had a fine home in Benedict Canyon, an Oscar, and a reputation for launching the careers of screen sirens—a reputation that helped him to snag a beautiful wife, an up-and-comer named Jean Harlow.

THE BEAUTY AND THE BRAIN

Harlow—the original platinum blonde—was born in 1911 in Missouri, as Harlean Carpenter. After dropping out of school at 16 and surviving a failed marriage, she was pushed into show business by her domineering mother, whose real name—Jean Harlow—Harlean now took as her own. By 1928 young Jean began making brief appearances in films before her big break in Howard Hughes's World War I epic *Hell's Angels* (1930). After Harlow's next film, *Platinum Blonde* (1931), her dazzling tresses were the rage among America's women, but her acting career wasn't taking off as quickly as she hoped.

Insecure despite a brash onscreen persona, the young actress was grateful when Paul Bern befriended her. Knowing she would shine in roles that were modern, comic, and sexy, he found Harlow a perfect vehicle, *Red-Headed Woman* (1932), a film so steamy, it was banned in England but made Harlow a superstar at home. Harlow and Bern's partnership yielded high box office receipts for MGM. It

"I'm sorry I didn't build you a stronger ship, young Rose."

also yielded a marriage between the two that summer. Two months later, Paul Bern was dead.

SECRETS AND LIES
More than 70 years after Paul Bern's death, mystery still surrounds the case. Most agree that it all stems from the butler's phone call to Jean Harlow at her mother's house; only Jean didn't take the call, her mother did. Instead of immediately reporting Bern's death to her daughter or to the police, Harlow's mom called MGM. Louis B. Mayer immediately rushed to the Benedict Canyon house with his chief of security and chief of publicity. Fearful that Harlow may have killed Bern, the executives had plenty of time to stage the suicide and manufacture the impotence scenario to protect both the star and the studio. They also severely restricted access to Jean, telling police she was too hysterical for questioning.

When Mayer told his staff that Paul Bern committed suicide because he wasn't "man enough" for his wife, no one argued with the story. Mayer hoped that as the scenario circulated and came to be accepted, interest in investigating Bern's death would die off. His plan worked pretty well, too—until news of another woman leaked out many years later.

MYSTERY WIFE
Who was this other woman? Dorothy Milette had lived with Bern as his common-law wife in New York before he moved to the West Coast. She had suffered a mental breakdown and entered a sanitarium, which caused Bern to leave her behind when he moved to California in 1922. He continued to pay for Milette's care but told very few people about her; those in the know said that visits with her left him emotionally devastated. Until he met Jean, he had never married because he felt responsible for his former love.

But Dorothy had not given up on the relationship. Two months before his marriage to Harlow, Dorothy moved to San Francisco hoping that Paul would take her back and make her a star. The producer discouraged her efforts, but he never fully broke contact. Finally, a desperate Dorothy showed up at the Benedict Canyon house on Labor Day weekend (some speculate that Bern knew of Dorothy's visit and sent Harlow on an overnight trip to her mother's). The next morning, Paul Bern was found dead—and Milette was gone. Could she have been the one to pull the trigger?

—Thomas Andrews (Victor Garber), *Titanic* (1997)

It is possible. The butler's wife later admitted she saw a woman fitting Milette's description running from Bern's home that night; she also remembered seeing a woman's swimsuit, two empty drinking glasses, and bloodstains near the pool. Studio records indicate that Bern had hired a car from MGM to drive someone to San Francisco. Milette did make it to San Francisco after her meeting with Bern.

Once there she checked out of her hotel and hopped a steamer to Sacramento—but she never arrived. Two weeks later, Milette's dead body was found in the Sacramento River; theories abound that she committed suicide, fell off the boat accidentally, or was pushed. Once again there was a quick inquest, and the official verdict was suicide, even though there were protests from local investigators. Milette, although destitute, was buried in Sacramento's fashionable East Lawn Cemetery; both her funeral and an expensive and ornate headstone were paid for by Jean Harlow. The name on the stone? Dorothy Bern.

BLOND WIDOW

After Bern's death, Harlow's career did not suffer. The studio's story of her husband's impotence and suicide won her public sympathy and saved her from publicly being a wronged wife, certain death for the reputation of a sex goddess. Harlow's personal demeanor did even more to keep her fans. A widow at only 21, her grief was obvious. Yet when she returned to making films, she was uncomplaining and hard working. When questioned by the press about Bern, all she would say was that she didn't understand the tragedy because their marriage had been happy. It was Harlow's talent, as well as her dignity in the face of scandals and grief that won her devoted fans.

After her husband's death, however, Harlow secretly began to drink, which contributed to her poor health. In 1937, at only 26 years old, she died from uremic poisoning brought on by kidney failure. With Jean's death, the last person who could have truly described the relationship between herself and Paul—and the triangle that included Dorothy—was gone.

BOX OFFICE BLOOPERS

Some of our favorites from new and classic films.

MOVIE: *E.T. The Extra-Terrestrial* (1982)
SCENE: When Elliott (Henry Thomas) first meets E.T. in his backyard, a crescent moon can be seen overhead.
BLOOPER: In the famous bike-flying scene, the silhouettes of Elliott and E.T. pass in front of a full moon, yet it's only three days later.

MOVIE: *Braveheart* (1995)
SCENE: In the beginning of the film, young William Wallace (James Robinson) is throwing rocks with his left hand.
BLOOPER: In the next scene, a grown-up William Wallace (Mel Gibson) is throwing rocks with his right hand.

MOVIE: *Terminator 3: Rise of the Machines* (2003)
SCENE: At the veterinary hospital, Kate (Claire Danes) is hiding only a few feet away from the T-X (Kristanna Loken).
BLOOPER: The T-X is the state-of-the-art Terminator, with heightened sensory awareness all around: sight, hearing, smell, even the ability to sense body heat. Yet somehow Kate—heavy breathing, sweating, and all—stays under the T-X's radar and escapes.

MOVIE: *Titanic* (1997)
SCENE: The passengers are all boarding the lifeboats.
BLOOPER: One of them is wearing a digital watch.

MOVIE: *Maid in Manhattan* (2002)
SCENE: Near the beginning of the movie, it's six days before Christmas. There's a fresh blanket of snow in the foreground.
BLOOPER: Someone forgot to tell the trees—in the next scene they all have green leaves.

MOVIE: *Forrest Gump* (1994)
SCENE: After Jenny (Robin Wright) dies, Forrest (Tom Hanks) is visiting her grave. He says, "You died on a Saturday."
BLOOPER: The gravestone reads March 12, 1982 (it's a Monday).

Really Big Fan: Myra Franklin of Cardiff, Wales, saw *The Sound of Music* 940 times.

MOVIE: *L.A. Confidential* (1997)
SCENE: Toward the end of the movie, Lynn Bracken (Kim Basinger) is talking to Detective Exley (Guy Pearce).
BLOOPER: An establishing shot shows them facing each other, but in each of their close-ups, the sun is behind their heads. Are there two suns in Los Angeles?

MOVIE: *Galaxy Quest* (1999)
SCENE: When Commander Taggert (Tim Allen) and Lieutenant Madison (Sigourney Weaver) first encounter the "chompers," Madison exclaims, "Oh, screw that!"
BLOOPER: That's what we hear, but it doesn't take a professional lip reader to see that she actually says . . . a word other than "screw."

MOVIE: *The Rocky Horror Picture Show* (1975)
SCENE: The audience is told that it is a "late November evening."
BLOOPER: In the very next scene, when Brad (Barry Bostwick) and Janet (Susan Sarandon) are in the car, Richard Nixon's resignation speech is playing on the radio. Nixon resigned in August.

MOVIE: *Pearl Harbor* (2001)
SCENE: When Evelyn (Kate Beckinsale) first arrives at Pearl Harbor, she walks past a tall building.
BLOOPER: The building has a sign that says "Est. 1953"—12 years after the actual attack.

MOVIE: *When Harry Met Sally* (1989)
SCENE: During a car ride when Harry (Billy Crystal) first gets to know Sally (Meg Ryan), Harry is spitting seeds out of an open window.
BLOOPER: An exterior shot shows that Harry's window is closed.

MOVIE: *There's Something About Mary* (1998)
SCENE: Ted Stroehmann (Ben Stiller) gets "stuck" in his zipper.
BLOOPER: While trying to get free of the zipper, Ted somehow manages to alternate between wearing his tuxedo jacket and not wearing it, from close-ups to wide shots.

Valley of the Dolls (1967) had its premiere aboard the Italian cruise ship *Princess Italia.*

THEIR BIG BREAKS, PART 2

More films that turned actors into stars. If you missed the first part, turn to page 61.

THE STAR: TOM CRUISE
THE FILM: *RISKY BUSINESS* (1983)
According to the *TLA Film and Video Guide*, Tom Cruise created a small sensation in his first starring role in this film about a college-bound teenager who turns his house into a brothel while his parents are on vacation. He won the part after Timothy Hutton, the producers' first choice, turned it down. Tom Hanks and Nicolas Cage were also considered before Cruise finally won the part.

There was only one problem—at 21, Cruise looked too old to play a teenager. To make his appearance more youthful, he underwent a rigorous and unusual training regimen. First, he worked out intensively seven days a week, until he lost 10 pounds. Then, he stopped working out altogether, and started pigging out on high-fat and high-calorie foods, in order to put on a layer of fat. This "baby fat," presumably, gave him that youthful, childlike appearance necessary for the part. Baby fat or not, no one who has seen this movie can forget the scene with Cruise dancing in his underwear.

THE STAR: CHARLIE SHEEN
THE FILM: *PLATOON* (1986)
Charlie Sheen's breakout role was in this searing exploration of war and its effects on its participants. He plays the part of Chris Taylor, a young recruit introduced to the horrors of war. Although the son of Martin Sheen, an established and well-respected Hollywood actor, Charlie was not a shoo-in for the part. The role of Chris was first offered to Kyle MacLachlan, who turned it down. When Sheen auditioned, he was considered too young for the role, and it was given to his older brother, Emilio Estevez. But production delays pushed back the filming, and by the time they were ready to resume, Estevez had other commitments. Charlie Sheen read for the part once more, and apparently he had aged enough that he was then just right to play Chris.

A *Variety* critic's review of the 1978 film *Movie Movie*: "Awful Awful."

Filming was not without its dangers, and Sheen came close to death. While riding in an open helicopter during one of the scenes, he was thrown toward the open door. He says he would have gone right through, had he not been grabbed by Keith David (who played the part of King), whom Sheen credits with saving his life.

You might also remember Charlie Sheen from his small, yet memorable role in *Ferris Bueller's Day Off* (1986). He played a burned-out teen who makes out with Jeanie Bueller (Jennifer Grey) in the police station. Reportedly, Sheen forced himself to stay awake for 48 hours before filming the scene, so he could be sure to look dissipated and addled enough for the part.

THE STAR: DIANE KEATON
THE FILM: *THE GODFATHER* (1972)

The Godfather was only Diane Keaton's second film appearance, and she was not happy with the part. She felt miscast and underappreciated. Yet her performance as Kay, Michael Corleone's WASP girlfriend, impressed critics. Her role pointed out the cultural chasm between the Mafia families and the outside world. She made a lasting impression and was soon to star in a string of Woody Allen films. *Play It Again, Sam,* with Keaton in the role of Linda Christie, came out later that same year.

THE STAR: DEBBIE REYNOLDS
THE FILM: *SINGIN' IN THE RAIN* (1952)

The breakout role for this actress/singer/dancer was *Singin' in the Rain.* She plays an aspiring actress (not too far from the mark) who is brought in to dub the voice and songs of a prominent silent-film star. During the course of this work, the male costar of the fictional film (Gene Kelly) falls madly in love with her—and goes singin' and hoofin' it up in a downpour.

The problem was that Debbie Reynolds, now known for her singing and dancing as well as her acting, had never before done either publicly. She felt inadequate next to her costars, who were established professional musical stars. Ironically, even though Reynolds played the part of the dubber in the film, her own voice was dubbed by someone else. Reynolds has said that this film and giving birth were the two hardest things she has ever done.

At the time of the filming, Debbie Reynolds was only 19 and

lived at home with her parents. She had to get up at 4:00 every morning and ride three different buses to get to the set each day.

THE STAR: ROBERT DUVALL
THE FILM: *TO KILL A MOCKINGBIRD* (1962)

To Kill a Mockingbird marked Robert Duvall's first screen appearance. His small part, that of Boo Radley, a reclusive and mysterious neighbor of the main characters, was pivotal to the plot's development. According to the *Internet Movie Database*, Duvall stayed out of the sun for six weeks and dyed his hair blond to lend veracity to the part of the shut-in Radley. In commemoration of the film, Duvall named a succession of his dogs Boo Radley. It's a good thing the movie didn't go to the dogs; it won numerous Academy Awards.

* * *

"The director is simply the audience. So the terrible burden of the director is to take the place of that yawning vacuum, to be the audience and to select from what happens during the day which movement shall be a disaster and which a gala night. His job is to preside over accidents."

—Orson Welles

* * *

TOP 10 FUNNIEST FILMS
From the American Film Institute's "100 Years, 100 Laughs" list

1. *Some Like It Hot* (1959)
2. *Tootsie* (1982)
3. *Dr. Strangelove or: How I Learned to Stop Worrying and Love the Bomb* (1964)
4. *Annie Hall* (1977)
5. *Duck Soup* (1933)
6. *Blazing Saddles* (1974)
7. *M*A*S*H* (1970)
8. *It Happened One Night* (1934)
9. *The Graduate* (1967)
10. *Airplane!* (1980)

. . . thriller *The Carpathian Eagle* (1980). It was his first part in a feature.

"I VANT TO BE IN PICTURES," PART 2

If Dracula had only made it onto the stage as a play
(see page 341), we probably never would have heard of him.
It was the 1931 Universal film, starring Bela Lugosi,
that finally made him a household name.

THE SILVER SCREEN

In 1930, impressed by the success of the Dracula stage play, Universal Pictures decided to buy it. They paid $40,000 for all rights to the novel and the stage plays so they would have the exclusive film rights to the Dracula character. Unfortunately, none of the play manuscripts proved to be suitable as a movie screenplay. So Universal brought it to Pulitzer Prize–winning novelist Louis Bromfield. And when the lavish sets and scenes called for in his ambitious screenplay threatened to bust the film's budget, two more writers were brought in to "help" him finish the job.

SPLIT PERSONALITY

But before he left Hollywood (never to return), Bromfield made one lasting contribution: he combined the older, nastier Dracula of Bram Stoker's novel with the suave young Count that had become popular on stage. Starved for fresh blood in Transylvania, the old, tired Dracula would regain his youth drinking fresh blood when he arrived in London.

JUNIOR PARTNER

Dracula would be Universal's first horror movie, but it wouldn't come without a fight: Studio head Carl Laemmle, Sr. was vehemently opposed to the idea of making scary movies. "I don't believe in horror pictures," he would later tell an interviewer. "It's morbid. None of our officers are for it. People don't want that sort of thing."

So why did he agree to make the film? Two reasons: First, Dracula was a hot property and he didn't want it to go to the competition. Second because, he explained, "Junior wanted it."

"Junior" was Laemmle's son Julius, who changed his name to Carl Jr. when his father made him head of Universal on his 21st birthday. Junior headed Universal until the studio was put up for sale in 1936, and his years at the helm were rocky ones. "His abilities and achievements are still a matter of debate," David Skal writes in *Hollywood Gothic*, "but he made one indelible contribution to American culture: the Hollywood horror movie, an obsessive new genre revolving around threatening, supernaturally powerful male monstrosities."

CASTING CALL
Once they actually decided to make the film, the search for an actor to play Dracula was on.

Silent film star Lon Chaney Sr. was the top contender for the part . . . until he was diagnosed with terminal throat cancer. At least five other actors were considered for the part, but none of them panned out.

Meanwhile, Bela Lugosi lobbied hard to win the role, trying to ingratiate himself with Universal by printing up publicity photos showing him posing as Dracula, praising the film in print interviews, and offering unsolicited suggestions on how the script could be improved. When the sale of the film rights was still pending, Lugosi had even tried to intercede with Bram Stoker's widow to get Universal a better price.

Lugosi apparently hoped that bowing and scraping would ingratiate him with the studio, but what it really did was make him appear desperate—which he was. Universal finally did offer him the part, of course, but for only $500 a week. The offer was an insult—David Manners, who received third billing as Jonathan Harker, signed for $2,000 a week. But Lugosi took it anyway. He'd already lost the role once by holding out for too much money, and he wasn't about to let it happen again.

ON THE SCREEN
To direct, Universal picked veteran horror filmmaker Ted Browning. Filming *Dracula* took seven weeks. Lugosi delivered a masterful performance, arguably the most memorable and influential ever. It was so convincing that a number of his co-stars wondered if he really was performing . . . or just being himself. "I never thought he was acting," David Manners remembered, "just

being the odd man he was. . . . I mainly remember Lugosi standing in front of a full-length mirror between scenes, intoning 'I
am Dracula.'"

DRACULA MUST DIE!

Dracula is tame by today's standards, but in its day it was a shocker.
When it was shown in previews, people actually demanded that it
be banned. "I saw the first fifteen minutes of it," wrote the PTA's
previewer, "and felt I could stand no more. . . . It should be withdrawn from public showing, as children, the weak-minded, and all
classes attend motion pictures indiscriminately." Even Universal
head Carl Laemmle Jr. was put off by scenes that he found to be
suggestively homoerotic. "Dracula should only go for women and
not men," he dashed off in an angry memo, and the offending
scenes were removed.

IT WAS A GRAVEYARD SMASH

The movie opened on February 12, 1931, and despite very mixed
reviews, *Dracula* turned out to be a crowd pleaser. The gothic horror film proved to be the kind of escapist fantasy filmgoers were
looking for as the country slid deeper into the Great Depression,
and the tale of ordinary mortals triumphing over seemingly insurmountable evil must have thrilled a public in the grips of seemingly
endless economic troubles.

Dracula went on to be one of the top-grossing films of 1931, and
Universal's biggest moneymaker for the year. Thanks to *Dracula*,
Universal turned a profit for the first time since 1928, and though
its financial problems continued for the rest of the decade, *Dracula*
is credited with earning Universal the money it needed to weather
the Great Depression.

Just seven weeks after *Dracula* opened in theatres, Universal
purchased the film rights to *Frankenstein*, setting it on a course to
become Hollywood's reigning horror studio through the 1930s
and into the 1940s, thrilling audiences (and its board of directors) with the Werewolf, the Mummy, and other classic
Hollywood monsters.

OSCAR, OSCAR, OSCAR

*For your reference, a list of facts and figures
about the Academy Awards.*

THE NEVERENDING CEREMONY
The first televised Oscar ceremony
On March 17, 1953, Oscar welcomed television cameras for the first time. The ceremony was divided between two hosts and two locations—Bob Hope at the RKO Pantages Theatre in Hollywood, and Conrad Nagal at the International Theatre in New York City. Cameras switched back and forth between the locations depending on where the presenter and the winner were.

The longest Oscar ceremony
Although many feel like it gets longer every year, the longest ceremony actually took place on March 21, 1999. It lasted for four hours two minutes.

The March 25, 1954, ceremony (and second Oscar telecast) was the first one to run long; it was slated to last two hours, and the overrun caused William Holden to cut his Best Actor acceptance speech (for *Stalag 17*) to just "Thank you."

Most ceremonies hosted
Alone and with cohosts, Bob Hope served as a master of ceremonies 16 times. (Donald Duck shared cohosting duties with him in 1958.)

YOUNG AND OLD
The youngest Oscar winner
Ten-year-old Tatum O'Neal won the Best Supporting Actress Oscar in 1974 for *Paper Moon*. Anna Paquin comes in second: she won her Best Supporting Actress Oscar for *The Piano* in 1994. She was 11.

. . .The role of Dorothy Boyd, played by Renee Zellweger, was written for Winona Ryder.

But what about Shirley Temple?
Technically Shirley Temple is the youngest recipient of an Oscar statue, but it wasn't for her work in one picture. When she received her miniature statue, she was just 55 days shy of her seventh birthday. The award was for "grateful recognition of her outstanding contribution to screen entertainment" in 1934.

The oldest winner
Jessica Tandy won the Best Actress Oscar for *Driving Miss Daisy* (1989) when she was 80.

AND THE WINNER IS . . .
The most total Oscar nominations
With 64 under his belt, Walt Disney has been up for more Oscars than anyone else. He's also won more than anyone else; he collected 26 awards total. He posthumously won his last in 1968 for the animated short *Winnie the Pooh and the Blustery Day.*

Which actor has the most nominations?
No slouch herself in Oscar winning (she's won twice), Meryl Streep has the most acting nominations with 13. She's been up for Best Supporting Actress three times and Best Actress 10 times. Jack Nicholson is right behind her with 12 nominations (nine for Best Actor and three for Best Supporting Actor). He's won three times.

Most "Best Acting" Oscars
Also nominated 12 times, Katherine Hepburn has the most wins with four statues for Best Actress in: *Morning Glory* (1933), *Guess Who's Coming to Dinner* (1967), *The Lion in Winter* (1968), and *On Golden Pond* (1981). After she won for *The Lion in Winter*, she said: "I was enormously touched. They don't usually give these things to the old girls, you know."

Most Best Directing wins
Only nominated five times, John Ford holds the record with four wins: *The Informer* (1935), *Grapes of Wrath* (1940), *How Green Was My Valley* (1941), and *The Quiet Man* (1953). His one loss was to Victor Fleming's work for *Gone With the Wind* (1939).

Robin Williams ad-libbed Adrian Cronauer's broadcasts in *Good Morning, Vietnam.*

AND THE OSCAR GOES TO . . .
The most nominated film
It's a tie between *All About Eve* (1950) and *Titanic* (1997). They both received 14 total nominations. *Eve* won six, and *Titanic* got 11.

The film with the most wins
Another tie: With 11 wins each, *Ben-Hur* (1959), *Titanic*, and *Lord of the Rings: The Return of the King* all share the record for most wins. Only *Lord of the Rings* won in every category for which it was nominated.

Most nominations, but no awards
It's a tie between *Turning Point* (1977) and *The Color Purple* (1986). Both movies received 11 nominations but won nothing.

Have any films won an Oscar "Grand Slam" (Best Picture, Actor, Actress, Director, and Screenplay)?
Two have: *It Happened One Night* (1934) and *The Silence of the Lambs* (1991).

The most valuable Oscar
Michael Jackson owns the world's most valuable Oscar, but he didn't win it. David O. Selznick actually won the Oscar for Best Film for *Gone With the Wind*. Jackson bought it for $1,542,000 in 1999 at a Sotheby's auction.

* * *

"She can't act. She can't talk. She's terrific."
—Director George Sidney after seeing Ava Gardner's screen test

* * *

"I was not a born actress. No one knows it better than I. If I had any latent talent, I have had to work hard, listen carefully, do things over and over and then over again in order to bring it out."
—Jean Harlow

Halle Berry's debut role: Vivian in Spike Lee's *Jungle Fever* (1991).

BRIDE OF THE POISON PEN: SECOND-RATE SEQUELS

*All sequels are not created equal. Some are great,
like* The Godfather, Part II, The Empire Strikes Back,
and Superman II. *Some, like the ones reviewed here, are
unworthy. But don't take our word for it.*

The Bad News Bears Go to Japan (1978)
"And they can stay there."
   —Ken Hanke, *Mountain Xpress* (Ashville, North Carolina)

Grease 2 (1982)
"The story can't even masquerade as an excuse for stringing the
songs together, which are . . . so hopelessly insubstantial that the
cast is forced to burst into melody about pastimes like bowling."
   —Janet Maslin, *The New York Times*

Staying Alive (1983)
 "So horrific are the musical sequences in this movie that you'll
swear you were having nightmares directed by Satan himself."
   —Scott Weinberg, *Apollo Guide.com*

Superman IV: The Quest for Peace (1987)
"More sluggish than a funeral barge, cheaper than a sale at Kmart,
it's a nerd, it's a shame, it's *Superman IV.*"
   —Desson Thomson, *Washington Post*

Arthur 2: On the Rocks (1988)
"This film never happened. Don't ask me about it again."
   —Widgett Walls, *Needcoffee.com*

Cocoon: The Return (1988)
"All the same actors are back, and they again appear as
elderly people enjoying a delirious resurgence of youth, but

"I never drink . . . wine."

. . . the net effect is one of being on a cruise ship to hell."

—Janet Maslin, *The New York Times*

Mannequin 2: On the Move (1991)
"*Mannequin 2* is so bad that you'd easily accept my supposition that the film was in fact directed by three spiders, a goat, and a dedicated gust of wind."

—Scott Weinberg, *Efilmcritic.com*

Child's Play 3 (1991)
"Slow, stupid and cheap, the ending effectively kills off any reason for *Child's Play 4*. We hope."

—Richard Harrington, *The Washington Post*

Return of the Blue Lagoon (1991)
"*Return to the Blue Lagoon* . . . makes the original *Blue Lagoon* look like *Citizen Kane*."

—Hal Hinson, *Washington Post*

Batman and Robin (1997)
"Holy creative breakdown, *Batman!*"

—Robin Dougherty, *Salon.com*

Speed 2: Cruise Control (1997)
"If *Speed 2* and let's say, *Kissed*, a dark comedy about a woman necrophile, were the very last two movies at the video store, I would pick *Kissed*."

—Judith Egerton, *Courier-Journal* (Louisville, Kentucky)

Book of Shadows: Blair Witch 2 (2000)
"Creating a movie that virtually everyone can hate is no small accomplishment. But filmmaker Joe Berlinger may just have pulled it off."

—Jay Boyar, *Orlando Sentinel*

Son of Mask (2005)
"This is the closest I've ever come to walking out halfway through the film, and now that I look back on the experience, I wish I had."

—Richard Roeper, *Ebert and Roeper*

—Count Dracula (Bela Lugosi), *Dracula* (1931)

MACHO, MACHO MOVIE

Feeling the need to tap into your inner he-man by watching some big-screen tough guys? Chock full of muscles, car chases, and explosions, here are some favorites to help ratchet up the testosterone.

FIRST BLOOD (1982)

A great big shoot-out ensues when a half-crazy Vietnam vet, John J. Rambo (Sylvester Stallone) stops in a small town for a bite to eat and gets on the bad side of the town sheriff (Brian Dennehy). Stallone punches his way out of jail, blows up a gas station, and fights a one-man war against the corrupt sheriff. The movie developed a reputation for gung-ho violence, even though only four people actually die in it. The body count for *Star Trek II: The Wrath of Khan* (rated PG), released the same year? More than a dozen.

Macho Line: "All I wanted was something to eat. But the man kept pushing, Sir."—John Rambo (Stallone)

BILLY JACK (1971)

Tom Laughlin played the half-Native American, half-Caucasian, ex-Green Beret Billy Jack, who uses his fighting skills to protect peace-loving kids from small-town fascists. Being a pacifist didn't stop Billy Jack from kicking some butt in this movie and the two sequels that followed, *The Trial of Billy Jack* (1974) and *Billy Jack Goes to Washington* (1977). In the 1980s and 1990s Tom Laughlin didn't do much acting, but he never stopped fighting for the social themes he infused into his popular 1970s flicks. In 2005 he did finally return to filmmaking with *Billy Jack's Crusade to End the War in Iraq and Restore America to Its Moral Purpose*.

Macho Line: "I'm gonna take this right foot, and I'm gonna whop you on that side of your face. And you wanna know something? There's not a damn thing you're gonna be able to do about it."
—Billy Jack (Laughlin)

Jason Patric turned down the role of Mitch in *The Firm.* The role went to Tom Cruise.

DEATH WISH (1974)

Charles Bronson plays a New York architect who goes from a self-confessed liberal to a pistol-packing vigilante after a brutal attack on his family. (At age 53, it was Bronson's break-through role.) After he hits the streets, just about anyone with bell-bottoms and a switchblade gets it. Audiences could relate to Bronson—a middle-aged everyman who isn't built like Mr. Universe—and were thrilled by how intimidating he could be. Next time *Death Wish* is on, play close attention to the first thug attacking Bronson's wife: it's Jeff Goldblum (*Jurassic Park*, *The Fly*) in his first film.

Macho Line: "What about the old American social custom of self-defense?"—Paul Kersey (Bronson)

THE SHOOTIST (1976)

John Wayne plays a gunfighter struggling to maintain his legacy while trying to die like a man. Just about every John Wayne film makes the macho list, but this one makes our list because "The Duke" had to be especially tough while filming it. In real life, he was dying from cancer and some days was too sick to film. But like the macho man he was, he rode it out and completed his last film. The film is full of bar fights and shoot-'em-ups. It ended Wayne's career in style.

Macho Line: "I won't be wronged. I won't be insulted. I won't be laid a-hand on. I don't do these things to other people, and I require the same from them."—J. B. Books (Wayne)

PREDATOR (1987)

Nothing says macho like going one-on-one with a man-hunting alien. Muscle-bound commandos Arnold Scwarzenegger, Jesse Ventura, and Carl Weathers are being stalked across a South American jungle by an extraterrestrial that likes to hunt humans and keep their skulls as trophies. The alien, a nine-foot-tall man-lizard with dreadlocks, fangs, and body armor, can turn invisible and swing from trees. Originally, Jean Claude Van Damme was the nameless body behind the alien suit, but he quit on the second day because he felt the work was beneath him.

Macho Line: "If it bleeds, we can kill it."
—Alan "Dutch" Schaeffer (Schwarzenegger)

The Firm went on to become the third-highest-grossing film of 1993.

THE GOOD, THE BAD AND THE UGLY (1966)

The third film in the Sergio Leone trilogy featuring Clint Eastwood as the Man With No Name is so macho that nobody says a word for the first 10 minutes. The spaghetti Western pits three men against each other in a search for buried treasure during the Civil War. The film was actually shot in Spain (not Southern Italy like the others), using over a thousand soldiers from the Spanish militia for extras. Eli Wallach, the guy who played Tuco (the ugly one), went on to write an autobiography entitled *The Good, the Bad, and Me.*

Macho Line: "You see, in this world there's two kinds of people, my friend: those with loaded guns and those who dig. You dig."
—The Man With No Name (Eastwood)

* * *

ON THE GLITZ AND GLAMOUR
OF HOLLYWOOD

"There were times when I drove along the Sunset Strip and looked at those buildings or when I watched the fashionable film colony arriving at some première . . . that I fully expected God in his wrath to obliterate the whole shebang."
—S. J. Perelman, screenwriter

"Hollywood held this double lure for me, tremendous sums of money for work that required no more effort than a game of pinochle."
—Ben Hecht, screenwriter

"A celebrity is a person who works hard all his life to become well known, then wears dark glasses to avoid being recognized."
—Fred Allen, comedian

"Hollywood money isn't money. It's congealed snow, melts in your hand, and there you are."
—Dorothy Parker

Kirsten Dunst turned down the Angela Hayes role in *American Beauty* (1999) . . .

GARY COOPER: BY THE NUMBERS

"Just make me the hero," Gary Cooper famously told one of his screen-writers. And it's a good thing he did. Cooper became the embodiment of the American hero, holding on to his honor and courage while beset by violence and corruption. A quick look at the legend.

0

Number of names named by Gary Cooper when he was called as a "friendly" witness before the House Un-American Activities Committee. Cooper was a solid conservative but had little interest in politics.

1

Number of Cooper's marriages. Coop's affairs, on the other hand, were innumerable. He romanced virtually every one of his costars. Here's the short list: Clara Bow, Lupe Velez (they had a torrid affair until Cooper's straitlaced mother stepped in), Marlene Dietrich, Carole Lombard, Tallulah Bankhead, Joan Crawford, Ingrid Bergman, Barbara Stanwyck, Patricia Neal (as close as Cooper ever came to leaving his wife), Grace Kelly, and Anita Ekberg.

1

In dollars, the first money young Cooper ever earned. A friend of his mother's wanted two birds to put on a hat, so Cooper went out and shot and stuffed a couple of them for the nice lady.

3

Number of movies Cooper's wife, Rocky, appeared in, using the name Sandra Shaw. Her most memorable scene was in the original *King Kong* (1933). She can be seen silhouetted and screaming in a high window as Kong climbs up the skyscraper.

6

Number of real life characters Cooper played on the screen: Wild Bill Hickok in *The Plainsman*, Marco Polo in *The Adventures of*

. . . which went to Mena Suvari.

Marco Polo, Sergeant Alvin C. York in *Sergeant York*, Lou Gehrig in *The Pride of the Yankees*, Dr. Corydon M. Wassell in *The Story of Dr. Wassell*, and General Billy Mitchell in *The Court-Martial of Billy Mitchell*.

8
Age at which Cooper's mother brought him and his brother, Arthur, from their home in Helena, Montana, to England to live with relatives and attend school for three years. Mrs. Cooper thought living in England would civilize her boys.

10
In dollars, what Frank Cooper (his real name) earned per day as a stuntman in Westerns when he started in films.

14
Number of silent movies Cooper appeared in. When talkies came in, his deep, resonant voice was perfect for the sort of characters he played.

22
Caliber of pistol Cooper used when indulging in his favorite sport in the 1930s: hunting bobcats in the Malibu hills.

64
In dollars, what Cooper invested in his own 20-second screen test, hoping to break out of the ranks of stuntmen. It worked; he was soon making $50 a week, first as an extra, then as a featured player in Westerns produced by Samuel Goldwyn.

100
Number of minutes in which the story of *High Noon* takes place, from 10:35 to 12:15. The movie is slightly longer.

125
Miles per hour Cooper was clocked at driving his custom-built Duesenberg down the boulevards of Hollywood in the 1930s.

2,000
In dollars, the amount that Cooper paid per month to a public

relations firm in the early 1950s to minimize the difference between his on-screen image of the true-blue hero and the philanderer he was in real life.

3,000
In dollars, what John Ford offered Cooper to star in *Stagecoach*. Cooper was making $150,000 a picture at the time, so he naturally turned it down. The role went to John Wayne and made him a star. Cooper was offered the role of Rhett Butler in *Gone With the Wind*, too, but turned that down, based on his prediction that it was "going to be the biggest flop in Hollywood history."

150,000
In dollars, what Ernest Hemingway made when he sold the film rights to *For Whom the Bell Tolls*—to make sure that his good friend Cooper would play the lead. (Cooper had starred in Hemingway's *A Farewell to Arms* in 1932.) Before the two even met, Hemingway had modeled the hero of *For Whom the Bell Tolls* on Cooper's looks and mannerisms.

482,826
In dollars, Gary Cooper's earnings in 1939, the highest salary in the United States. To put things in perspective, two thirds of American families earned between $1,000 and $2,000 that year.

* * *

"George Raft and Gary Cooper once played a scene in front of a cigar store, and it looked like the wooden Indian was overacting."
—George Burns

* * *

In 1975 the average cost of marketing a movie from a major studio was two million dollars. In 2003 it was thirty-five million.

. . . were blow-up mannequins with masks as faces and painted-on suits.

THE CREATION OF FRANKENSTEIN

*You might assume that the flat-headed, bolts-in-the-neck monster
we all know was taken directly from Mary Shelley's original novel.
Nope. It was created specifically for the movies. Here's the story
of how the world's most famous monster was born.*

FIRST FRIGHT

History books credit Thomas Alva Edison with inventing the lightbulb, the phonograph, the movie camera, and many other things. But one invention they usually leave off his resume is the horror movie. His Edison Film Company invented it in 1910, when they put Mary Shelley's 1818 novel *Frankenstein* on film for the first time.

Edison's *Frankenstein* was barely 16 minutes long and was only loosely based on the original. The filmmakers thought the book was too graphic, so they eliminated "all the . . . repulsive situations and concentrated on the mystic and psychological problems found in this weird tale."

CREATIONISM

But one scene in Shelley's book wasn't graphic enough for Edison executives: the "creation scene" in which Dr. Frankenstein brings the monster to life. Shelley devoted only two sentences to it:

> I collected the instruments of life around me, that I might infuse a spark of being into the lifeless thing that lay at my feet. It was already one in the morning; the rain pattered dismally against the panes, and my candle was nearly burnt out, when, by the glimmer of the half-extinguished light, I saw the dull yellow eye of the creature open; it breathed hard, and a convulsive motion agitated its limbs.

That was all Shelley wrote. So the folks at Edison used their imagination and decided to make a "cauldron of blazing chemicals" the source of the monster's life. Edison's monster looked nothing like the Frankenstein we know. It was a white-faced hunchback with matted hair and a hairy chest.

For *Whale Rider*, Keisha Castle-Hughes claimed she could swim—but she couldn't.

ON THE ROAD

Following the success of Edison's *Frankenstein*, other studios filmed their own versions of the story. The first full-length Frankenstein film, called *Life Without a Soul*, hit the silver screen in 1916, and an Italian film called *Il Mostro di Frankenstein* followed in 1920.

But the Frankenstein monster might never have become a Hollywood icon if it hadn't been for Hamilton Deane, an English actor who ran (and starred in) a traveling *Dracula* show during the 1920s. Tired of performing *Dracula* night after night, Deane began looking for material he could use as an alternate. He settled on *Frankenstein*.

In 1927 he asked a member of the *Dracula* troupe, Peggy Webling, to adapt *Frankenstein* into a play. Like the folks at Edison, she got creative with the story. For example:

- Webling saw the monster—whom Mary Shelley called Adam—as an alter ego of Dr. Victor Frankenstein. She became the first person ever to refer to both the man and the monster as Frankenstein. To make the connection obvious, she dressed the characters in identical clothing throughout the play.

- She changed the ending. In the novel, Dr. Frankenstein pursues the monster to the Arctic circle, where the monster strangles him, jumps onto an ice floe, and drifts off to a sure death. The scene made good reading, but it was boring onstage. So Webling had the monster jump off a cliff instead.

Unfortunately, Hamilton Deane, who played the monster, wasn't much of an athlete. As troupe member Ivan Butler recalled years later, the new ending was "very tame indeed, because of Deane's tentative jump." So Webling wrote a more exciting ending. "The final version was quite a bloodthirsty affair," Butler recalled, "with the monster apparently tearing his maker's throat out before being destroyed by lightning. Old Deanie revelled in it."

CLASSIC FRANKENSTEIN

Universal Pictures bought the screen rights to Deane's *Dracula* and cast Bela Lugosi in the starring role. Even before the film was released in 1931, studio executives knew it would be a hit. So they commissioned a Frankenstein film, too. They bought the rights to Webling's play, then hired fresh screenwriters to craft a brand-new script.

A WHALE OF A TALE

First, Universal hired director James Whale to work on the film. Whale had just finished work on *Hell's Angels* and *Journey's End*, two films about World War I, and Universal officials were so impressed with them that they offered Whale his pick of any of the dozens of film projects they had in the works. He chose *Frankenstein*. Why? As he later recalled:

> Of thirty available stories, *Frankenstein* was the strongest meat and gave me a chance to dabble in the macabre. I thought it would be amusing to try and make what everybody knows is a physical impossibility seem believable. . . . Also, it offered fine pictorial chances, had two grand characterizations, and had a subject matter that might go anywhere, and that is part of the fun of making pictures.

And besides, Whale was sick of working on war movies.

BEG, BORROW, AND STEAL

Once again, writers changed Shelley's story. Universal's screen-writers followed the novels only loosely, adding and deleting details as they saw fit. They also appropriated ideas from other films:

- An early draft of the script said the lab should be filled with electrical gadgets that were "something suggestive of the laboratory in Metropolis," a 1926 German film about a mad scientist.

- Dr. Frankenstein's lab was moved from the top floor of his house to an old watchtower. This idea was taken from *The Magician*, a 1926 film in which a student of the occult finds "the secret of the creation of human life . . . in an ancient sorcerer's tower."

- *The Magician* was also an inspiration for the creation scene. As in *Frankenstein*, lightning bolts that strike the tower create life.

- Both *Metropolis* and *The Magician* provided ideas for the character of Igor, Dr. Frankenstein's assistant. In both films, the mad scientist has a dwarf for an assistant. Whale's scriptwriters changed him from a dwarf to a hunchback.

- Universal scriptwriters moved the final scene to an abandoned windmill, where angry peasants trap Dr. Frankenstein and the monster inside and burn it to the ground. Why was a windmill chosen? Scriptwriter Robert Florey remembers, "I was living in a [Hollywood] apartment above a Van de Kamp bakery," which had a windmill as its company symbol. The sight of the company's "windmill rotating inspired me to place the final scene in an old mill."

- In Mary Shelley's *Frankenstein*, the monster is extremely articulate and drones on for entire chapters without stopping. But movie audiences were still getting used to the idea of people talking (and screaming) in movies, let alone monsters—so the scriptwriters decided to make the Frankenstein monster a mute. Throughout the film, all he does is grunt.

CREATING THE MONSTER
Whale cast an actor named Colin Clive to play Dr. Frankenstein and selected a woman named Mae Clarke to play Dr. Frankenstein's fiance. (Bette Davis was also considered for the part.)

Casting the monster turned out to be more difficult. Bela Lugosi, probably Universal's first choice for the part, filmed a full-dress screen test. But because the Frankenstein makeup hadn't yet been finalized, the makeup department gave Lugosi a big, fat head "about four times normal size," and "polished, clay-like skin."

Nobody knows if Lugosi's performance was any good; the screen test was lost shortly after it was filmed. But it didn't really matter— Lugosi figured the nonspeaking role was beneath him and worried that his fans wouldn't recognize him under all that makeup. The role went to someone else, someone who was almost completely unknown in Hollywood.

* * *

Mike Myers, Cameron Diaz, and Eddie Murphy were each paid ten million dollars for providing the voices of the main characters in *Shrek 2.*

* * *

In the first *Terminator*, Arnold Schwarzenegger had seventeen lines.

* * *

The first Batman movie earned three times as much from merchandise as from ticket sales.

—Roger De Bris (Christopher Hewitt), *The Producers* (1968)

INTO THE SUNSET

*If stars don't burn out, then they can quietly fade away
at the Motion Picture & Television Fund's retirement
home in Woodland Hills, California.*

Way out west, at the end of Mulholland Drive in Woodland Hills, California, is a 50-acre campus filled with golden oldies. It's the Motion Picture & Television Fund's retirement home and hospital, housing anyone who has worked in front of or behind the camera for 20 years or more. Women must be older than 55; men, older than 60. Extras, makeup artists, grips and gaffers, producers and directors can all find a place to retire in Woodland Hills.

WE TAKE CARE OF OUR OWN

Making movies has always been a volatile business, and even industry big shots were aware of how precarious it could be. To help fellow moviemakers who might be down on their luck, Hollywood big shots Mary Pickford, Douglas Fairbanks, Charlie Chaplin, and director D. W. Griffith founded the Motion Picture Relief Fund (MPRF) in 1921. The motto "We take care of our own" summed up the primary mission of the MPRF.

The first people to be helped were a husband and wife who fell on hard times when the husband, a veteran character actor, was partially paralyzed and unable to work. The fund arranged to pay their monthly rent and found a job for the wife. Gifts didn't have to be big to make a difference; the fund once purchased a toupee for an actor who needed it for a movie. The fund also came to the aid of those movie professionals who did not survive the transition from silent movies to talkies. Successful movie stars threw themselves into fund-raising events and galas; others participated in the Payroll Pledge Program, through which a percentage of their salaries could be donated to the fund.

THE OLD FOLKS AT HOME

Then, in 1939, actor and director Jean Hersholt came across an orange grove in Woodland Hills; he thought it a perfect spot for

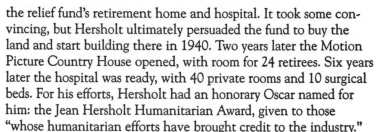

the relief fund's retirement home and hospital. It took some convincing, but Hersholt ultimately persuaded the fund to buy the land and start building there in 1940. Two years later the Motion Picture Country House opened, with room for 24 retirees. Six years later the hospital was ready, with 40 private rooms and 10 surgical beds. For his efforts, Hersholt had an honorary Oscar named for him: the Jean Hersholt Humanitarian Award, given to those "whose humanitarian efforts have brought credit to the industry."

Over the years the fund itself has grown to provide many health-care services to those in the industry. The hospital now has 250 acute-care beds. The retirement community has grown, too; it's expanded to accommodate as many as 400 residents with very different needs. Harry's Haven, donated by Kirk Douglas and named for his father, houses patients suffering from dementia and Alzheimer's disease. The Fran and Ray Stark Villa is the latest addition, with condos both for independent and assisted living.

Residents can stroll through the grounds, including the Roddy McDowall Memorial Rose Garden, where roses from McDowall's own garden have been replanted and a statue of McDowall (as he appeared in *Planet of the Apes*) stands. Residents have access to the Louis B. Mayer Theater, which seats 250 people and shows first-run features; they can also keep their motion picture skills sharp in the on-site production suite stacked with state-of-the-art equipment.

RETIRED RESIDENTS
Over the years many stars have been cared for there as well:

- **Norma Shearer,** Oscar winner, former Queen of MGM, and star of *The Women* (1939)

- **Hattie McDaniel,** winner of the Oscar for Best Supporting Actress for *Gone With The Wind* (1939)

- **Mary Astor,** actress who played the double-crossing Brigid O'Shaughnessy in *The Maltese Falcon* (1941)

- **Johnny Weissmuller,** better known as Tarzan. A notorious resident, he liked to roam the halls at night roaring the famous Tarzan yell—something the other residents didn't appreciate. To keep everybody happy, the fund administrators moved Weissmuller and his wife to a home in Mexico, complete with a staff to care for him, at no charge, until his death in 1984.

. . . how to use the swords and speak Japanese, among many other things.

Some of the movies' greatest achievers have also stayed at the motion picture home. You may not recognize some of their names, but you'll certainly recognize their accomplishments:

- **Bob Broughton,** special-effects guru for Walt Disney Studios. He helped create the giant squid in *20,000 Leagues Under the Sea* (1954) and the twin–Hayley Mills effect in *The Parent Trap* (1961).
- **Lothrop Worth,** the Father of 3-D Films. This cinematographer got his start in 1921 as a cameraman.
- **Jackie Alderman,** a propman who created and wagged the Cowardly Lion's tail in *The Wizard of Oz* (1939).
- **John Chambers,** the cosmetic mastermind who created the monkey makeup for *The Planet of the Apes* series. He was also the inventor of Scar 'Em (a molding plastic for fake scars and wounds) and the industry standard bald cap.

'TWAS THE NIGHT BEFORE THE OSCARS . . .

Today Hollywood still takes care of its own by raising money for the Motion Picture & Television Fund. One of the biggest events, called Night Before, takes place the night before the Oscars. The Beverly Hills Hotel puts decks over its pool to host the heavily attended party each year. Night Before attracts its fair share of corporate sponsors, too: Hewlett-Packard, *Variety* magazine, Ford, Coca-Cola, Target, and Krispy Kreme have all supported the party, whether by donating computers, cash, or donuts. In its first three years, the party managed to raise more than $10 million for the fund, so the future remains bright for the old stars' home.

* * *

ALIBI

Anthony Perkins was miles away when the shower scene in *Psycho* was filmed in Hollywood; he was in New York preparing for a play.

The kiss between Bill Murray and Scarlett Johansson at the end of *Lost in Translation*

B-MOVIE BASICS

*Everyone knows what a B movie is: quickly made, shoddily
produced, and usually short on plot. They're designed to appeal
to the lowest common denominator. In the 21st century,
they've become better known as direct-to-video flicks. But
how did the saga of the B movie begin?*

The B movie's tale begins in the Great Depression of the
early 1930s, when the number of people going to movie
theaters began to decline. When film producers cast about
looking for ways to entice cash-strapped audiences back into theaters, they discovered that people still liked movies, they just
wanted more movie for their money. Thus was born the double feature, offering two movies—plus cartoon shorts, newsreels, and
coming attractions—for the same admission price. It wouldn't do
for a movie studio to offer two of its best current releases on the
same bill. So studios came up with an alternative: the B movie.

BUDGETS, B MOVIES, AND BOTTOM LINES

B movies differed from main features in two ways—first, in their
production standards. While main features were lavish affairs with
big-name stars, top-flight directors, big budgets, and all the other
bells and whistles, B movies were designed to be shot cheaply and
quickly, using lesser-known actors and journeymen film crews. B
movies also tended to be shorter than main attractions. *Formulaic*
was not an insult to a B movie; that's just what the movie studios
were aiming for.

Second, movie studios made money from B movies differently
than they did from main features. Studios earned money from the
main features by taking a cut of the box office profits collected by
the theater owners (just like they do with films today). B movies,
however, were offered to theaters for a flat fee. For movie studios,
this meant there was only so much money that could be made from
B movies. On the other hand, it also meant studios would make
money no matter how these pictures did. "Small but safe" was the
B-movie slogan.

NOT ALL BAD

Although B movies were designed to be made quickly and cheaply, originally they weren't all bad. A number of horror and film noir classics (like 1942's *Cat People* and 1949's *Criss Cross*) were shot as B movies yet became influential later. However, the reputation of the B movie began to fall in the late 1940s when the major film studios, which had previously had their own B-movie divisions (called B units), got out of the business. This left the lower-card part of the double bill to Poverty Row studios, like Republic Pictures (famous for its cheap Westerns), whose production standards were lower than those of the major studios.

By the 1950s movies were no longer always formally bundled as double features. But there were quite a few quickie movie studios banging out cheap flicks for second-rate theaters; these exploitative and often shoddy (but also fun) flicks inherited the B-movie title from their predecessors. Some people even became famous for working in the genre. Director and producer Roger Corman, for example, rather notoriously banged out 1960's *The Little Shop of Horrors* in just two days; he has produced (to date) more than 360 films, none notably expensive. He also directly influenced A-list Hollywood by giving some of its most famous directors and stars their earliest breaks: Oscar-winning directors Francis Ford Coppola, Martin Scorsese, Jonathan Demme, Ron Howard and James Cameron all got their start working for Corman.

In the 1980s and 1990s B movies largely disappeared from U.S. movie screens. Producers began pumping their films directly into video stores, offering endless sequels to marginal horror films and cheaply produced action films.

MAKING OF A MODERN B MOVIE

Nowadays, the B movie is having something of a televised renaissance, as audiences intentionally go for the camp ridiculousness. Cable TV offers Sci Fi Channel's *Original Movie* series, which unashamedly apes the "quick and dirty" B-movie production experience, cheaply cranking out titles like *Alien Lockdown*, *Mansquito*, and *The Man with the Screaming Brain*. These films get surprisingly high ratings for the network and have even been written up in *Wired* magazine and *The New York Times*. Which goes to show, you might be able to take the B movie out of the movie theaters, but not out of the hearts of audiences.

Eli Wallach appears uncredited in *Mystic River* (2003) as a liquor store owner.

SOUNDSTAGES

*When sound was added to movies, it brought plenty
of highs and lows to the lives of those in showbiz.*

In 1927 Warner Bros. Studios released *The Jazz Singer*, the very
first film to offer scenes with synchronized sound. Crowds lined
up to purchase tickets and were delighted when the film's star,
Al Jolson, said the lines, "Wait a minute. Wait a minute. You ain't
heard nothing yet!"

The future belonged to sound, and the film industry plunged
into change. Directors no longer gave orders to their performers
while cameras were rolling; now everything had to be quiet on the
set. Big changes also came to performing—no more reliance on
broad pantomime and facial expressions. Now actors had to talk.
When silent movies were ultimately abandoned in 1929, there
were a lot of careers that hit the skids. But there were just as many
new hopefuls on the rise.

LEADING MEN
Silents Please: When John Gilbert was on the silent movie screen,
ladies' hearts fluttered. Gilbert started out as an extra in 1915 and
worked his way up to megastar status; by 1926 his films were setting
box office records. Gilbert seduced screen goddesses like Lillian Gish
and Greta Garbo (both on-screen and off), earning $10,000 a week
for the privilege. But it all ended in 1929 with *His Glorious Night*.

There are several theories as to why Gilbert's first talkie, *His
Glorious Night*, was so inglorious. For years the conventional wisdom was that Gilbert's voice in the film was too high pitched and
unmanly for a leading man. Others attached a conspiracy to
Gilbert's vocal woes. At Gilbert's aborted wedding to Greta Garbo
(she stood him up at the altar), studio head Louis B. Mayer
allegedly told Gilbert that marrying Garbo was unnecessary since
Gilbert had already slept with her. The infuriated groom punched
Mayer's lights out. According to some Hollywood historians, the
vengeful Mayer plotted against Gilbert during filming of *His
Glorious Night*. According to that theory, Mayer arranged to have
Gilbert's voice recorded with too much treble and no bass, making
him sound squeaky (and not studly).

Others believe that Gilbert's voice was fine, but it was his character's overwritten professions of undying devotion that made the audience giggle instead of swoon. Most likely all of the theories are somewhat true: a voice that wasn't what the audience expected, florid scripts, technical goofs, and the wrath of Mayer all put Gilbert in a steep career slide. He made several more films, but he couldn't score a comeback. A growing dependence on alcohol led to his death in 1936—only seven years after *His Glorious Night*.

Pump Up the Volume: Clark Gable was a struggling stage actor who worked in stock theater and never quite made it big onstage. In 1930 Lionel Barrymore saw Gable in a play in Los Angeles. Barrymore (who, incidently, directed John Gilbert in *His Glorious Night*) advised brawny, big-voiced Gable to make movies, saying, "The silent picture people don't talk so well."

Gable took Barrymore's advice, even though he had to tape back his outsized ears for his talkie debut as a villianous cowboy in *The Painted Desert* (1931). Within a year Gable's charisma, charm, and sex appeal made him a top box office draw—he had 19 pictures under his belt before his biggest hit in 1934. That year he starred with Claudette Colbert in *It Happened One Night* and changed the men's fashion industry (he famously did not wear an undershirt in one bare-chested scene—undershirt sales plummeted). He also won an Oscar for his trouble. As early as 1937 Spencer Tracy anointed Gable the King of Hollywood—and the title stuck.

LEADING LADIES
Silents Please: Clara Bow was 16 years old and living in Brooklyn when she won the 1921 Fame and Fortune Contest sponsored by *Motion Picture* magazine. Her prize? A tiny part in *Beyond the Rainbow* (1922). By the following year the young redhead had her first starring role, playing a tomboy in *Down to the Sea in Ships*. Constantly in films, the beautiful Clara Bow was an established success by 1925. Two years later she became Paramount's biggest star when she played a Jazz Age flapper and wild child in a film called *It* (1927). From then on Clara became known as the It Girl and was deluged with thousands of fan letters a week. Her future seemed assured—until the advent of sound.

Clara's expressive face was a natural at showing strong emotion for the screen, but her voice wasn't a natural for the microphone. She had a slight stammer and a strong Brooklyn accent. Another problem: Bow was largely illiterate and struggled to read scripts and memorize lines. Finally in 1931, while making *Kick In,* the stressed and emotionally fragile actress broke down. She recovered to make two successful talkies, but her accent typecast her, and scandals plagued her (she was—truthfully—connected to Gary Cooper and—falsely—connected to the USC football team). The It Girl had burned out by 1933, retiring at the ripe old age of 28.

Pump Up the Volume: Teenage Lucille Le Sueur danced her way from the Southwest to the Broadway chorus line, where she was spotted by an MGM talent scout in 1925. When she came to Hollywood, 21-year-old Lucille played bit parts and worked to stand out from the ranks of silent starlets. She even let Mayer change her name to Joan Crawford (which she wasn't wild about, thinking it sounded too much like *crawfish*).

In the next three years Joan made 20 silent movies, usually playing a free-spirited flapper. Her first starring role was in one of the last silent films made, 1928's *Our Dancing Daughters.* As they had for Clara Bow, the talkies posed a huge threat to Crawford's new star status. Joan was no stage actress, only a dancer who'd made the most of an opportunity to act. Now she'd have to learn voice techniques and shed her Texas accent.

Determined to succeed in the world of sound, Joan studied diction books, read newspapers aloud, and practiced saying difficult words over and over. In 1929 she performed in her first important talkie, *Untamed*; her husky, sultry voice seemed a perfect match with the sexy characters she played on-screen. Her transition to talkies would be a shoo-in.

In 1930, as talkies forced most other silent stars out of Hollywood, Crawford's hard work payed off. For a while she even rose above rivals such as Greta Garbo and Norma Shearer to become the glamorous Queen of MGM. After conquering sound, Crawford's career in films lasted 45 years—with more than 70 films and an Oscar for Best Actress to her credit.

FUNNY MEN
Silents Please: Buster Keaton starred in his parents' comic vaudeville act as "the Boy Who Can't Be Damaged." From the age of

---

Nicole Kidman did all of her own piano playing in *Cold Mountain* (2003).

four, Keaton performed pratfalls and physical comedy. He also learned that a serious expression made his physical gags seem funnier. In 1917 Fatty Arbuckle put Keaton in his first film, *The Butcher Boy*. Eventually starring in short and feature comedies to rave reviews, Buster Keaton—whose constant refusal to smile or laugh led to his nickname "the Great Stone Face"—became one of the silent era's most popular clowns.

Though Keaton made several talkies for MGM, his physical brand of comedy became less popular, sending his film career into decline. Keaton summed up his problems this way, "In every picture, it got tougher . . . They'd laugh their heads off at dialogue written by all your new writers. They were joke-happy. They didn't look for action; they were looking for funny things to say." After a series of unpopular films, Keaton was fired from MGM in 1933. By then alcoholism had become a major problem for him. He would not return to the limelight until his popular TV series in the 1950s, *The Buster Keaton Show*, where his old silents were resurrected for an appreciative new audience. In 1959 Keaton was presented an honorary Oscar for his life's work.

Pump Up the Volume: The Marx Brothers—Groucho, Harpo, Chico, and Zeppo (who would leave the act in 1933)—were stars on the vaudeville circuit. Their zany, verbal brand of humor packed houses on Broadway stages just as talkies were taking hold in Hollywood.

As pure physical slapstick went into a decline, studios searched for a new kind of comedy to put on films. If, as Buster Keaton suggested, producers of the early talkies were "joke-happy," it's no wonder that Paramount hired the Marx Brothers, who could rap wacky jokes at a frantic clip. (Groucho: "Time flies like an arrow. Fruit flies like a banana." Chico: "I don't remember when I was born, I was just a little baby." Groucho: "Love flies out the door when money comes innuendo.") In 1929, Paramount released *The Cocoanuts*, a filmed version of the trio's Broadway show. It was an instant hit, and for years the most popular comedy team of the talkies was the nutty Marx Brothers, whose appeal has not diminished over time. The American Film Institute put five Mark Brothers films on their list of America's Funniest Movies. The highest rated: *Duck Soup* (1933), at #5.

BOX OFFICE BLOOPERS

We all love bloopers. Here are a bunch of movie mistakes to look for in popular films. You can find more in a book called Film Flubs, *by Bill Givens.*

MOVIE: *The Wizard of Oz* (1939)
SCENE: Dorothy, the Tin Woodsman, and the Scarecrow dance down the Yellow Brick Road singing, "We're Off to See the Wizard."
BLOOPER: A crew member can be seen in the background among the trees. (For years rumors circulated in Hollywood that the crew member had committed suicide and hung himself from one of the trees on the set. The rumors were false.) *Note:* Also pay close attention to the length of Dorothy's hair. Because the scenes were filmed out of sequence, her hair changes from mid-length to long to short as the movie progresses.

MOVIE: *Spartacus* (1960)
SCENE: Peter Ustinov gets off of his horse.
BLOOPER: His jockey shorts are visible under his tunic as he climbs down.

MOVIE: *The Alamo* (1960)
SCENE: The battle sequences.
BLOOPER: Though the movie is a Western, you can see several mobile trailers in the distance. (And in another scene, you can see a stuntman falling into a mattress.)

MOVIE: *Children of a Lesser God* (1986)
SCENES: Several occasions in which Marlee Matlin (who is deaf and portrays a deaf character) and co-star William Hurt sign to each other during conversations in which Hurt is speaking.
BLOOPER: The sign language has nothing to do with the movie—it's about Matlin's and Hurt's private life. (At the time the movie was made, Matlin and Hurt were having an affair.)

MOVIE: *Abbot and Costello Go to Mars* (1953)
BLOOPER: In the movie they actually go to Venus.

—Maggie (Bridget Fonda), *Point of No Return* (1993)

MOVIE: *Rambo III* (1988)
SCENE: Rambo steals a "Russian" helicopter.
BLOOPER: A small American flag is clearly visible on the helicopter's rotor housing.

MOVIE: *Rear Window* (1954)
SCENE: Jimmy Stewart, in a cast and sitting in a wheelchair, argues with Grace Kelly.
BLOOPER: His cast switches from his left leg to his right.

MOVIE: *Raiders of the Lost Ark* (1982)
SCENE: German soldiers and Gestapo agents lift the ark.
BLOOPER: Paintings of C-3PO and R2-D2, the androids from *Star Wars* (another George Lucas film), are included among the hieroglyphics on the wall.

MOVIE: *Close Encounters of the Third Kind* (1977)
SCENE: Richard Dreyfus and Melinda Dillon smash through several road blocks as they near Devil's Tower.
BLOOPER: The license plate on their station wagon keeps changing.

MOVIE: *Camelot* (1967)
SCENE: King Arthur (Richard Harris) praises his medieval kingdom while speaking to some of his subjects.
BLOOPER: Harris is wearing a Band-Aid on his neck.

MOVIE: *The Fortune Cookie* (1966)
SCENE: Walter Matthau leaves one room and enters another—and appears to lose weight in the process.
BLOOPER: Matthau suffered a heart attack while this scene was being filmed; only half was completed before he entered the hospital. He returned five months later to finish the job—40 pounds lighter than he was in the first part of the scene.

MOVIE: *Diamonds Are Forever* (1971)
SCENE: James Bond tips his Ford Mustang up onto two wheels and drives through a narrow alley to escape from the bad guys.
BLOOPER: The Mustang enters the alley on its two right wheels—and leaves the alley on its two left wheels.

GOSSIP MAVENS

*Darling! Scoot yourself over here and we'll tell you
all about the cattiest gossips ever to hit the streets of
Hollywood: Louella Parsons and Hedda Hopper.*

You know, gossip just isn't what it used to be. Sure, there's
more of it—your supermarket check-out aisle would be posi-
tively bare if it weren't for all the magazines and tabloids
telling who did what with whom and how often. But the gossip
columnists slinging the tales of seamy celebs today just don't have
the—oh, what's the word—*oomph* of the gossip columnists of the
Golden Age of Hollywood. In those days, not only could a gossip
columnist tell millions of slavering housewives what your next
movie was, if she decided to slag that movie—and your performance in it—well, then, sweetheart, you simply wouldn't work in
this town again. Back to Iowa with you, darling. Iowa, ironically,
being where the most powerful of all gossip mavens was from.

LOUELLA PARSONS
Louella Parsons was a lonely, neglected wife in little Burlington,
Iowa, when one night in 1906 she decided to take in a movie at the
local picture show—*The Great Train Robbery*, to be precise. Well,
dearie, she was enthralled. Fast-forward to 1914, and Louella had
left that dreary Iowa town far behind for the lights and glamour of
Chicago, where she worked at the *Chicago Record-Herald* as the
world's first movie columnist. The lights! The camera! The action!

WORKING GIRL
Then, tragedy—the *Record-Herald* was bought by William Randolph
Hearst, who declared the paper didn't need a movie columnist. Out
on the streets, our plucky Louella picked herself right up and headed
to New York to bang out another movie column, this time for the
Morning Telegraph. Hearst may have run her out of Chicago, but in
New York, he was impressed with her style and made her a deal she
couldn't refuse—a job with his New York paper, the *American*. She
took the job in 1922, and in 1925 moved to Hollywood itself, the
very epicenter of glitz and glamour. Our heroine Louella would work
for Hearst, in fact, for the rest of her long career.

WITNESS

How did she manage a lifetime contract? Well, normally we wouldn't pass on gossip, but in this case we'll make an exception. In 1924 Louella and several other notables were on Hearst's boat when movie director Thomas Ince suddenly and tragically took ill and was rushed off the boat, thence to expire. Oh, the official story is that it was acute indigestion, but those who were there might tell you that if it was indigestion, it's because he ate a bullet. And the chief suspect was none other than Hearst himself, because he suspected Ince had a thing for Marion Davies. It would have been such the scandal, except that Hearst hushed all the witnesses with lavish gifts—in Louella's case a lifetime contract. It's just rumor, mind you. And you know what they say about rumors.

In any event, Louella paid back the favor for Hearst—when Orson Welles made *Citizen Kane*, Louella alerted Hearst to the fact that it was based largely on him ("Rosebud!"). She walloped Welles with scathing comments in her columns, and even allegedly organized a campaign to have Welles booed at the Oscars. Sure, he got an Oscar for Best Screenplay, but on the other hand, his career never did completely recover, did it? In her 1961 autobiography, *Tell It to Louella*, she said, "I have carried only one grudge for any length of time and that was against Orson Welles."

THE TERMINATOR

Louella could be even nastier behind the scenes, when she felt the need. On her Web site, B-movie actress Mamie Van Doren alleges that in the 1950s Louella Parsons launched a vicious whisper campaign against her, in part because Van Doren's manager was Parsons's own boyfriend and Louella was seeing green. Apparently Louella told some of the trashier tabloids that Mamie and her mother were, well, women of low repute. Oh, you know—hookers, darling. Scandalous—and not a bit of it true. Now you know why you wanted to stay on her good side.

HEDDA HOPPER

But if you couldn't stay on Louella's good side—say for instance, your name was Orson—there was one other option: Hedda Hopper. Not that that was her real name. Her real name was, and this is very rich, Elda Furry. And she came to the gossip game with a certain amount of experience on the other side of the publicity

---

Lawrence of Arabia (1962), though 227 minutes, has no women in speaking roles.

machine—she was an actress, primarily during the silent era, mostly playing the heroine's best friend, in more than 100 films. She got rid of "Furry" by marrying actor DeWolf Hopper (their son, William, had a long-running role in the early *Perry Mason* series on TV). But back in 1938 she left acting behind for a much more interesting job—gossip columnist for the *Los Angeles Times*. Her column was called "Under Hedda's Hat."

PUBLIC ENEMY
Of course, she and Louella became mortal enemies—how could they not?—and stars who were beloved of one were less than the dust beneath the pumps of the other. And vice-versa—while Louella was busy torching Orson Welles when *Citizen Kane* was in the theaters, Hedda had him as the featured guest for a week-long sit-down on her radio program. Their rivalry eventually even spawned a movie in itself: *Malice in Wonderland*. But it starred Liz Taylor! So that's good.

REDS
Like Louella, Hedda wasn't above being petty when it suited her. Hedda had a chatty relationship with FBI director J. Edgar Hoover, to whom she wrote long letters about all the communists in Hollywood. In one 1947 letter, for example, she swiped at Charlie Chaplin and other "commies": "I'd like to run every one of those rats out of the country starting with Charlie Chaplin. In no other country in the world would he have been allowed to do what he's done." And of course, Chaplin was eventually run out of the country! Coincidence? Possibly, but then again, possibly not.

HEDDA AND LOUELLA HANG UP THEIR HATS
So what happens to old gossip columnists? Why, the same thing that happens to old actors and actresses—they die, or they just fade away. Hedda died in 1966. Louella stopped writing her gossip column in 1965 and lived out her last years in a Santa Monica nursing home. Rumor has it that she spent her final days watching old movies on TV and talking to the images of the people whose careers she'd made or broken.

Country with the most movie theaters: U.S., with 32,992. Second: India, with 12,867.

MOVIE BRATS, PART 2

*Just when things were going so well for lovers of original,
quirky movies, along came two directors who share the glory—
and most of the blame—for changing Hollywood movies.
They weren't interested in imparting any deep, dark
truths. All they wanted to do was entertain. (For
the first part of this story, see page 334.)*

1977
GEORGE LUCAS—THE VISIONARY

Unlike his contemporary movie brats, Lucas didn't spend his childhood watching movies. Born in 1944 in Modesto, California, George Lucas spent his teen years racing cars as well as immersing himself in comic books (*Buck Rogers* and *Flash Gordon* were favorites). A serious accident three days before his high school graduation made him reconsider life as a race car driver. Instead, he turned to his other interests, storytelling and photography, and started the process that would get him into the University of Southern California's film school in Los Angeles. There he made the sci-fi short *Electronic Labyrinth THX 1138 4EB*, which took first prize at the 1967–68 National Student Film Festival. On the strength of that and his many other student awards, Lucas won USC's annual scholarship to become a production apprentice at Warner Bros.

The only film Warner had in production at the time was *Finian's Rainbow*, which was being directed by 27-year-old Francis Ford Coppola. The two directors-in-the-making became friends and supporters of each other's work. Coppola helped produce Lucas's first film, *American Graffiti*, a nostalgic look at the teenage art of cruising. The popularity and financial success of *Graffiti* gave Lucas the money and time to flesh out an idea he'd been hatching for a while: to write and direct his own science-fiction saga.

The Movie: In 1977 *Star Wars* exploded into the theaters. What made this tale of a farm boy who saves an imprisoned princess from a powerful villain so different was that the princess was being held captive inside a huge space station instead of a castle. The combination of mythological storytelling with science fiction and spectacular special effects made *Star Wars* an unprecedented phenomenon.

The Legacy: *Star Wars* broke all box office records and earned seven Oscars. More important for its filmmaker, the movie's success and huge following granted him instant independence from the Hollywood studio system. Lucas went on to create five more *Star Wars* films—sequels and prequels—and even though his most recent efforts have caught some critical flak from fans and reviewers alike, all the *Star Wars* films have been eagerly anticipated and every one of them has been a blockbuster.

Lucas's facilities, far from Hollywood in Northern California, were built on the success of *Star Wars*. Through various subsidiaries of Lucasfilm Ltd. and THX Group, he continues to explore and fund new technologies in cinema. But Lucas's most lasting legacy— with Stephen Spielberg—may be the blame they share for "the blockbuster syndrome."

1975
STEVEN SPIELBERG—THE KID

The baby of the brats, Spielberg was born in Cincinnati in 1946 and moved with his father (an electrical engineer) and mother (a concert pianist) to Phoenix, Arizona, while still a child. He started playing with his father's 8mm camera when he was eight. His parents encouraged his interests to the point of indulgence, and his parents and three younger sisters were his first acting troupe. By the time he was 12, he was using actors (albeit amateurs) in short films. At 16 he "released" *Firelight, a Close Encounters*–type movie, in a local theater his father had rented for the evening.

He dropped out of film school after three years at California State University, Long Beach; this was in 1968, the same year that he directed his first TV show, a 90-minute episode of the sophisticated crime series *The Name of the Game*. More TV work followed, including episodes of *Marcus Welby* and a *Columbo*, but Spielberg didn't make his mark until the made-for-TV movie *Duel* hit TV screens in 1971. It was the story of a business commuter (Dennis Weaver) who is terrorized by a malevolent tractor-trailer. The movie was nominated for a Golden Globe as the Best Movie Made for TV.

—Captain Kirk (William Shatner), *Star Trek II: The Wrath of Khan* (1982)

Spielberg's first feature film, *The Sugarland Express* (1974), was a relative success for Universal Studios and earned its director a nomination at Cannes. Little did the studio know that the next movie they assigned him would make them a profit beyond their wildest dreams—and would land 28-year-old Spielberg in the pantheon of Hollywood directors.

The Movie: *Jaws*, the story of a man-eating shark that terrorizes a seaside community, became an instant cultural phenomenon upon its release in 1975. Audiences had seen horror flicks before, but this one was different. Spielberg sprinkled the terror with humor; instead of serving up cardboard characters as victims for his scary shark, he gave them quirks and funny mannerisms—they were real. And the more real they were, the more viewers cared about them . . . and feared for them. Audiences went back to see *Jaws* again and again as if it were an amusement park thrill ride. That's how it became the first movie in history to gross more than $100 million.

The Legacy: Whereas George Lucas has stuck mostly to his *Star Wars* saga, Spielberg has experimented with a variety of genres including *Close Encounters of the Third Kind* (1977), which earned him his first Oscar nomination as director; *Raiders of the Lost Ark* (1981), the swashbuckling action pic suggested to him by friend George Lucas; and *Schindler's List* (1993), the heroic drama that, besides winning the Oscar for Best Film, earned Spielberg his first Best Director award at both the Oscars and the Golden Globes. He continues to pepper his surefire blockbusters with smaller movies like *Amistad* (1997) and *The Terminal* (2004), and has yet (except for a few that shall remain nameless) to make a bad movie.

The Lucas-Spielberg Legacy: Because of their massive success, *Star Wars* and *Jaws* are accused of being the reason that the studios replaced adult storytelling with formulaic action movies jam-packed with special effects. Well, okay, guilty as charged. But the problem with blaming Lucas and Spielberg is that their original intent wasn't to make blockbusters. They just wanted—like all the other movie brats—to follow their artistic vision and to bring original stories to the screen in original ways.

On the set, the clapboard snap starts a scene. Later on, filmmakers use the . . .

EPILOGUE

And so Hollywood's second Golden Age came to an end. But the decade in filmdom that Pauline Kael called her "favorite" wouldn't be complete without the mention of some of the other innovative filmmakers who made landmark films during the 1970s.

Robert Altman: M*A*S*H* (1970), *Nashville* (1975)

Hal Ashby: *Harold and Maude* (1971), *Shampoo* (1975)

Peter Bogdanovich: *The Last Picture Show* (1971)

Michael Cimino: *The Deer Hunter* (1978)

Brian De Palma: *Sisters* (1973)

William Friedkin: *The French Connection* (1971)

Terrence Malick: *Badlands* (1973)

Bob Rafelson: *Five Easy Pieces* (1970)

* * *

Singin' in the Rain (1952) spoofs the problems of the transition from silents to talkies. Don Lockwood (Gene Kelly) is a silent star making his first talkie. Like many silent stars, he studies with a diction coach. And, in a parody of *His Glorious Night*, Lockwood is given a script with such overwrought love lines that he improvises by comically repeating "I love you" over and over.

* * *

"Hollywood was born schizophrenic. For 75 years it has been both a town and a state of mind, an industry and an art form."
—Richard Corliss, critic

HUMPHREY BOGART: BY THE NUMBERS

A specialist in hard-boiled detectives and cynical tough guys, Bogie was a Hollywood treasure. Here's looking at him—by the numbers.

0
The number of live leeches in *The African Queen* (1951) on Bogart's chest. Bogart didn't like leeches, but director John Huston led the actor to believe that he had to use live ones for a crucial scene, which made Bogie uneasy and nervous—qualities needed for his facial close-ups. Ultimately, Huston only used rubber leeches on the shots Bogie appears in. For the close-up torso shots of the live leeches, the leech breeder, who was on the set, stood in for Bogie and put a live one on his chest.

1
Bogart's rank on the American Film Institute's list of the Greatest (Male) American Screen Legends. It's also the rank of *Casablanca* (1942) on the AFI's list of America's Greatest Love Stories.

1.5
Length, in years, of Bogart's first and shortest marriage, to Broadway star Helen Menken. He married two other actresses, Mary Philips and Mayo Methot, before meeting and marrying Lauren Bacall.

2
Number of ways Bogart's nickname can be spelled; he preferred Bogie to Bogey. It's also the number of starring roles George Raft turned down that Bogie took: Roy "Mad Dog" Earle in *High Sierra* (1941) and Sam Spade in *The Maltese Falcon* (1941). Both helped turn Bogie into a star.

3
Number of Best Actor Oscar nominations Bogart received during his career: for *Casablanca*, *The African Queen*, and *The Caine Mutiny* (1954). He won for *The African Queen*.

What do Jamie Lee Curtis, Terry Gilliam, Geraldine Page, Rodney Dangerfield,

4
Number of different stories of how Bogie earned the scar on his lip and, thereby, his lisp. One story says his father gave it to him when he was a child. Another that it was caused by shrapnel from a U-boat attack during his U.S. Naval service. Yet another version: a prisoner that Bogart was escorting to the brig asked for a light and then smashed his handcuffs into Bogie's face in an attempt to escape. Last but not least is the account told by his New York drinking buddies: the scar came from a speakeasy brawl.

5
In inches, the height of the platform shoes Bogart reportedly wore during the filming of Casablanca so that he'd be as tall as costars Ingrid Bergman and Paul Henreid. His medical reports alternately list his height as 5 feet 7 1/2 inches and 5 feet 9 1/2 inches.

6
Average number of movies per year Bogie made in the 1930s, among them such forgotten films as *Crime School* (1938), *Racket Busters* (1938), and *The Return of Doctor X* (1939).

11:30
Time of evening referred to in a quote by Dave Chasen, the owner of Chasen's, where Bogart often drank. "Bogart's a helluva nice guy until around 11:30. After that, he thinks he's Bogart."

17
Age at which Bogie ended his 11-year prep school career by getting kicked out of Philips Academy in Andover, Massachusetts, for "indifference and lack of effort." After four days back home in New York City, he enlisted in the navy, just a few months before the end of World War I.

19
Lauren Bacall's age when she was first introduced to Bogie. There were no sparks—until a few months later when they started filming *To Have and Have Not* (1944).

21
Age at which Bogie made his acting debut in a play in Brooklyn. He played a Japanese butler and had one line.

and Hoagy Carmichael have in common? The same birthday, November 22.

49

Bogie's age when his first child, Stephen Humphrey (named for his character in *To Have and Have Not*), was born in 1949. Three years later came one more child, Leslie Howard, named after the actor who co-starred with Bogie in *The Petrified Forest* (1936).

50

In cents, the price for a game of chess with a not-yet-famous Bogart. In 1933, when trying to earn some extra money, he became the house player for an arcade.

57

In years, age at his death in 1957, from cancer of the esophagus.

1800

In military time (that's 6 p.m. for you civilians), the time of the evening at which Bogie stopped working, as stipulated in his contract once he became a big star. At exactly 6:00 his assistant would hand him a scotch and water; he would drink it and then leave the set.

8,800

In dollars, Bogie's earnings for 1938's *Angels With Dirty Faces*. He was third-billed, after James Cagney and Pat O'Brien. Cagney's salary was nearly 10 times Bogie's: $85,667. Three years later, Bogie would make $36,667 for *Casablanca*. For *Sabrina*, in 1954, Bogie pulled in $300,000.

* * *

"I came out here with one suit and everybody said I looked like a bum. Twenty years later Marlon Brando came out with only a sweatshirt and the town drooled over him. That shows how much Hollywood has progressed."

—Humphrey Bogart

Before he became a movie mogul, Louis B. Mayer was a scrap metal dealer.

DIGITAL DREAMS

For more than a hundred years, the movies have come to audiences on celluloid film. Now all that is about to change.

In May 2002 George Lucas's *Star Wars: Episode II—Attack of the Clones* opened in theaters across the country. The millions who watched the movie were also seeing the opening salvo of a revolution. *Clones* was the first, big-budget movie shot in digital video. And the revolution that heralded digital cinema may be coming to your local theater soon.

For more than a century, movies have been shown by a projector that unwinds a reel of celluloid film past a light, in turn illuminating moving pictures on a theater screen below the projection booth. But the future belongs to digital video cameras, which record the movies as digital files—in bits and bytes that can be stored on magnetic tape and in computers. The movies, shot as digital files, will emerge as a stream of data called digital cinema.

Digital video technology has been important to Hollywood ever since 1977 when the pioneering Lucas used computer-generated images, or CGI, to create galactic battles in the first *Star Wars*. After CGI special effects (from the lawyer-eating dinosaur in *Jurassic Park* to the mammoth waves in *The Perfect Storm*) are created, however, they are then usually filmed on celluloid. But as digital technology keeps advancing, celluloid may become a thing of the past—some experts believe as soon as 2007.

MONEY MATTERS
Digital cinema changes the cost to make a film, distribute it, and show it in theaters.

Making a movie: Hollywood films are usually shot on professional-quality 35-millimeter film. That film stock is expensive and so are its processing costs. Digital videotape is far cheaper. And digital footage can be edited directly on a computer rather than converted to digital for editing and then reconverted to film for projection.

Building expensive sets or flying to a location can sometimes be eliminated. In the movie *Castaway*, the stranded character played by Tom Hanks stands on a lonely island cliff top and sees nothing but miles and miles of empty ocean. Hanks was actually standing in a Malibu parking lot, and a digital team replaced everything in the shot except the actor.

Overall, studios can make digital movies for about 1 percent of the cost of film. During the making of *Attack of the Clones*, it cost $16,000 to shoot 220 hours of digital tape. The cost to produce those hours on film? More than 100 times as much: $1.8 million!

Distributing a movie: When the studio wants to release a blockbuster, it must make thousands of prints of the movie from a master negative, at a cost of up to about $1,000 to $2,000 per print. The prints are then stored in cans and shipped to theaters around the world. A digital movie could be encrypted for piracy protection, then transmitted electronically to those same theaters directly from the studio, saving on the costs of the prints and the physical shipping—to the tune of millions.

Showing a movie: The cost of installing digital projectors is a big reason that most movies are still shot on film. A current 35 millimeter–film projector costs about $30,000 and lasts about 35 years. Digital projectors cost up to $150,000, and some theater owners doubt they will last 25 years. They also complain that digital projectors can be compared to early laptops—the technology is still first generation.

Independent movies: In 2002 the Sundance favorite *Tadpole* made more than $2 million at the box office. That would be a huge loss for a studio film. But *Tadpole* was an independent film, shot entirely with a digital video camera for $150,000, enabling it to make a tidy profit.

WHAT MATTERS TO MOVIEGOERS
Digital cinema may change what you can see at your local theater.
Cinematic quality of a movie: What would a change to digital movies mean to the way movies look on-screen? Depends on whom you ask. Director George Lucas and many of his colleagues, including James Cameron (*Titanic*) and Robert Rodriguez (*Sin City*), are eager to drop film to embrace digital cinema. They believe the look of digital is rapidly approaching the quality of celluloid. But the most popular director of our day, Steven Spielberg (*Jaws, Jurassic Park, E.T., War of the Worlds*, etc.), disagrees. He

believes there is "magic" in celluloid film, and that its grainy look lends artistry to his work that the clean blandness of digital can't provide. Says Spielberg, "I was one of the first people to use digital technology to enhance my films, but I'm going to be the last person to use digital technology to shoot my movies."

Once a digital movie is made, it has a big advantage. It never wears out. Digital cinema with its electronic transmission won't scratch, smudge, or break the way regular film does—celluloid movie film degrades with each showing until it's finally too damaged for use. A viewer will see the same quality digital movie if he or she goes to its first or thousandth showing.

Type of movie you'll see: Digital proponents say that in the new era, movies will be more imaginative because whatever can be imagined can be filmed. Without building sets, movies can explore any world that can be dreamed up in a script—using a computer screen. And digital will only make it easier to use CGI special effects.

Theaters will be able to change programming as easily as rearranging playlists on a computer. That means theaters could easily rearrange films at different showings. Popular films will be easy to see, because theaters can request them from studios and receive them instantly. And there'll likely be more edgy, independent movies, made on a shoestring budget available as the cost of digital moviemaking continues to fall.

But it won't all be esoteric or highbrow at the multiplex. The thrills of 3-D may soon return to the local Bijou. A single digital projector can beam images that trick the eye into perceiving depth.

* * *

"We have our factory, which is called a stage. We make a product, we color it, we title it, and we ship it out in cans."

—Cary Grant

* * *

"My stage successes have provided me with the greatest moments outside myself, my film successes the best moments, professionally, within myself."

—Sir Laurence Olivier

The alien puppet in *E.T.* cost $1 million to make, almost 10% of the film's budget.

REEL QUOTES

Here are some of our favorite lines from the silver screen.

ON DATING
Allen: "What are you doing Saturday night?"
Diana: "Committing suicide."
Allen: "What are you doing Friday night?"
—*Play It Again, Sam*

ON LOVE
Darrow: "You ever been in love, Hornbeck?"
Hornbeck: "Only with the sound of my own voice, thank God."
—*Inherit the Wind*

"Jane, since I've met you, I've noticed things I never knew were there before: birds singing . . . dew glistening on a newly formed leaf . . . stoplights . . ."
—Lt. Frank Drebin, *Naked Gun*

ON ANATOMY
Nick Charles: "I'm a hero. I was shot twice in the Tribune."
Nora Charles: "I read where you were shot five times in the tabloids."
Nick: "It's not true. They didn't come anywhere near my tabloids."
—*The Thin Man*

ON GOLF
"A golf course is nothing but a poolroom moved outdoors."
—Barry Fitzgerald, *Going My Way*

ON RELIGION
Sonja: "Of course there's a God. We're made in his image."
Boris: "You think I was made in God's image? Take a look at me. Do you think he wears glasses?"
Sonja: "Not with those frames . . . Boris, we must believe in God."
Boris: "If I could just see a miracle. Just one miracle. If I could see a burning bush, or the seas part, or my Uncle Sasha pick up a check."
—Woody Allen's *Love and Death*

ON BEING CLEAR
Ted Striker: "Surely, you can't be serious."
Dr. Rumack: "I am serious. And don't call me Shirley."
—*Airplane!*

Ollie: "You never met my wife, did you?"
Stan: "Yes, I never did."
—*Helpmates*

When Charlie Chaplin's *Modern Times* debuted in New York City in 1936, . . .

TARZAN OF THE MOVIES, PART 2: HERE'S JOHNNY!

*Besides Edgar Rice Burroughs, the person most associated with the
character of Tarzan is a swimmer-turned-actor named Johnny
Weissmuller. In fact, it wasn't until 1932, when Weismuller
took on the role, that Tarzan developed a stable personality
and face the public could get used to. But to Johnny, it
was just a job. Here's the rest of the story. (The
first part begins on page 310.)*

AFRICA SPEAKS

In 1927 MGM bought the film rights to *Trader Horn*, the memoirs of an African adventurer, and assigned director W. S. "Woody" Van Dyke to the picture. The studio originally planned to make it as a silent film, but then decided that *Trader Horn* would be their first talkie.

Making the leap from silent films to sound is considered the biggest technological advance in the history of filmmaking. MGM understood the significance of the coming of sound and wanted its first talkie to be larger than life. Money was no object—Trader Horn was going to be the best film possible.

ON THE ROAD

Van Dyke persuaded the studio that the only way to do the film justice was to film it on location. So in March 1929 Van Dyke— along with 35 cast and crew members, three sound trucks, and 90 tons of equipment—set sail for Africa. Over the next seven months, they (and 200 African natives) traveled more than 10,000 miles through Africa, shooting more than a million feet of film. Needless to say, the production ran over budget.

"The expense was worth it," John Taliaferro writes. "When *Trader Horn* was released in 1931 it was a huge hit and helped rekindle public interest in the continent of Africa. Even Ernest Hemingway credited *Trader Horn* with giving him his Africa 'bug.'"

MGM had more than just a hit film on its hands: it had thousands and thousands of feet of unused African film footage and the studio began looking for ways to put it to good use.

"Inevitably," Taliaferro says, "someone suggested Tarzan."

TOUGH BREAK
By 1931 MGM had bought the rights to *Tarzan the Ape Man* and hired Van Dyke to direct it. For the first time in the history of the Tarzan franchise, a movie studio was simply buying the right to make a movie about Burroughs's character and was free to come up with its own story.

Having Van Dyke direct the film was a good idea from a stylistic point of view: he was considered Hollywood's finest nature film-maker. But it made casting the film more difficult, because Van Dyke was a perfectionist who wasn't afraid to turn down Tinseltown's biggest stars if he felt they weren't right for the role. Clark Gable was one of the first actors rejected. "He has no body," Van Dyke complained. "What I want is a man who is young, strong, well-built, reasonably attractive, but not necessarily hand-some, and a competent actor. The most important thing is that he have a good physique. And I can't find him."

STROKE OF LUCK
Meanwhile, screenwriter Cyril Hume was hard at work in his hotel room cranking out the *Tarzan* screenplay. One afternoon he stepped out for a minute and happened to notice a powerfully built young man swimming in the hotel pool. It was 27-year-old Johnny Weissmuller, the greatest amateur swimmer the world had ever seen.

Between 1921 and 1928, Weissmuller had won 52 national titles, held every freestyle record, and broken his own records dozens of times. Weissmuller won three gold medals at the 1924 Olympics and two more at the 1928 games. Not long afterward he gave up his amateur status and signed on as the national spokesman for BVD swimwear and underwear. He was still model-ling for BVD when Cyril Hume discovered him.

MR. NATURAL
Hume was so impressed by Weissmuller that he arranged a meeting with Van Dyke. However, rather than give him a formal screen test, they just had him strip to his shorts to get a sense of what he'd

---

look like in a loincloth. Two things immediately struck them: 1) Weissmuller clearly had the right build for the part, and 2) he seemed perfectly at ease stripping down to his underpants in front of two men he hardly knew. He actually appeared comfortable in his skivvies, something almost unheard of in an age where most men still wore two-piece, shirt-and-shorts bathing suits on the beach. In fact, Weissmuller had spent so many years modeling underwear and wearing skimpy one-piece racing trunks that he was completely uninhibited about appearing semi-nude on film. Even though he was nearly naked, he somehow seemed wholesome.

"Other Tarzan actors, when they wore loincloths and leopard skins, seemed merely undressed," Taliaferro writes. "Weissmuller, by contrast, was clean-limbed in every sense. He gave the impression that he could have sold Bibles door to door wearing nothing but a G-string . . . There was no hint of either embarrassment or braggadocio in his comportment."

Weissmuller won the part hands (and pants) down . . . and just in case anyone failed to notice his unique abilities, in the publicity leading up to *Tarzan the Ape Man's* premiere, MGM's publicity agents billed Weissmuller as "the only man in Hollywood who's natural in the flesh and can act without clothes."

A CHANGED MAN
Weissmuller still didn't have much acting experience, but it didn't really matter—rather than change Weissmuller to make him better fit the role, MGM simply adjusted the Tarzan character to fit Weissmuller's strengths and weaknesses: the Tarzan of the Edgar Rice Burroughs novels was a self-educated, cultured gentleman who spoke several languages; the Tarzan of the Weissmuller films was someone who spoke very little and swam surprisingly often for a guy who lived in the middle of a jungle. "The role was right up my alley—it was just like stealing," Weissmuller recounted years later.

Not much of Burroughs's original Tarzan character had ever made it to the screen. But by the time MGM was through, the few remaining vestiges had been swept away. The screenplay made absolutely no mention of Tarzan's noble origins and didn't even bother to explain how he'd ended up in the jungle. Even the sound of Tarzan's name was changed: Burroughs had always pronounced it as TAR-zn, but MGM changed it to TAR-ZAN; and

—Gilda (Rita Hayworth), *Gilda* (1946)

TAR-ZAN it would stay. Burroughs had always resisted changes to his character in the past; this time he just accepted it. "I don't give a damn what they call him," he told a friend, "as long as their checks come regularly."

FINDING HIS VOICE

Because this was the first true *Tarzan* talkie, the filmmakers had to figure out what Tarzan's jungle yell would sound like. Nobody really knew what to do . . . until Weissmuller came up with the yell on his own. He recalled:

> When I was a kid, I used to read the Tarzan books, and they had kind of a shrill yell for Tarzan. I never thought I'd ever make Tarzan movies, but when I finally got the part, they were trying to do yells like that. And I remembered when I was a kid I used to yodel at the picnics on Sundays, so I said, "I know a yell!"

Nobody gave Weissmuller's yell much thought until after the film opened and MGM realized just how popular the yell was. They quickly invented a story that it was created by sound engineers who blended Weissmuller's voice "with a hyena's howl played backward, a camel's bleat, the pluck of a violin string, and a soprano's high C."

"It was a commentary on the mystique of talkies and the bizarre singularity of the yell itself," John Taliaferro writes in *Tarzan Forever*, "that the public accepted the studio's fib as fact."

LOVE INTEREST

MGM knew pretty quickly what Jane would look like—they cast a contract actress named Maureen O'Sullivan to play her. But it took a while to decide what she should wear. "First," O'Sullivan recalled, "they had the idea of having Jane wearing no bra—no brassiere at all—and she would always be covered with a branch. They tried that, and it didn't work. So they made a costume and it wasn't that bad at all. There was a little leather bra and a loincloth."

THE FILMING

The stage was set. Filming of *Tarzan the Ape Man* began on October 31, 1931, and finished eight weeks later. Total cost, even with the free leftover jungle footage from *Trader Horn*, was just over $650,000. The film had not come cheap, but it turned out to

---

The *Saturday Night Fever* soundtrack has sold more than 30 million copies.

be worth every penny: *Tarzan the Ape Man* opened to huge crowds and rave reviews in March 1932, and went on to become one of Top 10 box office hits of the year. The movie's success helped increase the popularity of the Tarzan novels and comic strips, whose sales had started to suffer in the grip of the Great Depression.

Weissmuller didn't have a lot of dialogue in the film, but his acting was surprisingly authentic. He became the hottest new star of 1932. "However credible or interesting Tarzan may be on the printed page," Thorton Delehanty wrote in the *New York Evening Post*, "I doubt very much if he emerges in such splendor as he does in the person of Johnny Weissmuller. . . .With his flowing hair, magnificently proportioned body, catlike walk, and virtuosity in the water, you could hardly ask anything more in the way of perfection."

Maureen O'Sullivan also won high praise for her performance and, like Weissmuller, set the standard by which all future Janes would be judged; to this day the six movies she starred in with Weissmuller are considered the best Tarzan films ever made.

THE SEQUEL

When *Tarzan the Ape Man* became a runaway hit, MGM paid Burroughs for the right to make a sequel called *Tarzan and His Mate*. They signed Weissmuller and O'Sullivan for an encore. Influenced by the success of *King Kong* the year before, the makers of *Tarzan and His Mate* spent a lot of money on animal and special effects, including a 20-foot-long steel-and-rubber mechanical crocodile that Weissmuller wrestles and kills in the film, and a live hippopotamus that was imported from a German zoo so that Weissmuller could ride on its back. Even Cheetah the chimp was given an expanded role to take advantage of the public's newfound fascination with primates.

BIG GAMBLE

The film ultimately cost $1.3 million, nearly double what *Tarzan the Apeman* cost and a huge sum for a Depression-era film. But like its predecessor, it played to packed theaters all over the country and, when it was released to foreign markets, all over the world. *Tarzan and His Mate* is considered the best of the Weissmuller Tarzan films and probably the best *Tarzan* film of all time.

Mel Brooks, Gilda Radner, John Cusack, and Kathy Bates all were born on June 28.

It is also famous for another reason: it features the most nudity of any of Weissmuller's *Tarzan* films. O'Sullivan wears a skimpy leather top and a loincloth comprised of one flap of leather in front and one in back, leaving her thighs and hips fully exposed. It "started such a furor," O'Sullivan remembered years later. "Thousands of women were objecting to my costume." MGM finally caved in and changed O'Sullivan's costume from "something suitable for the jungle" into "something resembling a suburban housedress," a la Wilma Flintstone. Even Weissmuller had to cover up for the next film in the series: he went from a revealing loincloth to what looked like "leather gym shorts."

BIG BUDGET
In July 1935 MGM began work on *The Capture of Tarzan*, its third *Tarzan* film. They planned to make it the most elaborate, most expensive, and (they hoped) most profitable one yet.

Set designers built a six-room treehouse for Tarzan and Jane that the Flintstones would have envied, complete with running water, an oven for baking, overhead fans operated by Cheetah, and an elevator powered by an elephant.

The Capture of Tarzan was also supposed to be much more graphic than the earlier films. In one scene, a safari party is captured by the Ganeolis tribe of natives and the captives are spread-eagled on the ground "to be butchered in a two-part ritual: a savage cutting with knives followed by a rock-swing to the head, cracking the skull open," but are rescued by Tarzan just in time. In another scene, the party crosses into a foggy marshland where they're attacked by pygmies, giant lizards, and vampire bats.

Unfortunately, when *The Capture of Tarzan* was shown to preview audiences in 1935, it "terrified children and brought outraged complaints from irate mothers and women's organizations," Gabe Essoe writes. "Afraid that *Capture* would alienate more people than it would attract, studio bosses ordered all gruesome scenes cut out and replaced with re-takes." When director Jim McKay objected to the changes, he was fired and replaced with John Farrow, who was himself later fired. (But not before falling in love with Maureen O'Sullivan and eventually marrying her, and fathering seven children—one of whom is actress Mia Farrow.) Next in line for director was Richard Thorpe, who stayed on as director for the rest of the MGM series.

WATCH OUT FOR THAT TREE!

Thorpe spent months shooting new scenes "as necessary" to make the film "appeal" to young and old alike, and changed the name to *Tarzan Escapes*. Thorpe also began the tradition of reusing scenes from older *Tarzan* films—in this case cutting out the vampire bat attack scene and replacing it with the crocodile fight from *Tarzan and His Mate*—and cheapening what had been considered a top-notch motion picture franchise. "In essence, this film marked a major step in lowering the *Tarzan* series to the child's level," Essoe writes.

With all of the rewriting, refilming, and reediting, *Tarzan Escapes* took 14 months to finish and cost more than the first two MGM *Tarzan* films combined. That would have been okay if it was a good film. But when it finally opened in New York in November 1936, it ran into harsh reviews and lousy ticket sales. "The tree-to-tree stuff has worn pretty thin for adult consumption," *Variety* complained. "While at first the sight of Tarzan doing everything but playing pinochle with his beast pals was a novelty, it's all pretty silly now. Derisive laughter greets the picture too often."

JUNGLE FAMILY VALUES

Johnny Weissmuller was content to continue as Tarzan, but Maureen O'Sullivan wasn't. When she learned that a fourth *Tarzan* film was in the works, she insisted on being written out of it. MGM offered to let her take a leave of absence, but she insisted on leaving permanently. So screenwriter Cyril Hume decided to kill her off with a spear wound at the end of the fourth film.

This created a problem: the female character helped attract women and families to Tarzan pictures, and the studio was afraid that if Tarzan went solo his audience would shrink. So they gave the couple a son—Boy. And to avoid controversy from censorship groups (because MGM's Tarzan and Jane never married), Boy was adopted. Tarzan and Jane find a baby in the jungle following a plane crash and raise him as their own.

MGM ran an ad in the *Hollywood Reporter* asking readers, "Do you have a Tarzan, Jr., in your backyard?" and auditioned more than 300 boys for the part before finally settling on seven-year-old Johnny Sheffield. (Sheffield's stunts were performed by a 32-year-old midget named Harry Monty, who billed himself as the "Midget Strong Man.")

BACK FROM THE DEAD

Edgar Rice Burroughs was furious when he learned MGM wanted to kill off his second-most important character. "MGM reminded Burroughs that while their contract forbade them to kill, mutilate, or undermine the character of Tarzan, it didn't mention Jane," Essoe writes. "MGM was free to rub her out and Burroughs was powerless to stop them."

In the end, though, MGM didn't "rub Jane out." Preview audiences were so upset at the prospect of Jane dying that the studio felt compelled to refilm the ending so that she survives. Not only that, O'Sullivan went on to play Jane in two more films before finally hanging it up for good.

TRAPPED IN THE JUNGLE

O'Sullivan made an average of three other films for every Tarzan she made, but Weissmuller wasn't that lucky. MGM wouldn't let Weissmuller play any other roles, fearing they'd damage his screen image. So although Johnny had been compared to Clark Gable in 1932, by the late 1930s he was hopelessly typecast.

Another thing that irked Weissmuller was that although he'd done so much to bring millions of dollars into MGM's coffers, the studio refused to give him a share of the profits. When MGM used up the last of its Tarzan movie rights making *Tarzan's New York Adventure* (1942), it decided not to buy any more, and let Weissmuller's option expire. Weissmuller moved over to RKO Pictures, the new owner of the *Tarzan* film rights, and made *Tarzan Triumphs*—the first of six RKO *Tarzan* films. But his deal there was the same as at MGM: no profit-sharing. Weissmuller earned his salary and nothing more.

LARGER THAN LIFE

In the years that followed, the *Tarzan* film budgets shrank as RKO relied more and more on reusing footage from earlier *Tarzan* movies, and the films themselves became shorter as they slipped from top billing to second place in double features. About the only thing that grew during the 1940s was Weissmuller's waistline: Now in his early 40s, his svelte swimmer's build had long since given way to the barrel-chested brawn of a middle-aged man who was having trouble staying in shape. Weissmuller gained as much as 30 pounds between *Tarzan* films, and he wasn't always able to take it all back off.

In 1948 Weissmuller finished *Tarzan and the Mermaids*, his 12th Tarzan film in 17 years. When talk of a 13th film began, Weissmuller again asked for a percentage of the profits. Rather than give it to him, producer Sol Lesser let Weissmuller go.

It wasn't the end of his career, though. Weissmuller wound up with the lead in a new series—*Jungle Jim*, based on a comic strip by the same name. This time he talked and wore clothes. He made 20 films between 1948 and 1956, and when he finished he began looking around for new roles to play. But no one would have him—after spending 26 years in the jungle, no one could see him playing any other kind of part. "Casting directors wouldn't even talk to him," Essoe writes. "After kicking around Hollywood for a while, Weissmuller went into a forced retirement."

After more than a quarter century in the movie business, Weissmuller had only one non-jungle film to his credit: the 1946 film *Swamp Fire*. "I played a Navy lieutenant in that one," he joked later. "I took one look and went back to the jungle."

Weissmuller died on January 20, 1984, at the age of 79. At his request, a tape recording of his famous Tarzan yell was played as his coffin was lowered into the ground.

* * *

THAT'S A WRAP
On April 29, 1944, the last "Our Gang" comedy was released. The very first had been produced in 1922 by Hal Roach, who continued to work on the shorts until he sold the rights to MGM in 1938. There are more than 100 films in the series, all featuring a band of kids getting into trouble and then trying to get out of it.

* * *

"People sometimes say that the way things happen in the movies is unreal, but actually it's the way things happen to you in life that's unreal. The movies make emotions look so strong and real, whereas when things really do happen to you, it's like watching television—you don't feel anything."

—Andy Warhol

According to our sources, in *West Side Story*, Robert Wise wanted Elvis to play Tony.

FROM D-DAY TO Z-DAY

Making war may be hell, but making war
movies isn't for the fainthearted, either.

THE FILM: *THE LONGEST DAY* (1962)

THE STORY
The tagline boasted that the *The Longest Day* "is the day that changed the world . . .When history held its breath." And indeed it was. *The Longest Day* chronicled the events of June 6, 1944: D-day, when the Allied powers surprised the German forces on the beaches of France. Told from the perspectives of both the Germans and the Allies, the movie had been shot on actual battle locations in France, giving it an authenticity that few other war films have. And it's all thanks to movie mogul Darryl F. Zanuck and his Z-day campaign.

THE BACK STORY
Darryl F. Zanuck was a studio boss at Twentieth Century Fox. But in his early 50s, he left Hollywood (and his wife) for Europe, where he independently produced movies.

Living in France surrounded by the battlefields and graveyards of World War II inspired the former Lieutenant Colonel Zanuck. He decided to make a movie on location in Europe that would repro-duce the massive D-day invasion. To do it, Zanuck put together his own campaign that industry insiders called Z-day (with the Z standing for Zanuck). His first battle? Raising money. First Zanuck went to Twentieth Century Fox for funds; but in 1961 the studio was hemorrhaging money from cost overruns for Elizabeth Taylor's *Cleopatra* and could only offer him a very tightly fixed budget. Unwilling to compromise his dream, Zanuck decided to contribute his own cash to the project.

It took Zanuck 365 days to re-create this one monumental day in history. He hired three directors, four cinematographers, 42 international stars (as the posters proclaimed), and a literal army of extras—23,000 actual troops supplied by the United States, England, and France. Seeking realism, Zanuck wanted the French characters to speak French and the Germans officers to speak

German (subtitles would be provided in the finished film). He even hired the perfect person to play the part of Private Millin, who played the bagpipes at the Normandy beach when the British commandos landed. It was Private Millin himself.

42 INTERNATIONAL STARS

The Longest Day was a hunk fest that included Henry Fonda, Robert Mitchum, John Wayne, Richard Burton, Sean Connery, Roddy McDowall, Peter Lawford, Mel Ferrer, Robert Wagner, and Richard Todd—an actual D-day vet. Having been a producer for decades, Zanuck had no trouble getting his Hollywood heroes at bargain rates. Richard Burton even showed up to work for free. Only John Wayne insisted on a salary of $250,000—about 10 times what the other actors were paid—because he was angry over a slight that Zanuck made in an interview (about Wayne's production of *The Alamo*). But Zanuck wanted Wayne—and Wayne got his $250,000.

ON LOCATION

There were more than 30 separate locations in *The Longest Day*, including five original beach landing sites: Utah, Omaha, Sword, Juno, and Gold. Like a true general, the imperious Zanuck flew in a helicopter from location to location, supervising important shots, a Havana cigar jutting from his teeth. To step back in time, flamethrowers cleared away 17 years of overgrowth to expose the original German fortifications from 1944. Zanuck even found and restored authentic Messerschmitts (German airplanes) like those that the Germans used to attack the Allied troops.

The Longest Day re-creates events in the places where they actually occurred. On D-day 1944, U.S. Rangers climbed 100-foot cliffs at Pointe du Hoc to destroy a nest of German guns (which were in a different location). On Z-day 1961, U.S. Marines reenacted the event on those same cliffs for "commander" Zanuck. During the location filming of the liberation of Sainte-Mère-Eglise—the small seaside village that had been the midnight landing site for paratroopers from the U.S. 82nd Airborne Division—Z-day took on some casualties of its own. In 1944 storm winds had marred the original drop and left paratroopers hanging from trees, hedges, and even the town's church steeple. In 1961 Zanuck tried to restage the event safely, shutting down the town's traffic and cutting off the

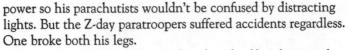

power so his parachutists wouldn't be confused by distracting lights. But the Z-day paratroopers suffered accidents regardless. One broke both his legs.

It was also at Sainte-Mère-Eglise that the film's historical accuracy nearly caused a local riot. Hundreds of citizens watched the filming of the town's battle for liberation. It all seemed so authentic that when the extras in German uniforms marched in, the townspeople (still smarting from occupation after 17 years) began shouting insults and hurling stones. The crowd settled down after being assured it was all pretend.

THE LEGACY
Though it can't be compared to the heroes who saved Europe, *The Longest Day* did save something: Twentieth Century Fox from financial disaster (brought on by overspending on Cleopatra). *The Longest Day* cost $10 million to make, but it made over $39 million for the studio and pulled it out of the red.

After four decades the film, which takes a viewer into the heart of the invasion, is still considered one of the great war movies, enjoyed by audiences and praised by historians. It exposes the mistakes of higher-ups, the evils of war, and the heroism of ordinary soldiers—not to mention the greatness of a day that gave hope to the world.

* * *

OFFICIAL TEENAGE UNIFORM
James Dean and Marlon Brando are both credited with creating the teenaged rebel look of a white T-shirt and jeans. (Allegedly, Brando once told Dean to stop copying him.) Brando once said, "I could've made more money if I'd just sold T-shirts with my name on them . . . they would have sold a million."

* * *

"Here's a tip to young directors. They never fire you midweek."
—Francis Ford Coppola

MUNCHING AT
THE MOVIES

*Let's all go to the lobby . . . and grab ourselves
some bite-sized snack facts.*

- M&Ms first became popular with American GIs during World
War II. In 1941 the candies were packaged in cardboard tubes
and sold to soldiers overseas because the hard candy shell
allowed M&Ms to travel well in different climates.

- When Whoppers malted milk balls first came out in the 1940s,
they weren't packaged—they were sold loose in drugstores: two
for a penny.

- The Junior Mint was named after the candy executive James
Welch's favorite Broadway play, *Junior Miss*. The play ran for
two years (1941–1943). Over 60 years later, the candy continues to outlive its namesake.

- Goobers, the chocolate-covered peanut candies, were named
after Southern slang for peanuts.

- Good-N-Plenty is the snack for those watching their weight.
According to the Center for Science in the Public Interest, the
licorice pellets have just 255 calories per box (about half the
calories of most other concession candies).

- Need caffeine? Just eat 50 Raisinets candies, which have more
caffeine than a cup of coffee.

- Almost a million miles of Twizzlers strawberry-flavored licorice
candy is made each year—enough to tie it around the equator
more than 40 times.

- Cinnamon-flavored Hot Tamales candy has zero grams of fat. A
real tamale? Nearly 50 grams of fat per serving.

- Jujubes have their origins in China. Originally they were gelati-
nous lozenges flavored with the juice of a Chinese date
(*Ziziphus jujuba*), a tiny, thorny fruit that's been harvested in
China for nearly 4,000 years. In the 19th century Westerners
used Jujubes as cough medicine, but soon people ate them
because they liked the taste.

The first copyrighted motion picture is of a man sneezing.

VIDEO GAMES GO HOLLYWOOD, PART 2

The gaming industry continues to churn out new games for Hollywood's new releases. But what about the classic films of yesteryear like Jaws *and* The Godfather? *Luckily somebody had the bright idea to explore these films, too—through the magic of video game technology. The story begins on page 375.*

The story begins on page 375.

J ust because a movie came out before the age of video games doesn't mean it can't one day have a game of its own. One of the latest trends in gaming is aimed squarely at anyone who wants to turn back the clock to step inside those all-time faves.

JAWS Unleashed
Let's face it—it's more fun being the bad guy sometimes. JAWS Unleashed puts you into the infamous Spielberg-inspired world of fish terror. But this time you're the shark! You get to eat just about everything in or near the water, evade fisherman, kill lifeguards, and, in general, terrorize everyone. The graphics are great, too—with beautiful underwater panoramas and intricate portrayals of sea life, right up until you eat whatever it was you were looking at.

James Bond 007: From Russia with Love
Enough with the bad guys. Put on your white hat (and your black tuxedo, as the case may be) for another exciting and authentic Bond blast. The original Bond, Sean Connery himself, does the voice-overs for this amazing Bondfest of London shoot-outs, flying jetpacks, and Zurich firefights. The game even features that classic silver Aston Martin from the original 1963 flick. And, of course, there's the beautiful daughter of an ambassador. The graphics are great, the bad guys wily, and the music pure 007.

The Godfather
Inspired by the 1972 Paramount Pictures flick, *The Godfather* game challenges players to, "earn respect through loyalty and fear as they

---

"I figured the Rocky Mountains would be a little rockier than this."

rise through the ranks to become the Don in a living 1945–1955 New York." You start out doing odd "jobs," then work your way into the Corleone family, where the real fun begins. Original cast members from the film (including the Godfather himself, Marlon Brando, in one of his last acting jobs) granted use of their likenesses as well as providing a few voice-overs to give the game the true patina of the original picture. Just like the Don, you have to use your brain, not just your brass knuckles. Sure, you get to carry out Mob hits and bank heists, but to really get ahead in the game takes diplomacy and strategy.

Scarface: The World Is Yours
Vivendi Universal went all out for this new take on the 1983 cult gangster (and capitalist) classic *Scarface*, released in 2006. The game picks up as if Tony Montana (played by Al Pacino in the movie) survives the final shootout from the movie and must fight his way to the top of his drug empire all over again. Al Pacino officially lent his likeness to the game, and original cast members Robert Loggia and Steven Baeur did voice-overs for their characters. Fast-paced action, high-powered graphics, and guns blazing are part of the new storyline written by a Hollywood script wizard, David McKenna, who makes sure that fans of the gangster flick and gangster game alike are "saying hello to this little friend." Like the movie it's based on, this one is for adults.

* * *

A LONG TIME AGO, IN AN ARCADE FAR, FAR AWAY . . .

Video games based on *Star Wars* have been popular since the movies first came out. One of the first was the arcade version that came out in 1983. Just like Luke Skywalker, players piloted an X-Wing fighter to destroy the Death Star. Today, the game still remains popular. In 2005 to celebrate the opening of *Episode III: Revenge of the Sith*, Brandon Erickson, a teacher from Portland, Oregon, set a new record for the longest recorded game of the original arcade version of *Star Wars*: 54 hours, 10 minutes. He was also attempting to beat the scoring record (300 million points) set way back in 1983 when *Return of the Jedi* debuted, but he fell about 80 million points short. (Better luck next time!)

—Lloyd Christmas (Jim Carrey), *Dumb and Dumber* (1994)

MOVIE TRIVIA YOU CAN'T REFUSE

Francis Ford Coppola's Godfather *trilogy is one of the most well-known and well-loved series of movies. But there may be more to the movies than you know. Check out these facts.*

- Remember that horse's head in the bed in *The Godfather*? Well, it was no fake. It was real and came from a dog-food factory.
- Laurence Olivier and Edward G. Robinson were both up for the role of Vito Corleone.
- Dustin Hoffman, Robert Redford, Martin Sheen, and . . . Burt Reynolds were considered for the part of Michael Corleone.
- Francis Ford Coppola was not the first choice to direct *The Godfather*. Sergio Leone, director of *The Good, The Bad, and The Ugly*, was tapped first but refused the offer.
- Coppola wasn't excited about directing *The Godfather*, but George Lucas encouraged him to take the job.
- Former wrestler Lenny Montana was hanging around the set and working as a bodyguard when he was noticed and tapped to play bodyguard Luca Brasi.
- Paramount executives hated Nino Rota's music composed for the film. Coppola refused to let the studio change it and told them that if Rota's score went, then he went, too. Paramount kept the composer.
- The Italian Civil Rights League had a sit-down with producers because the League was upset by the portrayals of Italian Americans as gangsters and thugs. To appease them, producers agreed not to use the words *Mafia* and *Cosa Nostra* in the film.
- In the scene where Sonny Corleone (James Caan) beats up his brother-in-law Carlo (Gianni Russo), Caan got a little carried away. He broke two of Russo's ribs and chipped his elbow.

Rudolph Valentino was arrested for bigamy in 1922. A judge found that he had . . .

- Sofia Coppola, Francis's daughter and now a movie director herself, has appeared in all three *Godfather* movies. She is the baptized infant in the first movie, played an immigrant child in the second, and is Michael Corleone's daughter Mary in *The Godfather: Part III*.

- Marlon Brando and Robert De Niro are the only two actors to ever win an Oscar for playing the same role: Vito Corleone.

- Talia Shire, who played Connie Corleone, is also known as Talia Coppola, Francis Ford's sister.

- John Cazale, who played Fredo, the weakest Corleone brother, had a brief but brilliant career. Before his death from bone cancer in 1978, he made only five films (*The Godfather, The Conversation, The Godfather: Part II, Dog Day Afternoon,* and *The Deerhunter*)—and each was nominated for best picture. Three of them (the two *Godfathers* and *The Deer Hunter*) won.

* * *

GREATEST AMERICAN MOVIE MUSIC
From the American Film Institute's "100 Years, 100 Songs" list

1. "Over the Rainbow," *The Wizard of Oz* (1939)
2. "As Time Goes By," *Casablanca* (1942)
3. "Singin' in the Rain," *Singin' in the Rain* (1952)
4. "Moon River," *Breakfast at Tiffany's* (1961)
5. "White Christmas," *Holiday Inn* (1942)
6. "Mrs. Robinson," *The Graduate* (1967)
7. "When You Wish Upon A Star," *Pinocchio* (1940)
8. "The Way We Were," *The Way We Were* (1973)
9. "Stayin' Alive," *Saturday Night Fever* (1977)
10. "The Sound of Music," *The Sound of Music* (1965)

BEFORE HIS TIME: RIVER PHOENIX

River Phoenix was one of his generation's most talented young actors, which makes his loss at age 23 all the greater.

O f all the ways to become a film star, River Phoenix's may be the strangest. In 1970 he was born to parents John and Arlyn Bottom on an Oregon hippie commune. His name came from the river of life in the Hermann Hesse novel *Siddhartha*. A few years later, little River Bottom (!) became River Phoenix when his parents were initiated into the Children of God, an evangelistic cult. The entire family was given the Biblical name "Phoenix" to represent the rise from the ashes of their past. In 1974 the Phoenix family (which now included River's sister, Rain, and would soon include brother Joaquin) set off on a divine mission to save the world—starting in Venezuela.

The family had always been close to broke, but in Venezuela they became destitute. At ages five and three, River and Rain sang on the streets for money. Finally, in 1977, disillusioned by the wealthy and hypocritical leader and disturbing allegations of sexual abuse practices during the children's initiations, the Phoenixes stowed away on a freighter bound for Florida. Once there, they settled into a more normal lifestyle. But one thing didn't change: when money got tight, the five talented Phoenix kids (by now Liberty and Summer had been born) went to work.

River, who'd been given a guitar in Venezuela, played and sang with Rain at fairs across central Florida. A *St. Petersburg Times* article about them made its way to Paramount, prompting a letter from the studio inviting the kids to an interview if they were ever in Hollywood. The family climbed into their VW van and set off for California.

A STAR IS BORN
Success came quickly for the talented boy. By age 10, the blond, charismatic River was doing commercials; at 12 he was a regular on the TV series *Seven Brides for Seven Brothers*. By 15 he was famous

---

Hamlet (1948) was filmed on location in Elsinore, Denmark.

for his performance as a tough, but vulnerable kid in *Stand By Me*. That same year he made *The Mosquito Coast* with Harrison Ford, a movie that strangely mirrored his own life, about a father who drags his family off to Guatemala to escape civilization. River thought of it as his best work and "more meaningful than anything else [he'd] ever done." He played the young Indiana Jones in the opening scenes of *Indiana Jones and the Last Crusade*. At 17, River's intense performance in *Running on Empty* (as the eldest son of former 60s radicals hiding from the government) won him a nomination for Best Supporting Actor.

His astonishing good looks and natural style helped him make the transition from child to adult actor. He charmed the critics in the 1991 indie *Dogfight* and won the 1991 Best Actor award at the Venice Film Festival for his portrayal of a hustler in the cult classic *My Private Idaho*. The former street urchin was now considered one of the best actors of his generation. Moviegoers wondered where his talents would take him next.

THE END IS NEAR
On October 30, 1993, at the Viper Room, Johnny Depp's Los Angeles nightclub, Phoenix, his brother Joaquin, his sister Rain, and his girlfriend Samantha Mathis all arrived with a group of friends shortly after midnight. River had brought his guitar and hoped to perform that night. He wasn't at the club for very long before he began acting strangely and having problems breathing. His brother and girlfriend helped him leave the club, but he fell to the sidewalk outside, thrashing and convulsing violently. Joaquin called 911 and had his brother rushed to the hospital. There, at 1:51 a.m., River Phoenix was pronounced dead from heart failure; later, an autopsy found cocaine and heroin in his system. His death was ruled accidental, caused by "acute multiple drug intoxication." He was only 23.

POSTMORTEM
Phoenix's death shocked family, friends, and fans alike. In life, Phoenix had been a strict vegan, an animal rights advocate who wouldn't wear leather, and an environmentalist who bought hundreds of acres of rain forest to preserve them. Phoenix was famous for his idealism, but the less-than-ideal events surrounding his death surprised those who were closest to him. There are many opinions about what drove River Phoenix to succumb to drugs: the pressures

of child stardom, the responsibility of supporting his family, a way of dealing with his unusual childhood, or just the adolescent rites of passage that he'd missed out on because he'd been so busy working.

THE LEGEND
Phoenix's brief life has been constantly explored in books and documentaries. Fellow musicians, including Natalie Merchant, the Red Hot Chili Peppers, and REM, have composed tributes to him. Fellow actors mourned him but fondly remembered his work. Harrison Ford said, "He played my son once, and I came to love him like a son, and was proud to watch him grow into a man of such talent and integrity and compassion." Phil Alden Robinson, who directed Phoenix in the film *Sneakers* (1992), said, "He was an extraordinarily honest actor . . . He could portray great sensitivity and great vulnerability and still be exciting to watch. There was nothing soft about him when he did it. It came out of strength. It's a great tragedy." His ideals are still inspirational, and his pain-edged performances in *Stand By Me*, *Running on Empty*, and *My Private Idaho* are eloquent reminders of how tough it is to be young.

* * *

THE MOVIES OF RIVER PHOENIX

Explorers (1985)

Stand by Me (1986)

The Mosquito Coast (1986)

A Night in the Life of Jimmy Reardon (1988)

Little Nikita (1988)

Running on Empty (1988)

I Love You to Death (1990)

My Own Private Idaho (1991)

Dogfight (1991)

Sneakers (1992)

Dark Blood (unfinished) (1993)

* * *

"It's a great feeling to think that I can be a friend to so many people through my movies."

—River Phoenix

UNCLE SAM GOES TO HOLLYWOOD

*Propaganda can be as blatant as a swastika or as subtle as a voice-over.
And after Pearl Harbor, when an isolationist America was plunged into
war overnight and thousands of new recruits needed to be educated
and inspired, propaganda was just what Uncle Sam ordered.*

In February 1942 Army Chief of Staff George C. Marshall asked
Hollywood director Frank Capra to make a series of documentaries "that will explain to our boys in the Army why we are
fighting, and the principles for which we are fighting." Capra was
reluctant—he'd never filmed a documentary before. But Marshall
told him: "Capra, I've never been a chief of staff before. Thousands
of young Americans have never had their legs shot off before. Boys
are commanding ships today, who a year ago had never seen the
ocean before." Capra apologized and promised "the best damned
documentary films ever made."

GOODBYE, CRUEL WORLD
Of all the directors in Hollywood, Capra was the perfect choice.
His upbeat movies, like *Mr. Deeds Goes to Town* and *Mr. Smith
Goes to Washington*, featured idealistic young heroes who win the
day in a selfish and brutal world. They gave people a good feeling
about being American and a sense of hope that, given American
gumption and character, things would inevitably get better. All the
director had to do was replace his young hero with America, and
that brutal world with the Axis powers: Germany, Japan, and Italy.

FUNNY THING
Capra had, in fact, been born in Italy and came to America when
he was six; he loved his adopted country with a passion unique to
immigrants. He'd grown up in Los Angeles and earned a degree in
chemical engineering, but Hollywood seemed more like home to
him. So he started in the business as a gag writer for producers Hal
Roach (of the "Our Gang" comedies), Mack Sennett (the
Keystone Kops), and comic actor Harry Langdon.

He'd directed a few Langdon movies when he was discovered by movie mogul Harry Cohn in 1929. Cohn was smart enough to give the young director complete autonomy and creative freedom. In return Capra's movies saved Columbia Pictures and even propelled it into the big leagues when *It Happened One Night* (1934) became the first movie to win all five top Oscars: Best Picture, Director, Actor, Actress, and Writing (Adaptation). Capra won two more Best Director Oscars for *Mr. Deeds Goes to Town* (1936) and *You Can't Take It With You* (1938).

Capra dabbled in movies with dark philosophical themes—*The Bitter Tea of General Yen* (1933) and *Lost Horizon* (1937)—but they didn't do well at the box office, so he would always fall back on his comedies with the little-guy-battles-the-forces-of-evil theme.

To prepare for his first documentary, Capra watched millions of feet of newsreels and commercial and propaganda movies to see how other countries—both allies and enemies—used the art of propaganda over the years.

REVOLTING BEHAVIOR

The Bolsheviks were pioneers in the use of propaganda—particularly on film. When they came to power in Russia in 1917, they wasted no time in taking control of the country's budding film industry. Because the documentary style, unlike narrative film, is less concerned with the telling of a story, the Soviet filmmakers focused on the psychological impact of visual images, in particular the way that images strung together would affect the emotional reactions of viewers.

Sergei Eisenstein's *Battleship Potemkin* (1925) tells the story of an uprising among the sailors aboard the ship. The revolt spreads to the steps of Odessa's harbor, where Cossacks of the czarist army gun down innocent civilians. By intercutting the action with close-ups of the characters as they were massacred, the sequence aroused viewer sympathy so strong that most people today believe that there actually was fighting on the Odessa steps during the Russian Revolution.

CUT TO GERMANY

After Germany's humbling defeat in World War I, the government produced a spate of propaganda films that portrayed the glory that had been the fatherland's before the war. When Adolf Hitler came

---

Vivien Leigh often wore gloves because she thought her hands were too large.

to power, he appointed Joseph Goebbels as Propaganda Minister. Goebbels called together the heads of the major German film studios and screened *Battleship Potemkin* for them. After the showing, he's reputed to have said, "Gentlemen, that's an idea of what I want from you."

The first films produced by the Nazis were so obvious and simplistic that they had little propaganda value. But under Goebbels's tutelage, they became more pointed: "hate" films that exhorted audiences to hate the Jews, hate the British, and hate anyone who didn't sympathize with the Nazi cause. Movie theaters in Germany were required by law to show newsreels and documentaries (with Nazi messages) before they could present any other films. By 1939, under Goebbels's influence, those nonfiction "shorts" lasted as long as 40 minutes.

LENI'S TRIUMPH
When she was 20, Leni Riefenstahl heard Adolf Hitler speak at a rally; she was so impressed that she offered her services as a filmmaker. (She'd directed one film, *The Blue Light*, in 1932.) At Hitler's request, Riefenstahl recorded on film the first Nazi convention in Nuremberg, starring all the leading lights of the movement—Himmler, Göring, Goebbels, Hess—after which she edited the footage into a film she called *Triumph of the Will* (1935). Using carefully designed camera angles and editing, she depicted Hitler as a godlike figure, revered by the masses who were in the throes of near-religious fervor. The Führer was so pleased with the film that he praised its "incomparable glorification of the power and beauty of our Movement."

MEANWHILE, BACK IN HOLLYWOOD
Frank Capra studied Riefenstahl's impressive work and similar Japanese and Italian propaganda movies in particular, noting how the Axis powers liked to flaunt their strength with parades of troops and machines of war, and with leaders shouting and gesticulating from high platforms surrounded by thousands of devoted subjects. Which gave Capra the brilliant idea of using the enemy's own propaganda against itself—by editing those movies into his own, cleverly juxtaposing the menacing faces and words of the enemy against the bright hope and accomplishments of the American people and their allies, England, France, and the Soviet Union.

Jack Nicholson's first role: Jimmy Walker in *Cry Baby Killer* (1958).

THE GOOD FIGHT
The result was a series of seven films called *Why We Fight* that were required viewing for millions of American soldiers:

- *Prelude to War* (1942): The development of the Axis dictatorships and the simultaneous rise of anti-militarism and isolationism in the U.S.; a look at enemy propaganda and the first acts of aggression.
- *The Nazis Strike* (1943): Nazi international aggression leading up to the British and French declarations of war.
- *Divide and Conquer* (1943): The European theater of war from the point of view of the Allies; the English and French entry into the war to the fall of France.
- *The Battle of Britain* (1943): Great Britain's stand against the Nazi war machine after the Dunkirk evacuation.
- *The Battle of Russia* (1943): The fight between the Soviet Union and Germany.
- *The Battle of China* (1944): The Chinese defense against Japanese aggression.
- *War Comes to America* (1945): The factors leading up to America's entry into the World War II.

DEMOCRACY'S DYNAMITE
The trailer for *Prelude to War* was pure Hollywood: "55 minutes of Democracy's Dynamite! . . . the greatest gangster movie ever filmed . . . the inside story of how the mobsters plotted to grab the world! More vicious . . . more diabolical . . . more horrible than any horror-movie you ever saw!"

The Allies were carrying the "Torch of Freedom" to a world threatened by the darkness of the Axis powers. In Capra's own words, "Let our boys hear the Nazis and the Japanese shout their own claims of master-race crud, and our fighting men will know why they are in uniform."

BOFFO AT THE BOX OFFICE
The films became critical and commercial successes. President Franklin Roosevelt liked *Prelude to War* so much that he suggested releasing it to the general public; the film went on to win the Academy Award for Best Documentary of 1942. It and the rest of the series became required viewing for American soldiers and were

distributed abroad, dubbed in French, Spanish, Russian, and Chinese.

V-E DAY TO V-J DAY

Three more Capra-made films were released in 1945. *Your Job in Germany*, written by Theodor Geisel, aka Dr. Seuss, was about peace in Europe after the war. *Two Down and One to Go* was written and filmed after Italy and Germany had surrendered, to remind the Allied soldiers of their one remaining task in the Pacific. *Know Your Enemy: Japan* was released on August 9, 1945—the day American planes dropped the atomic bomb on Nagasaki—and withdrawn on orders of General Douglas MacArthur on August 28, two weeks after Japan had surrendered.

HAPPY ENDING

When the war was over, Frank Capra returned to making commercial movies. But he didn't get out of the business of propaganda (that is, if you define propaganda as anything that carries a message). His next movie was possibly the sweetest propaganda movie ever made, and just what the country needed: *It's a Wonderful Life*, in which Jimmy Stewart battles his own demons and comes to realize that living the life of a small-town American is the best of all possible worlds.

* * *

DISNEYWORLD WAR II

The government had asked Walt Disney to participate, too. At one point during World War II, 94 percent of the Disney facilities and staff of more than 1,000 artists, animators, writers, and technicians were engaged in the production of training films and propaganda shorts, from the silly-serious cartoon *Der Fuehrer's Face*, in which Donald Duck wakes up in Nutziland, where even the trees are shaped like swastikas, to the ultraserious drama, *Education for Death*, the story of a boy growing up in Nazi Germany, who is humiliated for having feelings of compassion and who ultimately marches and dies with his fellow brainwashed soldiers. When the war ended, Disney went back to his prewar agenda and began to build his now-enormous empire.

—Norma Desmond (Gloria Swanson), *Sunset Blvd.* (1950)

THE POISON PEN STRIKES BACK: GAME OVER

Games are fun, and movies are fun. But sometimes when the two get together, the critics wonder if it would have been better to stay apart.

Clue (1985)
"Inspired by the Parker Brothers board game, *Clue* . . . quickly grows tedious. The more you struggle to keep track of the constantly multiplying plot developments, the harder it gets to care who did it."

—Kevin Thomas, *Los Angeles Times*

Super Mario Bros. (1993)
"They should have used cheat codes to make this a winner."

—Gerry Shamray, *Sun Newspapers of Cleveland*

Double Dragon (1994)
"A double shot of stupidity"

—Rick Gershman, *St. Petersburg Times (Florida)*

Street Fighter (1994)
"What can you say when a video game is more exciting and entertaining than the big-budget feature film it inspires? Not much."

—Richard Harrington, *Washington Post*

Mortal Kombat (1995)
"I mean, it's bad enough Hollywood is dredging up old TV shows for inspiration—but video games? What's next—a film version of Yahtzee?"

—Russell Evansen, *Wisconsin State Journal*

Mortal Kombat: Annihilation (1997)
"There is nothing . . . I repeat, nothing worthwhile in this film."

—Madeleine Williams, *Cinematter.com*

World War II made filming in Europe impossible, so a Welsh mining town . . .

Pokémon: The First Movie (1999)
"If your kids give you the choice between seeing this movie and a poke in the eye, go for the latter. The pain will pass sooner."
—Matt Mullins, *Wisconsin State Journal*

Dungeons & Dragons (2000)
"Dungeons & Dragons is as laughably bad as a first-level wizard."
—Marc Savlov, *The Austin Chronicle*

Lara Croft: Tomb Raider (2001)
"Angelina Jolie was born to play the fierce PlayStation heroine who scales archeological landscapes looking for hidden treasures. Too bad she's trapped inside Atari's Frogger."
—Ed Gonzalez, *Slant Magazine.com*

Resident Evil (2002)
"Add it to the list of efforts that only a joystick jockey could love."
—Dennis King, *Tulsa World* (Oklahoma)

Lara Croft Tomb Raider: The Cradle of Life (2003)
"At least now we have a clue about what's in Pandora's Box: It's movies like this."
—Mark Wolf, *Rocky Mountain News* (Denver, Colorado)

House of the Dead (2003)
"You'd have more fun standing in an arcade and watching someone else play the game."
—Scott Von Doviak, *Fort Worth Star Telegram*

Alone in the Dark (2005)
"As video game adaptations go, even *Pong: The Movie* would have a lot more personality."
—Michael Rechtshaffen, *The Hollywood Reporter*

Doom (2005)
"Doom is like some kid came over and is using your computer and won't let you play."
—Roger Ebert, *Chicago Sun Times*

THE FALL GUYS AND GALS

*Starring the brave unsung heroes and heroines of
action-packed filmmaking: the stunt doubles of Hollywood.*

Everyone who's seen an action movie knows that isn't really Bruce Willis who's falling off that 27-story building. And there are two good reasons why. For one thing, no insurance company would write the policy for it. For another, movies are so often filmed out of sequence that if a main character suffered even a minor injury—a fat lip or a bad scratch on the face—and the next day's filming involved a scene that preceded the stunt, shooting would have to be held up until the injury healed. In Hollywood, time is money.

THE OLDEN DAYS

At first, actors and actresses did whatever their parts called for, including the dangerous stuff. In her autobiography, Lillian Gish reminisces about the 1920 filming of D. W. Griffith's *Way Down East*. In it she is first driven from her home into a (real) howling blizzard, then to a river where she leaps from ice floe to ice floe, then she collapses onto one as it floats toward a waterfall. The river wasn't really heading for a waterfall, and the ice floes were really big pieces of wood. But Gish's own idea of letting her hand drift in the water was real—and left her with pain in that hand for the rest of her life.

If they wanted hair-raising action in their moving pictures, early filmmakers had two choices. They could hire people who could do the job, like the acrobats and race car drivers that Mack Sennett hired to be his incredibly inept *Keystone Kops* in 1912. Or they could hire people who would do the job: When dangerous sequences were planned, like the chariot race scene in 1925's *Ben-Hur*, the extras (who were earning $5 a day) would be canvassed for volunteers. Anyone chosen would be rewarded with an extra fiver.

The liquor industry offered director Billy Wilder $5 million to bury *The Lost Weekend.*

THOSE MAGNIFICENT MEN . . .

Movies about flying (a genre unto itself) required the services of real pilots like Ormer Locklear, aka the King of the Wing Walkers. Locklear's experience as a barnstormer and his daring creations like "the transfer," going from a moving car into a moving plane, got him the starring role in two early movies: *The Great Air Robbery* (1919) and *The Skywayman* (1920). Locklear made only the two films; he and his copilot were killed in a plane crash on the last day of filming *The Skywayman*.

By the time *Wings*, a drama about World War I fighter pilots, won the first Best Picture Oscar in 1927, real actors were doing the acting and stunt doubles were assigned the really dangerous stuff. The star Charles "Buddy" Rogers learned how to fly a plane during the filming of *Wings*. In close-up scenes he's actually piloting the plane himself and, like the other actors up there, working a camera. But the serious job of crashing the plane was left to aerial stuntman Dick Grace. He emerged from the wreck with a smile, posed for a picture next to the downed plane, and then collapsed. He'd broken his neck and crushed four vertebrae. Doctors told Grace that he should take a year off from stunt work, but he was back on his feet in six weeks.

SAFETY FIRST FOR SAFETY LAST

Legend has it that Harold Lloyd—an extraordinary athlete and the biggest box office draw of the 1920s—always did his own stunts. Well, almost. Lloyd most often appeared as "The Boy," an Everyman in horn-rim glasses who managed to survive death-defying predicaments through optimism and luck. In his most famous scene, from the film *Safety Last!* (1923), Lloyd struggles to hold onto the hands of a large clock atop a skyscraper. Lloyd did the close-up work. But in the long shots, the person suspended so precariously was stunt player Harvey Parry, who had an agreement with the studios not to divulge his role as long as Lloyd was alive. (In Lloyd's defense, it should be mentioned that the actor was missing the thumb and index finger of his right hand—which he lost in an on-set accident with a bomb that was supposed to be a prop . . . but wasn't.)

HORSING AROUND

The rise of the Western cemented the need for stunt players. As one prominent stuntman put it, "Car work is for sissies. Horse work

---

Sandra Bullock's debut: Lisa Edwards in a low-budget CIA thriller, *Hangmen* (1987).

is for men." The stuff of old Westerns was hazardous all right: chase scenes on horseback, stampedes, and falls from balconies. There was an urgent need for cowboys to jump from one moving conveyance to another (from horses to trains, from stagecoaches to horses, or any combination thereof), not to mention to take part in the ubiquitous saloon fights. Directors of Western movies found the perfect stunt players on the rodeo circuit.

EASY RIDER

One of John Wayne's regular stunt doubles was a former rodeo rider named Yakima Canutt. His specialty involved speeding wagons: jumping on and off them, sliding under them, and, in his most famous stunt (in 1939's *Stagecoach*), being run over by one. Canutt also pioneered the concept of choreographed fight scenes. He taught camera operators how to best capture a staged punch—the punching actor should face the camera, which is filming over the shoulder of the actor about to take the blow. After some serious injuries forced Canutt to retire from the actual performing of stunts, he became a stunt coordinator. He sometimes combined that job with directing second units (the crews responsible for action sequences and other scenes not requiring the main cast members), and worked on action-packed hits like *Spartacus*, *Rio Bravo*, and 1959's *Ben-Hur*, for which he created the climactic chariot race.

DON'T SEND A MAN TO DO A WOMAN'S WORK

Meanwhile, in the outside world, the advent of the women's liberation movement in the 1960s proved to be the perfect opening for female stunt players, who'd been clamoring for a chance to get in on the action.

Back in the silent era, an actress named Pearl White had built her career on performing her own stunts. The 20 chapters that make up the serial *The Perils of Pauline* (1914) are just a few of the hundreds of shorts that White starred in. But once she got to be a star, she became a commodity, and the studios decided it was time for a stunt double. Her use of a stand-in was a well-kept secret until 1922, when her double, John Stevenson, was killed during filming. After the rumor that it was White herself who'd been killed died down, audiences reacted with indignation—they'd been fooled! But they weren't surprised that her stunt double was a man; that was standard operating procedure. And so it was for decades to come, until the 1960s.

THE MORE VULNERABLE SEX
Any stunt player will tell you that women's stunts tend to be more dangerous than comparable stunts by men because women are usually wearing less clothing—men can get away with layers of padding under their clothes. But the women who do stunts couldn't care less.

Veteran stuntwoman Jeannie Epper started in the stunt business in her teens on TV shows like *Maverick* and *77 Sunset Strip*, and worked her way up (largely uncredited, as all stunt players were at the time) through action films like *The Poseidon Adventure* (1972) and *The Towering Inferno* (1974) to be Lynda Carter's double on TV's *Wonder Woman*. Epper's most famous stunt might be the Kathleen Turner mudslide scene in *Romancing the Stone* (1984).

FEELING NO PAIN
What makes stunt players different from the rest of us is that they accept the dangers of what they do—and the pain that accompanies it. Jeannie Epper has said, "I had stitches . . . But that's nothing. You get stitched up and you go back to work." Another veteran put it this way: "You know you're going to get hurt. The trick is not minding."

CREDIT WHERE CREDIT IS DUE
Stunt players are nicely rewarded for the chances they take: a good one can make upward of $200,000 per year, and a stunt coordinator can earn more than double that. But there's one thing that stunt players think is missing—and his name is Oscar.

Oh, sure, Yakima Canutt got one of those Lifetime Achievement awards in 1966 for his stunt work and the safety devices he engineered. But it wasn't the kind of Oscar that an actor, makeup person, or sound engineer can win for a specific movie in a specific year.

—Crystal Allen (Joan Crawford), *The Women* (1939)

BEST IN SHOW, 2005

There's a movement afoot to make stunts an official Academy Awards category. But in the meantime, since 2001, the industry has been holding its own ceremony, the Taurus World Stunt Awards. The 2005 awards show, hosted by Dwayne "the Rock" Johnson, honored these films: *The Bourne Supremacy* for the Best Vehicle Stunt and Best Stunt Coordination; *Spider-Man 2* for Best Stunt by a Man; and *Kill Bill: Vol. 2* for Best Fight and Best Female Stunt (both awards were won by Monica Staggs and Zoe Bell, for the fight scene between Daryl Hannah and Uma Thurman, respectively). Stuntwoman Jeannie Epper was on hand, too, to present the award to the Action Movie Director of the Year, Quentin Tarantino.

* * *

"There's only one thing that can kill the movies, and that's education."

—Will Rogers

* * *

HER HARSHEST CRITIC

"*The Temptress* has now been shown here—terrible . . . It is no exaggeration to say that I was dreadful. I was tired, I couldn't sleep and everything went wrong. But the main reason is, I suppose, that I'm no actress."

—Greta Garbo, in a letter to a friend. *The Temptress* (1926) was her second movie.

* * *

LONG LINES

When *The Wizard of Oz* premiered in New York City, 15,000 people stood in line to see it.

WEIGHT LESS IN HOLLYWOOD

If you're one of the 127 million Americans who are overweight,
or just a fan who gorges on Hollywood minutiae, here's what
some celebs have done to shed those extra pounds.

DESSERT! (Uma Thurman)
When *Pulp Fiction* princess Uma Thurman needed to slim down
fast to play a starring role in the 2003 Quentin Tarantino film, *Kill
Bill*, she kept to a strict dessert-only regimen. After losing 25
pounds, she said, "I know it sounds crazy, but I ate desserts, I had
ice cream, chocolate mousse, the whole lot, but I didn't have anything else."

JELL-O (John Malkovich)
As a teenager, John Malkovich (*Dangerous Liaisons* and *The
Hitchhiker's Guide to the Galaxy*) transformed himself by losing 70
pounds in six months by eating nothing but Jell-O! The jiggling
dessert paid off—Malkovich was named one of the 100 Sexiest
Stars in film history by *Empire*, a British movie magazine.

BOILED EGGS (Adrien Brody)
Brody, who won the Best Actor Oscar for his portrayal of Polish-
Jewish musician Wladyslaw Szpilman in the 2002 film *The Pianist*,
got ready for the part by losing 30 pounds on a diet of boiled eggs,
green tea, and only a little bit of chicken and veggies for dinner
each day. He'd only weighed 160 pounds to begin with, but the
role demanded a gaunt look, since Szpilman spent most of his time
hungry and in hiding.

WORK—AND LOTS OF IT (Francis Ford Coppola)
Sometimes the movie business doesn't give you enough time to
gain weight. Director Francis Ford Coppola lost 100 pounds during
the filming of *Apocalypse Now*, his legendary takeoff on Joseph
Conrad's novel *Heart of Darkness*. The combination of intense
work, stress, and enormous production challenges triggered the
weight loss.

Vincent Price's last on-screen role was the Inventor in *Edward Scissorhands* (1990).

FOOD COMBINING (Catherine Zeta-Jones)

Zeta-Jones uses a technique called food combining, which is actually more about what you don't combine, the concept being that your body has an easier time digesting various foods when they're eaten either alone or with compatible foods. Not the diet for those who like their meat and potatoes at the same meal, bananas on their cereal, or melons with anything else.

POTATOES (Howard Stern)

Private Parts (1997) star and shock jock Howard Stern dropped more than 20 pounds before filming his flick by eating nothing but steamed potatoes six times a day. He noted that his own private parts looked better next to his thinner body.

GRAPEFRUIT (Jerry Lewis)

For his role in the bizarre (and unreleased) film *The Day the Clown Cried* (1972), Lewis lost 30 pounds on the Grapefruit Diet, restricting himself to about 800 calories a day taken over three meals—with grapefruit. Proponents say grapefruit contains a plant compound that cuts insulin production and leads to weight loss, but critics think the diet is a lot of hooey.

HARDLY ANY FOOD (Christian Bale)

Bale went from 180 to 120 pounds for his role as a man who hasn't slept in a year in *The Machinist* (2004). His secret? He ate only a can of tuna and an apple a day. Bale said his hunger led to a Zen-like experience on the set—but that might have been the starvation talking.

NO FAT, NO SUGAR (Matt Damon)

Prepping for his role as a Gulf War veteran in the 1996 movie *Courage Under Fire*, Damon went cold turkey on all fats and sugars, and ran 10 miles a day to lose an impressive 40 pounds.

RAW FOOD (Demi Moore)

The 40-something star of *Ghost* (1990), *Indecent Proposal* (1993), and *Striptease* (1996) went on a vegan raw-food diet—eating only unprocessed and uncooked fruits, veggies, and nuts—to get even slimmer than usual for a bikini-clad scene with 30-something Cameron Diaz in *Charlie's Angels: Full Throttle* (2003).

Throughout *The Big Lebowski,* the Dude (Jeff Bridges) drinks nine White Russians.

BULKING UP

The record holders for the biggest weight gains in movie history:

- Tom Hanks had to gain, and then lose, 50 pounds for his role as a FedEx employee stranded on a desert island in 2000's *Cast Away*. (He'd also had to lose more than 25 pounds for his performance as an AIDS victim in 1993's *Philadelphia*.)
- Robert De Niro added 60 pounds for his role in the 1980 boxing movie *Raging Bull*, for which he won an Oscar for Best Actor.
- De Niro's record was broken by Vincent D'Onofrio when he put on an amazing 70 pounds for his role as Private Lawrence in the 1987 Stanley Kubrick Vietnam classic *Full Metal Jacket*. He shed the weight and now looks more like his real self on *Law & Order: Criminal Intent*.

* * *

CREATION OF A CLIFFHANGER

On March 3, 1914, the *Perils of Pauline* was first released. Starring Pearl White, this 20-part serial became the first international serial success—largely due to its use of cliffhangers at the end of every episode, forcing audiences to come back to see if Pauline escaped from her perils.

* * *

I WANT MY MOVIE TV!

MTV got in on the Hollywood act when it covered *Purple Rain*'s Hollywood movie premiere live in 1984. The movie starred Prince (who was essentially playing himself) as a struggling Minneapolis musician. Critics didn't rave about his acting, but fans loved his soundtrack, which sold over 10 million copies by the end of the year.

Marilyn Monroe took her first screen test in 1946.

THE RIGHT DIRECTION, PART 2

*Two more pioneers from Hollywood's golden age, these
visionaries created movies considered by many to be
some of the best ever made. Part 1 is on page 259.*

OSCAR'S PAL—William Wyler (1902–1981)
Born in Mulhouse, in the province of Alsace, then part of
Germany, Wilhelm (Willi) Weiller was the son of a Swiss merchant. He was studying the violin at the National Music
Conservatory in Paris when he met his distant cousin—Carl
Laemmle, the head of Universal Studios. Laemmle was notorious
for his nepotism, so he offered Wyler a job. Shortly thereafter, first
in New York, then in Hollywood, Wyler started working his way
up from publicity to prop man to script clerk to casting director to
assistant director (the Lon Chaney version of *The Hunchback of
Notre Dame*, 1923).

At the age of 23, Wyler made his debut as a director; the film
was a two-reel Western called *Crook Buster*. During those first few
years as a director, he turned out more than 40 two-reel Westerns.
In 1930 he directed *Hell's Heroes*, Universal's first all-sound movie
shot outside a studio and his own first feature-length A film. *Hell's
Heroes* turned out to be both a commercial and critical success.
From then on, Wyler directed just about every kind of movie: dramas, comedies, romances, thrillers, and costume epics, in a career
that lasted for another 40-plus years.

Wyler was married twice: the first time to actress Margaret
Sullavan (for a year and a half); the second time to actress Margaret
Tallichet, who quit the business a few years later. The couple had four
children and were married for 42 years, until Wyler's death.

THE MOVIES: Wyler has received more Oscar nominations as
Best Director (12) than any other director, and his films hold the
record for the most nominations for Best Picture (13). He first rose
to the academy's notice in 1936 with *Dodsworth*, an adult drama of
a comfortable business tycoon caught in a loveless marriage. Seven

years later the popular *Mrs. Miniver*, a tale of ordinary people in Britain coping with the extraordinary events of World War II, won him the directing award. In 1946 Wyler won an Oscar for his most critically acclaimed film, *The Best Years of Our Lives*, a tough take on the problems facing veterans returning from World War II. In 1959 he won again for *Ben-Hur*, the biblical epic that swept the Oscars with 11 wins. (Only 1997's *Titanic*, and *The Lord of the Rings: The Return of the King* have equaled that achievement.)

THE LEGACY: A key to Wyler's success was his perfectionism. Nicknamed 40-Take Wyler, he would shoot long scenes over and over until perfect. His movies benefited, but his actors suffered, particularly since the director knew what he wanted, but was unable to explain it to anyone else. Once, after many takes, Henry Fonda asked him for direction; Wyler's helpful reply was, "It stinks. Do it again."

Despite that, Wyler managed to drag some great performances out of his actors. He launched the stardom of Laurence Olivier in *Wuthering Heights*, Audrey Hepburn in *Roman Holiday*, and discovered Harold Russell, the only actor to receive two Oscars for the same film, Wyler's *The Best Years of Our Lives*. While training paratroopers, Russell had lost both hands when some TNT he was handling blew up; his moving, low-key performance as a handicapped veteran won Best Supporting Actor and an honorary Oscar for bringing "hope and courage" to other vets.

Quality movies and performances were Wyler's trademarks. His stories are told eloquently and powerfully. And although he was originally criticized for not putting a more personal stamp on his stories and characters, he's since been rediscovered by young filmmakers and fans who praise him for his commitment to letting his stories and actors shine—while keeping himself out of the picture.

THE BOY WONDER—(George) Orson Welles (1915–1985)
Born in Kenosha, Wisconsin, raised in Chicago, and educated at home in his early years, little Orson was putting on Shakespeare's plays in his playroom while other kids were out shooting marbles. He was every parent's dream of a gifted child. By age 16, he was starring onstage in Dublin, Ireland; at 18, he was touring in a Shakespeare company. He shot his first short film at 19 (starring himself and first wife, Virginia Nicholson), and by 21, he was producing and performing in shows on radio and Broadway to rave

reviews. With John Houseman (*The Paper Chase*), Welles founded the Mercury Theatre, which became famous for its bold, original productions and the start it gave to talented actors like Joseph Cotten and Agnes Moorehead. In 1938 his radio production of H. G. Wells's novel *The War of the Worlds*, performed as an emergency news broadcast, convinced the nation that aliens had landed! At the ripe old age of 23, Welles found himself on the cover of *Time*—and Hollywood beckoned.

At age 25, Orson Welles produced, directed, cowrote, and starred in *Citizen Kane*, the story of a newspaper tycoon who possesses everything except the ability to love. Welles had based *Citizen Kane* on the life of William Randolph Hearst, a real newspaper mogul—who immediately tried to suppress the film. The Hearst papers launched an advertising boycott pressuring theater chains not to show *Kane*. But the studio, RKO, held firm. It released the movie, which was hailed as a masterpiece but didn't do well at the box office. As a result, the studio tightened its reins on the Boy Wonder, to the detriment of his future films. The next one, an adaptation of Booth Tarkington's prize-winning novel *The Magnificent Ambersons*, was edited by the studio while Welles was working in South America so that it could be part of a double bill (with, as it turned out, a Lupe Velez comedy, *Mexican Spitfire Sees a Ghost*). Welles disowned the resulting film and from then on kept himself on the outskirts of Hollywood.

In 1943 Welles married screen siren Rita Hayworth (he'd been divorced from his first wife for three years) and took up acting again; the following year, he starred as Mr. Rochester in *Jane Eyre* opposite Joan Fontaine. Producer Sam Spiegel gave him a chance to direct 1946's *The Stranger*, and his workmanlike attitude on that film got him another: *The Lady from Shanghai* (1947), in which he starred with Hayworth. As soon as filming was over, Hayworth sued for divorce. And when the movie wasn't received well, Welles packed up and left Hollywood for Europe. There he acted in films, among them *The Third Man* (1949), for other directors, while trying to save money to make his own (mostly Shakespearean) movies. In 1955 he married Italian actress Paola Mori; their marriage lasted until his death.

Thirty years later the prodigal son returned to the United States, was honored in 1975 with an American Film Institute Life Achievement Award, and built a solid career in movies and television. To younger generations he's probably best remembered as the TV pitchman for Paul Masson wines: "We will sell no wine before its time."

THE MOVIES: There's been some controversy over the authorship of *Citizen Kane* (Welles was forced to add the name of his collaborator, Herman J. Mankiewicz, to the credits), but there's no question about who directed it. The movie is included on nearly every Great American Film list, and the scholarly American Film Institute ranks it as #1.

Despite its mutilation by the studio, Welles's second movie, *The Magnificent Ambersons,* is still considered a superior contribution to film. The *Lady from Shanghai*—as bizarre and confusing as it is—has some brilliant scenes, notably the climactic "hall of mirrors" sequence in which Rita Hayworth and her on-screen husband, Everett Sloane, shoot at each other and die in a shower of broken glass. Welles's stylized and surrealistic *Macbeth* (1948) is considered a failure, but his daring and visually exciting *Othello* (1952) won the Palme d'Or, the ultimate award at Cannes. A few years after that, Welles was given a chance to direct an American film, *Touch of Evil* (1958)—not on his own merit, but because the star, Charlton Heston, insisted on it. The stylish black-and-white thriller about an American husband and wife embroiled with the Mexican underworld was a critical success in the United States and Europe, but it flopped at the box office. The movie has a cult following, and some of its fans think it may have inspired Hitchcock's *Psycho.*

THE LEGACY: Welles pushed film in new directions. He is famous for his use of deep-focus photography (the technique by which all parts of a frame can be seen equally clearly, thus allowing viewers to choose what to look at, rather than having their attention directed to a specific point), unusual camera angles (like the scene in *Citizen Kane* that was shot from a hole in the floor to make Kane look larger than life), flashbacks, and overlapping dialogue. And Welles knew how to convey sophisticated, meaningful stories with realistic—as opposed to melodramatic—acting.

Forced to work outside the studio system, Welles became a symbol of the director as auteur—a director who defied the commercialism of Hollywood and brought his own artistry to moviemaking. In fact, modern directors have picked up so many techniques from Welles that he's often called the most influential moviemaker of all time.

WHAT THE #$@*? HOLLYWOOD'S RATING SYSTEM

Ever wonder what those ratings mean or how they are determined? As a public service, Uncle John explains it all to you.

FREE AT LAST!
Once the Hays Production Code was abandoned in 1968, filmmakers had a field day. The 1960s were a time of radical social change in the United States; new attitudes toward race relations, civil rights, sexuality, and women's rights flew in the face of older social traditions. It wasn't surprising that Hollywood's movies would reflect the changing times. Filmmakers had also been exposed to the freewheeling cinema of Europe, with its frank attitude toward sex and nudity. Reveling in their new freedom, American filmmakers could embrace more sensitive subjects and formerly forbidden topics; movies became explicit in their treatment of sex, violence, and language. But not everyone was happy about it.

Although many people welcomed the new open attitudes in films, parents were faced with a new problem. From the very beginnings of film, young people took to the movies. But how could parents tell what films were age appropriate for their children? Once the little ones were seated in the darkened theater, it was too late for parents to realize that what was about to be shown on the screen wasn't what they wanted their children exposed to. Judging a film just by its title or advertising poster was too difficult.

RATE THIS
The Motion Picture Association of America (MPAA) president, Jack Valenti, was worried. In 1966, just a few weeks after taking office, he faced his first controversy, about several lines of dialogue in *Who's Afraid of Virginia Woolf?* Valenti, studio executives from Warner Bros., and the MPAA lawyer sat for hours discussing whether to delete or keep the words *hump* and *screw* in the picture

(they kept *hump* and dropped *screw*). Valenti saw a crisis coming, in which every little controversial detail within a film would have to haggled over. Something had to be done.

The MPAA sat down with the National Association of Theatre Owners (NATO) to hammer out a system, something that wouldn't censor the studios, but would give consumers an educated choice in what they saw at the cinema. On November 1, 1968, they announced the birth of the first ratings system. It was quite simple and consisted of just four categories:

G: Suggested for GENERAL audiences (all ages admitted)

M: Suggested for MATURE audiences: parental discretion advised (all ages admitted)

R: RESTRICTED: Children under 16 (later changed to 17) not admitted unless accompanied by a parent or adult guardian (over 21, at many theater chains)

X: No one under 17 admitted

THE PROBLEM IS . . .
For some reason many people had difficulty understanding what the symbols really meant. Some thought that M (for mature) contained more adult material than R (restricted). This led to some confusion. So in 1969 the M rating was changed to GP: General audiences, parental guidance suggested. A year later they flip-flopped the letters and changed the rating to its current PG.

G STANDS FOR "GAAAH!"
Although a number of films of interest to adults were released with G ratings in the late 1960s, including *2001: A Space Odyssey*, *Planet of the Apes*, and *The Odd Couple*, many people came to believe that G designated a movie for children. A G rating became the kiss of death for anything but a children's movie. Few G-rated films have been commercial successes. Some filmmakers went so far as to deliberately lace dialogue with naughty words, to bump their ratings from a G to a PG.

FIE ON YOU, STEVEN SPIELBERG!
In 1984 two Steven Spielberg movies were released with a PG rating: *Gremlins* (which he produced) and *Indiana Jones and the Temple*

—Charlie Allnut (Humphrey Bogart), *The African Queen* (1951)

of Doom (which he directed). Many people objected to the level of violence in such PG movies. So the MPAA tweaked their system once more and added the PG-13 designation. Although children under the age of 13 could be admitted without guardians to movies so designated, parents were now "strongly cautioned" that the films included violent and/or sexual content. According to Jack Valenti, "PG-13 meant a higher level of intensity than was to be found in a film rated PG." The first movie to be released with a PG-13 rating was *Red Dawn* in 1984.

THE SYSTEM WASN'T PERFECT
There was another problem with the rating system, involving the X rating. Originally, it was not intended to be for pornographic films, but for films with serious adult themes. *A Clockwork Orange* (1971), *Last Tango in Paris* (1973), and *Medium Cool* (1969) were all X-rated when originally released. *Midnight Cowboy*, another X-rated film, even won an Oscar. But the X rating was not trade-marked, so anyone could brand their film with an X. And the adult-film industry just loved that! They started posting as many Xs as they could fit on a movie marquee, to show how packed with adult material their films had to be. Consequently, many legitimate theater owners refused to exhibit films with an X rating. This left many genuinely artistic, but adult-themed, films out in the cold.

But the MPAA rating system did adapt. In November 1990 the association instituted yet another rating category, NC-17: No one under 17 admitted. The first movie with an NC-17 rating was *Henry & June*, a biography of novelist Henry Miller. Some film-makers shied away from this rating, fearing that audiences might stay away because of the stricter rating. *South Park: Bigger, Longer & Uncut* (1999) received an NC-17 rating for its prolific use of profanity; then they cut a few swear words here and there to bring the rating down to R. But other films, like *Showgirls* (1995), used the controversial new rating to lure audiences in with shocking adult material.

HOW THEY DECIDE
Here are a few of the guidelines used by the MPAA in determining the rating of a film:

- If a film uses "one of the harsher sexually derived words" (such

Top Gun (1988) is dedicated to Art Scholl, a stunt pilot who died during filming.

as the F-word) once, it remains eligible for a PG-13 rating, provided that the word is used as an expletive and not in a sexual context.

- If such language is used more than once, or once if in a sexual context, it usually receives an R rating.
- A reference to drugs usually gets a movie a PG-13 at a minimum, though a few movies were rated PG for "mild" drug references.
- A "graphic" or "explicit" drug scene earns a film an R, at the minimum.
- Nudity: While total female nudity is permitted in an R-rated movie, any full-frontal display of male genitalia will (usually) result in an NC-17 rating. Non-sexual male nudity is the one exception.

IT'S VOLUNTARY
The MPAA rating is entirely voluntary. That means that the makers of any film can opt not to have it rated. The film is identified as Unrated. Viewers then have to decide on a case-by-case basis which movie to see at the theater.

* * *

A MOMENT OF SILENCE
After the death of legendary director D. W. Griffith, all major Hollywood studios observed three minutes of silence in honor of his funeral on July 28, 1948. Lionel Barrymore, Charlie Chaplin, and Cecil B. DeMille served as pallbearers.

* * *

A SCENE AT THE RACES
When *Ben-Hur* premiered in 1959, the chariot-racing scene amazed audiences. It should have. It took five weeks to film, required 15,000 extras, and an 18-acre set. Eighteen chariots were built, but only nine made it into the film (the other nine were used for practice).

THE QUOTABLE VAMPIRE

A collection of favorite vampire quotes from books, TV, and film.

"All I know is I haven't had a suntan in one hundred and thirty-six years. . . . I'd give anything just to go to the beach for at least fifteen minutes."
—Suzy the vampire,
Vampire Hookers (1986)

"There's no getting around it, kid, vampires drink blood. We suggest pigs' blood—B negative. I think you'll find it surprisingly, um, full-bodied, with a smooth flavor."
—Modoc, *My Best Friend Is a Vampire* (1988)

"Look. The night. It's so bright it'll blind you."
—The vampire Mae,
Near Dark (1987)

"This part of the seduction is quite simple, really. Just take away everything that she has, then give her everything she needs."
—The vampire Maxmillian,
Vampire in Brooklyn (1995)

"Fun? How would you like to go around dressed like a head-waiter for seven hundred years? Just once I'd like to go to dinner dressed in a turtleneck and a sports jacket."
—Dracula to Renfield, *Love at First Bite* (1979)

"I buried myself for 100 years to get away from you. Can't you take a hint?"
—The vampire Angelique,
Nightlife (1989)

"Humans are prey, they are sustenance, cattle. Do you converse with a hamburger before you eat it? Do you converse with a milkshake?"
—Jacob, *To Sleep with a Vampire* (1992)

"I may never see the sunrise, but I can take you to worlds beyond your dreams. I can teach you about the stars. We'll dance in their light—for eternity."
—The vampire Carmilla,
Carmilla (1990)

The non-scary *Stand by Me* (1986) is based on Stephen King's short story *The Body*.

"You shall pay, black prince. I shall place a curse of suffering on you that will doom you to a living hell. A hunger, a wild gnawing animal hunger will grow in you, a hunger for human blood."

> —Dracula,
> *Blacula* (1972)

"I'll take a lite . . . Blood Lite."

> —Vampire in a vampire bar, *Nightlife* (1989)

"There's only one way you can be with me, but you have to do something you've never done before . . . commit yourself . . . forever."

> —The vampire Louise, *The Girl with the Hungry Eyes* (1993)

"For centuries I have known the magical powers of blood—powers greater even than those of holy water. That fountain of youth that withstands the ravages of time."

> —Countess Dracula, *Mama Dracula* (1980)

"I think I should warn you I have certain unusual habits. I'm a late riser, very late. . . . When I'm sleeping I must never be disturbed. . . . And I'm on a liquid diet."

> —The vampire Angelique, *Nightlife* (1989)

"Vampires get such a crummy deal. Not only do we have to sleep in worm-eaten old coffins and wear these smelly old clothes, but we can't even look in the mirror when we want to fix ourselves up a little bit."

> —The vampire Anna to her human friend Tony, *The Vampire Moves In* (1985)

"We have lived in this country for four generations. We're Americans—Carpathian-Americans. We work here, we live here, we pay taxes, we're entitled to the protection of the law. I think it's time we came out of the damn coffin."

> —Harry, to his vampire family, *Blood Ties* (1991)

* * *

DRIVE-IN THEATERS

During the golden age of drive-in theaters (from the 1940s to the 1960s), more than 4,000 of the outdoor theaters were in operation in the United States. Today, just over 400 remain. Alaska, Hawaii, and Louisiana have none.

The plot of *Strange Brew* (1983), starring Bob and Doug McKenzie, is based on *Hamlet*.

HOLLYWOOD PHYSICS

*The movies have perfected the art of making the
impossible look real. You've seen these things happen
in the movies, but can you tell the science from the fiction?*

FICTION: After falling off a cliff, a car will burst into flames on impact.
SCIENCE: A car will only burst into flames if the gas tank is severely damaged, the gasoline has been vaporized, and there is a source of ignition. Like a lit match.

FICTION: Stray bullets give off a spark or a flash of light when they strike a surface.
SCIENCE: Most handgun bullets are made of copper-lead or lead alloys, which don't spark when they strike a surface, even if the surface is made of steel.

FICTION: Automatic weapons can fire off thousands of rounds for several minutes at a time without being reloaded.
SCIENCE: It's true that automatic weapons can fire off thousands of bullets—but only for a few seconds at a time. Sustaining a ten-minute gun battle would not only require tens of thousands of bullets, it would also overheat the guns and cause them to malfunction.

FICTION: When shot, a person is propelled backward.
SCIENCE: Because a bullet is much lighter than a person, it doesn't have enough force to propel a person backward.

FICTION: Falls from great heights are easy to walk away from.
SCIENCE: Stunt players seem to do it all the time, but falls from as "high" as three feet (like falling out of bed) can make for serious injuries. Just remember that the farther a body falls, the harder it lands.

FICTION: A spaceship needs to bank when turning to compensate for the effects of centrifugal force.
SCIENCE: In Earth's atmosphere, aircraft have to bank to create a pressure difference on the two wings that produces the turning force. Despite what you've seen small spacecraft do in the *Star Wars* movies, the only forces necessary for them to change direction in the vacuum of space are the rockets that propel them.

FICTION: When a space station explodes it makes a deafening noise.
SCIENCE: There's no air in outer space to transmit sound waves, so those big explosions you hear in *Star Wars* are pure fiction.

FICTION: Laser beams are visible.
SCIENCE: Though the end point is visible, the beam itself is only visible when reflected by the fine particles in mist or smoke.

FICTION: A lit cigarette carelessly tossed into a puddle of gasoline is likely to start a fire.
SCIENCE: A mixture of gasoline vapor and air is highly explosive, but liquid gasoline will be wicked up by the cigarette paper and extinguish the burning ember.

* * *

KIDDIE COCKTAIL

Many Hollywood celebrities had drinks named for them, but few have stood the test of time like the Shirley Temple, a non-alcoholic favorite since the 1930s. Made of lemon-lime soda (or ginger ale), grenadine syrup, and a maraschino cherry, the Brown Derby restaurant in Los Angeles is credited with creating the drink. But the real Shirley Temple isn't a big fan of the concoction. She says it's too sweet for her.

—Deep Throat (Hal Holbrook), *All the President's Men* (1976)

FIRST FILMS

People like Arnold Schwarzenegger would probably just as soon
you forgot about the films they had to make before hitting it big. But
Jami Bernard didn't forget—she wrote First Films, a book we used
to research this section. We recommend it. The best of its kind.

MERYL STREEP
First Film: *Julia* (1976)
The Role: She plays a snooty, shallow friend of the lead characters
(played by Jane Fonda and Vanessa Redgrave). If you blink, you
might miss her—her two scenes last a total of 61 seconds and her
back is to the camera most of the time. She's also wearing a black
wig (which she hated).
Memorable Line: "Oooh . . . you're so famous."

PAUL NEWMAN
First Film: *The Silver Chalice* (1954)
The Role: Newman plays Basil, a Roman slave selected to make
the chalice for Jesus' last meal because he can whittle better than
anyone in Jerusalem. Publicity posters called it The Mightiest
Story of Good and Evil Ever Told, Ever Lived, Ever Made into a
Motion Picture! Newman called it "the worst film made in the
entirety of the 1950s." At one point, he even took out a magazine
ad urging people not to see it.

ARNOLD SCHWARZENEGGER
First Film: *Hercules in New York* (1969)—rereleased on video as
Hercules Goes Bananas
The Role: Arnold plays Hercules, of course. Viewers got their first
look at his pumped-up body (including a ludicrous scene in which
he "bounces one pectoral muscle at a time"). But they never heard
his voice. The 22-year-old Austrian's accent was so thick, no one
could understand him. Result: His entire part (but only his) had to
be dubbed. The film is so bad that Schwarzenegger—who was originally billed as "Arnold Strong"—won't acknowledge it.
Memorable Line: "Bucks? Doe? What is all this zoological talk
about the male and female species?"

JANE FONDA
First Film: *Tall Story* (1960)
The Role: Not what you'd expect. The future feminist plays June, a 21-year-old home economics major and cheerleader who's got her sights set on the school's basketball star and top scholar (Anthony Perkins). Once she gets him—about a third of the way through the film—she fades into the background. The story then focuses on Perkins's basketball dramas.
Memorable line: (On why she came to college) "The same reason that every girl, if she's honest, comes to college—to get married."

NICOLAS CAGE
First Film: *Fast Times at Ridgemont High* (1982)
The Role: "Brad's Bud"—a part so small that the writers didn't even bother giving him a name (or any lines). Most of his part was cut out, but you can still see him looking miserable behind the grill at All-American Burger. He was billed as Nicolas Coppola, but got so much flak from the cast about being director Francis Coppola's nephew that by his next film he'd changed his name to Cage.

MICHELLE PFEIFFER
First Film: *Hollywood Knights* (1980)
The Role: "Sporting her old nose and too much eye-liner . . . she [plays] Suzy Q, a carhop at Tubby's Drive-In, where her job requires her to wear tall, white go-go boots." On the side, she's an aspiring actress and girlfriend to Tony Danza—who also makes his screen debut in this "low-rent ripoff of American Graffiti."
Memorable line: "I have an audition in the morning."

TOM HANKS
First Film: *He Knows You're Alone* (1980)
The Role: Hanks is on for three and a half minutes in this low-budget psycho-slasher film. He plays a college student who meets two of the killer's future victims and takes them on a date to a Staten Island amusement park. That's about it.
Memorable line: "Want a goober?"

Neve Campbell's first name is also her mother's maiden name; it means "snow."

DAHLIA M FOR MURDER

Moving to Hollywood and becoming a star is the Hollywood Dream, but the story of Elizabeth Short could be called the Hollywood Nightmare. Elizabeth (better known as the Black Dahlia) moved west to chase stardom but never found success as an actress. She did, however, become famous for one thing—being the murder victim in one of Hollywood's most notorious unsolved cases.

On the morning of January 15, 1947, a young woman was walking near an abandoned field at South Norton Avenue in the Leimert Park section of Los Angeles. As she passed it, she spotted a broken department store dummy lying in the overgrown weeds. It seemed odd to her, so she took a closer look. It wasn't a broken mannequin at all. It was the body of young would-be actress Elizabeth Short.

The battered corpse had been cleanly cut in half and laid carefully posed in the grass. Not a drop of blood was found at the scene; it appeared the nude body had been washed before being brought to the lot and abandoned. Her clothes were missing, and no personal belongings were found. It was the beginning of one of Hollywood's most gruesome mysteries, the unsolved Black Dahlia murder.

WHO WAS ELIZABETH SHORT?
Known as either Betty or Beth to her friends and family, Elizabeth Short was born July 29, 1924, in Hyde Park, Massachusetts. She grew up in Medford, just outside Boston, and had four sisters. During her childhood, Short lost her father after his business failed during the Depression; his abandoned car was found near a bridge, and he was believed to have committed suicide. Her family struggled to make ends meet, but one luxury they could afford was the movies, which inspired young Elizabeth to become a movie star someday.

After the death of James "Scotty" Doohan, at age 84, in July 2005 . . .

When she was a teen, Elizabeth received some shocking news: her father was not dead at all but alive and well in California; he had faked his suicide and moved out west to start over after his financial ruin. The family remained estranged from him, but Elizabeth wrote to her father often and finally moved to California to live with him at age 19.

By then, Short had grown into a pretty young woman; her dark hair and fair skin were set off by the red lipstick and nail polish she favored. She worked at Camp Cooke as a clerk (she won a beauty contest there), and hoped that her good looks would help her break into films. Once in California, she had tried to seek out people she thought could give her an entrée into the film business, but her efforts didn't yield results. Her acting career never took off.

Her relationship with her father grew strained (he complained that she was messy, boy-crazy, and stayed out to all hours of the night). She moved out and started living with friends. Short's frustrations with her career and her love life made her restless and unsettled. Money was often a problem for her; she borrowed from a series of friends and acquaintances. It has been said that she only ate when other people—usually dates—were paying. She still kept horrendous hours, partying with movie people until late into the night.

But Short wasn't a loose woman. She longed to get married and settle down. She dated frequently but did not develop a reputation for being easy (some went as far as to call her a tease). Her most serious relationship was with a pilot who wanted to marry her, but it ended in 1945 when he died in a plane crash. Short was despondent over the loss. Some say she even became mentally unstable after his death. She continued to date despite the loss. At the time of her death, she was seeing a married handyman from Los Angeles, Robert "Red" Manley, who was also the last man to see her alive. Manley parted ways with her at the Biltmore Hotel on January 9, 1947. Six days later, Short's battered remains were discovered in Leimert Park. She was only 22.

THE INVESTIGATION
The murder caused a sensation in Los Angeles. Police were baffled, and the press sensationalized the case by covering every angle and

detail. It was nicknamed the Black Dahlia murder because, some say, that was Short's nickname in reference to her jet-black hair and fondness for dark clothing. Others say the press came up with the name after a 1946 movie, *The Blue Dahlia* (starring Veronica Lake and Alan Ladd).

A month after Short's body was found, the *Los Angeles Examiner* received a strange package with a note: "Here is the Dahlia's belongings. Letter to follow." Inside they found Short's social security card, birth certificate, business cards, address book, photographs of her with various men, and claim checks for suitcases she had stowed at the bus depot. The police determined that all the items in the package had been washed with gasoline to remove any fingerprints. Nevertheless, they painstakingly hunted down every lead—they traced every name on the business cards and in the address book to no avail. The letters, when they came, contained no usable clues.

At first, the leading suspect was Manley, the last person to see Short alive. They had spent the night together before he drove her from San Diego (where she had been visiting friends) back to L.A. He paid for a hotel room and slept on the bed; Short, complaining of illness, slept in a chair. The next day Short told Manley that she was returning home to Massachusetts and asked him for a ride to the Biltmore Hotel, where she was meeting her sister. Manley dropped her off in the hotel and last saw her speaking on the lobby telephone. After extensive police interrogation and two passed polygraph tests, the LAPD cleared him. Nevertheless, the interrogation took a serious toll on Manley, who eventually suffered a nervous breakdown and was committed to a psychiatric hospital.

To complicate matters, police were inundated with false confessions. More than 50 "Confessing Sams" confessed to the murder and cost the cops valuable time trying to rule them out. No strong leads emerged, and the case has remained open indefinitely.

THEORIES
But just because a case is unsolved doesn't mean there are any shortage of theories and suspects.

Jack Wilson: Author John Gilmore, a former child actor turned writer, published *Severed: The True Story of the Black Dahlia Murder* (1998). In it, he fingers Jack Wilson as the killer. Forty years after the murder, in the early 1980s, an informant told the LAPD that he had a taped recording of a man named Arnold Smith, who claimed that a sexual deviant named Al Morrison had confessed the murder to him. The Smith tape recounted the murder with graphic details—some of which had never been made public. According to this tape, Short had gone to Morrison's hotel room but refused to have sex with him. Morrison had become enraged and tied her up, brutalized her, and killed her.

The police were convinced that Smith and Morrison were the same person and that Smith needed to brag about getting away with the notorious crime for so long and had invented a fictitious perpetrator to protect himself. Upon further investigation, the LAPD learned that both Al Morrison and Arnold Smith were aliases of a violent sex offender named Jack Wilson. All that remained to be done was to find Jack Wilson, and the crime would be solved.

The informant did not know where Smith/Morrison/Wilson lived but eventually tracked him down. In 1982 a meeting was arranged between a police detective and Wilson, but it never took place. A few days prior, Wilson fell asleep while smoking in bed; he died in the fire that followed. Wilson's death may have seemed suspicious, but he did have a history of starting fires by smoking in bed. The Los Angeles District Attorney's office could not close the case, because their leading suspect was dead. The case remained open.

George Knowlton: In 1995 Janice Knowlton wrote *Daddy Was the Black Dahlia Killer*. Through the retrieval of repressed memories, Knowlton, a self-described victim of paternal incest, claimed to remember watching her father kill Elizabeth Short. Knowlton claims her father and Short were having an affair and even refers to Short as "Aunt Betty." Some experts are skeptical of her claims. Knowlton cannot be questioned further: in March 2004, she committed suicide.

Dr. George Hodel: In 2003, Steve Hodel, a former police detective, wrote *Black Dahlia Avenger*, in which he claimed that his own

—Rick Blaine (Humphrey Bogart) *Casablanca* (1942)

father, George, a surgeon and businessman with a spectacular IQ and connections with the LAPD, had committed the crime. According to Hodel, his father was immune from investigation for the murder because he had the goods on LAPD members—he had treated many of them for venereal disease and provided a number of them with illegal abortion services. Steve Hodel based his theory in large part on photographs he had discovered among his father's possessions when the elder Hodel died. His conviction that the photos were of Elizabeth Short is not shared by everyone.

Dr. Walter Bayley: Writer Larry Harnisch's theory fingers an elderly surgeon named Walter Bayley as the killer. Dr. Bayley was acquainted with Short's older married sister Virginia, who lived close to his own home on South Norton Avenue, just one block from where Short's body was found in 1947. Bayley had been a prominent physician in the early 1940s, but in late 1946, Bayley's life was falling apart; he had lost his spot as chief of staff at County Hospital, left his wife, and was showing signs of dementia. Harnisch theorizes that Short sought refuge with Bayley, a family friend with an office just five blocks from the Biltmore. He made a pass at her, and she rejected him. Then he became enraged, killed her, and took her mutilated body to place it near his former home on South Norton Avenue to frighten his estranged wife. Dr. Bayley died in 1948 of pneumonia; his death certificate lists a condition called encephalomalacia, which involves shrinkage of the brain and would have caused a mental impairment.

EPILOGUE

We'll probably never know for sure just what happened to Elizabeth Short, but almost 60 years later, interest in the Black Dahlia case continues unabated. There are more books in the works, and Internet chat rooms continue to offer outlets for the many people who cannot let go of speculations and theories. The case remains open.

Myrna Loy's second husband was car rental heir John Hertz Jr.

ANSWERS

AT THE OSCARS (page 83)

1. C 5. D
2. A 6. D
3. B 7. C
4. B 8. A

Note: Streep has been nominated thirteen times—10 as Best Actress and 3 times as Best Supporting Actress—and has won twice. Hepburn was nominated for 12 Best Actress Oscars and won four. Davis is not far behind: 11 Best Actress nominations, two wins. Pickford was nominated once and won for *Coquette*, in 1930. She won an honorary award in 1975.

SILVER SCREEN CEO QUIZ (page 166)

1. F 6. B
2. E 7. J
3. D 8. C
4. H 9. A
5. G 10. I

How many matches did you get right?
8–12 Big-time player
5–7 Middle management
1–4 You're fired!

TAGLINES OF TERROR (page 234)

1. H. *The Blob* (1958)
2. K. *Halloween* (1978)
3. C. *The Mummy* (1932)
4. E. *Bride of Frankenstein* (1935)
5. L. *Prom Night* (1980)

6. F. *Cat People* (1942)
7. G. *House of Wax* (1953)
8. A. *Dracula* (1931)
9. D. *The Invisible Man* (1933)
10. J. *Blacula* (1972)
11. B. *Frankenstein* (1931)
12. I. *House on Haunted Hill* (1959)
13. M. *Child's Play* (1988)
14. N. *Scream* (1996)

CAST OF CHARACTERS (page 277)

1. Clarice Starling, H. *The Silence of the Lambs* (Jodie Foster)
2. Jimmy "Popeye" Doyle, E. *The French Connection* (Gene Hackman)
3. William Wallace, I. *Braveheart* (Mel Gibson)
4. Margo Channing, B. *All About Eve* (Bette Davis)
5. Pu Yi, G. *The Last Emperor* (John Lone)
6. Phileas Fogg, C. *Around the World in Eighty Days* (David Niven)
7. Frodo Baggins, J. *The Lord of the Rings: The Return of the King* (Elijah Wood)
8. Ratso Rizzo, D. *Midnight Cowboy* (Dustin Hoffman)
9. Richard Blaine, A. *Casablanca* (Humphrey Bogart)
10. Randle P. McMurphy, F. *One Flew Over the Cuckoo's Nest* (Jack Nicholson)

AKA (page 303)

1. **D.** As a boy, young Marion had an Airedale named Little Duke. He and his dog were inseparable, earning Marion the nickname Big Duke. As he got older, he preferred to just go by Duke, a tougher sounding name than Marion.

2. **B.** De Niro, who grew up in New York's Greenwich Village and was a real-life member of a Little Italy street gang, was known as Bobby Milk because of his pale complexion.

3. **A.** Humphrey Bogart. His marriage with third-wife Mayo Methot earned them the nickname "the Battling Bogarts." During their marriage, he bought a sailboat and named it Sluggy after her.

4. **E.** Keanu Reeves. He got the name by playing the goalie position. Reeves may not look imposing on-screen, but the 6'1" Canadian knows his way around a hockey rink. In fact, one of his first big screen appearances was as an ice hockey player in *Youngblood*, a 1986 flick starring Rob Lowe and Patrick Swayze.

5. **D.** Her stage named used to be Whoopi Cushion because, indeed, she was known for her excessive flatulence. A high school dropout and reformed heroin addict, she cleaned up her act and moved to California in 1974. There she worked both as a bricklayer and in a mortuary before becoming a huge success.

6. **A.** Smith was born and raised in Philadelphia's Wynnefield section, and wasn't as underprivileged as his TV series suggested (his father owned a refrigeration company). A natural-born charmer, he earned the name Prince while still in school.

7. **B.** Chase was born into a wealthy New York family, and Chevy was a childhood name his grandmother gave him. Just before joining SNL, the future *Fletch* and *National Lampoon's Vacation* star had his name officially changed to Chevy.

8. **B.** In addition to acting talent, Ms. Moore has an uncanny ability to negotiate for more money and better benefits. She was the first actress to reach the $10 million salary mark.

Bonus nickname trivia:
- Brad Pitt's nickname in high school was the Pit-bull.
- Sir Laurence Olivier's family called him Kim.
- Bill Paxton is known as Wild Bill to his friends because of his wild sense of humor and bent for practical jokes.
- Jerry Lewis earned the nickname Picchiatello, which means "crazy" in Italian.